Rapprochement
or Rivalry?

Russia and Eurasia Books
from the Carnegie Endowment

BELARUS AT THE CROSSROADS
Sherman W. Garnett and Robert Legvold, Editors

GETTING IT WRONG: Regional Cooperation and the Commonwealth of
   Independent States
Martha Brill Olcott, Anders Åslund, and Sherman W. Garnett

KEYSTONE IN THE ARCH: Ukraine in the Emerging Security Environment
   of Central and Eastern Europe
Sherman W. Garnett

RUSSIA AFTER COMMUNISM
Anders Åslund and Martha Brill Olcott, Editors

RUSSIA IN THE WORLD ARMS TRADE
Andrew Pierre and Dmitri Trenin, Editors

YELTSIN'S RUSSIA: Myths and Reality
Lilia Shevtsova

Rapprochement or Rivalry?

Russia-China Relations in a Changing Asia

Sherman W. Garnett
Editor

Carnegie Endowment for International Peace
Washington, D.C.

© 2000 Carnegie Endowment for International Peace
1779 Massachusetts Avenue, N.W.
Washington, D.C. 20036
Tel. 202-483-7600
Fax. 202-483-1840
www.ceip.org

To order, contact Carnegie's distributor:
The Brookings Institution Press
Department 029, Washington, D.C. 20042-0029, USA
Tel: 1-800-275-1447 or 202-797-6258
Fax: 202-797-6004, E-mail: bibooks@brook.edu

Library of Congress Cataloging-in-Publication Data
Rapprochement or rivalry? : Russia-China relations in a changing Asia /
Sherman W. Garnett
   p. cm.
  Includes bibliographical references.
  ISBN 0-87003-125-2
  1. Russia (Federation)—Foreign relations—China. 2. China—Foreign
Relations—Russia   (Federation). 3. China—Foreign   relations—1976-
  I. Garnett, Sherman W., 1955- .
DK68.7.C6R37 1999
327.47051—dc21   99-16517
                                                    CIP

Printed on acid-free, recycled paper.
Cover design by Laurie Rosenthal.

Contents

Foreword

The collapse of the Soviet Union and the economic rise of China in the early 1990s profoundly changed the strategic balance and security environment of the world. A decade after the end of the Cold War, the leaders of Russia and China have referred to their new relationship as a "strategic partnership." However, if that is what it is, its realities and potential to force a major realignment in great power relations and global security remain to be seen.

Joint Sino-Russian communiqués, often implicitly directed at the United States, declare the two countries' responsibility for opposing hegemony and establishing a multipolar world. Yet while both countries are exploring the possibilities of drawing closer together on the global as well as local scene, they are being pulled apart and toward the United States. Indeed, at the present time, their relationships with the United States remain more important for each country than their relationship with each other.

Even without factoring in the influence of the United States and Western Europe, the Russo-Chinese relationship does not lack for present-day complications, and the historical record is plagued by hostility and mistrust. While the interests of the two countries often converge on what they oppose, their interests most often diverge on what they seek to promote.

Rapprochement or Rivalry? Russia-China Relations in a Changing Asia brings together leading American, Russian, and Chinese experts on Sino-Russian relations. Edited by Sherman Garnett, a former senior associate at the Carnegie Endowment for International Peace and now Dean of James Madison College of the Michigan State University, the book explores from different perspectives the many aspects of this complex relationship. It probes the realities of the Sino-Russian "partnership," the challenges to and opportunities for its development, and its impact on the world.

The book is a product of the Carnegie Endowment's Russian and Eurasian Program, which seeks to improve U.S.-Russian relations through joint research that develops understanding of the region and generates new policy solutions. This book is the latest in a series of publications assessing Russian domestic and foreign policy. Other books include *Yeltsin's Russia: Myths and Reality,* by Lilia Shevtsova; *Russia After Communism,* edited by Anders Åslund and Martha Brill Olcott; *Getting It Wrong: Regional Cooperation and the Commonwealth of Independent States,* by Olcott, Åslund and Sherman Garnett.

This important study was made possible by the Smith Richardson Foundation. We are grateful for their support.

JESSICA T. MATHEWS
President
Carnegie Endowment for
International Peace

Acknowledgements

This book is the result of a three-year collaboration between American, Russian, and Chinese analysts, generously supported by the Smith Richardson Foundation. I would never have been able to undertake such a project without the encouragement and advice of Morton Abramowitz, then the president of the Carnegie Endowment and his vice-president, Paul Balaran. Both are serious students of China and were of great help to me in establishing contacts with both American Sinologists and key academics and officials in China and Japan. There would in fact be no project at all without their help.

I am also grateful for the support I received throughout this project from the senior leadership and staff at the Carnegie Endowment for International Peace. Jessica Mathews, Steve Sestanovich, Arnold Horelick, and David Kramer provided steady support and sound advice. Jennifer Little and the Carnegie Endowment's library always found the material I needed. Natalia Udalova came to my rescue at various times to provide editorial assistance and translations. Carmen Cook did a superb job in tidying up the manuscript. Vanda Felbabova has shepherded this large manuscript through its final stages, while I took up a new job in Michigan. Sherry Pettie also deserves special mention for her invaluable work on the final stages.

My Moscow partners, Irina Kobrinskaya and Dmitri Trenin, made every visit to Russia easy and intellectually productive. Throughout I have had the good fortune to have the very best possible research work from Anita Seth, Elizabeth Reisch, Rachel Lebenson, and Marcus Fellman, outstanding examples of the Endowment's Junior Fellows program. I owe them more than I can convey.

I must also thank literally dozens of officials, analysts, and scholars who took the time to meet with me in Moscow, Tokyo, Beijing, and Harbin. The project benefited greatly from their insight. I want to single out Vilya Gelbras, Li Jingjie, and Lu Nanquan for their willingness to tutor me on China. But certainly this project and this volume in particular would not have been possible without the work of Professor Gilbert Rozman of Princeton University. He took a lively interest in the project from the beginning, helped establish important contacts for me, and took me on an unforgettable research trip to Beijing and Harbin in January 1997. Though busy with his own work, he was always willing to look at my drafts or those of other authors. His mastery of the sources and languages, analytical insight, and generosity of spirit are present throughout this volume, not only in his two insightful contributions.

This project also brings to an end my work as a senior associate at the Carnegie Endowment for International Peace. I can imagine no better place to work or a better group of colleagues. I am grateful for the five years I spent as a part of this great institution and its Russian and Eurasian Program.

SHERMAN GARNETT
Dean, James Madison College
Michigan State University

PART ONE

Introduction

1
Limited Partnership

Sherman W. Garnett

Russia and China have formed what they describe as a "strategic partnership of equality, mutual confidence and mutual coordination aimed towards the 21st century."[1] At a time of Russian setbacks, both internal and external, this partnership represents one of the few successes in Russian diplomacy and is widely trumpeted as such. For China, the relationship symbolizes less a singular success than another sign of its increasing diplomatic reach. Cooperation with Russia dramatically alters China's northern border, completing the process begun with the first stages of Sino-Soviet thaw in the 1980s—winding down decades of military confrontation, border disputes, and bitter ideological conflict. The change for the better in bilateral relations between the two largest land powers in Asia is an accomplished fact.

It is not surprising that its chief architects believe that their new partnership will be a significant force "for the establishment of a new international order."[2] Although both parties deny they are forming an alliance, their statements at the highest levels proclaim solidarity on issues ranging from Taiwan to the enlargement of NATO. The two countries welcome the coming "multipolar world" and, in thinly disguised swipes at Washington, denounce "hegemonism." Bilateral trade has fluctuated from year to year, reaching a high of nearly $7 billion in 1996 and dropping to close to $6 billion in 1997.[3] China has been Russia's largest single customer of arms and defense technology. Both sides want to expand economic ties, setting an ambitious and probably unrealizable goal of $20 billion in trade by the year 2000. They have almost completely resolved a long-standing border dispute, reduced military forces near this border, and expanded military cooperation. Since the breakthrough summit of April 1996, the two sides have institutionalized their relationship, holding frequent summits and ministerial meetings and establishing working groups designed to break through deadlocks on trade, military cooperation, energy, and other key issues.

Yet, these ambitions and accomplishments raise more questions than they answer. Many observers are left wondering what this new partnership might yet become, how enduring it will be, and what it means for Asia as a whole. Those asking these questions are not only Western critics, suspicious of what they see as a reversal of the dynamics of the old strategic triangle, but also Russian analysts. Although the Chinese press maintains a rigid and sunny political correctness about the relationship, it is not hard to find observers in Beijing who doubt whether Russia will prove a reliable partner, in the end, because of either its internal shortcomings or the reemergence of old strategic tensions.

The authors in this volume, from China, Russia, and the United States, joined together in a two-year effort, organized by the Carnegie Endowment for International Peace and generously funded by the Smith Richardson Foundation, to study the shape and future of Russian-Chinese relations. As the following essays demonstrate, they came to no common view.[1] Indeed, it would have been odd if a group reflecting such a wide range of disciplines, experiences, perspectives, and origins came to a single conclusion. But their work reveals a rich set of insights into three major issues key to understanding the past, present, and future of Sino-Russian strategic partnership: (1) the shape of the Russian-Chinese relationship and its possible future; (2) the future challenge posed by a weak Russian Far East; and (3) the impact of this relationship on Central and East Asia. These three overarching categories form the basic divisions of both this introduction and the volume as a whole.

THE SHAPE OF THE RELATIONSHIP

Let us begin with a closer look at the relationship itself, the ties that currently bind the two states together, and the attitudes of those involved in maintaining and analyzing the relationship. The essays of Dmitri Trenin, Li Jingjie, Lu Nanquan, Alexei Voskressenski, and Gilbert Rozman illuminate the Russian-Chinese strategic partnership from a variety of perspectives, offering special insight into where the partnership came from, what the two sides think about each other, and where this relationship is headed.

None of these authors find the improvement itself much of a surprise. The old pattern of strategic competition was both dangerous and wasteful of resources, particularly for a China turning to economic reform. The authors likewise agree that the foundations of the current partnership were laid during the Soviet period. Our Chinese colleagues are, by and large, the most optimistic about what has been accomplished to date, although Lu Nanquan offers a serious critique of why, from the Chinese perspective, Russian economic reforms thus far have faltered. Trenin and Voskressenski both focus on potential problems and limitations. Neither of these authors regret normalization. Both of them would like to see cooperation continue, but each describes a set of "objective constraints [that] limit how far the relationship is likely to go." Even Gilbert Rozman, who offers the most expansive view of what the current relationship has accomplished, believes that while "the strategic partnership is likely to endure and even to strengthen, [it will not] advance in the manner or to the degree envisioned."

Underlying Interests and Trends

In part, the limitations are already present in the very trends that have brought the two states closer together. One set of these trends grows out of Russia's internal problems, which have produced a weak state, a contracting influence, and, in particular, great vulnerabilities in Russia's Asian lands. The collapse of the Soviet Union meant the end of the highly centralized Soviet center. As President Yeltsin has regularly complained, no steady state structure has yet emerged to give Russian internal and external policy a consistency of purpose or the material base that effective policy requires. Russia's economic crisis and the attempts of the Primakov government to address it are the latest chapter in Russia's struggle with the internal challenges and constraints.

This weakened state must also cope with an expanding set of foreign policy actors, from regional governors and traders to arms sellers and other financial and business sectors. The rise of these competing interests is a positive sign of greater pluralism in Russian foreign policy; however, these expanded interests are not well coordinated or managed by the government. As Dmitri Trenin points out in his essay, relations with China deserve better, for "China is gradually becoming a major external factor capable of influencing not only Russia's foreign relations but increasingly also its domestic environment, to the extent of even reshaping the very nature of Russia—its government structure, ethnic composition, and its general orientation in a changing Eurasia."

A weakened Russia needs breathing space to concentrate on internal problems. It needs to reduce external challenges, and a tense Sino-Russian relationship would expose the growing weaknesses of Russia's Siberian and Far Eastern lands. Russia has ceased to be an Asian power of consequence for the immediate future. Russia has never been a major economic actor in Asia, and its other sources of influence have contracted or collapsed. Russian military power, in particular, has eroded. The Pacific Fleet and the ground and air forces deployed by the USSR in response to the border clashes with China in the late 1960s have shrunk in size and dramatically declined in quality. Even if these military assets, so crucial to Soviet influence in Cold War Asia, were as formidable as they were in the past, they would not today offer Russia the same leverage in a post–Cold War Asia moved more by trade and investment flows than by the balance of military power.

China has also been, until recently, Russia's only real option for cooperation in Asia. Until Japanese Prime Minister Hashimoto's mid-1997 Russia initiative and the "no neckties" summit between Hashimoto and Yeltsin in November of that same year, Russian-Japanese relations were largely frozen in place over the unresolved status of the Kurile Islands. Japan continues to claim these islands, which the Soviet Union occupied during the waning days of World War II and later annexed. Both Russia and Japan now agree that this problem should not hold up the development of strong bilateral ties. Russia's economic plunge in August 1998 and Japan's continued economic troubles, however, underscore the problems in making the Russian-Japanese relationship as dynamic as the Russian-Chinese one. Russia, in particular, has to make painful internal adjustments in order to attract Japanese investment and other economic benefits. China will take Russia as it is.

Indeed, for China, relations with Russia are less a centerpiece of its foreign policy than a part of its overarching effort to emerge as a world power after more than a century and a half of backwardness and exploitation. China wants material and political support for this goal, particularly for its economic and military modernization. It does not want this support to be so concentrated in U.S. or Western hands that it limits its own internal or external options. As Chinese power grows and regional and global perceptions of its significance take shape, China also wants to avoid the prospect of a foreign coalition of powers attempting to delay, contain, or even roll back its ambitions. Normalization of relations with Russia is a part of Beijing's larger strategy, not the centerpiece.

In addition, China has several specific reasons for improving ties with Russia. Sources of tension that remain from the Sino-Soviet period can now be resolved in terms China can accept. China can now settle these issues and concentrate its energies and ambitions internally and to the south and east. Moreover, Russia has technologies important to China, especially military technologies. Chinese aerospace and defense industries are already benefiting from exchanges with Russian firms.

In light of its growing economy and expanding energy needs, China desires access to the gas and oil reserves of Russia and the other states of the former USSR. Thus, China wants specialized Russian ties to supplement—not to replace—its critical economic ties with the United States, Japan, and the West. China also shares with Russia a desire to limit instability, ethnic separatism, and challenges to the political status quo throughout Inner Asia.

Ties That Bind

Yet, if one turns from the foundations to the accomplishments of the past several years, the results are impressive. The current Russia-China "warming" goes far beyond stated interests and future ambitions. As the essays in this volume show, there has been real and substantial progress on a number of fronts. These successes—eight of which are listed below—are now the ties that bind the two countries together.

Demilitarization and Arms Reductions. Perhaps the most impressive achievement of Russo-Chinese rapprochement has been the reversal of security relations. After a rise in tensions and armed clashes over disputed islands in the Amur, Ussuri, and Argun rivers in the 1960s and 1970s, the Soviet Union expanded its military presence in Siberia and the Far East to more than fifty divisions and built up both the surface and nuclear submarine portions of the Pacific Fleet. China likewise devoted large military resources to its northern borders. In recent years, however, military tensions and military capabilities have been decreasing. Mikhail Gorbachev's policies, including specific conventional and nuclear force reductions, gave this process real momentum.

In 1992, Gorbachev's promised withdrawal of Soviet forces from Mongolia was completed under Boris Yeltsin. In 1994, the two sides agreed to measures that would reduce the risk of dangerous military incidents. They have expanded military-to-military contacts, particularly at high levels. Arms sales and military technical cooperation (further discussed below) have flourished. In April 1996, the leaders of Russia, China, and three Central Asian states—Kazakhstan, Kyrgyzstan, and Tajikistan—agreed to a set of confidence-building and transparency measures on their shared borders. The agreement calls for the regular exchange of information on military exercises and activities, and limits the size of exercises to fewer than 40,000 personnel.[5] At the April 1997 summit, Russia agreed to reduce the size of its forces in the 100-kilometer border zone by 15 percent. Although the details are still somewhat unclear, press reports suggest the treaty limits a wide range of ground, air defense, and frontal aviation equipment and personnel.[6] These new lower levels probably reflect actual holdings—not future reductions—on the Russian side, given the unilateral reductions in force structure that have been taking place since the early 1990s.

As Trenin and Voskressenski make apparent, parts of the military, Western-oriented reformers, and certain nationalists have doubts about long-term Chinese military intentions. Suspicion of China—especially of a China on the verge of becoming a world power in its own right—runs deep among some in the Russian military and foreign policy community. In December 1996, Igor Rodionov, who was then defense minister, included China on the list of countries that were potential threats, although he later recanted this view under pressure from those in the government who are responsible for relations with Beijing.[7] Russia's military doctrine, announced in November 1993, renounced the doctrine of "no first use" of nuclear weapons—a step seen by key Russian analysts as a hedge against

China. In September 1994, however, Russia and China agreed bilaterally to observe a "no first use" pledge and to detarget their nuclear warheads. While these are positive, substantial developments in the security field, they received an enormous boost from the erosion of Soviet and Russian military capabilities and China's own unilateral reductions. In interviews conducted by the Carnegie Endowment project in Beijing, Chinese experts on Russia were nearly unanimous in emphasizing the weakness of Russia and the disappearance of a military threat from the North for the foreseeable future. These experts were confident that long-term developments would remain favorable to China.[8]

Border Demarcation. There has also been a decisive turn on border demarcation. In 1991, the Soviet Union and China—after nearly thirty years of on-again, off-again negotiations—concluded the first agreement juridically establishing borders along a 4,300-kilometer stretch in the East. In 1994, the two countries signed a second agreement on a shorter section of the western border. In 1997, they again reaffirmed their commitment to resolve outstanding border issues quickly.[9] In November 1997, they signed a joint statement indicating near-resolution of all border issues. Two islands in the Amur River and one in the Argun River remain outside these agreements.[10] Their unresolved status continues to be a source of regional and nationalist discontent on the Russian side. The work of the treaty-mandated demarcation commission is also proceeding, though not without occasional interruptions. In 1996, one of the commission's Russian members resigned in protest of the surrender of Russian land to China. So far, the Russian leadership has managed to contain the fallout from such disruptions and to move ahead with the demarcation and normalization of what was once one of the world's most tense borders. Nevertheless, the issue will continue to sow tension between central and regional authorities in Russia and between Russians and Chinese in the affected areas of Siberia and the Russian Far East.

Economic and Trade Issues. Improved bilateral relations have led to expanded trade, opening up the formerly closed and militarized border between China's Northeast provinces and the Russian Far East. Russian-Chinese trade has expanded from negligible levels in the early 1980s to slightly less than $7 billion in 1996. The leaders of the two countries have, as already mentioned, set a $20-billion target for bilateral trade in the year 2000. Arms sales and nuclear power are the most active sectors in bilateral trade. In contrast, border trade between Northeast China and the Russian Far East—which will be considered in the next section—has been subject to cycles of expansion and contraction.

The past six years have put to rest the notion that the alleged "complementarity" between the two economies—a synergy resulting from the early and broad-based Soviet contribution to China's defense and manufacturing sector—would be a significant factor in bilateral trade. China has not sought to upgrade its aging, Soviet technology base in heavy industry, military production, and other sectors. If it had done so, the Russians would have had a genuine advantage.

Rather, China has sought full modernization, often starting from scratch in many enterprises (much to the economic disadvantage of the Northeast, which remains China's "rust belt"). China wants airplanes from Boeing or Airbus, not Tupelev; it has sought joint ventures with Audi and General Motors, not Lada. In some sectors, for example the construction of nuclear power plants or defense technology, Russia has competitive advantages that China has recognized. Even in these sectors, however, Chinese-Russian deals have not led to upgrading old Chinese enterprises. China's purchase of a license to produce its own SU-27 aircraft in 1996 will not revitalize old defense plants in the Northeast. Instead, it will create new opportunities for more modern facilities elsewhere in China.

The hoped-for benefits to Russian industry from such deals also have not materialized. In the first few years, barter predominated, leaving Russian manufacturers with less than they had bargained for, as they received Chinese goods, not hard currency, for their products. Corruption and rent-seeking have made many rich but seldom have made the enterprises or their workers better off. Although widespread benefits are usually touted when deals are signed—proceeds from Russian-Chinese arms sales in late summer 1997 were designated to pay the salary arrears of Russian officers—little seems to trickle down beyond the senior enterprise and government officials who are the prime beneficiaries of such deals.

Bilateral trade undoubtedly will expand. There simply are too many potential benefits for both sides to prevent such expansion.

As the past six years have shown, however, obstacles remain in the way of a broad-based and swift expansion to the levels envisioned by the two presidents.

Noninterference in Internal Affairs. Neither Russia nor China has ambitions to transform the internal political or economic system of its partner. Indeed, each side has made it plain that the internal affairs of the other are inviolable. Russia has strongly supported a "One China" policy, explicitly backing China on the status of both Taiwan and Tibet. China has, in turn, expressed its understanding of Russia's policy toward Chechnya.[11] In striking contrast to the Sino-Soviet past, the two sides have said nothing about ideological questions, although Chinese analysts continue to compare the success of Deng's approach to reform with what they perceive as Gorbachev's and Yeltsin's failures. Russia, for its part, has kept silent on human rights in China. It will be a "Tiananmen-proof" partner, not risking the political, diplomatic, security, or commercial benefits of the new relationship by criticizing the internal failings of the Chinese regime.

A Shared View of Regional and Global Issues. The Russia-China summit meetings in 1996 and 1997 featured a public display of solidarity and convergence on key regional and global issues. Indeed, the major accomplishment of the April 1997 summit in Moscow was a joint declaration that expressed the determination of both countries "to facilitate the development of a multipolar world and the establishment of a new international order."[12] The statement denounces "hegemonic" policies—a thinly veiled criticism of the United States. It describes the Commonwealth of Independent States (CIS) as "an important factor of stability and development in Eurasia" and expresses concern over "attempts to expand and strengthen military blocs."

The declaration also reflects a shared Chinese and Russian caution on the use of UN sanctions, a view that united the two countries in their approach to Iraq in late 1997. Moreover, in the declaration, the two sides agree on the dangers of ethnic separatism, particularly in Central Asia and Chechnya. These statements—and additional official and scholarly commentary on both sides—reflect a convergence of views on stability in Eurasia. China recognizes Russia's leading role in the CIS and desires that Russia exercise its leadership in the interests of stability along China's border. Russia, for its part, has no interest in seeing separatism grow in either Tibet or Xinjiang.

This growing solidarity gives many U.S. observers great anxiety over the future of Russo-Chinese relations, particularly as these relations develop in tandem with Russian or Chinese cooperation with Iran. Our own essayists divide over whether these expressions of solidarity are meaningful or not. Gilbert Rozman argues that the two sides' aim is "nothing less than a counterthrust against a new world order led by the United States." Trenin and Voskressenski are more reserved, stressing the tactical benefits of solidarity but raising doubts about its operational significance. The two sides, in fact, still do not see eye-to-eye on key Asian matters. The Chinese have expressed concern over the April 17, 1996, U.S.-Japanese Joint Declaration on Security. Russia has kept silent on the matter. China has made no attempt to expand the four-power efforts on Korea to include Russia. My own interviews with Chinese specialists and government officials in January 1997 revealed a great deal of cynical appreciation of the leverage NATO enlargement has given China over Russia. They were willing to pay a small rhetorical price in terms of joint statements to exercise this leverage. Similarly, Russia's support of a "One China" policy is largely ceremonial. Moscow follows the example of other nations in eschewing formal recognition of Taiwan but looking to Taipei for expanded trade and informal links.

Arms Sales. Russo-Chinese rapprochement is sustained by arms sales. At a January 1998 meeting at the Carnegie Moscow Center, one Chinese participant called arms sales "the glue" of the bilateral relationship and a key to whether the two countries will approach the $20-billion target set for bilateral trade by the two countries' leaders. More than a quarter-century after the breakdown of serious Sino-Soviet military cooperation, renewed discussions on arms sales began with General Liu Huaqing's June 1990 visit to the USSR. The organized transfer of defense technology through scientific exchanges began in 1992. Russian defense exports to China were an estimated $2.1 billion in 1996, comprising almost 70 percent of China's arms purchases in foreign markets.

China's military modernization requires substantial improvements in its air force, command, control and communications, naval power projection, and space technology capabilities. Russia has accommodated or appears willing to accommodate China in all these areas. It has sold China a range of electronics, air-to-air and surface-to-air missiles and air defense systems, armored fighting vehicles and T-72 tanks, and SU-27 fighters (including, in April 1996, the license to manufacture this aircraft). China has placed orders for four Kilo-class submarines. There are reports that China has acquired or is seeking other advanced aircraft, such as the TU-22M "Backfire" bomber, as well as Russian cruise-missile technology, missile guidance and satellite systems, and nuclear weapons–related technology.[13]

Arms sales are responsible for much of U.S. and Western anxiety about the future of Sino-Russian ties. For the foreseeable future, China will have an obvious and enduring military need for Russian military technology and systems, and Russia will need to sell both to help sustain its declining defense industries. Official statements by senior Russian defense officials indicate they believe Russia has at least a fifteen-year lead on China in key military capabilities. In this perspective, the current sales do not create a military threat to Russia itself.

These calculations, however, could be mistaken. Russia's sales to China and other Asian countries have the potential to upset regional military balances in areas of vital U.S. interest in East and Southeast Asia or the Taiwan Strait. At the very least, the upgrading of key Chinese military capabilities places an added burden on the United States and its regional allies in future crises. Improved Chinese capabilities inevitably raise awkward questions about U.S. staying power in an altered strategic environment. These problems are more the result of the fit between China's military modernization and Russia's collapsing defense industrial base than of a common strategic policy. Arms sellers, not strategic planners, are the driving force on the Russian side.

Energy. The two countries are also drawn together by a fit between China's rising energy requirements and Russia's gas and oil. As China's economy continues to grow, it will require higher volumes of energy—a resource that mainland China does not possess. China naturally has looked to Russia to supply this need from Russia's large reserves of gas and oil in its Far East and Siberia. China has also taken an increasing interest in oil from Kazakhstan, which could potentially put it in competition with Russian and Western energy firms. Russia and China have embarked on several energy projects endorsed by recent summits. At the 15th World Petroleum Conference in October 1997, Russian and Chinese energy officials discussed plans to build two pipelines—one that would connect the natural gas reserves of Russia's Irkutsk region with China's Shandong Province and ultimately reach Korea and Japan, and one that would run from western Siberia to Shanghai, via the Xinjiang Province, to supply China's vibrant Southeast. Moreover, China is not the only Asian economy that will require significant increases in energy in the decades ahead.

Three hurdles face joint Russian and Chinese efforts to extract and transport energy from Siberia and the Russian Far East: (1) the lack of pipelines; (2) the lack of capital to construct and maintain the pipelines (Russia and China cannot follow through on their intentions in this area without outside help); and (3) Russia's unstable political and investment environment, especially in the Russian Far East.

At the late October 1997 round of the "Gore-Chernomyrdin" Commission (the U.S.-Russian Joint Commission on Economic and Technological Cooperation), U.S. oil companies criticized Russia for not making progress on joint U.S.-Russian projects. Exxon has also protested the Russian government's decision to invalidate a tender that Exxon had won to develop oil fields at the Timan-Pechora site. Russia's weak infrastructure and fragmented decision-making bodies at the center and in the region make it difficult to sustain momentum on joint production deals. Indeed, in 1998, "Gore-Chernomyrdin" itself changed briefly to "Gore-Kiryenko" only to settle on "Gore-Primakov." China will have no special advantage when these same obstacles confront it. Russian-Chinese joint production efforts are potentially even more vulnerable, since both countries need outside capital.

As Martha Olcott argues, two 1997 deals between China and Kazakhstan suggest that, for China, Central Asia may eclipse the Russian Far East and Siberia as an energy source. In September 1997, Chinese Premier Li Peng visited Kazakhstan, cementing two deals earlier signed by the Chinese National Petroleum Company to build a pipeline from the western part of Kazakhstan to China. The first, modest shipment of oil from Kazakhstan to China—a shipment of 1,700 metric tons of Kazakh crude by rail to refineries in China's Xinjiang Province—was sent in late October 1997.[14] Russia is likely to try to benefit from this project—either by linking it to western Siberian oil, which would have a shorter and cheaper route, or by bidding to supply the pipe for the project. Yet, there are interests in Russia that do not welcome alternative pipelines or direct competition to Russian export routes. Thus, energy may well be a source of both cooperation and friction in the Sino-Russian relationship in the years ahead.

The Mechanisms of Cooperation. Over the past six years, the two sides have built up important mechanisms of cooperation. They hold regular meetings of heads of state and senior ministers. They have formed various intergovernmental working groups to realize the agreements reached at senior levels. These groups include special structures on trade, defense cooperation, and energy. The two sides have had real successes in resolving or at least ameliorating long-standing sources of tension in the relationship—achievements ranging from the steady progress on delineating and demarcating Asia's longest shared border to the five-nation agreements on confidence building and military restraint. One should not underestimate the influence of these successes or of the structural adjustments that both governments have made to accommodate and expand bilateral ties. At the very least, these build up a hedge against the sudden reversal of dynamics in the relationship, ensuring that problems that arise have ready-made structures in which they can be addressed.

Mutual Assessments

A key contribution of the essays in the first section is their outline of Russian and Chinese mutual assessments.[15] These assessments are important, as Gilbert Rozman argues, for "the Sino-Russian partnership has developed unexpectedly and could change in ways not yet well incorporated into projections of great-power relations." The four essays that address this issue—those of Li, Lu, Voskressenski, and Rozman—each provide a slightly different framework for understanding the development of mutual assessments through time and across the Russian and Chinese analytical spectrum.

Li Jingjie's essay, for example, describes three distinct periods in the development of the bilateral partnership, stressing, in particular, key moments in the Chinese debate about ties with Russia during each period. The first period, 1989–1992, is one of intermingled thaw and anxiety. The warming of bilateral ties was unmistakable, but many Chinese analysts feared that the fall of the USSR would bring about Russia's close integration with the West and potentially create a solid bloc surrounding China. The collapse of the Russian-Japanese summit and Yeltsin's trip to Beijing in 1992 signaled the start of a second period, which Li sees as encompassing 1993–1994. This period saw closer cooperation between the two governments, progress on border issues, and the flourishing of border trade. This period also brought problems, including the management of border trade and Russian fears of illegal immigration. Chinese analysts argued about the extent of the constraints on Russian power and whether Russia had come to a more or less stable outcome internally or lived under a system of continuing "dual power."

The most recent period, from 1995 to the present, features the maturing of a full-fledged strategic partnership and state-to-state contacts at the highest levels and through working groups designed to give that partnership meaning. This period is also marked by a consensus among Chinese analysts that Russian foreign policy has reached a steady and consistent state, defined by traditional Russian national interests, such as the protection of Russian influence in lands long under Moscow's sway. Many analysts believe the framework provided by national interests will prove enduring, whether or not communists come to power. Despite its survey of Chinese debates, Li's essay leaves the reader with an appreciation for the underlying unity of Chinese and Russian policy and the commitment of the leaders of both countries to create and sustain a genuine partnership.

By contrast, Alexei Voskressenski maps out the various Russian perspectives on relations with China, dividing Russian analysts into three categories: optimists, pessimists, and pragmatists. Pragmatists recognize the inherent limits in the bilateral partnership and the inherent disadvantages for Russia in embracing an ambitious, politically driven model of partnership. Optimists see the expansion of Chinese power and the advantages a strong China has for Russia; pessimists see that power's expansion, but focus on the potential negative consequences for Russia of a stronger China.

Lu Nanquan's aptly titled chapter, "Chinese Views of the New Russia," discusses Russia's economic and political struggles as seen by the major schools of thought in the Chinese foreign policy community. The author summarizes Chinese views of Russia's economic reform and its future, its great-power potential, and the possibility of Russia regaining great-power status as a future pole in an "irreversible" multipolar world. In addition, the author intersperses his chapter with his own personal recommendations on how Russia could alleviate some of its social, economic, and political difficulties. His recipes tend toward what he sees as China's successful experience, yet Lu equally stresses a broad-based Chinese view that the choice of a political and economic course is Russia's own, declaring that "no matter how Russia carries out its economic reforms, no matter what kind of model it chooses, the reforms are Russia's own affair."

Gilbert Rozman presents his analysis by examining Russian and Chinese views on several topics crucial to the future of the strategic partnership. These include assessments of national strength, the partnership itself, the emerging world order, and predictions about the future development of Sino-Russian relations. Each of these topics reveals a core common understanding that cements the partnership, even though doubters and skeptics also have something to say. In fact, Rozman sketches out the most ambitious view of what the two countries have accomplished to date, seeing the creation of a relationship "virtually synonymous with a peacetime alliance. Indeed, through coordination of arms supplies and joint efforts to shape the global strategic environment, what is promised could be one of the significant collaborations of modern times."

The issue of how the two countries view one another's national strengths may, in fact, turn out to be a crucial future determinant of the relationship. As all the authors in this section demonstrate, the majority of Russian and Chinese policy makers and analysts believe that power is shifting away from Russia and toward China. Many in Russia, perhaps prematurely, already credit China with superpower or near-superpower status. While almost all the Russians we spoke with during the course of this project expressed the notion that Russia should become one of the major centers of power in a multipolar world, many of these same people doubt that it can accomplish this goal. Russia continues to enjoy an advantage over

China in military power, but even this advantage is hostage to stalled military reform at home and a belief that China's military modernization will not produce a superior army anytime soon.

Moreover, Russia has never been a strong economic power in Asia and still seems a long way from becoming one. China, however, has one of the fastest growing economies in the world—although whether it can sustain such high growth rates in the future, particularly in light of the economic crisis in East Asia, is open to serious question. China also intends to become a well-rounded world power, including a military power. Although it is unlikely to achieve such status quickly, its potential to do so is widely recognized and even taken for granted by an increasing number of Russian observers. If China's progress in this direction continues, it will bring about— some even say it already has brought about—a dramatic strategic role reversal in which Russia will increasingly find itself playing the *demandeur* or even junior partner to a strong China.

In Beijing, we found a number of Chinese specialists and policy makers optimistic that China would continue to hold an economic and political advantage in the relationship. In Moscow, those who said they favored strong Russian-Chinese ties nevertheless acknowledged China's growing might; in both Moscow and the Russian Far East, those who were skeptical about the partnership with Beijing viewed the shifting balance of power with profound anxiety. Nearly all those interviewed acknowledged that Russia is, at best, unaccustomed to such a role and will find it a difficult one to manage gracefully. Yet, if the Russian-Chinese relationship is to continue developing, both sides must manage what both see as a rising power gap.

THE RUSSIAN FAR EAST

The two sides must also manage a serious future challenge from the Russian Far East. The second section of this volume provides a detailed overview of the potential sources of this future problem. Gilbert Rozman provides a comprehensive overview of the problem in transforming a region structured to play the role of a fortress into a free trade zone. Elizabeth Wishnick and Tamara Troyakova focus specifically on the problems of Sino-Russian relations as seen from Heilongjiang and the Russian Far East, respectively. Both authors report the frustration of early expectations for mutually beneficial trade, the growing corruption, and what can only be called "civilizational" frictions and prejudices. Judith Thornton, Michael McFaul, and three migration experts—Galina Vitkovskaya, Zhanna Zayonchkovskaya, and Kathleen Newland—present extended analysis of the economic, political, and demographic roots of the current crisis in the Russian Far East.

Russia is an Asian power geographically, militarily, and politically—but not demographically or economically. The Russian Far East region is underpopulated, especially in comparison with adjacent Chinese provinces. Moreover, there has been a steady Russian out-migration from the region since the late Soviet period. Siberia and the Russian Far East produce more than 90 percent of the country's gas and oil, all the diamonds, and a great share of other important natural resources.

In the Soviet period, however, economic life in these regions was sustained by a system of government subsidies for transportation, energy, and food, as well as higher salaries and housing incentives. This made the region especially vulnerable to the collapse of the Soviet system. As this system and its subsidies disappeared, residents of the Russian Far East came face-to-face with market realities. It was no longer possible to rely on Moscow and European Russia as a market; the real costs of energy and shipping made the products of the Russian Far East uncompetitive there. The region's adjustment to a world of more open markets and open borders was further complicated by its role as security outpost of the former USSR. Many in the region still harbor Soviet-era suspicion of the outside world, particularly of China.

Moscow received a lesson of its own from the collapse of the old system: the central government's influence can no longer depend on imperial or Soviet command methods. Even now, the center is not without real instruments of influence—it is richer and controls a system of laws and tariffs that it uses to its advantage. Yet, it is also immeasurably weaker than it has been in generations. Moscow must find a new way of managing its relations with the regions— and perhaps the most important test cases, alongside the ethnically diverse regions of the North Caucasus, will be the geographically distant regions of Siberia and the Russian Far East. Neither the regions nor the central government have yet found a satisfactory and stable substitute for the old relationship under the Soviet system. The likelihood that this internal struggle between Moscow and the Far Eastern regions will continue for some years to come undoubtedly has geopolitical consequences, especially in Russian-Chinese relations. At a minimum, Russia's Far Eastern regions continue to show Russia's weakest face to the world's most dynamic area.

The Political Struggle between the Center and the Regions. Both the center and the regions are weakened by a political struggle laid out, from different perspectives, in Michael McFaul's and Tamara Troyakova's chapters. This struggle seeks to define the structure of federal relations and the division of property and power that this implies. Moscow can no longer afford to dominate, coerce, or subsidize the Russian Far East. This change is not simply a consequence of the economic decline that Russia has experienced as it attempts a transition from a command economy to a market-oriented one. Moscow would not have been able to maintain its earlier spending even if it had retained a command economy; the economy had been in decline since the mid-1970s. At most, Moscow could have put off reassessing its spending in the Far East for a few years.

Not surprisingly, these circumstances have engendered fierce contention for political and economic power between the center and the regions. "Paradoxically," McFaul writes, "as the republican challenge to Russian federalism has subsided, the federal compromise between Moscow and Russian oblasts has grown increasingly strained." There is no more striking case of this conflict than the tensions between Moscow and Primorskii Krai Governor Yevgeniy Nazdratenko. In this case, McFaul states that the center "represents the cause of liberal policies and institutions. . . . Decentralization has allowed the Primorskii governor to consolidate a local authoritarian regime." Troyakova, herself a resident of the Russian Far East, sees things from a different perspective. She acknowledges the strong-arm tactics of Nazdratenko but makes plain that federal efforts have been largely ineffective or, in the case of the Federal Program on Economic and Social Development of the Far Eastern and the Trans-Baikal Regions in 1996–2005, largely for show. She sees this program as announced "only to increase Yeltsin's chances for garnering votes from the region in the 1996 reelection," noting that funding dried up soon after the elections were over. Troyakova also ranges beyond

Primorskii Krai to contrast Nazdratenko's politics with those of neighboring governors.

The struggle to define the appropriate division of powers between center and region is not likely to end soon. The regions, including the Russian Far East, are not seeking to secede from the Russian Federation but merely to increase their rights and control. Moscow could not reimpose the old controls even if it wished to do so. Yet, the outlines of a new balance of power between the center and the regions still are not clear. As long as the struggle to define them continues, the Russian political scene, especially in the Russian Far East, will be defined by a divided and distracted government, revenue shortfalls, and the absence of the basic regulations and enforcement mechanisms necessary for a normal market economy and stable political relations.

Regional Economic Realities. Judith Thornton, Elizabeth Wishnick, and Gilbert Rozman all provide insight into the underlying economic obstacles to prosperity in the region. Although Siberia and the Russian Far East are frequently invoked—especially in Moscow—as the future engine of Russia's economic revival, the transition to a market economy complicates Moscow's ties with the region. Much of the industry built up in the past is unprofitable under market conditions. Under Soviet rule, the region was little more than a resource colony and military outpost of the center. It sent fish, timber, minerals, and military equipment to European Russia and elsewhere in the USSR. More than half the food and fuel consumed in the region came from other parts of Russia.

Judith Thornton details these problems in a comprehensive overview of regional economic issues. She argues that the region's economic problems lie in continued overregulation by the center, the unprofitability of local processing industries, and nonmarket constraints such as bribery and extortion, which force would-be entrepreneurs to pay security fees. Moreover, key industries are producing goods that are worth less than the raw materials used to make them. Ferrous metals, coal, and agriculture could not cover costs if wages were at world market levels. In addition, although the Russian Far East traditionally has sent its goods and resources to European Russia, its natural trade partners are the neighboring regions of China, Korea, and Japan. Although strong cultural tensions still divide the local Russians from their Asian neighbors, attitudes are slowly changing, especially among the Russian elite, who already engage in profitable (though gray- and black-market) international trade.

Rozman, Wishnick, and Troyakova record the cycle of boom and bust that has marked border trade. In the first years of the opening of the China-Russia border, the regions most affected—Khabarovsk, Amur, and Primorsk in Russia, and Heilongjiang in China—provided a crucial impetus to the explosion of bilateral trade. By 1992, a kind of "border fever" had broken out on both sides. Wishnick's essay describes in great detail the high expectations engendered in Heilongjiang for profit from this trade. Deng Xiaoping gave China's northern border regions preferential treatment. Although the terms were not as generous as those earlier given to the free economic zones in southern China, they boosted economic activity. Chinese companies that had flourished in the southern free economic zones rushed north to open new branches. Beijing also gave Heilongjiang and neighboring northeastern regions the authority to license companies. As a result, it became very easy for interested Chinese to secure rights to engage in cross-border trade.

Northeast China—especially Heilongjiang, a disadvantaged region compared with the southern regions—nurtured high expectations about its newfound role as supplier to the needy Russian Far East. The border districts of Heilongjiang Province benefited greatly from access to both the province's Russian neighbor and China's southern regions. Average income in these districts increased from 400 yuan to 2,000 yuan from 1988 to 1995.[16] In Heilongjiang, the standard of living improved dramatically. Russia's border regions also benefited. Russian economic reform policies required the center to discontinue the hefty energy and transportation subsidies to the regions that, in Soviet times, had made the economy function and had hidden the real costs of both from the consumer. After the collapse of the Soviet Union, when severe shortages appeared and Russian production fell into disarray, Chinese traders were there to fulfill demand. Inexpensive—and sometimes shoddy—Chinese goods filled an important niche.

Border trade in this form could not be sustained, however. Gilbert Rozman, Judith Thornton, and Elizabeth Wishnick provide complementary accounts to explain why. The emergency shortages immediately following the collapse of the USSR and continuing into 1992 were quickly filled, and, by 1993, low-quality Chinese goods had saturated the market and earned an unfavorable reputation in Russia. In 1993–1994, Beijing imposed tighter controls on its economy, reducing large-scale construction projects on which Russia had counted for its steel and concrete exports. It also reintroduced quotas on goods imported from the Russian Far East. Numerous factors contributed to the eventual decline in cross-border trade in 1994, among them the lack of an administrative infrastructure at the borders; the prevalence of barter trade; congestion, petty regulation, and corruption at the border crossings; and general suspicion and misunderstanding on both sides. While China underestimated the impact of regional problems on bilateral relations, Russia was too distracted to perceive the economic tensions between Beijing and its provinces. China hopes more regulation in the near term will restore Russian confidence, permitting an expansion of border trade in the long run; it has tightened the visa regime and exercised greater supervision over the actions of its traders.

Control of the region's rich resources clearly is an aspect of the political struggle with the center. As Moscow-based politicians, banks, and financial-industrial groups vie with their regional counterparts for power and wealth, the only thing about which they agree is that foreign competitors must be kept out.

The center's economic policies hinder the region's development. Moscow has imposed export license quotas, requires regional producers to sell their products to central trading authorities, and mandates the surrender of foreign exchange at below-market rates. These measures have encouraged widespread rent-seeking, corruption, and evasion of existing laws and regulations. Most observers understand that the large discrepancy between Russian and Japanese reports of fish exports reflects the enormous gray and black markets that exist in fisheries—a direct result of the government's policies.[17] Thus, even if the center prevails in the struggle with the regions, it will neither restore the order necessary for normal economic life at home nor attract much-needed capital from abroad. The economy of the Russian Far East will remain overregulated, unpredictable, and very risky for outside investors. This lack of economic normalcy in turn ensures the continued deterioration of the economy, which already features energy shortages, high prices, and serious underemployment and unemployment.

Demographic Imbalances. Only 7.5 million of nearly 150 million Russian citizens live in the Russian Far East. As one 1994 study put it, "the demographic potential . . . of the Far East is clearly insufficient for the development of the natural resources located there. . . ."[18] The situation continues to deteriorate, and no early reversal is on the horizon. In 1990–1992, for perhaps the first time since Russia annexed the region in the nineteenth century, there was a net out-migration of more than 225,000. Moreover, the rate of out-migration was increasing, with 12 per 10,000 leaving in 1991 and 56 per 10,000 leaving in 1992.[19] During the same period, there was a net drop in population of about 2 percent—a result of declining birthrates, rising death rates, and out-migration. Early in this century, between 1906 and 1914, state-sponsored migration brought perhaps 2 million people to the region. Russian and outside observers agree that the Russian state lacks the capabilities to launch and sustain a similar policy, while the residents themselves are already voting with their feet.

Between 2005 and 2010, Russia is expected to experience a natural decline of some 15 percent in the working population. These figures foreshadow a precipitous decline in available labor. Many European countries have faced a similar situation; in all cases, they attracted immigrants to fill the empty places in the economy. Russia will not be able to avoid a similar approach, although the local populations tend to see the prospect of Chinese or Korean immigrant labor as a "yellow peril," not as an act of salvation for the local economy. In the next decade, the tensions between the anxieties of the local Russian population and the needs of the labor market will deepen. Thus, Russia must not only develop a sound immigration policy but also work hard to lay the groundwork for such a policy. Neither the center nor the regions have even begun this work.

Disproportionate settlement along the border in China is another part of the problem. Only about 7.5 million Russians live in the Russian Far East; some 120 million Chinese live across the border in Heilongjiang. The figures for Primorskii Krai and its neighboring region in China are 2.3 million and 70 million, respectively. These numbers alone represent tremendous potential pressures for change—in defiance of the best wishes of diplomats and statesmen in Moscow and Beijing. Both sides have tightened visa and border regimes. They have delayed planned bridges across the Amur River and the improvement of other transportation infrastructure.

These measures have had an effect. As Vitkovskaya, Zayonchkov-skaya, and Newland note, the wild exaggerations of the numbers of illegal Chinese immigrants in Russia cannot be substantiated by any serious governmental or academic source. They write,

> The scale of Chinese migration to the Far East and Eastern Siberia has been routinely exaggerated in the Russian press and political debate. Estimates of as many as 2 million have commonly been cited. More sober local estimates were in the 100,000–200,000 range, not all of them (perhaps not even the majority) permanent. The Chinese government estimates that 300,000 Chinese reside in all the CIS countries put together, and it has repeatedly felt compelled to deny any territorial ambitions in the Russian Far East.

The demographic problem, however, is not far from the minds of any of our Russian authors. They fear that Russian economic conditions, and perhaps Chinese social conditions in the Northeast as well, will not support the maintenance of a regime of restrictions indefinitely. The demographic pressures will not be reversed. Their existence does not, itself, mean that large-scale Chinese immigration will occur; policies may continue to try to hold the line. It should be remembered, however, that historically the Chinese as well as the Japanese and Koreans have settled in these regions, and that they continued to live there under Russian rule until Stalin's forced migrations and increased tensions between the USSR and the People's Republic of China turned the border into a zone of ethnic separation. Today, any of the large-scale economic projects that have been proposed—such as the pipeline that both sides agreed to pursue at the April 1997 summit or other plans for large-scale resource extraction or port upgrades—are likely to require vast supplies of labor that neither Asiatic nor European Russia can provide. Over time, the pressures of the market and the open frontier could subject the region to a thoroughgoing Sinicization, transforming the region and its links with both Moscow and Beijing.

Beijing does not have a policy of colonizing Russian land. In fact, China has worked hard to diffuse Russian anxieties about any present and future population shifts. The "pull" pressures may, however, become too great for Beijing to control. Large-scale Chinese migration clearly would transform the demographic makeup, trade patterns, culture, and political orientations of this part of Russia.

This migration would not necessarily—though it, indeed, could—spark conflict between the two states. But Sinicization of the region would, at the very least, alter the terms of Russo-Chinese cooperation. It would build in Chinese influence in the future development of Siberia and the Russian Far East. Greater cooperation with China would, thus, become a necessity, not a matter of choice.

Clearly demographic pressures will exert influence on the region for decades to come, complicating the task of maintaining stable Sino-Russian relations and adding to tensions, should relations become more fragile. Because illegal Chinese migration is still small, however, there is still time to lay the groundwork for a "soft landing" on Chinese migration. Such a soft landing requires the end—or at least the moderation—of political and economic competition between center and regional elites, so that effective government can begin. It requires that political leaders in both the center and the regions understand Russia's long-term labor requirements and adopt a more flexible notion of both immigration and guest workers. It particularly requires Russia to overcome lingering fears and anxieties about the coming "yellow peril." No observer can look at either the central or the regional authorities most concerned and conclude that the breathing space currently allotted is being used to carry out these pressing tasks.

CENTRAL AND EAST ASIA

The third and final section of the book looks at Sino-Soviet relations through the prism of larger Asian issues. Martha Olcott analyzes the role Central Asia has played and will continue to play in Sino-Russian relations. Harry Gelman concludes this section with a consideration of the link between developments in Japan and the Korean peninsula and Sino-Russian relations.

Stability in Central Asia is paramount for Russia and China as well as for the states of the region. Russia and China are geographically separated by inexperienced and potentially unstable Muslim states. The two big powers and the three Central Asian border states have agreed that instability and ethnic separatism are common threats. The Sino-Russian partnership includes a division of labor in Central Asia built around each country taking the lead on its side of the old Sino-Soviet border. China will, of course, police its own territory.

Russia is presumed to be the primary agent of stability on the other side of the old Sino-Soviet border, working directly with its Central Asian neighbors. The economies, transportation and communication nets, political structures, and security orientations of the new states still reflect the long history of czarist and Soviet rule. Olcott describes the past century of Sino-Russian encounters in this region, a review that underscores both the importance of the region for each country and the shift in power now under way from Moscow to Beijing; much of this historical review depicts an assertive Russia, conceiving of its interests as deeply engaged in China's Northwest and often intervening to pursue those interests.

Yet, the current division of labor in Central Asia may not be stable. Olcott, in fact, stresses that "long-term Chinese advantage in the Central Asian states is not compromised by allowing Russia near-term advantage in the region." Russia is deeply concerned about cross-border conflicts in Afghanistan and Tajikistan, its own military weakness and internal distractions, and the stability of the Central Asian regimes themselves. Russia appears just strong enough to contain existing conflicts in the region, but not strong enough to resolve or suppress them. Indeed, it can be argued that even if Russian military power were sufficient to resolve the conflicts, the Central Asian states would not consent to the Russian presence necessary to do so.

Thus, the combination of declining Russian military capabilities and the desire of Central Asian states to disengage from a dominating security relationship with Russia defines the current security structure in Central Asia. Yet, this structure is unlikely to produce stability. In the longer term, the region as a whole will forge expanded linkages with the outside world. In the next five years or more, such ties will not be sufficient to erode Moscow's position, but they will eventually create economic, political, and even security alternatives to Moscow's currently dominant role. But anyone looking at Russia's declining economic, political, and military reach has to wonder how long it will be before Russia cannot fulfill its part of the bargain. China cannot afford an unruly Central Asia. Should instability in Xinjiang and Central Asia grow, China would have intervene.

Russia and China face still other security threats. Russia fears that the spread of Islamic fundamentalism in Central Asia would alienate the region even more from Russia. China's foremost fear is ethnic separatism, which in its western regions takes the form of Islamic fundamentalism. While both Russia and China are interested in preserving the status quo with regard to security, no such restraint is apparent in trade and other economic activities. China is already working to transform Central Asia into a dynamic place from which it can benefit. The Sino-Kazakh pipeline deals highlight this interest. Russia, for its part, prefers stagnation to an economic dynamism that would leave it out of the game. The rise of Uzbekistan to the status of a regional power will also complicate Russia's current political, military, and security arrangements.

All these trends are at work, even if China is content to let Russia handle problems on its side of the border. Yet, there is no guarantee that Russia can handle them. If it proves unable to do so, China's own economic development and the links it forges between important energy and other resources in Central Asia in a decade's time may very well require China to take a more active role in protecting its interests there. China could not ignore either support for separatism within Northwest China coming from Central Asia, or political and social chaos there that could inspire similar conditions in Xinjiang. If Russia fails to police its side of the border, China will undoubtedly find itself forced to do the job. Thus, China's interests in its own stability could overwhelm the current Russian-Chinese division of labor in Central Asia.

Harry Gelman's paper draws our attention to the interconnections between Sino-Russian rapprochement and a complex, unfinished security agenda in East Asia. Indeed, this bilateral relationship historically "has conditioned the strategic environment in East Asia. And each time, too, changes in the Asian landscape in their turn had an impact on the behavior of Moscow and Beijing toward each other and helped (along with other factors) to change the relationship." Gelman's essay singles out several issues to illustrate his point, including Russian arms and technology transfers to China; the future of Taiwan; ongoing changes in Japan's security policy; and future challenges from the Korean peninsula. In each of these issues, he sees "discontinuities in the regional geopolitical environment [that] have already begun to create a new divergence of Russian and Chinese interests." In short, important questions for the future stability of East Asia are likely to fray the Sino-Russian partnership.

On the Korean peninsula, for example, Russia and China share a common interest in wanting to prevent large-scale conflict or collapse. Yet, little else draws them together in East Asia. China has seen little reason to upset the four-power talks on the future of the Korean peninsula by insisting on Russia's presence at the table. In North Korea, Russia has lost—in part, willingly sacrificed—its former influence. In South Korea, Russia has made much less headway than China. In addition to lacking the centuries-old ties that China has with the entire peninsula, Russia also cannot hope to compete with the economic ties that South Korea and China have established over the past decade.

The U.S.-Japanese alliance is another fundamental Asian issue on which China and Russia seem to disagree. The upgrading of that alliance at the Clinton-Hashimoto summit in April 1996 was greeted with suspicion in China. Russia, however, has made clear that it sees little of concern in strong U.S.-Japanese ties. Former defense minister Rodionov stated as much during his visit to Tokyo in May 1997, much to Beijing's dissatisfaction. News agencies quoted him as saying that he "welcomes that Japan and the U.S. are building even closer security ties."[20] Both Russia and Japan have made the improvement of bilateral ties a strategic priority, although the economic effects of the Asian financial crisis on both countries rob this effort of much of its momentum. Nevertheless, high-level meetings, including the November 1997 "no neckties" summit, have restarted a long-stalled peace treaty and led to a new agreement over fishing rights. Both sides now agree that the thorny issue of the Kurile Islands must not be an obstacle to better relations, although neither side has figured out a way to resolve the issue. Japan is the Asian partner of choice of many Russian economic reformers. Yet, a relationship with Japan will require Russia to take serious steps to adapt its own economy—steps made more difficult now by the current economic and political crisis. Indeed, the full benefits of ties with Japan will not emerge unless the Russian economy becomes more open, orderly, and predictable. China, however, needs no such changes in Russia either to sustain its ties or derive benefits from the Sino-Russian partnership. Nevertheless, despite current economic and political obstacles to sustaining Russo-Japanese ties, Japan will likely be a decisive factor in shaping the future of the Sino-Russian partnership.

CONCLUSION

Russo-Chinese rapprochement is now a well-established feature of the Asian diplomatic landscape, but its future will be determined by how both countries manage the challenges outlined in this book. These challenges from the Russian Far East, Central Asia, and East Asia are likely to limit the scope of bilateral strategic cooperation. Russia's economic crisis and the resulting political efforts that have and will be made to address it will certainly constrain Russian actions. On key issues of the emerging world order, the two sides will often speak as one. Whether they will coordinate their actions is an open question. As the Kosovo crisis demonstrates, however, both sides will find tactical opportunities to join together to the detriment of U.S. policy. Russo-Chinese partnership in such areas could prove to be a serious irritant to the United States, yet it will fall far short of an alliance seeking to reduce the options of the United States in Asia.

The most likely trajectory of the relationship is that Russia and China will continue to deepen their cooperation. Each will see bilateral ties not as a grand alliance or as an alternative to ties with the United States and the West, but rather as something that increases its own options. China needs a tranquil northern and northwestern border. It benefits from Russian defense technologies. These things alone are enough to sustain interest from China's side. Russia, however, has to weigh gains and losses. The Russian-Chinese relationship is perhaps Moscow's most visible foreign policy success. It shores up Russia's position in Asia and has served as a striking reminder of the potential for Russia to look beyond the West for partners. Yet, Russia faces the looming problems of a weak Russian Far East, China's rising influence as its own declines, and the lack of expected economic benefits from the relationship in areas other than arms sales.

Political linkages, a shared worldview, and arms sales give the relationship durability. Yet, substantial constraints restrict the development of trade, confine serious security cooperation to arms sales and the expression of ideological solidarity, and create future regional rough spots that both sides must address. In this context, the partnership will remain but can only develop so far. Sooner or later, these two nations, with their different strengths and prospects, will confront an array of problems arising along the old Sino-Soviet frontier. In these encounters, perhaps a decade or more hence, Russia is likely to discover that it can no longer manage an equal partnership with China. The Sinicization of the Russian Far East or a more assertive Chinese stance in Central Asia will certainly challenge the views of those in Moscow who are most committed to developing a strategic partnership with Beijing. In the event of such problems and tensions, neither side has an interest in a return to military confrontation.

Russia will have to either acquiesce to growing Chinese power, becoming a junior partner in an increasingly unequal relationship, or attempt to balance its relations with China by reaching out to other Asian and global partners. The latter is the option Russia is attempting to follow now, particularly in its high-profile expansion of relations with Japan. Yet, for such a balanced Russian policy toward Asia to emerge, economic conditions within Russia would have to become more stable, and Russia's presumed partners, particularly Japan and the United States, would have to devote substantial energy to supporting the emergence of such a policy.

A less likely trajectory, but one that cannot be ignored, is a maturing of the current partnership into something deeper and more anti-Western. A number of still unlikely trends would have to develop to make this scenario more plausible, beginning with Russia's acceptance of China as the senior partner guiding such an arrangement. In addition, the United States would have to mishandle relations with both China and Russia so badly as to destroy the strong incentives that each has to maintain pragmatic ties to Washington. The makings of such mishandling might be prompted by an escalation of the Taiwan problem into a Chinese-U.S. conflict and a simultaneous breakdown in U.S.-Russian relations.

A third trajectory might arise if China experiences serious internal problems similar to those that plagued the Soviet Union in its last years. If China were to undergo a substantial weakening of its central government in response to an internal political and economic crisis—a scenario that many China experts consider unlikely but not impossible—this pressure could create a frontier every bit as unstable as that in Afghanistan and Tajikistan. This frontier would contribute to the emergence of a new arc of crisis from the Russian Far East to Afghanistan, dominated by regional powers attempting to cope with continental pressures of population movements, scarce resources, and violence. Such dangerous developments would only deepen the problems of managing security in an already complex East Asia.

Whichever way the relationship develops, there are important implications for U.S. interests in Asia. Sino-Russian relations are an underappreciated factor in an increasingly unpredictable East Asian security environment. There is, however, no reason for the United States and its Asian allies to overreact to the current Russia-China rapprochement. The United States in particular, and the Western world in general, will continue to be the major external influence on both Russia and China. A transformation of the China-Russia relationship into a competing alliance is likely only if Washington badly misplays its hand with both countries. The United States should be prepared for the two countries to act together in some cases to oppose or try to modify U.S. policy, as they did in opposing the use of force against Iraq in early 1998.

Despite present and future problems posed by Sino-Russian cooperation, the United States and its allies directly benefit from the relaxation of tensions along the old Sino-Soviet border. Steps to reduce military forces there and the expansion of bilateral and regional trade from nearly zero to the present level make conflict between Asia's two greatest land powers unlikely and Asia more stable. In fact, some measure of Russo-Chinese cooperation is essential if the two countries are to manage future problems in East and Central Asia that, if unchecked, could add to Asian instability.

Although strong U.S. ties to both Russia and China are, indeed, the best guarantee to keep the relationship from becoming an anti-Western alliance, other important actors also influence the course of the Sino-Russian relationship. Japan's role in particular is important. U.S. policy makers ought to work with both Moscow and Tokyo to sustain the normalization of their bilateral relationship currently under way. As both nations face daunting economic challenges, they need this support all the more. In the long run, a strong relationship with Japan will lend greater support to the political and economic reforms that Russia needs to carry out. In the near and medium term, sustaining cooperative ties with Japan will be a difficult undertaking for Russia precisely because real economic transformation is required. The relationship with China makes no such demands on

Russia. Stronger Japanese-Russian ties require more effort to sustain and therefore greater encouragement from the United States and other Western countries, especially now, when both Russia and Japan face serious, though different, economic challenges of their own.

Russia's weak position in Asia as a future source of instability and tension needs to be factored into the calculations in every Asian capital. The Russian Far East will be one of the most politically vulnerable and economically troubled parts of Russia for some time to come. This vulnerability will not lead to secession; rather, the region will be subject to a set of demographic, political, and economic pressures that will continue to worry Moscow and to concern other powers in Asia. The future of Northeast Asia is complicated enough without the emergence of chaos in the Russian Far East. No one's interests—least of all the United States's and Japan's—are served by a challenge to the territorial status quo in Northeast Asia or by prolonged instability there. The potential dangers of Russia's weakness in its Far Eastern regions—and in Asia, more generally— need to be addressed in diplomatic discussions, particularly those involving the four major powers of the region: the United States, Russia, China, and Japan. An important element of such discussions must be the encouragement of substantial economic reform in this region of Russia and its integration into the economic dynamism of the Pacific Rim. Japan and South Korea will be key to the success of this effort.

There is room for cautious multilateralism in Northeast Asia. Given the still underdeveloped state of bilateral relations in the region, including continued tensions between key U.S. allies such as Japan and South Korea, it is premature to recommend a full-fledged multilateral structure, such as one modeled on the European Organization on Security and Cooperation in Europe, to address looming problems. Some cautious efforts need to be made, however, to inculcate a greater habit of multilateral cooperation among countries and regions. Regional cooperation is required to limit the scope and impact of illegal fishing, organized crime, and smuggling. Certainly, multilateral economic support must be found to help sustain economic reforms in Russia and the first positive steps in Russo-Japanese relations. Multilateral cooperation will continue to be required to manage the movement of goods and especially people.

The solution to the latter is not bigger fences or tighter visa regimes but broad-based cooperation between Russia's center, its Far Eastern regions, and its Asian neighbors. It is, in fact, hard to imagine an economic recovery in the Russian Far East that does not involve the orderly influx of capital and labor from these neighboring countries.

Finally, the integration of the resources of the Russian Far East and Central Asia into the Pacific Rim and world economies is crucial to the long-term stability of Russia itself and the peace of the region. As East Asian energy demand rises, the connection between a stable and prosperous East Asia and the stability of the Russian Far East, Siberia, and Central Asia will become clearer. What many U.S. analysts regard as Asia's "backside" or even "backwater" is already becoming increasingly linked to lands on Asia's rim. Thus, areas once remote from U.S. strategic planning will have an increasingly direct influence on areas of vital interest in East Asia and the Persian Gulf. Certainly, the expansion of energy and transportation links, new regional and subregional systems for security and economic cooperation, and the potential for large-scale cross-border migration make it important to understand these linkages before they surprise the West or its allies. To anticipate these developments, more attention must be given to understanding Russia's role in Asia, the Russia-China relationship, and the impact that the Russian Far East, Siberia, and Central Asia will have on shaping the future of all Asia.

NOTES

[1] *Xinhua*, April 25, 1996.

[2] "Russian-Chinese Joint Declaration on a Multipolar World and the Formation of a New International Order," *Rossiyskaya gazeta*, April 25, 1997.

[3] The figures for 1998 suggest that the level of trade is still falling, while senior Russian officials—including Prime Minister Primakov—have called in early 1999 for expanded high-technology trade with China as a way of improving trade volumes.

[4] The U.S. members of this group described the outlines of this consensus in a study group report entitled *Limited Partnership: Russia-China Relations in a Changing Asia* (Washington, D.C.: Carnegie Endowment for International Peace, 1998). This introductory essay borrows generously from this report. It also builds upon two other of the author's previous essays: "The Russian Far East as a Factor in Russian-Chinese Relations," *SAIS Review*, vol. XVI,

no. 2 (Summer-Fall 1996), pp. 1–20, and "Slow Dance: The Evolution of Sino-Russian Relations," *The Harvard International Review* (Winter 1996–1997), pp. 26–29.

[5]"Agreement between the Russian Federation, the Republic of Kazakhstan, the Kyrgyz Republic, the Republic of Tajikistan and the People's Republic of China on Confidence Building in the Military Field in the Border Area" (unofficial translation, Ministry of Foreign Affairs, Russian Federation, 1996), author's copy.

[6]*Trud*, April 26, 1997, p. 3. Kazakhstan, Tajikistan, and Kyrgyzstan also joined this agreement but declared that they would implement complete troop withdrawals from their borders with China. *Strait Times*, October 10, 1997.

[7]Rodionov's list of potential threats is variously reported in the leading newspapers. China is among those listed in the report run in *Kommersant-Daily*, December 26, 1996, p. 1.

[8]Personal notes from interviews conducted by Sherman Garnett and Gilbert Rozman in Beijing, January 1997.

[9]"Chernomyrdin, Jiang Zemin Satisfied with Evolution of Ties," in *ITAR-TASS*, June 7, 1997 *(FBIS Daily Reports)*.

[10]At a regular session of the border demarcation working group in July 1999, the two countries failed once again to reach an agreement on the status of the two islands. "Regional Border Talks End in Beijing," in *ITAR-TASS*, July 3, 1999 *(FBIS Daily Reports)*.

[11]See, for example, the April 1996 communiqué from *Xinhua*, April 25, 1996.

[12]"Russian-Chinese Joint Declaration on a Multipolar World and the Formation of a New International Order," *Rossiyskaya gazeta*, April 25, 1997, p. 3.

[13]On Russian arms sales to China, see Bates Gill and Taeho Kim, *China's Arms Acquisitions from Abroad: A Quest for 'Superb and Secret Weapons'* (Oxford and New York: Oxford University Press, 1995), pp. 48–70; Christoph Bluth, "Beijing's attitude to arms control," *Jane's Intelligence Review* (July 1996), p. 330; Stephen Blank, "The Dynamics of Russian Weapons Sales to China" (prepared for the Conference on Chinese Naval Power, Leesburg, Virginia, July 11–12, 1996); and Stephen Blank, "Russia's Clearance Sale," *Jane's Intelligence Review* (November 1, 1997). For a Russian view, see Pavel Felgengauer, "An Uneasy Partnership: Sino-Russian Defense Cooperation and Arms Sales," in Andrew J. Pierre and Dmitri V. Trenin, eds., *Russia in the World Arms Trade* (Washington, D.C.: Carnegie Endowment for International Peace, 1997).

[14]*ITAR-TASS*, October 21, 1997.

[15]Our project enjoyed the benefits of a separate but related effort led by Gilbert Rozman and financed by the National Research Council to look precisely at Russian and Chinese mutual assessments.

[16]See Elizabeth Wishnick's chapter entitled "Chinese Perspectives on Cross-Border Relations" in this volume.

[17]For a detailed look at the Russian-Japanese fishing trade, see Boris Reznik, "Mafia i More" (The Mafia and the Sea), *Izvestia*, October 21, 1997.

[18]A. G. Visnevskiy, *Naseleniye Rossii* (The Population of Russia) (Moscow: Yevraziya, 1994), p. 38.

[19]Pavel A. Minaker, ed., and Gregory L. Freeze, translator, *The Russian Far East: An Economic Handbook* (Armonk, N.Y., and London: M. E. Sharpe, 1994), p. 21. In 1992–1996, the region lost 559,000 people, or 7 percent of its population. Northern territories got hit the hardest, but people are also leaving the southern areas. Khabarovskii Krai and Amur Oblast lost 3.3 percent of their population each; Primorskii Krai, 1.5 percent. Eastern Siberia's Chita Oblast, which neighbors China, lost 3.1 percent of its population. Losses in internal migration are only partially recovered (by approximately 30 percent) by migration from the CIS countries. Most migrants are Russian expatriates reuniting with their relatives, or Koreans returning from Central Asia and Kazakhstan, where they were forcibly expelled during Stalin's purges. Koreans, however, are not welcomed to the areas they once inhabited for fear that they will take away property from current occupants or even seek an autonomous district. Statistics taken from *Chislenost, Sostav i Migratsiya Naseleniya* (Number, Composition, and Movement of Population) (Moscow: Russian Federation, Central Statistical Office, 1992), p. 12.

[20]*Moscow Times*, May 20, 1997; and *Asia Times*, May 21, 1997.

PART TWO

The Present and Future Shape of the Strategic Partnership

2

The China Factor: Challenge and Chance for Russia

Dmitri Trenin

The elevation of China to the status of a world power has changed the entire geometry of international relations. This process became especially clear against the backdrop of the decline and fall of the USSR and, of course, of Russia's current troubled times. While the rise of China affects the interests of all its many neighbors, as well as the United States and Europe, no major country is likely to be influenced by that process more than Russia. The reason is not the proverbial 4,300-kilometer-long common border itself. It is the inevitable interaction across that border that is beginning to change things in a serious, but also very unusual, way. China is gradually becoming a major external factor capable of influencing not only Russia's foreign relations but increasingly also its domestic environment, to the extent of even reshaping the very nature of Russia—its government structure, ethnic composition, and general orientation in a changing Eurasia.

Not all this influence is self-evident today. After several decades of grueling hostility with Beijing, official Moscow quite rightly considers improved relations with China a major achievement in its foreign policy. Unlike the case in Europe, Moscow managed to end its parallel Cold War in the East on what looked like honorable terms. No territory was lost. Troop withdrawals were confined to the evacuation of some 75,000 men from Mongolia. The end of alliance relations with that country, and also with Vietnam and North Korea, mostly meant the contraction of financial and economic obligations that under the new circumstances became impossible for Russia to honor. At the same time, none of the former allies has turned against the Kremlin. What a contrast to the way the Warsaw Pact collapsed, not to mention the breakdown of the Soviet Union itself.

To many, this "soft" weakening of Russian power in the region appeared to be more than counterbalanced by the end of the thirty-year-long conflict with China. Ever since they reconciled their quarrel in 1989, both Moscow and Beijing repeatedly underlined the essential equality of their new relationship and, since 1996, promoted the idea of a "multipolar world without leaders and the ones who are being led."[1] The 1990s have, so far, witnessed no serious disagreements, let alone crises, between China and Russia. No wonder words like stability, predictability, and mutual respect are frequently heard from both capitals. Moscow remains predominantly optimistic about the future. The Russian government evidently fears that pessimism will become a self-fulfilling prophecy and, thus, hardly welcomes doubters in its ranks. Occasionally, questioning Beijing's intentions is shrugged off as a U.S. ploy to keep Russia and China wide apart.[2] The result is complacency.

Even in the official portrayal, however, Russo-Chinese relations look superficial and sterile. The highfalutin and unwieldy formula, from the April 1996 Summit Communiqué, of "constructive interaction growing into a strategic partnership oriented into the 21st century" rings hollow.[3] At least in the Russian case, there is no long-term strategy beyond the usual platitudes. Despite the exponential rise in official contacts, Russian elites do not spend much time trying to understand their Chinese partners and generally do not care. Economic ties, proclaimed the backbone of the new relationship, are too much dependent on individual shuttle traders and arms dealers. Cultural contacts are few. It is emblematic that the Russian-Chinese Friendship Committee created in 1997 is a bureaucratic backwater, totally ineffectual.

The widespread fear of the "yellow peril" is the complete opposite of official complacency and self-satisfaction. That fear has existed always—even at the peak of Soviet grandeur—if only in the form of jokes about a "Sino-Finnish border" and the "pessimists who are learning Chinese" (as opposed to the optimists studying English). What is new is that what seemed a remote prospect decades ago is now perceived to be rapidly becoming a reality. Mistrust and disdain toward the Chinese are taking root in various strata of the society, and the Far Eastern regions are especially affected. True, the concern is not so much about a sudden invasion by the People's Liberation Army (PLA) across the Amur River; rather, it is a potentially endless stream of Chinese immigrants to Asiatic Russia. Many warn that the thin dyke of the border protecting the underpopulated Russian areas from the overpopulated Chinese provinces is already leaky and, in the future, can be swept away entirely. Hard evidence of the "Chinese demographic expansion" is lacking, but figures of 1–2 million illegal settlers are commonly cited.[4] Chinese migration, real and imagined, alongside Russia's concessions under the border settlement agreement have become major political issues in the Far East, with a number of local politicians adopting nationalistic and alarmist positions.

Nothing better illustrates the prevailing ambiguity among the Russian elites than the predicament of the military establishment: it has to approve massive Russian arms sales to China in order to salvage something from the crumbling national defense industrial base, while at the same time counting China among Russia's potential adversaries for the future.

Both smug complacency and inordinate fears may be fed from the same source: poor knowledge of China by the Russian elites and their lack of serious interest in Asia. For centuries, the Russians regarded their East Asian neighbors with superiority and a pinch of contempt. The place accorded to China in their thinking was always secondary, at best. It is revealing that when some members of the Russian elite mused about ways of countering NATO enlargement and came up with the idea of a Moscow-Beijing axis, it never occurred to them to first inquire about the Chinese attitude toward such a proposition. Characteristically, China appeared important not per se, but as an informal partner against the United States.[5] Matters are not helped by the paucity of academic experts on China and the little attention paid to the country by the Russian media, all of which shows how far most Russians are from appreciating their "China problem"—as regards both China's increasing international gravity and Russia's antiquated view of its Eastern neighbor.

WHITHER CHINA AND WHAT IT MEANS FOR RUSSIA

The current Sino-Russian relations are unprecedented. Never since the late seventeenth century, when the two countries first came into contact, has Russia lagged behind so far in terms of power, economic performance, or international influence. Russia's China problem is that already today China significantly surpasses Russia in the aggregate national capacity, with very few Russians realizing its implications. If and when Russia finally emerges from its present predicament, its relative decline—vis-à-vis China—is likely to continue. The change came incredibly quickly: at the beginning of the 1990s China still lagged behind the USSR, but by the end of the decade it surpassed Russia's GDP fivefold.

Of course, past growth rates should not be extrapolated into the future. But even assuming that the Chinese growth rate drops to 6 percent and Russia starts its long-awaited economic bottoming-out and advances at 4–6 percent a year, the gap between the two countries' GDP would continue to widen, so that by 2015 China's economy may dwarf Russia's by a factor of ten to one. This example is nothing but an illustration of a current trend, but it is very telling nonetheless.

China's population is 1,200 million people, while Russia's is a mere 146 million. A much higher per capita GDP has always been the source of national pride for Russians in their dealings with the Chinese. At the height of the Sino-Soviet dispute, the difference was sevenfold. Even now, Russia continues to stay ahead of China in this area, although the gap has significantly decreased: the Chinese indicator is about 60 percent of the Russian one,[6] and many coastal cities in China have already surpassed the average Russian level. In the beginning of the twenty-first century, China may very well overtake Russia in this sense as well, although the differences in the volume and quality of the accumulated national wealth will remain for a longer period.

Thus, Russia is becoming not only weaker than its neighbor but also poorer. Should the Chinese reforms fail, Russia is likely to lose even more, for it could be easily swamped by millions of hungry and desolate Chinese fleeing across the border from domestic misery and conflict. In any event, the fact remains that one-fifth of the population of the globe has been shifted away from traditional ways of work and life toward individualism and consumption values that destroy the former society. Leading Russian Sinologists conclude that the situation where everybody stood to gain from reforms is nearing its end.[7] Ironically, the mounting difficulties are the direct consequence of the successful development of the country over the past twenty years.

If as few as 5 million out of the expected 200–300 million Chinese migrants cross the Russian border in search of a better opportunity, this number will be enough to equal the entire Russian population of the Far East. True, China itself has vast unoccupied territories with difficult natural and climatic conditions, but this fact does not mean that the Russian territory may not, in principle, attract Chinese economic migrants. The Maritime region (Primorie) and the Amur area (Priamurie) offer migrants living and economic conditions very similar to those of neighboring Manchuria.

Russia's considerable advantage over China has been—and remains—its much wider and richer resource base. The terms for China's access to those resources will be one of the salient problems in future Russian-Chinese relations. The worsening environmental pollution in China raises a different kind of problem. As a neighboring country, Russia inevitably feels the consequences of this large-scale ecological catastrophe.[8]

For China's neighbors and partners, including Russia, the gradual transformation of the communist authoritarian regime has indefinite consequences. On the one hand, democratic China will undoubtedly become an important factor in Asian peace and stability and in the world at large. On the other hand, the democratization of Chinese society is obviously a lengthy process, an epoch, as can be seen from Russia's example. Moreover, the experience of the post-Soviet states shows a link between the process of democratization and the growth of nationalism and aggressive behavior.

Generational changes in China will eventually eliminate leaders who studied in the USSR. Soon, China and Russia may be the only two major countries in the world whose elites will be near total strangers to each other. This ignorance is hardly compensated for by the emergence of virtual Chinatowns in Moscow and other Russian cities, where Chinese rarely come into contact with Russian society, except to bribe the authorities.[9]

In both China and Russia, the regions are becoming more assertive. Ironically, those that border on the other country are among the more depressed, in the Russian case, or the less thriving, in the case of China. Their failure to cooperate closely is not surprising but serves as an indication of a serious disconnection between the two countries.

The return of Hong Kong under Beijing's rule in 1997 became a symbolic end of the era of Western superiority. The Russians have yet to realize that the Chinese firmly associate them with the European imperialists, and their historical grievances include unequal border agreements, the subjugation of Manchuria, the suppression of the Boxer Rebellion in Beijing, as well as later attempts to dominate China from the standpoint of an "elder brother" in the socialist camp.

At present, China is focused on its domestic needs even more than today's Russia. Beijing's foreign policy is clearly subordinated to the policy of economic and social transformation of the country. As a result, China is often called a country interested in maintaining the international status quo. This conclusion is imprecise. China is a country that is capable of being satisfied rather than one that is already satisfied. Starting with establishing control over Tibet in 1950, China has expanded its territory. In the future, as China's power grows, the status quo—not just territorial—will continue to change in its favor.

Beijing declares the maturity of its foreign policy, the policy's nonideological nature and restraint, and the desire for dialogue and cooperation with all countries, especially neighboring ones. Indeed, China needs a peaceful foreign environment for an extended period. Nothing shows that Deng Xiaoping suffered from the "nightmare of coalitions" as did Bismark, but the heirs of the "patriarch of Chinese reforms" will keep in mind the hypothetical scenario of China being "surrounded" by the United States and its allies, partners, and clients. In principle, there exist in East and Central Asia and in the western Pacific conditions for the use of the balance-of-forces mechanism and the formation of a coalition intended to restrain the growth of China's power. Besides, China's dependence on the outside world, above all on the West, constantly increases. Consequently, the good-neighbor policy is not charity or a goodwill gesture from China but rather an urgent need.

The Chinese leadership comprises a group of mostly traditionally minded officials for whom the state is the ultimate value. In this sense, Beijing's foreign policy is quite "normal" and predictable. The essence of China's foreign policy strategy is no secret either: it is aimed at the strategic gain of the time needed to accumulate economic, political, and military power and, in the end, to make China a first-rate global, rather than only Asian, power.

Beijing will hardly use traditional military expansion for these purposes. China's current behavior is not aggressive; it is quite capable, however, of suppressing the will of others with its own weight. It will try to win without entering an open fight, to divide potential competitors without entering into alliances that will tie it down. One of the lessons of the 1997 financial crisis for China is the realization that China and other countries have important common interests. Yet, China's basic interests are clearly more important for Chinese leaders than the interests of the international community. Using economic power as the main instrument of its foreign policy, Beijing, if necessary, is quite capable of using military force.

In its relations with the West, China takes an intentionally contradictory position. On the one hand, Beijing does not completely reject its former position as leader of the "world's poor," while on the other hand it is delighted to be a candidate member of the "world government." The West continues to doubt whether China has already become a "system player" or, once inside the system, will play against it.

Russia does not have these qualms. Russo-Chinese relations are to a large extent a function of both countries' attitudes toward the West, in particular the United States. Beijing publicly sided with Moscow regarding the expansion of NATO. It seems this is not simply a quid pro quo in response to Moscow's support of Chinese positions. If in the long-term prospect Moscow and the North Atlantic Alliance get closer, it will complicate China's strategic position, whereas institutionalized Russia-NATO confrontation or at least the continuation of the current mutual estrangement could serve as a sort of guarantee against the encirclement of China by the West. Both Russia and China branded the NATO air strikes against Yugoslavia as acts of aggression. But it becomes ever more obvious that Beijing, unlike Moscow, is concerned not with the Balkans or the accession of Central European countries to NATO but with the intensified activities of the alliance and the United States in Central Asia. China's strategic interests are concentrated in precisely this region, which is rich in the fuel and energy resources so much needed in China and which serves as a potential hinterland for Xinjiang separatists. Beijing takes no joy in seeing the economic, political, and military influence of the West, above all the United States, grow in this Chinese periphery, replacing the weakening Russian influence.

China, the United States, and Russia have moved away from the Cold War model of triangular relations. The famous triangle has, at the very least, lost its former rigidity.[10] It may even seem that diplomatic actions of the three countries positively stimulate each other. In reality, Russia is turning from a corner into a piece, albeit an important one, in the U.S.-Chinese arrangement. The United States and China much more often speak about a different triangle—this time a regional one with the participation of Japan.

Relations with Russia form for Beijing part of the policy intended to establish a favorable external environment. The main goal is to remove the potential threat from the North and the prospects of a political-military confrontation. In the early 1990s, Chinese leaders were still apprehensive of what they termed Russian imperialism or militarism. During the short-lived honeymoon in Russian-U.S. relations, they became even more worried at the prospect of Moscow becoming Washington's junior partner. Currently, China may be satisfied: there is no threat to it from Russia in the foreseeable future. The essence of strategic partnership with Moscow is to strengthen this favorable condition. Partnership will guarantee that Russia will not participate in any potential anti-Chinese coalitions. No matter how relations between China and the West develop in the future, the isolation of China will never be complete thanks to the Russian "safety valve."

The material basis for Russian-Chinese normalization is the border agreement among Russia, China, and Central Asian states. The positive significance of the 1991, 1994, 1996, and 1997 agreements can hardly be overestimated. For the first time, the entire length of the border is not only accurately delimitated (except for three islands) but also marked, except for small sections. Limitation of armaments and confidence-building measures in the 100-kilometer zone on both sides of the border reinforce political stabilization with a military and technical one. The resolution of the former Soviet-Chinese border problem made an enormous contribution to the security of East and Central Asia. Russians, however, should not forget that Chinese continue to regard the 1858 and 1860 treaties that underlie the present state and territorial delimitation between the two countries as unequal and imposed by czarist Russia on Qing China. Deng Xiaoping's behest contains clear indications that all consequences of the imperialist policies by European countries toward China must be overcome in the future. In principle, the will of the Chinese nation should, in the final analysis, overcome the unjust treaties of the past. Therefore, it seems it would be more appropriate for Russians to consider the latest agreements the regulation of the present borderline rather than the "final" border treaty. One cannot preclude that in the future the entire problem will be raised again in order to be solved on a "rational and just" basis.

So far, Chinese leaders have behaved themselves nearly impeccably with regard to Russia. China is one of the few countries that spare Russia's injured vanity. Beijing especially emphasizes the equal nature of relations with Moscow and echoes Moscow in speaking about a multipolar world and the unacceptability of hegemony. One could conclude that the Chinese are confident that their northern neighbor is suffering temporary difficulties and that in the future Russia will inevitably become one of the poles in the new international construction. Such a conclusion, however, will be too optimistic for the Russian Federation.

Clearly, new serious troubles in Russia or, worse still, the collapse of the country would present a source of serious danger for China. Beijing even rejects direct relations with individual Russian regions, such as Yakutia, strictly limiting those ties to the interregional level. China is interested in the stable development of Russia but not in its becoming considerably stronger. Beijing does not seek to include Moscow in the China–United States–Japan triangle in Northeast Asia or in the quadripartite (China, United States, and the two Koreas) talks on Korea. Although Chinese leaders have learned to play up to the remnants of Russian greatness, they are not convinced Russia is truly capable of becoming an independent pole in the system of international relations. Consequently, Beijing faces an important consideration for the future: to watch as Russia moves closer to a united Europe or the United States or to try delicately to attract it toward China.

Apart from its geopolitical and geostrategic significance, Russia is interesting for China as a source of energy and raw materials—though not the only one and probably less attractive than Central Asian countries. China believes that Russia is still capable of playing a stabilizing role in Central Asian countries, including countering pan-Turkic movements and political Islam that might threaten Beijing's control over Xinjiang.

China is not interested in Russia yet as a major economic partner, with the significant exception of military-technical cooperation. Russian arms are an attractive means for the modernization of the PLA, given their high quality and low cost. China will not buy Russian arms in mass quantities; it is more interested in purchasing technology to organize its own production.[11] Another potentially promising direction is organizing—with Chinese funding—the development of advance weapons systems jointly with Russia. If it happens, China will be able to achieve a qualitative shift of the military balance in Asia in its favor. The post-Kosovo environment makes such a scenario more likely.

China's growing economic might implies greater resources that can be directed for defense. With the GDP—calculated in purchasing-power parity terms—at more than one-third that of the United States, China can allocate for military purposes up to $50–70 billion a year without damaging economic and social development. This sum is no more than 2 percent of its GDP, roughly half of what today's Russia can afford to spend.

Officially, Beijing presents the modernization of the Chinese defense sphere as justified and long overdue. Indeed, military arsenals of China's neighbors contain today greater numbers of modern military equipment than do China's. It is urgently necessary to turn the PLA into a smaller but professional military organization. Despite growing military spending, the scale of the task is such that the pace of military modernization can hardly be called accelerated. China obviously expects a long break during which a major war, especially a nuclear one, is unlikely. Officially, China does not consider any state its potential adversary and remains the only state that declared it would not be the first to use nuclear weapons.[12] Russian military analysts are also unanimous in their opinion that in the next ten years China's political-military aspirations will not be directed against Russia.

Military détente with Russia ensures for China a reliable rear in the North and a certain stability in the Northeast. Priority development of the rapid deployment forces, the navy and the air force, rather than the ground forces, indicates that Russia has not yet seen

China as either a potential aggressor or as the most probable theater of military operation. Thus, Beijing is able to concentrate on strategic directions that are more important for it—the southern and southeastern ones. At the same time, Russian observers have doubts. China, in their view, is not yet ready for close collaboration in the sphere of cooperative international security and comprehensive arms control. The Chinese defense sphere continues to be closed to the outside world. The military doctrine and budget, personnel strength, armament, location of units, and formations are all secret. Weapons and technology purchases from abroad, including from Russia, are made under a cloud of secrecy.

So far, Russia's relative military weakness guarantees a strategic break for China for a minimum of fifteen years. China, however, is developing nuclear systems with multiple independent reentry vehicles. These efforts may be given an additional boost by the Indian and Pakistani nuclear tests of 1998 and 1999.[13] By 2010–2015, a parity in the number of nuclear warheads may emerge between the Peoples Republic of China and the Russian Federation, at the level of 700–1,000 warheads.[14] Because of China's military and strategic situation, this capability will more likely be directed against Russia than against the United States. But in Russia many people believe that the Chinese are intrinsically incapable of catching up with Russia in terms of military technologies and that they can only copy obsolete Soviet equipment. Given such an approach, Russia might easily fall into the mistake of self-complacency.

China's international weight is significantly increasing, but, at the same time, the dependence of the country on the global economic and financial systems grows, too. In the next ten years, Beijing will probably conduct a "frugal" foreign and security policy involving self-limitation and avoiding conflicts with other countries. But in the early twenty-first century, this self-restraint will most likely give way to a more active policy intended to gradually create not only a China-friendly, but also to a large degree a pro-Chinese, East and Central Asia. If this policy is successful, the basis for future Asian stability may well be not a multilateral security system but a version of *Pax Sinica*. The implications for Russia are most serious.

In the twenty-first century, China and the Chinese factor will influence Russia's foreign, defense, and domestic policies; economy; and development of demographic processes more than any other state. Russia thus far is not only unprepared for this eventuality, but also both the elites and the society at large have not yet grasped such a prospect. At the same time, the answer to the question "Which China is more preferable to Russia?" is quite obvious. Russia is interested in a prospering China that can satisfy the needs of its huge population and that will open its market to Russian goods and services. Alternatively, chaos in the Celestial Empire may turn into a nightmare for its neighbors. Armies of Chinese migrants can easily swamp the Russian Far East and Siberia.

PROSPECTS FOR RUSSIAN-CHINESE INTERACTION

Despite the commitment of the significant part of Russian elites to the old-fashioned geopolitical vision of the world and an obvious predisposition toward such cozy formulas as multipolar world and strategic partnership, major prospects for Russian-Chinese interaction lie in the economic, scientific, technical, and information spheres.

Russia's vital interests in the region "to the east of the Urals" consist in maintaining the sovereignty and territorial integrity of the Federation, achieving economic and cultural prosperity, and achieving integration into the world economic system, first of all with the countries of the Asia-Pacific region. Keeping a monocultural identity and unchanged ethnic composition can hardly be considered vital interests. The problem is that these state interests are not easily compatible with the private interests of individual players in the center and in the regions. Numerous governmental bodies, regional administrations, some sectors of the economy, and individual oligarchies have their own, often competitive, agendas in the relations with China. The officially proclaimed Russian goals do not always correspond to Russia's reduced capabilities.[15]

Economic Ties

China is important to Russia first of all as a vast market capable of consuming not only Russian raw materials but also industrial production and services. China is also important as a source of human and, in the future, investment resources necessary for the development of the Russian Far East and Siberia.

After the exuberant but chaotic development at the turn of 1990s, the economic ties between the two countries have entered a period of stagnation. The volume of trade in 1998 amounted to $5.8 billion—ten times less than that between China and the United States. This bilateral trade turnover is a far cry from the declared goal of $20 billion by the year 2000. The main items exported by Russia into China are weapons and military equipment. In 1997, Russian companies were unpleasantly surprised when they failed to win a tender for energy-producing equipment for the Three Gorges Hydropower Station project. Finally, also in 1997, the United States removed unilateral limitations on the supplies of nuclear power station equipment, becoming a powerful competitor to the Russian nuclear industry in China.

For Russian interests regarding China to be realized, Russia not only has to become more attractive economically but also must adjust its current attitudes significantly. For one, it should stop thinking of China as a market capable of consuming goods intrinsically noncompetitive in Europe and the United States. It is also time Russia abandoned the hope that China will match its political loyalty to the Sino-Russian partnership with lucrative industrial orders from Russian firms. There should be no illusions about Russia's part in modernizing China's heavy industry enterprises built with the help of the USSR in 1950s; China seeks more advanced equipment than Russia can offer today. The frequently repeated thesis about mutual complementarity of the Russian and Chinese economies needs a closer examination: sometimes it is only a myth.[16]

In dealing with Russians, Chinese note not only the muddle at the state, regional, and local levels but also that Russian businesses lack strategy, wanting to sell everything at once and at superhigh prices, too. Russians, on their part, resent the ability of Chinese to use Russian weaknesses and difficulties to buy certain goods, technologies, and know-how for peanuts. Yet, Russians must realize that if they cannot ensure development of the Far East and Siberia, Russia will lose those territories one way or another. Somebody else will develop them. A no less obvious truth is that Russia alone will not be able to develop its Asian provinces in the foreseeable future. The required investment can be, in principle, obtained from various sources, including the United States, Japan, and South Korea, while the work force to a greater degree will have to be imported from China.[17] Large-scale use of a Chinese labor force, which is cheaper and more disciplined than the local Russian one, may become a key to the development of the Far East and regions to the east of Lake Baikal.

PROSPECTS OF POLITICAL PARTNERSHIP

Close relations with China are not a luxury for Russia or even a matter of choice but an absolute and long-term necessity. In 1991–1992, the links with China—barter trade in food and industrial goods—literally kept the Far East alive. For at least the next fifteen years, Moscow cannot afford a confrontation or even tense relations with China. Russia has to a considerable degree lost its former military power—the only serious basis for its positions in Asia. Despite the invitation to join Asia-Pacific Economic Cooperation (APEC), Russia so far is economically and commercially absent in Asia and the Pacific. Thus, privileged political relations with the rising continental and world power expand Russia's possibilities for political maneuver. Fearing to find itself in isolation in its opposition to Washington, Moscow feels more confident when acting in the UN Security Council in the framework of an informal coalition with Beijing and Paris. There is a positive effect in Asia as well: the development of Russian-Chinese relations already influenced Tokyo in 1997 to put forward an initiative of improving relations with Moscow.

Russia and China have a number of interests in common. The desire to limit U.S. influence in the regions of the world that are important for Moscow and Beijing has already been mentioned. It should be noted here that possibilities for joint or coordinated antihegemony actions are narrow. Both states are interested in stability in Central Asia and on the Korean peninsula, as well as in the continuation of the peaceful and "demilitarized" foreign policy of Japan. Central Asia will be discussed below. Regarding Korea, China clearly is not prepared to use its influence to allow Russia to participate in the talks. At the same time, Russia and China mutually support each other's territorial integrity and do not question each other about the methods of warfare in Chechnya and the stabilization of Xinjiang. The Russian government prefers not to notice the problem of human rights or the persecution of ethnic or religious minorities in China while public pressure on the Russian authorities so far is too weak.

Of course, there is no possibility of a stable bloc between Moscow and Beijing or of a political alliance between them, which Russian politicians and even officials sometimes discuss. China feels no need for alliances, especially with a weak and unpredictable Russia, and will never agree to Moscow's leadership. Russian constructions of various axes, be they Moscow-Beijing-Delhi or Moscow-Beijing-Teheran or any others, are only monuments to the Russian political thought of a certain period and nothing more. Russian policies are not consistent in nature; Russia's proclaimed political goals are the result of more or less spontaneous interests.

In reality, the military-strategic aspect of Russian-Chinese relations does not occupy an especially important place. Most Russian strategists do not see China among potential military allies. Former defense minister Igor Rodionov in December 1996 mentioned China among Russia's potential adversaries, obviously reflecting the collective apprehensions of the General Staff rather than simply a personal opinion of the head of the defense establishment. Military cooperation with China is not included as a separate item in the main policy documents on the Russian military reform, contrasting with the way that cooperation with the CIS (Commonwealth of Independent States), NATO, or even Central and Eastern Europe was (at least before Kosovo) prominently featured. Despite the agreement on mutual nontargeting of strategic nuclear missiles and the regime of military transparency in the border area, the degree of trust between the Russian and Chinese military is lower than that in Central Europe at the end of the Cold War, and their contacts are probably less profound than those between the Chinese and U.S. military.[18] Supplies of Russian arms to China—the basis for not only military but also economic cooperation of the two countries—are of a forced nature and are mostly driven by commercial considerations.[19] Meanwhile, Russia is also supplying arms to India, Vietnam, and South Korea—all countries with potential problems with China.

At the same time, the Russian-Chinese agenda looks very narrow and is basically limited to traditional geopolitical issues. It practically does not include foreign economic, monetary, financial, or environmental problems. Although Russia and China are on the verge of joining the World Trade Organization (WTO), this issue also does not feature prominently in their relationship. Unlike their U.S. and European colleagues, Russian politicians in their communication with Chinese officials are content to limit themselves to the symbols of "high politics" and do not condescend to the "low politics" of commercial contracts. This is understandable: Russian globalism so far remains essentially archaic, emphasizing geopolitical and geostrategic subjects.[20]

Humanitarian Cooperation

Contacts between Russians and Chinese have never been so close and free as in recent decades. Ideological barriers have been removed. Possibilities for private visits appeared, as well as the opportunity to earn money during such trips. Several million Russian and Chinese visitors travel back and forth each year. Russian researchers and specialists work in China again, and Chinese communities have appeared in many Russian cities, including Moscow. Even taking into account the fact that this explosion of contacts has often brought not the best part of Russian society together with not the best part of the Chinese society, it is obvious that contacts have had a positive influence.

At the same time, Russians seem to lose numerous opportunities. Past experience is more of a hurdle than an asset to them. The Russian-Chinese Committee for Peace, Friendship and Development established in 1997 resembles a Soviet-era friendship society. Russia has not yet gotten out of the remnants of its superiority complex regarding its neighbors. Russians do not show any active interest in China, its language and culture, and prefer that the Chinese learn their language. Russians do not quite understand how Russia is viewed in China. Russian imperialism for Chinese is not a propaganda cliché but part of their history. Contacts between governmental officials or military officers are shallow in nature. Exchanges at the governmental level are infrequent, and when they do happen it is on the Chinese initiative or in Chinese interests. Finally, many Russians are terrified at the prospect of a more or less significant Chinese population appearing in Russia. During the three-quarters of a century in which the Far East served as a fortress against the outside world, many residents have forgotten that before the First World War 300,000–500,000 Chinese lived in the region. The tolerance of Russian Far Easterners toward Chinese as well as Korean immigrants is exceptionally low, which in the future may not only slow down the development of the region but also can become a source of real danger.

THREATS AND CHALLENGES FOR RUSSIA

The main danger for Russia in connection with the rise of China is to believe in the reality of a "yellow peril." If this were to happen, the Russian political scene, economy, and media would be deformed by an obsession with China and Chinese immigrants, doing much damage to Russia's national interests, regardless of the Chinese reaction.

No less dangerous is the quiet, gradual withdrawal of Russia from the Far East and Siberia as a result of the center's decreasing interest in the region, the continuing exodus of ethnic Russians, and the growth of separatist trends in the regions and their reorientation toward Asian power centers and, above all, toward Beijing.

A third danger is the emergence of Russia's excessive economic and political dependence on China, depriving Moscow of its freedom to maneuver in foreign policy and, to a certain extent, in domestic policy, as well. Such dependence is in no way a consequence of the growing difference in the two countries' weights but may rather result from unskilled policies. Russia is accustomed to playing from a position of strength but has been recently losing more and more. It has yet to learn to play from a position of relative weakness and in so doing attempt to gain benefits, especially since the stakes are seldom zero-sum.

In the economic sphere, Russia should be wary of becoming China's raw materials appendage, both in general and in specific regions of the country (for example, the Maritime region, the Khabarovskii Krai, and the Transbaikal area).

In the demographic sphere, the danger is not primarily the "demographic overhang" of Chinese provinces over the Russian Far East, which cannot be eliminated in any case, especially through the inconsistent or inefficient immigration policies of the Russian authorities. Indeed, major flows of Chinese migration are oriented to the South rather than the North. Yet, only a small portion of Chinese migrants will suffice to completely upset the current ethnic and political balance. Integration of significant groups of Chinese and Koreans in Russian society is necessary and, perhaps, inevitable. One study forecasts that by the mid-twenty-first century there will be 7–10 million Chinese living in Russia, who will thus become the second largest ethnic group in Russia after Russians themselves.[21] This possibility alone should revolutionize Russian thinking and mobilize the will of the authorities. In these conditions, the lack of clear and consistently implemented immigration policies virtually guarantees frictions on an interethnic basis that may easily lead to an interstate conflict between Russia and China.[22]

Such a conflict may result in the resumption of the Russian-Chinese military standoff, but this time on terms much less advantageous for Moscow. Both the Russian military forces and Russian presence in Asia are decreasing.[23] Having left Mongolia, Russia has lost even the theoretical possibility of repeating the Manchurian operation of August 1945 that arguably formed the foundation of strategic planning in the 1970s and 1980s. Although the defense of the Russian Far East involves great difficulties, the combat potential of the Russian armed forces, especially the combat readiness of the units and formations, is at the lowest level in the past fifty years.

Facing Chinese superiority in conventional forces, a growing Chinese nuclear deterrent, and a set of military and geographical circumstances that favor China, Russia is evidently ready to adopt a strategic concept similar to NATO's flexible response. Moscow will have to place new emphasis on nuclear weapons, both strategic and tactical (mostly air-based),[24] as well as develop the capability for transcontinental redeployment of reinforcements to the Far East in case of conflict with China.[25] The attempt to fulfil this twofold task will require more than just huge resources. Russia might well provoke China into a massive increase of its nuclear potential, resulting in a strategic parity between the two countries and the loss of Russia's current advantage.

Central Asia may become a serious problem for Russia and China, where growing contradictions between ethnic, clan, and religious groups, as well as problems over borders, water use, and natural resources, may surface in the next ten years, causing conflicts and provoking outside interference. The states that formed here after the collapse of the Soviet Union have managed to survive but remain weak, and the transfer of power in any of them to new leaders may lead to serious shocks. In this respect, China is probably interested, as a minimum, in strengthening its influence in the region so rich in energy resources, while Russia wants to keep Central Asia as a strategic buffer. Beijing is already successful in having its interests—not only economic but also political—taken into account by Astana and Bishkek, Moscow's closest CIS partners in the region.[26] Moscow analysts now foresee the possibility of a Russian-Chinese clash in Central Asia and propose that territorial integrity of the CIS countries be ensured with the help of the Russian nuclear umbrella.

Other possible threats from China are much less important for Russia. A forcible solution to the Taiwan problem will not disturb Sino-Russian relations. Moscow might even try to gain some benefits from the tension between Beijing and Washington (although a China-U.S. clash is unlikely).[27] The conflict in the South China Sea and the tensions in the Taiwan Strait area will naturally divert Chinese leadership's attention from the northern borders and will even create a possibility for opportunistic Russian leaders to achieve advantages through the supplies of Russian arms to all the potential parties of the confrontation: China, Vietnam, Indonesia, the Philippines, and Malaysia.

Russia will try to close its eyes to the internal conflict in Xinjiang, but this effort will become more difficult if Beijing, frustrated in its attempts to counter Turkic and Muslim separatism, attempts direct interference in the territories of Central Asian countries, which Russia considers to be the zone of its vital interests.

A separate issue is that of Mongolia. The country has for a long time been the ally of the USSR—first against Japan, then against China. The presence of 75,000 Soviet forces in Mongolia gave the USSR the capability to wage a powerful offensive against the Chinese capital in case of a war with China. The present Mongolia, for the first time in its history, enjoys real political independence. It is trying to establish relations with third countries (especially the United States and Japan) to escape the custody of both Russia and China, its historical hegemons. China is, however, used to seeing Mongolia as its vassal, a part of the historical Chinese Empire. Stronger Chinese positions in the region may lead to the reestablishment of Chinese suzerainty over Mongolia in one form or another. Mongolia's transition to the Chinese orbit cannot present a threat to Russia as such; the transition may become threatening only in the case of Chinese occupation of Mongolia, in other words, a mirrorlike repetition of the arrangement that existed throughout the 1970s and 1980s.

STRATEGIC OPTIONS FOR RUSSIA

So far Russia, unlike China, does not have any definite strategy for the development of relations with its neighbor. Moscow's China policy results from activities of various forces that usually cater to their short-term interests. How will Russian-Chinese relations develop in the future? The official optimism insists on the mutually advantageous peaceful partnership of the two power centers in a multipolar world. "Realists" hope that everybody, including China, the United States, and Japan, need a strong Russia as a stabilizing force in international relations.[28] Pessimists predict inevitably growing contradictions between a weakening Russia and an ever more up-and-coming China, and a resulting conflict between them. More pragmatic analysts prefer saying that China is both a prospective partner and a potential adversary for Russia. In their view, a transition to hostility, if any, will not be initiated by Russia, although it may be provoked by some Russian activities.[29]

In my view, the fundamental and instrumental factor is the growing gap between China and Russia in major indicators of national capacity and the gradual increase of Chinese influence on various aspects of Russian society. It is this fact, rather than ideological, geopolitical, civilizational, or any other preferences of elite groups (anticommunist-minded liberals; patriots fearing the Chinese threat; communists sympathizing with China; or pragmatists constantly balancing between the West, the South, and the East) that will set the framework of Russia's China policy. Finding itself in this situation, Russia could, in principle, choose one of the two basic strategies: side with the strongest or find a new balance of relations with the neighbor who became stronger.

Vassalization or Vampirization

The side-with-the-strongest strategy could have two scenarios: *vassalization of Russia* or the so-called *vampirization of China*. Vassalization would entail Russia agreeing to become China's junior partner and, hence, its association with "progressive Asia" against "the rotten West." In so doing, Moscow would retain sovereignty over Siberia. There are advocates of such a partnership in Russia today, and in the future the pro-Chinese lobby will definitely grow, yet chances that the vassalization option will be implemented are slim.

First, Russia's submission to another country, especially one with such a different civilization, would be rejected by the majority of the country. They would see such a union with China as a second edition of the Mongolian yoke. Second, while the advocates of submission to China want to sting the United States more than anything else, a struggle with the United States and its allies—for which purpose Moscow supposedly might offer a nuclear umbrella to China[30]—will not necessarily form the basis of Beijing's foreign policy. Beijing may want to accommodate itself to the West, seeing little value in Russia as a partner. Finally, China is unlikely to accept a formal alliance with Russia in the future, even if it guarantees a leading role to Beijing. The logical final result of vassalization is Moscow's "voluntary" acquiescence to Beijing's dominating influence in the territory east of the Urals.

Vampirization would mean a purely temporary and pragmatic closeness with China in order to receive the necessary nourishment—for instance, in the development of the Far East and Siberia. If that goal were achieved, the policy would be sharply reversed. To an extent, such an option would repeat the 1950s, except that Moscow and Beijing swap roles. The flaw of this strategy is that it initially implies a sharp shift from "eternal friendship" to an acute and prolonged conflict. The cost of the latter would overshadow the near-term benefits of "friendship." All other things being equal, it would be much more difficult to repatriate Chinese workers, farmers, and dealers than it was Soviet engineers and technicians in the past.

The Search for Balance

The search for balance may take several versions, too. The traditional rigid version implies *deterrence of China*. Russia itself does not have and will not have the resources to pursue such a course. To do so, Russia must join with others, which logically leads to the need to join an anti-Chinese coalition, best of all the one led by the United States. The problem is that historical processes cannot be reconstructed. The United States and China do not aim at confrontation, and, although one cannot in principle exclude a conflict between them, in the future it is difficult to imagine the circumstances in which China will play the role of Stalin's Soviet Union; Russia, the role of postwar Western Europe; and the future U.S. president, the role of Harry Truman.

A strategy based on the *interaction of interests* rather than the inevitably zero-sum balance of forces would be a lot more effective. The key elements of such a strategy would include: (1) priority development of the Far East and Siberia involving private Russian and foreign capital (Western, Japanese, Asian) and work force (from the CIS countries, China, Korea); (2) creating a system of economic, scientific, and technical mutual (rather than one-sided, as now) dependence with China; and (3) comprehensive development of relations with Japan, Korea, the United States, and other Asian and Pacific countries. The broadest possible internationalization of the development of the Russian Far East and Siberia will not only accelerate the process but also will prevent unilateral Sinicization of the territories. In other words, to keep what it has, Russia should change; if it tries to maintain hold of everything it currently has without any fundamental changes, it will risk losing everything in the end.

CONCLUSION AND RECOMMENDATIONS

Despite the impressive strides that have been made in the Russian-Chinese relationship in the past few years, Russia will still face an enormous China problem in the coming decade. As this article has argued, important concrete steps must be taken for Russia to understand the shape of this problem and to prepare an effective response.

First and foremost, the Russian government, foreign policy and business elites, and society at large must embrace a new "Eastern paradigm" in their thinking about the future. Russian elites and society at large need to realize that the main challenge for Russia in the early twenty-first century is unfolding in the East. How Russia handles it will determine the future of not only the Far East region but also of the country as a whole. Russians have yet to demilitarize their mentality, to reject the paradigm of a besieged fortress (geopolitical, civilizational, demographic, and so on) and not only embrace the ideas of interdependence but also implement them in political practice. Russia will manage to save itself only if it makes significant changes not only in outward behavior but also in its internal structures as well—in particular in the ethnic structure and cultural diversity of the population.

The imperial model of Russia's rebirth is doomed to failure—first of all in Northeast Asia where Russia currently is, and will be for the foreseeable future, the weakest power. Success may await an intellectual, businesslike, open Russia. Russians need to make a fundamental turn in mentality and practical deeds; this change, in principle, is possible. Historically, Russia's basic idea was to expand its territory. This goal resulted in a unique conglomerate of nations and cultures that did not dissolve in a super-ethnos yet became accustomed to cooperation and interaction. In the future, this ethnic and cultural diversity that has become a natural state for Russia may help it adapt to new realities and integrate more successfully into the outside world. In other words, the imperial heritage may assist in the development of a fundamentally new postimperial model of Russia. If Russia manages to turn its Far East into a site of active interaction with its close and remote neighbors, it will take its place in Asia; if not, it will be pushed to the periphery of the region, at best, or outside the region, at worst.

Another part of the solution is situated in Moscow offices and headquarters. The stumbling blocks are the traditional Eurocentrism, remnants of the imperial mentality, and the new vogue of geopolitics leading back to the nineteenth century. More significant obstacles are the nearly complete domination of private and group interests in the Russian elite and a lack of consolidation at the top, which breeds alienation of an atomized society from a "privatized" and— for most Russians—still nonexistent state.

Second, Russia must take measures to stimulate the economic development and political and demographic stability of its Far Eastern regions. In a general sense, the basic outlines of the solution of the Chinese problem are obvious if Russian can turn its East into a territory attractive for Russian and international business. The basic building blocks of economic stability there include custom and tax breaks; curbing corruption; limiting administrative interference and muddle; and creating the necessary transportation, financial, economic, and telecommunications infrastructure. It is also absolutely clear that Russia alone or even mostly alone will not manage to do it. A consistent policy of attracting and encouraging foreign investment is required as the main instrument of development. Specific attention should be paid to recreating favorable conditions for medium- and even small-scale projects that can dramatically change the business atmosphere in the region.

New economic policies demand a complementary demographic initiative intended to make the region more attractive in the eyes of its inhabitants and potential resettlers from the former Soviet republics. If resettlers are offered a significant package of benefits and the present population of the Far East is guaranteed employment, the negative demographic trends of the past decade could be stopped and reversed. Of course, a new "Stolypin policy"[31] of encouraging immigration to the region through the distribution of land and other economic incentives is beyond the economic means of the current government and is unlikely to work in any case. Out of approximately 3 million people who might permanently move to Russia, the Far East will be able to accommodate no more than 10–15 percent of them, even fewer if current economic woes continue. Moreover, according to UN estimates, the population of Russia will probably continue to decline, reaching 130 million by 2050 (17 million less than at present). Ethnic Russians from the European part of the country or from Central Asia and other regions of the former Soviet Union alone will not provide the numbers needed to solve new tasks or even to restore the balance at the former level.

Therefore, the demographic initiative must be supplemented by a new immigration policy.[32] Russia of the twenty-first century may become the country of immigration. Immigrants from East Asia will be the majority of new permanent arrivals. Spontaneous development of the process may lead to instability and conflicts, while skilled management of the process would considerably increase Russia's resources. A detailed system of quotas and immigration requirements—developed on the basis of U.S., Canadian, and Australian experience—might provide both highly needed workers as well as future active and loyal citizens. Such a Russia will no longer be seen as alien in Asia—it will be linked to other countries of the region by a multimillion-strong human bridge.

To successfully integrate new settlers into Russian society and acquaint Russians with Asian peoples, a large-scale educational and cultural initiative would be required. On the one hand, efforts should be expanded to train Russian experts on China, Japan, and Korea; the experts could then help Russian elites and the more active groups of the emerging middle class to a better understanding of Asian countries. On the other hand, Russia needs to think seriously about its image in the eyes of Asian elites.

Third, Russia has to broaden its economic ties with China and more actively manage its weapons and technology trade. Economic ties between Russia and China should not be limited to the Far East and Siberia, that is, underdeveloped regions. Today, when geographic proximity no longer plays the decisive role in choosing economic partners, Russia would do well to stimulate contacts of its major industrial and research centers with China. Russia must concentrate on energy diplomacy as well as winning and maintaining niches in China's markets. These aspects will be crucial tests of the staying power of the Sino-Russian relationship. Implementation of oil, gas, and electric energy projects in Siberia and the Far East as well as in Central Asia—with the participation of Russian companies—might help Russia acquire instruments that will give it confidence in its ability to hold up its end of the partnership.

In the sales of arms and military technologies, Russia urgently needs stronger export controls that would preclude unauthorized supplies of arms, technologies, and know-how. It is in Russia's interests to apply the statewide approach, not to succumb to the lobbyist influence on the part of producers and sellers of this or that type of weapons, of banks servicing those deals, and so on. The question is not whether to sell but rather which weapons categories and systems may be sold to China and which may not. Naturally, it would be ill-advised to sell the newest equipment to neighbors. But this is not the only point.

Because China is seeking not so much weapons supplies as access to technology that opens the way to starting its own production, Russia should be especially vigilant in the transfer of technology. Yet, the situation is even less clear in this sphere than in the area of arms sales. After Kosovo, there are signs that Russia may be prepared to relax its control over the transfer of military technology to China.[33] Short-term and even long-term advantages to the military-industrial complex are not the only factors worth considering. Russia may lose its military technology edge on China, which so far is its most important advantage in the field of defense. Military and technical cooperation in its present format is more in the interests of China than Russia: Russia is helping China modernize its armed forces in exchange for modest economic compensation that cannot save, let alone modernize, the Russian military-industrial complex.

Fourth, Russia has to begin to shape its strategic relationship with China in ways that will encourage a positive outcome for itself and a more stable outcome for Asia. Russia could use its position as a virtual monopolist in the Chinese market of arms to gradually involve China in a bilateral dialogue on military aspects of security. For starters, joint seminars could be organized, as well as exchanges of professors, researchers, and students of military academies. In the course of such contacts with the Chinese, Russians ought to seek—on a mutual basis—greater transparency of security policy, military doctrine, and trends in the development of the armed forces in China.

Later, Russia might directly commence shaping strategic relations with China, bringing in elements of the START treaties and other measures and applying them to bilateral defense issues. The two sides could begin with agreement on mutual notification of ballistic missile launches, for example. Both Russia and the international community at large are interested in ensuring that a rising China is also a more internationally integrated China, taking upon itself obligations in the field of international security similar to those the United States and Russia have taken. Moscow might assist in involving China in the multilateral process of control over nuclear and conventional weapons. Passing from the category of a near pariah state to the ranks of the international establishment, China cannot be interested in further proliferation of nuclear arms and missile technologies. China's adherence to the missile technology control regime (MTCR) and to the Wassenaar agreements on the control of transfers of conventional arms ought to become part of the agenda. No matter what Russia's problems are with its weakened conventional forces, it would be insane to provoke China into a nuclear arms race that Russia most likely would lose.

Fifth, Russia has to place its relations with China within the context of a new Asian diplomacy. Russia needs a logical Asian policy along the lines of the traditional European one. Such a policy implies better coordination of the Chinese dimension with policies regarding other countries of the emerging Asian geoeconomic and geopolitical space, from Tokyo to Delhi, from Akmola to Jakarta. Within this space, Russia will have to play from the position of relative weakness, using what resources it has, its friends in the region, the existing balances of power and interests, and international institutions.

Relations between Russia and China will be more balanced if Moscow is simultaneously successful in expanding its ties to Korea and Japan. Lacking developed relations with Japan, Russia will simply be unable to integrate into the "progressive Asia." The inflow of Japanese capital and technology is decisive for the rise of the Far East and Siberia. Neither the United States nor for that matter South Korea can substitute for Japan in this respect. But Japan, which at the turn of the century is facing a number of challenges of its own, might well find improved relations with Russia useful as a minimum and in certain cases vital. Tokyo and Moscow, for the first time in history, seriously need each other as a support for a stable and balanced new Asia. In these conditions, finding a solution for the territorial problem in the framework of a future peace treaty is vital. If the problem of the Kurile Islands again becomes an insurmountable hurdle for the transition to stable partnership between the two countries, it will testify to the near-sightedness and provincial mentality of the ruling Russian and Japanese elites. It should be emphasized that Moscow does not need to make a choice between Tokyo and Beijing—to maintain stability, Russia needs stable relations and broad interaction with both countries.

Russia and China are interested in the peaceful development of the Korean peninsula, where Moscow's influence, however, cannot compare with Beijing's. This influence is unlikely to change. Some opportunities may emerge for Moscow in the future. The Russian Federation and united Korea being the two weakest countries in Northeast Asia might find, for that reason, some grounds for mutual cooperation. They certainly have nothing to fear from one another and would profit from stronger and closer contacts. Russia may become a kind of a "safety valve" for Korea, squeezed between China and Japan; for Russia the "Korean factor" in the development of the Far East may partially balance Chinese and Japanese influence.

Russia and China will not stumble over one another in Korea. Mongolia and especially the countries of Central Asia, however, could pose serious problems for the relationship. After the collapse of the USSR, Mongolia—a former unannounced "sixteenth republic" of the Soviet Union—ceased to be of any interest to Moscow. Such disregard for that country is shortsighted from the standpoint of Russian interests. Given the growing influence of China over its former vassal territory, the strengthening of the political independence of Mongolia requires Russia's interaction with the United States and Japan.

In view of the changes in South, Central, and East Asia, it would be appropriate for Moscow to conduct an inventory of both the opportunities and the problems in the Russian-Indian strategic partnership, which ostensibly continues to be conceptually based on the memories of a different historical era and in practice is limited to the supplies of Russian arms and technologies to India. Now that India and Pakistan have joined the ranks of nuclear powers, Russia has to decide what its interests in the region are. The main one is obviously to assist regional stability through promoting New Delhi's and Islamabad's mutual restraint and their increased responsibility for this or that trend in foreign or defense policy. Russian interests will in no way be served if Russia and India find themselves in one camp while Pakistan and China are in the opposite one. There is enough common ground to warrant close interaction on the South Asian nuclear issue among the United States, China, and Russia.

Sixth, Russia has to anchor its new Asian policy with a new and stronger partnership with Kazakhstan and Kyrgyzstan in Central Asia. This region is crucial for Russian national interest, and Moscow still has a reasonable chance to maintain more or less significant influence there. Kazakhstan and Kyrgyzstan have a decisive influence on how the relations between Russia and China will develop in the region. Partnership with Akmola and Bishkek in the economic and security fields could go hand in hand with Moscow's support of regional cooperation within the Central Asian Union and with the development of Russia's bilateral relations with Uzbekistan and other countries of the region. Russia could use for those purposes the cooperation with international organizations such as the Organization for Security and Cooperation in Europe and NATO (including the framework of the Partnership for Peace program).

Finally, Russia must not forget that the United States is its immediate neighbor in the Pacific. In the next century, Russian-U.S. interaction will probably be more intensive in Asia than in Europe. In any case, Asian security is going to become a more acute subject than security in Europe. It is only natural that the Asian security model will differ from the European one. What is important is that the political Asia will grow out of the multitude of relations between pairs of states and the few multilateral institutions. Not only Russia's possibilities but also its will and aspirations will determine the role it will play there.

What has been termed elsewhere "Russia's China Problem" holds both a challenge and a chance for Russia.[34] A challenge can better than anything else concentrate the will and stimulate changes necessary not only for survival but also for positive development. Successful and timely changes will in their turn make it possible to integrate Russia into global processes not only in the West but also in the East.

NOTES

[1]*Rossiyskaya gazeta*, January 15, 1997, p. 7.

[2]See Karen Brutents, "Rossia i Azia," *Nezavisimaya gazeta*, June 22, 1999, p. 8.

[3]See "Joint Statement on Russian-Chinese Relations on the Threshold of the 21st Century," *Problemy Dalnego Vostoka*, no. 1 (1999), pp. 11–15. See, also, Brutents, "Rossia i Azia," p. 8.

[4]These figures are wildly off the mark. Local researchers in Primorie, for example, report the number of Chinese traders at any one time is around 20,000, plus some 6,000 seasonal workers (mainly in the agriculture and construction sectors).

[5]Alexei Arbatov, "Konsensus v rossiiskoi vneshnei politike" (Consensus in Russia's Foreign Policy), *Nezavisimaya gazeta*, February 8, 1997, p. 6.

[6]Based on the purchasing-power parity criterion, the per capita GDP in 1995 dollars for Russia was $4,480; for China it was $2,920, or 65 percent of Russia's level. See The World Bank, *The World Development Report: The State in a Changing World* (New York: Oxford University Press, 1997), pp. 213–14.

[7]Mikhail Titarenko, director of the Institute of Far Eastern Studies of the Russian Academy of Sciences, is one such Sinologist.

[8]Publications on this subject are so far infrequent in the Russian press. For some recent ones, see, for example, the *Nezavisimaya gazeta* supplement *NG-regiony* (NG-Regions), April 1998, p. 1.

[9]The number of Chinese living in the capital of Russia, often illegally, is estimated to be 50,000–100,000 persons.

[10]Not everybody, of course, agrees with this statement. A part of the Russian governing circles believes that Washington "cannot allow a stronger link between Russia and China." See, for example, V. Kuzar, "Rossiya-Kitai: Na rubezhe tysyacheletii" (Russia-China: At the Turn of the Millennium), *Krasnaya Zvezda*, November 6, 1997, p. 3.

[11]During a series of seminars sponsored by the Carnegie Moscow Center in 1997–1998, a number of participants stated that the large supplies to China of the newest Russian military technologies could become a material basis for long-term unity between China and Russia.

[12]The USSR declared a no-first-use doctrine in 1980, but the Russian Federation revoked it in 1993. India has a tentative no-first-use doctrine, but this policy has not yet been officially accepted (www.indianembassy.org/policy/CTBT/nuclear_doctrine_aug_17_1999.html).

[13]It is generally accepted that China has a MIRV capability, but this belief has not yet been officially confirmed, and China has not yet deployed MIRVs.

[14]Alexei Arbatov, "Realnost mnogopolyarnogo mira" (Reality of the Multipolar World), *Mezhdunarodnaya Zhizn'*, no. 11–12 (1997), pp. 124–27.

[15]For a good regional perspective on the Russo-Chinese relationship, see Viktor L. Larin, *Kitay i Dalniy Vostok Rossii v pervoy polovine 90-kh: problemy regialnogo Vzaimodeystvia* (Vladivostok: Institute of History, Archaeology, and Ethnography of the Peoples of the Far East, 1998).

[16]The Chinese ambassador to Russia, in a presentation at the Institute of Far Eastern Studies of the Russian Academy of Sciences, December 4, 1997, frankly recognized that the current level of economic cooperation of the two countries approximately corresponds to their level of economic development.

[17]Only 11,200 forced migrants from the CIS and Baltic countries have resettled in 1992–1997 in the Far East—about 1 percent of their total number. See Zhanna Zayonchkovskaya, "Vynuzhdennaya Migratsiya iz stran SNG i Baltiiv Rossiyu" (Forced Migration from the CIS and Baltic Countries into Russia), *Mir Rossii*, vol. VI, no. 4 (1997), p. 29.

[18]For the latter, see, for example, Joseph Nye and Robert Blackwill, project leaders, *The China Initiative*, John F. Kennedy School of Government, Harvard University, February 1998.

[19]For further details about Russian-Chinese military and technical cooperation, see Pavel Felgengauer, "Oruzhiye dlya Kitaya i natsionalnaya bezopasnost Rossii" (Weapons for China and Russia's National Security), in Andrew Pierre and Dmitri Trenin, eds., *Russia in the World Arms Trade: Strategy, Policy, Economy* (in Russian) (Moscow: Carnegie Endowment for International Peace, 1996), pp. 121–42; Steven Blanc, "Dinamika rossiisko-kitaiskoi torgovli Oruzhiyem" (Dynamics of the Russian-Chinese Arms Trade), in Dmitri Trenin, ed., *Rossiisko-kitaiskiye otnosheniya glazami amerikantsev* (Russian-Chinese Relations through the Eyes of Americans) (Moscow: Carnegie Endowment for International Peace, 1997), Academic Reports, no. 20, pp. 23–51; Pyotr Vlasov, "Osobennosti rossiiskogo exporta obychnykh vooruzhenii v Indiyu I Kitai" (Features of Russian Conventional Arms Exports to India and China), *Export obychnykh vooruzhenii* (Export of Conventional Arms) (Moscow: PIR-Center, 1997), no. 10–11, pp. 10–18; Konstantin Makienko, "Opasno li torgovat' oruzhiyem s Kitayem?" (Is It Dangerous to Trade in Arms with China?), *Pro et Contra*, vol. 3, no. 1 (Winter 1998), pp. 41–57.

[20]In the fall of 1997, when comparing the Russian-Chinese and Chinese-U.S. summits, a Moscow newspaper ran the following headline later quoted by the ambassador of China to Russia: "Pekin-Washington: sotrudnichestvo bez santimentov; Pekin-Moskva: santimenty bez sotrudnichestva" (Beijing-Washington: Cooperation without Sentiments; Beijing-Moscow: Sentiments without Cooperation).

[21]Zhanna Zayonchkovskaya, "Vozmozhno li organizovat' pereseleniye na Dalnii Vostok?" (Is It Possible to Organize Resettlement to the Far East?), *Migratsiya*, no. 3 (1997), pp. 13–14.

[22]An alarming symptom is greater activity of neo-Nazi groups in Moscow and other Russian cities, which have declared a "war on Asians." From beatings of Chinese and other Asian students, neo-Nazis have turned to threats of murdering them. See *Nezavisimaya gazeta*, April 18 and 21, 1998.

[23]The strength of the Russian armed forces (2.5 million troops in 1992) decreased by two times in five years, including in the Far East—from 500,000 to 200,000 troops. In the future, Russia may be able to have no more than 700,000–800,000 troops. In view of financial difficulties, Russia is considering reducing the number of troops located in Tajikistan (22,000–23,000), Kazakhstan (23,000–25,000), and Kyrgyzstan (2,000–2,500). See Yuri Golotyuk, "Rossiiskoi armii prikazano otstupat" (The Russian Army Is Ordered to Retreat), *Russki Telegraph*, April 9, 1998, p. 2.

[24]Alexei Arbatov, "Military Reform in Russia. Dilemmas, Obstacles, and Prospects," *International Security*, vol. 22, no. 4, p. 95; "Kontseptsiya printsipov voyennoi reformy" (The Concept of Principles of the Military Reform), prepared by the Council on Foreign and Defense Policies in 1997.

[25]See "Konseptsiya printsipov voyennoi reformy" (The Concept of Principles of the Military Reform), prepared by the Council on Foreign and Defense Policies in 1997.

[26]Noticeably, in April 1998 President of Kyrgyzstan Askar Akaev chose not to change the previously agreed dates of his visit to Beijing and was absent at the Moscow CIS summit.

[27]See A.G. Larin, "Taivan'skaya problema. Perspektivy i varianty resheniya" (The Taiwan Problem. Prospects and Options for Solution), notes for a presentation at the Carnegie Moscow Center, November 25, 1997, p. 4.

[28]From the standpoint of U.S. "realists," for instance, it does not matter who specifically will control the resources of the Russian Far East and Siberia; the important thing is that this "someone" is not China. But at the same time, from the point of view of the United States, an international conflict over the control of resources of Asian Russia must be avoided.

[29]For a more detailed review of Russian attitudes toward China, see Alexei Voskressenski's chapter in this volume, and Vilya Gelbras, "Kitayskiy faktor vnutrenney i vneshney politiki Rossii," in Galina Vitkovskaya, Dmitri Trenin, eds., *Perspektivy Dalnevostochnovo Regiona. Mezhstanovye Vzaimodeystvia*, Carnegie Moscow Center (Moscow: Gendalf, 1999), pp. 43–73.

[30]See Dmitri Minin, "Tsunami—pered nami" (Tsunami Is Here), *Zavtra*, no. 218 (February 1998), p. 5.

[31]Named after Pyotr Stolypin, Russia's prime minister in 1906–1911, who organized a large-scale voluntary resettlement program into Siberia and the Russian Far East.

[32]Alexander Lomanov, "Na periferii stolknoveniya tsivilizatsii" (On the Periphery of the "Clash of Civilizations"), *Pro et Contra*, vol. 3, no. 3, (Winter 1998), pp. 20–21.

[33]"Moskva-Pekin: Bratya navek," *Izvestia*, June 9, 1999, p. 1.

[34]See Dmitri Trenin, *Russia's China Problem* (Moscow: Carnegie Endowment for International Peace, 1999).

3
From Good Neighbors to Strategic Partners

Li Jingjie

After World War II, relations between China and the Soviet Union, as the two largest states on the Eurasian continent, shaped the geopolitics and geostrategic conditions not only of the region but also of international relations as a whole. Sino-Soviet relations were thus a persistent center of world attention. After the breakup of the Soviet Union, Sino-Russian relations emerged, having some important roots in the old bilateral relationship, but also becoming important in their own right for the security and development of both countries, as well as for the peace and security of Asia and the world. Sino-Russian relations, like Sino-Soviet relations, have become a central factor in shaping the international environment.

Already many articles have appeared in and outside of China concerning Sino-Russian relations. I made my own contributions to that literature in 1994 and 1997, providing comprehensive overviews of Sino-Russian relations.[1] This article, however, is not a general description and analysis of the process of change in Sino-Russian relations; it focuses instead on how Chinese scholars and political leaders have understood and analyzed the relationship during three crucial periods of its formation: 1989–1992, 1993–1994, and 1995–1997. I also intend, in my conclusion, to show how the key trends from these three periods have continued to shape Sino-Russian relations through 1998. By surveying Chinese attitudes and opinions, I hope to provide an important perspective on developing relations between Russia and China. In addition to citing the views of China's political leaders, I will use specialized materials to expound the current Sino-Russian strategic partnership and Sino-Russian relations among great-power relations, which is another distinctive feature of this article.

After the breakup of the Soviet Union, there were many different conjectures about the possible shape of Sino-Russian relations. Several years of experience have proved that the development of Sino-Russian relations has been quite smooth. In each stage, they have achieved concrete and even remarkable advances. Taken as a whole, this past decade has been extremely important for Sino-Russian relations, not only by laying a good foundation for the development of bilateral relations, but also by providing clues to the future development of these crucial ties.

FROM SINO-SOVIET RELATIONS TO SINO-RUSSIAN RELATIONS: 1989–1992

Let us begin with the legacy of Sino-Soviet relations. In May 1989 Soviet President and General Party Secretary Mikhail Gorbachev broke a twenty-year hiatus of summit meetings with his visit to China. Gorbachev's visit normalized bilateral and biparty relations, an achievement reflected in the Sino-Soviet Joint Communiqué issued at the conclusion of the meeting. In May 1991, PRC Chairman and General Secretary Jiang Zemin visited the Soviet Union. The two sides signed a second Sino-Soviet Joint Communiqué and various other documents. The Sino-Soviet summit meetings reached fundamental agreements on several key issues:

- the development of good-neighbor relations on the basis of five principles of peaceful coexistence[2]

- the willingness to resolve all disputes peacefully, without using force or the threat of force

- the start of talks to cut military forces and to undertake confidence-building measures in the border areas

- the resolution of problems on the eastern section of the Sino-Soviet border, while agreeing to continue to advance talks on still unresolved questions on the border

- the expansion of bilateral trade and scientific and technological cooperation, broadening contacts between citizens of the two countries, and exchanges and cooperation in various areas

- Soviet support for China's position on Taiwan, recognizing that Taiwan is an indivisible part of the PRC

- joint promotion of the establishment of a new international political and economic order.[3]

As I will show, this legacy left by Sino-Soviet relations has clearly shaped Sino-Russian relations and is at the core of several key accomplishments of the new strategic partnership between Beijing and Moscow.

On December 25, 1991, the Soviet Union ceased to be. Two days later, a high-level Chinese delegation visited Moscow, reflecting a political decision in Beijing to take a positive approach to these great changes. At this meeting, China and Russia agreed on several points that ensured the momentum from the thaw in Sino-Soviet relations would not be lost. China recognized Russia as the successor to the Soviet Union and a permanent member of the UN Security Council. Both sides accepted past treaties and diplomatic agreements, stating in particular that the fundamental principles of the Sino-Soviet Joint Communiqués would be the guiding principles for Sino-Russian bilateral relations. They agreed that negotiations on the reduction of military forces, confidence-building measures in border areas, and border issues would continue. The Russian side stated that it was prepared to continue Gorbachev's China policy, although it would seek to make even more progress in the relationship than had been achieved in the past three years.[4]

The Soviet Union did not participate in sanctions against China after the July 1989 incident on Tiananmen Square but, instead, continued to expand bilateral ties. China was obviously concerned that the momentous changes in the former USSR would produce a Russia that might renounce this legacy or at least ignore China. The great transformation in Eastern Europe, the one-by-one fall of communist parties, and the subsequent breakup of the Soviet Union did, in fact, interrupt relations with China. At first, the new Russian leadership ranked China behind Japan, India, and South Korea in its Asian foreign policy priorities. The democratic faction still rebuked China on human rights and democracy questions, from time to time. Under these circumstances, many Chinese political leaders and analysts estimated that the international situation had become extremely serious, worrying that a united West joined by the new Russia might be able to concentrate pressure on China as the only remaining socialist power.

Around the time of the Soviet breakup, Chinese political and academic experts, in accord with Deng Xiaoping's instruction to "calmly observe, coolly cope," held internal discussions and debates on the post–Cold War international environment facing China. At that time Du Gong, who directed the Institute of International Affairs directly under the Chinese Foreign Ministry, and a group of senior specialists on international affairs compiled a 1992 book entitled *The World Framework in Changing Course*.[5] This book provided the first comprehensive analysis of Sino-Russian relations, analyzing trends in the light of the first steps taken in Sino-Russian relations. *The World Framework* largely rejected the notion of crisis in Sino-Russian relations but pointed toward an uneven impact on China from the breakup of the USSR.

First, the normalization of Sino-Soviet relations and Russia's adherence to the former Soviet Union's policies toward China promised to preserve trends that had been of fundamental benefit to China. In particular, China benefited from the striking demilitarization of relations in the North and Northwest: "For the first time China has removed direct military confrontation with all surrounding great powers. China has greatly developed good-neighbor relations with all surrounding countries. This historically is our country's best period of relations with surrounding countries."[6]

Second, the book's authors also noted that Russia could not adopt an offensive foreign policy strategy, because it was involved in a complex and difficult transition process that would last for some years to come. "[Russia's] national strength is weak," the authors noted, "its society shaken; it must concentrate its resources on internal affairs, while to the outside it can only adopt a contracting and defensive posture."[7]

Finally, however, Russia's ruling democratic faction had adopted anticommunist policies on internal matters and had attempted to establish a strategic alliance with the West based on a common ideology and values. China could thus not rule out Russia's being drawn closer to the West in politics, economics, and security, perhaps leading to "a tendency toward East-West integration" and "Russia and the U.S. possibly joining hands to cope together with some Third World countries."[8] The first and second points were sufficient to encourage China to adopt a positive attitude in relations with Russia, but the third urged China to "calmly observe" Russian developments.

On January 31, 1992, Premier Li Peng and President Yeltsin held a meeting in New York on the margins of a meeting of the UN Security Council. This meeting was the first time a Chinese leader met with Yeltsin. In May 1991, when Jiang Zemin visited Moscow, he had refused to step in the middle of a controversial political situation and meet Yeltsin. Although Li Peng and Yeltsin's meeting was a brief one, it played a big role in removing China's doubts about Russian policy. Yeltsin said that Russia highly valued good relations with China and sought expanded economic cooperation. Yeltsin also promised to do all he could to ratify quickly the already signed agreement on eastern border demarcation. Yeltsin also stated that Russia's China policy would not be influenced by the West.

During 1992, Russia provided other signals of reassurance. On July 14, Yeltsin said Russia was "firmly and unmovably heading to the East" and would "establish closer relations" with Eastern countries, including China.[9] On November 24, Yeltsin told visiting Chinese Foreign Minister Qian Qichen, "In Russian foreign policy there are many new viewpoints, and we recognize China as a powerful nation. Not only in our Asian policy, but even in our world foreign policy, China occupies a priority position."[10] At the same time, the Russian Foreign Ministry declared that China was included in the preferential position of the "near abroad" in Russian foreign policy, that is, countries that had the highest priority for Russian foreign policy.[11] These statements made plain to most Chinese officials that Yeltsin's anticommunism was not anti-China. This conclusion had a great influence on subsequent efforts to establish relations of trust between the leaders of the two countries.

In February 1992, the Russian Parliament and the Permanent Committee of the Chinese People's Congress separately ratified the Soviet-Chinese Agreement on the Border in the Eastern Section. In late March, talks resumed on Sino-Russian border troop reductions and confidence building in the military and security aspects of the relationship. At the end of June, the Sino-Russian united border demarcation committee met for the first time. During this year, China and Russia exchanged mutual visits of their foreign ministers and defense ministers.

If China exhibited, in the beginning, a somewhat cautious approach to the development of Sino-Russian political relations, no such caution existed in the development of economic relations. Many Chinese officials and analysts believed that after the end of the Cold War the competition among states was shifting from the military sphere to the economic sphere. Therefore, many analysts proposed that China's policy on Russia should shift from the past geopolitical strategy to a geoeconomic one:

> International relations and diplomatic relations are increasingly becoming economic. This is an important quality of the current world's developing international relations. Economic and trade relations for China and Russia are both now especially important; for strengthening and developing Sino-Russian relations and advancing friendship between citizens of the two countries, their relations are extremely significant.[12]

After Deng Xiaoping's speech in 1992 in South China, a new tide of reform and openness arose in China. China wanted to open not only coastal areas but also inland provincial capitals, even border areas where in the past foreigners were not allowed to set foot. China opened its border cities to Russia and gave policy privileges to the enterprises and companies of border areas. Residents of border provinces who long had lived in closed and poor conditions seemed to recognize an opportunity to get rich, giving rise to the popular saying "If you want to make money, go to the CIS [Commonwealth of Independent States]."

After the breakup of the Soviet Union, Russia experienced economic difficulties and shortages of consumer goods. Many Russians had an extremely positive attitude toward developing economic relations with China. At the beginning of March 1992, the two sides signed the Agreement between the PRC and the Russian Federation for Economic and Trade Relations, which established mutual most-favored nation status. The Russian side also proposed to abolish the original Sino-Soviet rule that required bilateral trade to use foreign currency. The deputy premiers in charge of foreign economic relations paid mutual visits, and the Committee for Economic, Trade, and Scientific and Technological Cooperation began to function again.

In 1992 the bilateral trade figure reached $5.062 billion, a 69 percent increase over 1991 Sino-Soviet trade. More than 80 percent of this figure came through border and local trade. In August 1992 when Deputy Premier Tian Jiyun, who was in charge of foreign economic relations, visited the Russian Far East, he consulted with local leaders on both sides. He concluded that the prospects were good for future bilateral trade. He stated that "to develop Sino-Russian trade ties is a great good fortune to enrich the state, to profit the people, to bring good-neighbor relations and peace."[13]

In this period, China and Russia both avoided steps that would bring ideological differences to the fore of the bilateral relationship. Chinese leaders repeatedly declared that events in the former Soviet Union were Russia's internal affairs. China respected the free choice of the Russian people. China declared its willingness to develop good relations with Russia regardless of its present or future political system. This approach is a marked change from China's expression of sympathy toward the coup d'état in August 1991. At that time, some Chinese scholars even published articles openly criticizing Gorbachev as a traitor to communism. China's clear support of the principle of noninterference doubtless contributed to helping assuage Russian doubts and resolve lingering misunderstandings it may have had toward China. Sino-Russian relations thus enjoyed a nonideological character from the very beginning.

Sino-Russian relations were also aided by increasing tension in Russia's relations with the West. China's earlier fears that Russia would enter the Western camp had proved groundless. In the second half of 1992, China keenly observed that Russia was beginning to adjust its excessively pro-Western foreign policy and carry out a foreign policy of "facing the West" as well as "facing the East." In addition, China had become the primary focus of Russia's Asian policy. These favorable trends caused China in turn to accelerate its efforts toward developing comprehensive relations with Russia. Both sides showed an optimistic and pragmatic attitude toward the prospects of Sino-Russian relations.

On November 11–13, 1992, scholars of both countries held a conference in Beijing on the subject Sino-Russian Relations under the New Situation. Chinese and Russian scholars at the conference jointly concluded that a huge latent potential and a vast future existed for improving Sino-Russian relations. Furthermore, they argued that the two countries had a series of parallel or common interests. They had forty-two years' experience of Sino-Soviet relations, some of it difficult and tense; neither side wanted to go through those dark periods again. Both countries thoughtfully and carefully handled differences. Both sides understood the limits of what they could and could not do in their bilateral ties. Top leaders in both countries placed great emphasis on good-neighbor relations and looked at the other as the "first surrounding country." Most of the border questions were already settled. The two countries possessed a colossal geographic advantage and economic structures that were mutually complementary. In short, the overwhelming opinion of the attendees at this conference was that China and Russia could cooperate in any area, and Sino-Russian relations would surpass Sino-Soviet relations.[14]

On December 17–19, 1992, Yeltsin visited China. This was the first, extended top-level meeting between China and Russia. The two sides issued the Joint Declaration Concerning the Fundamentals of Relations between the People's Republic of China and the Russian Federation (hereafter, the Joint Declaration).[15] This declaration clearly defined the fundamental principles guiding the development of bilateral relations:

- China and Russia see each other as friendly nations.

- They will develop good-neighbor and mutually cooperative relations in accord with the five principles of peaceful coexistence.

- Both nations will respect the right of each country's citizens to freely select their country's path of domestic development.

- They will resolve disputes in a peaceful manner; they will not participate in military or political alliances directed against the other.

- They will not conclude with any third country any kind of treaty or agreement that will harm the other country's sovereignty and security; nor will they allow a third country to use their territory to harm the other country's sovereignty and security interests.

- Russia respects that Taiwan is an inseparable part of Chinese territory and guarantees that it will not develop official relations with Taiwan; Russia and Taiwan will maintain bilateral talks and cooperation at each level, based on the existing treaties.

- Russia and China will continue to conduct negotiations on still unresolved border demarcation questions, reduce border-area military forces, and strengthen confidence between the two militaries.

This Joint Declaration is obviously a continuation and development of the two Sino-Soviet Joint Communiqués, with much more detail and substance than the two original documents. It is, in fact, similar to a friendship and mutual nonaggression treaty. During this same summit, the two sides also signed twenty-four documents to advance cooperation in trade, science and technology, and culture, thus establishing a political and legal foundation for the all-around development of Sino-Russian relations. A leading Chinese analyst and former PRC president, Yang Shangkun, expressed a common view among his colleagues in highly valuing this summit: "The Sino-Russian summit meeting not only is a conclusion of the development of the two countries' relationship for the past year, but also marks that this relationship has entered a new stage."[16]

FROM GOOD NEIGHBORS TO CONSTRUCTIVE PARTNERS: 1993–1994

The pivotal period for Russia was 1993. At this time, the Russian domestic condition grew increasingly complex. The economy plunged into crisis. The internal struggle for power intensified and, for a time, there even appeared "dual power," with legislative and executive branches pitted against one another. In October 1993, the bloody Moscow events ended this struggle.

Chinese Analytical Views

Chinese scholars closely observed the changes in Russia's domestic environment and foreign policy and formed their own analyses and evaluations. Their main conclusions concerning Sino-Russian relations during this period can be summarized as follows.

For one group of scholars and analysts, Russian liberal reform had failed, spawning a nationalist backlash. These scholars generally believed that the democratic faction overlooked Russia's national peculiarities in constructing its policies. They argued that, following the proposals of various Western strategists and the demands of international organizations, Russia's democrats conducted radical, free-market economic reforms that inevitably induced a severe economic crisis and an intense, internal political struggle. In the December 1993 parliamentary elections, nationalist forces gained the upper hand, a domestic counterreaction to "shock therapy."

This group of scholars was especially sensitive to Russia's diminished status as a source of political mobilization. The Soviet Union stood face-to-face with the United States as a superpower. Russia, in contrast, did not. After the Soviet Union broke up, Russian politics became fractious, the economy worsened, and Russia's international standing fell precipitously. Economically, Russia had to rely on Western aid, and politically it had to follow the lead of the West in its actions. Such an arrangement had to produce a counterreaction. An intense national sense of humiliation and crisis gathered steam, and it became difficult to control the wave of nationalism. Facing a rising and unabating nationalist wave in society, any politician, if he thought about maintaining Russian unity, advancing reform, and reviving the economy, had to raise the banner of nationalism in order to gain the support of the masses.[17] Thus, this group tended to see Russia as deeply divided, stagnant, or going backward, and on the edge of a nationalist backlash.

For a second group, Russia had entered a period of relatively steady development. Scholars who supported this viewpoint cited the following reasons. First, after the October 1993 bloodshed, Russia adopted a new constitution, established a presidential system of control, and eliminated the possibility of renewed "dual power." Second, having experienced repeated tests of strength, the general "rules of the game" for political struggle were now accepted by the vast majority of political parties and organizations. The multiparty struggle was moving from disorder to order. This in turn would help develop a civilized and rational direction for social and political development, as well as stabilize the political situation and the society. Finally, Yeltsin's hold in office was based on constitutional and legal provisions that lent a new predictability to executive power in Russia.[18] In sum, this group of scholars saw Russia in the process of slow recovery or at least muddling its way up.

A third group—largely focused on foreign and security policy—argued that Russian policies had made a comprehensive adjustment to the new situation and to changes in the balance of domestic political forces. These scholars argued that the overall aims of foreign policy were to revive the nation, establish its great-power position, and create favorable foreign conditions for domestic reform. In relations with the West, in order to stabilize the domestic situation and to win citizens' support, Russia's approach would likely be more difficult, less accommodating, and perhaps more defiant. With regard to areas of the former Soviet Union, Russia would seek to intensify its influence and control, actively maintaining its leading position. In order to establish its position as a Eurasian great power, to balance its Eastern and Western diplomacy, Russia would further emphasize the Asia-Pacific region and third world countries.[19]

Regarding relations with China, the majority of scholars were optimistic, although some worried that Russian nationalism could interfere in the development of Sino-Russian relations. Scholars of the Institute of Contemporary International Relations argued that Russia

> places relations with China in a "preferential direction" of its foreign policy, which will not be influenced by internal political changes. . . . this policy of the Russian government has also won parliamentary support. . . . 1994 is Russia's "China year." When Jiang Zemin visits Russia, Sino-Russian relations can be raised to a new level.[20]

In the view of all three groups of Chinese scholars, dramatic changes in Russia's internal condition or with the West would not exert a negative influence on Sino-Russian relations. On the contrary, because its contradictions with the West were increasing, Russia would need to draw even closer to China.

Bilateral Developments

Chinese analysis was right on the mark. After Yeltsin visited China in December 1992, Sino-Russian relations entered a new stage of comprehensive development. Russia was in fact drawn closer to China. Bilateral relations in economics, politics, military affairs, science and technology, and culture evolved smoothly. Both countries maintained high-level diplomatic contacts and exchanges. In May 1994, Prime Minister Chernomyrdin visited China. In September of that same year, Chairman Jiang Zemin visited Moscow. Exchanges between the two countries' parliaments and government ministries also became increasingly close. In 1993, Russia sent delegations of more than twenty-five deputy ministers to China, and in 1994 there were thirty-six such delegations. In 1994, the foreign ministries of the two sides signed an agreement on consultations. China and Russia then reached agreement on the western border.

In the area of military affairs and security, the defense ministries of the two countries signed a cooperative agreement resulting in numerous exchanges of military leaders. Cooperation in military technology followed these exchanges. During Jiang Zemin's visit to Russia, the two heads of state signed the Joint Declaration Concerning Non-Targeting of Strategic Nuclear Weapons at the Other Side. Economic relations also developed. The two sides opened twenty-one pairs of ports in border areas. In 1993, trade reached $7.68 billion, an increase of 52 percent compared with 1992, and the vast majority occurred without government involvement. The development of trade brought with it a large flow of people, among whom were myriad traders rushing onto the other country's territory. This situation reached a peak in 1993.

Beijing and Moscow also discussed how to bring bilateral relations to a new level—one that would provide a long-term, stable relationship. President Yeltsin sent a letter to Chairman Jiang Zemin in January 1994 proposing a "constructive partnership aimed at the 21st century," to which the Chinese side responded positively. On May 28 of the same year, Chairman Jiang Zemin told Russian Prime Minister Chernomyrdin on a visit to China: "Our thinking is completely in accord concerning establishing bilateral, long-term, stable, good-neighbor, and mutually cooperative relations. I also consider that we ought to look toward the 21st century, examining and managing Sino-Russian relations from the strategic high level."[21]

On September 2–6, 1994, Jiang Zemin visited Russia. The two heads of state carried on a deep discussion of how to construct Sino-Russian relations in the next century. Jiang Zemin summed up this discussion in describing the strategic and national basis for Sino-Russian partnership and its future development:

> China and Russia both are great powers and neighbors. After our two countries' relations have experienced a few stormy decades, they are gradually maturing. Neither confrontation nor alliance corresponds to the fundamental interests of the two peoples. Only if we establish good-neighbor relations and mutually cooperative relations on the foundation of the five principles of peaceful coexistence will we satisfy the fundamental interests of the two countries and peoples. Since this will also be beneficial for world peace and development, it is the best choice.[22]

A new Sino-Russian Joint Declaration resulted from that meeting. The declaration noted the development of a constructive partnership based on principles of peaceful coexistence and good-neighbor relations. It also mentioned that China and Russia were not involved in an alliance "directed against third countries."[23] If the first top-level bilateral summit established a foundation for the all-around development of bilateral relations, then the 1994 meeting established a foundation for the long-term and stable development of Sino-Russian relations.

Dealing with Problems

Although Sino-Russian relations were developing smoothly, problems also appeared. They fell into three broad categories: cross-border trade and contacts, the border agreement itself, and slipping economic relations.

Cross-Border Trade and Contacts. Although Sino-Russian relations at the central level were greatly improving, tensions appeared at the local level. Initially, exchanges between border regions were chaotic. A mass of Chinese flowed unexpectedly into Russia and provoked talk in Russia of hundreds of thousands or even millions of Chinese migrants. Even more serious was the reappearance of articles devoted to the alleged "yellow peril." Newspapers and journals of central Russia, the Far East, and Siberia had published roughly 100 articles since 1992 criticizing China's "expansion" into the Russian Far East. Some articles even manufactured the myth that the Chinese government, in order to realize its territorial demands toward Russia, devised a plan for large-scale migration to the Far East and Siberia.

It was comforting that the Chinese and Russian governments adopted an understanding, calm, and realistic attitude toward this situation. Chairman Jiang Zemin clearly expressed the Chinese government's position on this question when speaking to the Russian mass media during his visit to Moscow in September 1994:

> In recent years, under circumstances of rapid increases in mutual exchanges on both sides, mainly in border trade and personnel exchanges, some disorderly phenomena appeared. First, no matter which side gave rise to the problems, the

cause was always individual behavior, not the policies of the two governments. Second, these are problems that arise in the context of progress and development [of the relationship], problems that have appeared in the rapid transition from the closed borders of the past to openness and exchange. . . . They have not and ought not to influence the whole situation of the development of bilateral relations. Third, the principled standpoint of the Chinese government is to support and maintain orderly and legitimate trade activities . . . consistently opposing illegal migrants, and resolutely attacking criminal elements engaged in illegal migration activities. It does not permit Chinese citizens to do things harmful to bilateral good-neighbor relations.[24]

In 1993–1994, Chinese and Russian law enforcement organs cooperated closely, attacking criminal elements and organized groups violating Russia's borders. In order to develop bilateral personnel exchanges of a healthy and orderly nature, in January 1994 both China and Russia began implementing a visa system and made efforts to strengthen the legal and physical infrastructure of the border area. Under these circumstances the "yellow peril" theory dissipated. Through it all, Chinese scholars did not pay "yellow peril" writings a great deal of attention, dismissing them—when they were discussed at all—as a "nationalistic manifestation."

The Sino-Russian Border Agreement. Inside Russia, opposition to the Sino-Russian border agreement arose. Sino-Russian border negotiations had been proceeding for nearly thirty years, only at the very end achieving agreements on both the eastern and western borders. But in the process of implementing the eastern border agreement, the demarcation work was blocked by certain local leaders of the Russian Far East. The governor of Primorskii Krai agitated for a revision of the Sino-Russian eastern section border agreement, refusing to give up any territory. The governor of Khabarovskii Krai also raised an objection concerning the free navigation clause in the agreement. In April 1994, the Russian Parliament conducted a special hearing on the Sino-Russian border, in which diplomats, local leaders, and scholars participated. The conclusion of the hearing rejected the demands of certain leaders of the Russian Far East.

Yeltsin himself declared that "the signed bilateral Russian-Chinese border agreement is sacred. It cannot be changed, and the Russian side will resolutely implement it."[25] The Chinese made no public reaction to this problem, because Russian officials were clearly acting in accordance with Yeltsin's policy. Furthermore, the Chinese understood that certain regional leaders of the Russian Far East were using the border demarcation issue as a weapon in Russia's internal political struggle, not as a serious policy against Beijing.

Economic Problems. As Sino-Russian political relations developed positively, economic relations in 1994 slipped. Total trade in 1994 dropped 30 percent in comparison with the year before. The majority of Chinese scholars recognized that economic relations do not correspond with bilateral political relations; as bilateral trade develops from lower to higher volume and from irregular to regular trade, this discrepancy is an unavoidable phenomenon.

Partly in response, leaders of the two countries stressed trade and expanded cooperation in science and technology. In May 1994, when Prime Minister Chernomyrdin visited China, he focused on these exact issues. In the economic area, the two sides discussed strengthening macroeconomic management, raising the quality of goods, expanding areas of economic cooperation, and completing the infrastructure and legal foundation, and they managed to reach a broad consensus. During the visit, the two sides then signed agreements on the border management system, avoidance of double taxation, overall agricultural and industrial cooperation, sea transport cooperation, environmental protection, preservation of maritime resources in border waterways, and other issues.

FROM A CONSTRUCTIVE PARTNERSHIP TOWARD A STRATEGIC PARTNERSHIP: 1995–1997

In 1995–96, several internal and external events influenced Russian foreign policy. Russia entered the Chechen morass and could not get itself out. The economy continued to decline. Parliamentary elections at the end of December 1995 gave the Communist Party the largest number of seats. In the 1996 presidential elections, the communist leader Zyuganov became Yeltsin's only competitive opponent. Abroad, NATO expansion became an irreversible fact, and the split between Russia and the West became ever more apparent in their policies toward the CIS and the former Yugoslavia. At the beginning of 1996, Foreign Minister Andrey Kozyrev was ousted in favor of a more traditionally oriented figure, Yevgeny Primakov.

Chinese Assessments

Chinese scholars argued that the change in foreign ministers indicated the complete bankruptcy of Russia's pro-Western foreign policy and the final establishment of an independent and sovereign great-power foreign policy. This change had consequences for Sino-Russian relations. If at the beginning of the Sino-Russian rapprochement, Chinese scholars had doubts about Russia entering the "great family of the Western civilized world," they now focused on the increasing contradictions between Russia and the West, especially concerning Eastern Europe and the area of the former Soviet Union. As one scholar put it:

> Russia's foreign policy strategy puts its own national interests at the top, and the West's "common democratic values" cannot remove differences in fundamental national interests and long-term strategic objectives. In fact, Western assistance and support for the "democratic faction," headed by the U.S. great power, is to prevent the Communist Party from staging a comeback and to preserve this area's stability. Therefore, this aid is really to support Western interests and not to create a strong Russia. On the contrary, the Western great powers continuously showed concern about preventing and weakening Russia, to block it from being able to strive for supremacy through its revival as a world great power. This is fundamentally opposed to Russia's basic goal of restoring its great-power position.[26]

In this period, Chinese scholars and officials were extremely optimistic regarding the development of Sino-Russian relations. Shi Ze, deputy director of the Institute of International Relations, for example, gave a glowing review of the course of Sino-Russian relations:

> The experience of the development of Sino-Russian relations in the new period shows that bilateral relations have passed through three levels of different stages, but throughout have followed a healthy path of forward development. Sino-Russian relations year after year are striding forward in a new march, each area of cooperation is filled with vitality.[27]

Scholars from Shanghai recognized that "in current relations among the globe's great powers, Sino-Russian relations are comparatively stable. . . . From now on, no matter what Russian party has power, the overall tendency in the development of Sino-Russian relations cannot change."[28] It is interesting, however, that many scholars believed that if the Russian Communist Party rose to power, it would not necessarily be advantageous for the development of Sino-Russian relations. They anxiously said that "if the Russian communists rise to power, their policy toward China will still be mainly based on Russia's national interests. . . . On this point, China should soberly realize that it cannot have too optimistic an attitude."[29]

Political Developments

During this period, as in the previous one, relations were characterized by three main features: the institutionalization of the relationship, including the expansion of the frequency and range of contacts; the internationalization of the focus of bilateral ties, with both sides turning for the first time to issues of global significance; and substantial progress in addressing the problems and obstacles that had emerged.

First, let us look at the institutionalization of the relationship. High-level exchanges increased, mutual trust further intensified, and Sino-Russian relations rose to a new level. Chinese and Russian leaders again expressed their commitment to developing closer relations on May 8, 1995, when Chairman Jiang Zemin visited Moscow for the fiftieth anniversary of Russia's victory in the antifascist war. On June 5–8, 1995, Chinese Premier Li Peng visited Russia, where leaders resolved to push bilateral trade and scientific and technological cooperation to a new stage, using modernized methods of cooperation, pursuing mutual investments, establishing a new model of long-term cooperation in border areas, and realizing cooperation in large-scale production and scientific and technological projects. The two sides then signed concrete agreements for building the Amur River bridge, forest fire prevention, recognition of academic diplomas, vegetation disease-prevention and protection, information cooperation, bilateral machine ministry cooperation, and other projects.

High-level visits persisted throughout 1996 despite Russia's domestic concerns, including both a presidential election and a presidential health crisis. On April 23, while en route to China, Yeltsin suggested a revision in the already prepared Sino-Russian Joint Declaration, changing the draft phrase "to develop long-term, stable, good-neighbor, mutually cooperative, constructive partnership relations facing the 21st century" to new language, namely, "to develop an equal and trustworthy strategic partnership aimed at the 21st century." Yeltsin's proposal received a positive response from the Chinese side. The Sino-Russian Joint Declaration issued after the summit declared that the two sides would resolutely "develop an equal and trustworthy strategic partnership aimed at the 21st century." They also agreed to establish regularly scheduled summits of the two countries' leaders, to create a special telephone communications line between Beijing and Moscow, and to establish a Sino-Russian Friendship, Peace, and Development Committee of representatives from various circles in the two societies.[30] In Shanghai, another big achievement of President Yeltsin's visit to China occurred: the heads of state of China, Russia, Kazakhstan, Kyrgyzstan, and Tajikistan signed the Agreement to Strengthen Confidence in the Military Field in Border Areas.

As a second major trend, Sino-Russian relations internationalized. After its foreign policy adjustment, Russia sought increased cooperation with China on international questions, beginning in 1994. The Chinese side welcomed this. In March 1995, Chairman Jiang Zemin made it clear when he met with Russian Foreign Minister Kozyrev that "China and Russia are both great powers, which have a responsibility in opposing hegemony and maintaining world peace, and also have common interests."[31] China and Russia both believe the post–Cold War world will be a multipolar one. Both countries are opposed to the establishment of a unipolar world where one country or a group of countries monopolizes and controls international affairs. China and Russia have, since this time, daily increased their mutual support and cooperation on this front.

Finally, the two countries are striving to overcome problems that appeared in the previous stage of bilateral relations. The premiers and relevant ministers of the two countries have worked hard to develop bilateral economic and trade relations and strengthen government regulation over potential areas of difficulty or disagreement. As a result, in 1995 Sino-Russian trade began to increase again, growing 7.6 percent over the prior year and reaching $5.46 billion. In 1996 there was another comparatively big increase. In order to strengthen management of border areas, the two sides, in August 1995, signed an agreement for cooperative policing of the border. In September of that year, the Russian Border Guards also separately signed cooperative agreements with the Chinese Defense Ministry, State Security Ministry, and Public Security Ministry.

THE PRACTICE AND DEVELOPMENT OF THE SINO-RUSSIAN STRATEGIC PARTNERSHIP: 1997–1999

During 1997–1999, the contents of the Sino-Russian strategic, cooperative partnership solidified and developed. First, in this period, summits of the leaders of the two countries became more frequent. In 1997, during the course of one year, the heads of the two countries conducted two summits: one in April when Jiang Zemin visited Russia and conducted the fourth bilateral summit, and one in November when Yeltsin visited China for the fifth summit. In November 1998, Jiang visited Moscow for the first time in a "no necktie" style summit. The next informal summit of heads of state— the seventh—was set for Beijing in the second half of 1999.

In April 1996, when Yeltsin visited Beijing, the two countries decided to establish a system of regular summits between their political heads. In December of the same year Chinese Prime Minister Li Peng visited Moscow. The Chinese side regards this visit as "formally starting off the system of regular summits between Chinese and Russian political heads."[32] In February 1999, Prime Minister Zhu Rongji visited Russia in what was already the fourth regular summit of heads under the new system.

In 1997–1999, the development of bilateral relations also realized a major breakthrough. The breakthrough was first manifested in the bilateral border question. In November 1998, China and Russia issued the Joint Declaration Concerning the Sino-Russian Border Question, indicating that "the open field work on demarcating the Sino-Russian western border is already completed. With this, for the first time in the history of bilateral relations the border demarcation in the two eastern and western sections had been exactly marked out on the spot."[33]

Besides this breakthrough, in a follow-up to the April 1996 Sino-Russian and Kazakhstan, Kyrgyzstan, and Tajikistan five-country border area agreement for strengthening trust in the military area, in April 1997 the five countries again signed a border disarmament agreement. It stipulated that within the limits of 100 kilometers on either side of the land border of more than 7,000 kilometers each side's personnel in the army, air force, and air defenses will not exceed 130,400 after reductions.

In this period, the common consciousness and interests of China and Russia on international questions grew ever greater, thus causing the contents of the strategic partnership to become more solid. In November 1997, the two countries' heads signed the Joint Statement of China and Russia Concerning World Multi-Polarization and Building a New International Order. To issue a joint statement specifically on international questions is a rarity in the history of bilateral relations. In November 1998, the joint statement Sino-Russian Relations at the Turn of the Century, issued as a result of the summit at the highest level, also expressed the common views and standpoints of both sides on world multipolarization, the diversification of world civilization, the globalization of the world economy, the United Nations, post–Cold War great-power relations, and other questions. Moreover, consultations of the foreign ministries and general staffs of the two countries regularly occur. In light of the U.S. plan for preparations to deploy an antimissile system, China and Russia in April 1999 conferred on upholding the stability of the 1972 Treaty to Limit Anti-Ballistic Missile Systems. In April to June of 1999, when NATO, led by the United States, conducted an air attack on Yugoslavia, the highest leaders of China and Russia not only maintained "hot line" contacts to stop this unjust war and cause the conflict to turn to peaceful resolution, but also they used various channels for coordinating their positions and cooperation.

In 1997–1999, Sino-Russian bilateral economic and trade relations did not develop as anticipated, especially in 1998, when bilateral trade even slipped because of the financial crisis arising in Russia. But in this period the two countries were exploring new cooperative forms and areas, especially making important progress in advancing cooperation on big projects. Russian assistance to China in building a nuclear energy station is proceeding smoothly. Construction of a natural gas pipeline from Eastern Siberia to China's eastern coastline is already in the stage of economic and technological certification.

CONTENTS AND FEATURES OF THE SINO-RUSSIAN STRATEGIC PARTNERSHIP

The first eight years of Sino-Russian relations, beginning as Sino-Soviet relations in 1989, may be broken down into three distinct stages, passing from, in the language of communiqués, the initial stage of "seeing each other as friendly nations" to a second, more ambitious stage of establishing "constructive partnership relations." The third stage, which the two countries are still in today, works to establish relations defined by "a strategic cooperative partnership." Chinese scholars consider that bilateral relations have already smoothly passed through their "time of friction," rising to a path of stable, healthy, and comprehensive development.

The Sino-Russian declaration of a strategic partnership is not an empty statement; it has real substance. I tried to define this substance in an article published in China, relying not only on my own assessments but also on those of official statements and the work of other Chinese colleagues.[34] I believe there are six basic pillars supporting the current Sino-Russian strategic partnership.

The first is mutual respect and equality. Both China and Russia recognize that mutual respect and equality are important principles for maintaining and developing formal, healthy national relations. China has not, as the West did, used the Soviet Union's breakup and the internal crisis of Russia for its own ends. Russia similarly did not take advantage of China's internal so-called human rights and democracy questions to join with the West in causing problems for China. In mutual exchanges, neither China nor Russia behave like humiliated nations. Mutual respect and equality also mean that efforts are made to support each other in maintaining national sovereignty and territorial integrity. China supports Russia's attempts to uphold national unity and considers the Chechen problem an internal Russian matter. Russia in turn declares that Taiwan is an indivisible part of the territory of the PRC and will not develop official relations with Taiwan. It is no exaggeration to say that the relations China and Russia have established on the basis of mutual respect and equality are a model for post–Cold War great-power relations.

The second pillar is the work to create a new security system, peaceful borders, and security cooperation. More than 95 percent of the Sino-Russian border problem has been resolved, which establishes a reliable foundation for the development of long-term and stable relations. As mentioned above, in April 1996, China, Russia, Kazakhstan, Kyrgyzstan, and Tajikistan signed the Agreement on Strengthening Confidence in Military Field in the Border Area and, in April 1997, signed the Agreement on Mutual Reduction of Military Forces in the Border Area. The latter stipulates that the number of ground, air, and air defense forces stationed in the zones within 200 kilometers of the 7,300-kilometer-long border does not exceed 130,400 persons. This event not only is of great political and strategic significance for the development of the relations between China, Russia, and Central Asian states, but it also plays an important role in the Asia-Pacific region and beyond.

In my view, there exist two completely different kinds of policies related to rebuilding the world security system in the post–Cold War era. The first one, as the United States and its allies have done in Europe and Asia, is to build upon the political and military alliances of the Cold War. The alternative approach, embraced by China and Russia with respect to their relations, is to establish a new security system and the basis for cooperation through confidence-building measures and large-scale reductions in military forces. The second approach is better suited to creating a strategic partnership and supporting the multipolar trends of the post–Cold War era.

A third pillar of Russian-Chinese partnership is active cooperation in support of the other partner and in issues of mutual interest. With geographical advantages, great economic complementarity, rich endowment of natural resources, and huge markets, China and Russia consider each other important partners in the economic and technological spheres. Such cooperation has become an important part of the strategic partnership. In 1996, China and Russia reached an agreement that established a regular governmental consultation committee, chaired by the vice premiers from each side, to help prepare and implement the decisions made in the regular meetings of the leaders of the two countries. Within the framework of this agreement, several subcommittees on economics, trade and technological cooperation, energy, transportation, and military technology were set up. The new subcommittees have been established to meet present and future needs. With this step, Sino-Russian economic and trade cooperation have been given a more reliable political foundation, generating results in agriculture, energy, transportation, the peaceful use of atomic energy, air transport, finance, military technology, and other areas.

The fourth is continued bilateral efforts to advance the development of world multilateralism, which will establish a new international political and economic order. Over the past three years, after changes in the international environment and adjustments in Russia's foreign policies, the Sino-Russian consensus on post–Cold War international relations has been growing. Both consider that the world is becoming multipolar. Both are opposed to establishing a unipolar world and to hegemony and power politics. Russia supports China's standpoint on Taiwan and Tibet, not approving the West's use of so-called human rights as an excuse for interfering in China's internal affairs. China joins Russia in opposing NATO expansion. It supports integrated development of the CIS and Russia's full integration into Asia-Pacific institutions like APEC. China and Russia conduct an ongoing and intense dialogue on world strategic questions, including Asia-Pacific security. In the United Nations, China and Russia pursue effective cooperation to raise the organization's efficiency and ability to act, achieve disarmament, resolve regional conflicts, and establish a new international political and economic order.

The fifth is the institutionalization of high-level meetings. Bilateral relations have evolved smoothly—a consequence of consistent support for each stratum and channel of regular dialogue. The highest-level contacts and deliberations have an especially decisive influence on pushing bilateral relations forward and deepening and strengthening bilateral cooperation in various fields. In April 1996, during Yeltsin's visit to China, the two sides established a system of regular meetings of high-level leaders. Each year the top leaders of both countries will meet twice, once in China and once in Russia. Numerous ministerial and subministerial contacts are a part of this growing partnership. This structure will last. In the early 1990s, high-level leaders began to consider and discuss the long-range future of the relationship. The course of relations since shows that the basic relationship will not change, even if there are changes in the two countries' domestic conditions or in the international environment as a whole.

Finally, the sixth is the nature of Russian-Chinese partnership. It is not an alliance, nor is it directed against any third country. It is an act of mutual strengthening and self-protection, not an instrument for outside aggression or assertiveness. The world has nothing to fear from the development of this partnership nor from its future.

SINO-RUSSIAN RELATIONS AMONG WORLD GREAT-POWER RELATIONS

One of China's most authoritative party documents states plainly that "the world now is in a historical period of great change. Various forces are again separating and coming together, and the world is facing development in the direction of multipolarity. Peace and development are the present world's two great themes."[35] This statement reflects Deng Xiaoping's insight from the 1980s that the main contents of the current epoch are not war and revolution—as Lenin and Stalin stated—but peace and development.[36] Deriving policy insight from a new consciousness of the epoch, China has formulated a peaceful foreign policy of independent sovereignty and the development of friendly and cooperative relations with all the countries of the world on the basis of the five principles of peaceful coexistence. Understanding China's theory of the epoch is an important path to understanding China's foreign policy.

Multipolarity (*duojihua*) is also fundamental to China's post–Cold War world consciousness. Multipolarity means that relations among the United States, Japan, Germany (or the European Community), Russia, and China determine, to a large degree, the course of international relations. Although Russian national power has already weakened compared with that of the former Soviet Union, it is still a world great power and an important pole in the multipolar world. China—as the largest developing country and a permanent member of the UN Security Council—wants more flexibility on the international stage. In order to achieve this flexibility and exert a positive influence on international affairs, Beijing should maintain good relations with all the world's great powers, including Russia.

In China, there is widespread support for developing a strategic partnership with Russia. There are many reasons for doing so, as I have made plain in this article. They include a common border of 4,300 kilometers, economic complementarity, a tradition of friendship, a common task of internal reform, and a common need for a peaceful international environment. Recently, some analysts have stressed an additional factor, the need to counterbalance the United States: "The demand for Sino-Russian strategic cooperation arises because China feels increased pressure from the U.S., and that a clash in national interests between Russia and the U.S. is unavoidable."[37] In

Europe, for example, the United States sees Russia as a latent opponent and plans to expand NATO to contain it. In Asia, the United States sees China as a latent opponent and plans to strengthen the U.S.-Japanese alliance to contain it. Japan is not an independent factor in this line of thinking. Few Chinese think that the development of Sino-Russian relations has a serious impact on Japanese foreign policy or Japanese-Russian relations. In the views of many Chinese scholars, Japan does not have independent foreign policy. Japan is a follower of U.S. foreign policy.

The author of the book *China's Great Strategic Choices for the 21st Century: Foreign Policy Strategy*, Xi Laiwang, notes striking changes in the two triangles of Sino-Russian-U.S. relations and Sino-U.S.-Japanese relations. These changes offer new opportunities and challenges to China. China and Russia, Xi Laiwang notes, have established a strategic partnership, and relations in the Sino-Russian-U.S. triangle have changed to the disadvantage of the United States. The improvement and warming of Sino-Russian relations have caused a significant improvement in China's security environment. The United States and Japan have strengthened their security alliance relations, and this has created a change in the Sino-U.S.-Japanese triangle disadvantageous for China. "Looking at the Asia-Pacific region," Xi Laiwang writes, "Moscow must lean on Sino-Russian relations to contain the U.S. and Japan. Simultaneously, Russia also must rely on China's position and influence to gain a place in Asia-Pacific affairs."[38] The view that Sino-Russian cooperation might result from common challenges from the United States was also expressed in the popular book *A China That Can Say No.*[39] Though not expressing the results of scholarly research or an official policy, the book reflects the attitudes and sentiments in recent years of a broad mass of Chinese, especially the younger generation.

Although many in the West doubt the staying power and significance of Sino-Russian relations, after more than eight years of development, China and Russia have achieved something of value. Moreover, factors within and outside the bilateral relationship are likely to make it grow. At the end of 1996, Jiang Zemin summarized China's long-term aims toward Russia in sixteen characters, which can be translated as "good neighbors, equality and trust, mutual advantage and cooperation, joint development."[40] If I were to try to find sixteen characters to represent the direction in recent years of China's efforts toward the United States for comparison, they might be "increasing trust, reducing troubles, developing cooperation, not acting in confrontation." These characters represent a more constructive and positive set than might have been chosen in 1989 or 1996, but they still fall far short of Jiang Zemin's summation of what now and in the future describes relations between Beijing and Moscow. The Sino-Russian strategic partnership will prove an enduring and positive influence on the multipolar world of the next century.

NOTES

[1]"Xin shiqi de ZhongE guanxi" (Sino-Russian Relations in the New Period), *Dongou Zhongya yanjiu*, no. 1 (1994), pp. 8–17; "Shilun ZhongE zhanlue xiezuo huoban guanxi" (On Sino-Russian Strategic Partnership), *Dongou Zhongya yanjiu*, no. 2, (1997), pp. 3–15.

[2]The five principles for handling state-to-state relations advocated in the 1950s by China, India, and other countries are mutual respect for sovereignty and territorial integrity; mutual nonaggression; mutual noninterference in their respective internal affairs; mutual benefit; and peaceful coexistence.

[3]*Renmin Ribao*, May 19, 1989, p. 1; May 20, 1991, p. 1.

[4]Ibid., December 29, 1991, p. 6; December 31, 1991, p. 6.

[5]Du Gong and Yi Liyu, *Zhuangui zhong de shijie geju* (The World Framework in Changing Course) (Beijing: Shijiezhishi Publication, 1992).

[6]Ibid.

[7]Ibid.

[8]Ibid., pp. 46, 47, 54, 287.

[9]*ITAR-TASS*, July 14, 1992.

[10]*Renmin Ribao*, November 26, 1992, p. 1.

[11]*ITAR-TASS*, December 4, 1992.

[12]Lu Nanquan, "Jinyibu fazhan ZhongE jingmao guanxi de ruogan wenti" (Some Issues on Further Development of Sino-Russian Economic and Trade Relations), *Dongou Zhongya yanjiu*, no. 1 (1993), pp. 30, 43.

[13]*Renmin Ribao*, August 23, 1992, p. 6.

[14]"Summary of the International Conference: Sino-Russian Relations in the New Situation," *Xiandai guoji guanxi* (Contemporary International Relations), no. 1 (1993).

[15]*Renmin Ribao*, December 19, 1992, pp. 1, 4.

[16]Ibid., December 17, 1992, p. 1.

[17]"MeiE guanxi yantaohui jiyao" (Summary of the Seminar on U.S.-Russian Relations), *Xiandai guoji guanxi*, no. 11 (1994).

[18]Pan Deli, "1993 nian eluosi zhengzhi xingshi huigu he qianjing fenxi" (A Look Back at the 1993 Russian Political Situation and Analysis of Prospects), *Dongou Zhongya yanjiu*, no. 1 (1994), pp. 59–63.

[19]Rong Min, "Xi Eluosi waijiao shiji de xin tedian" (Analysis of New Features in the Practice of Russia's Diplomacy), *Dongou Zhongya yanjiu*, no. 2 (1994).

[20]Gu Guanfu and Tian Runfeng, "Yanjin zhong de Eluosi duiwai zhengce" (Russia's Foreign Policy in Changing Course), *Xiandai guoji guanxi* (Contemporary International Relations), no. 8 (1994).

[21]*Renmin Ribao*, May 28, 1994, p. 1.

[22]Ibid., September 3, 1994, p. 1.

[23]Ibid., September 4, 1994, pp. 1, 4.

[24]Ibid., September 4, 1994, p. 6.

[25]Ibid., May 9, 1995, p. 1.

[26]Wen Pingyang, "Eluosi Yatai zhengce de huigu yu qianzhan" (To Look Back and to Look Forward on Russia's Policy toward the Asia-Pacific Region), *Guoji wenti yanjiu*, no. 2 (1996).

[27]Shi Ze, "Lun xin shiqi de ZhongE guanxi" (On Sino-Russian Relations in the New Period), *Guoji wenti yanjiu* (International Politics Studies), no. 2 (1996).

[28]"Jinqi Eluosi zhengzhi jinji xingshi ji ZhongE guanxi yantaohui congshu" (Summary of Seminar on Russia's Political and Economic Situation and Sino-Russian Relations), *Dongbeiya yanjiu* (Northeast Asian Studies), no. 2 (1996).

[29]Ibid.

[30]*Renmin Ribao*, April 26, 1996, p. 1.

[31]Ibid.

[32]Ibid., April 28, 1996.

[33]Ibid., November 24, 1998.

[34]Li Jingjie, "Shilun ZhongE zhanlue xiezuo huoban guanxi," *Dongou Zhongya yanjiu*, no. 2 (1997), pp. 3–15.

[35]*Zhongguo gongchangdang dishisici quanguo daibiao dahui wenjian huibian* (Collection of Documents of the 15th Congress of the Communist Party of China), p. 43.

[36]*Deng Xiaoping wenxuan* (Collected Works of Deng Xiaoping), vol. 3, pp. 104, 105.

[37]"Jinqi Eluosi zhengzhi jingi xingshi ji ZhongE guanxi yantaohui congshu," *Dongbeiya yanjiu* (Northeast Asian Studies), no. 2 (1996).

[38]Xi Laiwang, *21 shiji Zhongguo zhanlue dacehua waijiao moulue* (China's Great Strategic Choices for the 21st Century) (Beijing: Hongqi Publication, 1996), p. 60.

[39]Wang Lingyun and Li Shuyi, *A China That Can Say No* (Zhonyguo keyi shuo bu) (Beijing: Zhonghua gongshang lianhe chubanshe, 1996).

[40]"Jiang Zemin's Meeting with Russia's Foreign Minister," *Renmin Ribao*, December 19, 1996, p. 1.

4
Chinese Views of the New Russia

Lu Nanquan

At 7:39 on the evening of December 25, 1991, in the Kremlin, the Soviet flag was taken down as the white, blue, and red flag representing Russia was raised in its place. Speculation about the course of independent Russia has been a hot topic ever since. As Russia's next-door neighbor and a co-sponsor of twentieth-century communism, China is naturally interested in how Russia develops. While the range of issues that are important for Chinese-Russian relations is wide, I will focus on four of the most critical ones: economic reform, future prospects for economic development, economic great-power status in a multipolar world, and the direction of social development.

CHINESE VIEWS OF RUSSIAN ECONOMIC REFORM

"Shock therapy" became the center of debate for Chinese scholars after 1991, and opinions continue to be divided on the topic. Most Chinese observers hold one of three basic views. The first, held by the majority, completely rejects Russia's shock therapy. Its supporters argue that three fundamental conditions ought to exist before a country applies this therapy: (1) the basic foundations of a market economy—a system that is moving away from state monopolies and has at least the rudiments of a market system; (2) an already established private sector—including private property—occupying a substantial or leading position in the national economy; and (3) modern and market-oriented financial, credit, and currency systems.

According to these analysts, Russia was simply not ready for shock therapy. Russia's highly centralized planned economic system, in operation for seventy years, required smaller transitional steps. In addition, the economy's focus on military production rather than on consumer goods, the perennial shortages of those goods and backwardness of services, and the monopolistic nature of industrial production were difficult to change overnight. The economy was not ready for the social shock of price liberalization. When prices were liberalized, living standards dropped dramatically and brought about a still unreversed slide in production. The private sector was extremely small, with little real private property. Russia's domestic industries were plainly unready for free trade, because of the uncompetitive quality of Russian goods. The fall of the USSR had disrupted Russia's economic links to the other newly independent states. Western credits and investment in Russia, which were expected to stabilize the economy and provide the decisive conditions for switching to a market economy, never materialized at the levels required. Finally and most important, economic reform came at the same time as great changes in political institutions and society as a whole, creating instability and political conflict.[1]

A second viewpoint holds that Russia had no choice but to use shock therapy or a radical mode of economic transformation. Russia's reforms, in this view, are a continuation of past Soviet reforms, beginning as early as 1957. These reforms were pursued in fits and starts, often languishing, for more than thirty years under Khrushchev, Brezhnev, and Gorbachev. These gradual efforts failed, leaving accumulated contradictions difficult to overcome without shock therapy. Moreover, at the time of the USSR's collapse, shortages were especially severe. In order to suppress the pent-up demand for goods, Russia was driven to shock therapy with price liberalization at its core. As the USSR entered the 1980s, it was clear that reforms could no longer be confined to the economy. They had to be applied to the political sphere, giving rise to an intense, life-and-death struggle of political forces. When rightist forces gained political power in the new Russia, they had to raise the flag of shock therapy to consolidate their political control and to manage state economic policy.

These analysts also point to an important external factor. Soviet reforms were hampered by the failure to sustain stable and constructive relations with the West, especially the United States. Thus, as these relations became more difficult, the military burden on the economy grew heavier. There were simply not enough resources to sustain economic reform and superpower military capabilities. The new Russian reforms were linked from the beginning to a reduction in tensions with the West, although Western rhetoric for support far exceeded concrete assistance. Analysts holding the second viewpoint agree with those of the first that radical measures were not suitable for transforming the Russian economy; however, the second group of analysts argues that the political and economic environment made such measures unavoidable.[2]

A third approach among Chinese analysts focuses on an assessment of both positive and negative consequences of radical economic reform. In this view, the principal negative result is a decline in economic power, since many key economic indicators fell to levels reached ten years ago or more. Reforms have not returned the economic system to balance but rather have further destabilized it, replacing the former emphasis on heavy industry with a production decline and an erosion of native producers in many areas of both heavy industry and consumer goods. The reforms have created a perpetual crisis of the state budget, which must live with deficits every year. Other negative consequences include the inter-enterprise financial crisis, a steep decline in living standards for large portions of the Russian population, and social polarization.

On the positive side of the balance sheet, this approach points to the increasing diversification of the Russian economy; the enormous change in people's thinking, with a large increase in market consciousness; and the appearance of genuine market elements in the economy, although the work of transforming the Russian economy into a true market economy is far from complete.[3] Analysts of this approach see Russia's economic reform effort primarily as price liberalization, large-scale privatization, some tax reform, currency reform, elimination of the state monopoly over foreign trade, and expanded openness to the outside.[4]

Russia's privatization program has also engendered serious debate in China. Like the discussion on shock therapy, this debate reveals enduring differences of opinion on the difficulty of reforming the inherited economic system and the wisdom of borrowing an approach from the West. Chinese analysts see Russian privatization as a governmental political program as well as a concrete economic policy. It is a means to preserve elements of both a market-style economy and a mixed economy.

While small-scale privatization has produced clear results, large-scale privatization is still awaiting a positive outcome, especially in terms of production. Currently, large-scale privatization in Russia is confronting a host of problems, the most important of which is the severe erosion of state control and the lack of market controls and a sense of ownership to take its place. Vouchers have not made the Russian masses owners in any real sense. Although the title of the factory may have changed hands, the managerial system has not been transformed. Efficiency has not yet been increased. For most enterprises, privatization has not brought new investment or introduced new technology or products. Chinese officials have a negative attitude toward Russian privatization. Repeatedly stressing that China does not engage in privatization, they warn that state property cannot be dispersed to individuals without compensation.

After privatization in Russia, can the newly appearing private ownership class become a pillar of democracy? People quickly becoming millionaires are members of the former privileged groups and their children, managers of the former shadow economy, a percentage of store renters and contract recipients of properties, and some individual households (known in Chinese as *getihu*). These strata have grown rich fast, and often this new wealth is linked to a bending or breaking of the law. Their good fortune increases the distance between them and the rest of Russian society. According to some sources, Russian private owners now constitute 15 percent of the population. Although many are able to help develop the Russian economy, more are engaged in asset stripping, rent seeking, or conducting criminal activities under the slogan of privatization. Their hundreds of millions of dollars in property are not the result of legal work. They do not support the kind of democracy that the government desires but, on the contrary, fear openness, parliamentary oversight, and public opinion. To think that these people could become pillars of democracy is too naive. Because Russian privatization was not based on fair competition, and all the power of privatization continued to be concentrated in the hands of bureaucrats and official organs, the results have been disappointing.[5]

As for privatization, in the past few years Chinese scholars with a critical outlook have become increasingly numerous. They regard the principal problems of Russian privatization to be the following: (1) political aims of privatization took precedence over economic ones, and as a result coercive measures were erroneously adopted; (2) a serious leakage of state-owned property was produced; (3) after privatization, enterprises did not become independent commercial producers, and consequently the enterprise management system could not change very quickly and it was also difficult to raise economic efficiency; and (4) after privatization, many social problems were born, the number of unemployed rose, economic crime grew ever more severe, social polarization was accelerated, and so on.[6]

Looking at Russia's economic reforms over the past few years, I think that Russia has not yet found a suitable structural model for its national circumstances. The development of basic reforms and sound policy lacks consistency. Moreover, no strong political leadership cadre has emerged to ensure that important reform policies can be carried to completion. Under such conditions, it is difficult for reforms to achieve the success they should.

According to the widely held opinion of Chinese officials and analysts, no matter how Russia carries out its economic reforms, no matter what kind of model it chooses, the reforms are Russia's own affair. Each country has its own concrete circumstances and must rely on these in deciding its own direction and policies. History does not offer a precedent for the kind of transition that Russia is making, from a traditional, centralized planned economic system to a market economy. It must start at the beginning and grope its own way forward. China's reform also has had a lot of problems that have not been resolved, such as the reform of state-owned, large and middle-sized enterprises. In Russia, leaders have always had an ambivalent outlook on China's reforms, on the one hand believing that the reforms do not suit Russia and in no way are applicable, and on the other hand believing that China's reform path is worth Russia's close attention. Chinese officials strive to avoid allowing differences in economic reform to influence the normal development of bilateral relations.

From my own perspective, Russia made four main mistakes in economic reform. First, for the past seven years, Russia has shaped its economy according to the free-market model with Western monetarist theory at its core. The experience of these years demonstrates that this kind of model does not apply to Russia. Second, in 1992, Russia adopted a series of measures that were aimed at radical transformation into a market economy that did not correspond to

Russia's circumstances. Later, Russia tried to adjust these policies to national circumstances, but the process was difficult. Third, Russia has not made state-managed enterprises compatible with a market economy. Russia's mistake was using command methods to accelerate privatization. In this way, it destroyed the past strength of state enterprises, deepening the economic crisis.

Finally, Russia did not manage well the delicate balancing of reform, economic development, and stability. The objective of reform is to develop production and on this foundation to raise living standards, thus creating a stable environment for further reform. Russia did not manage well the relationship of these three factors for seven years. It did not adequately consider the social and political problems produced by reform. During this period, Russia's top local leaders wasted a great deal of effort in internal political struggles, as they found themselves caught in one political conflict after another. Under these circumstances, Russia could not concentrate its energy on reform and the economy. The economy, in turn, could not escape from crisis; standards of living fell greatly; and unstable elements in society multiplied. These conditions also blocked the advance of reform policies.

PROSPECTS FOR RUSSIAN ECONOMIC DEVELOPMENT

Few Chinese writings examine the prospects of Russian economic development over a comparatively long period. Short-term forecasts, such as year-by-year predictions of the coming year, are quite common. Often the short-term forecasts are far removed from real results. Forecasting the economic condition in 1994, for example, many analysts expected the Russian economy to make a sizable improvement, reaching bottom and starting up again. The actual result, however, was a decline that far exceeded that of 1992 and 1993. Analyses for the 1995 economic condition generally anticipated further development of the Russian economic crisis with a decline in production by 10 percent, but the actual decrease was much less. The GDP fell by only 4 percent. When predicting the 1996 economic condition, several scholars said a rise of 0–2 percent could be realized,[7] but the actual figure was a decline of 6 percent. This poor track record is unlikely to change in the near future.

On the one hand, these inaccurate forecasts can be explained by the complexity of the Russian economy. On the other hand, Chinese analysts still do not understand the basic structures and trends of the Russian economy in the first period of transformation. Chinese research in this area has so far been inadequate.[8]

As for prospects for Russian economic development, the number of Chinese scholars taking a pessimistic view grows ever larger because of Russian political uncertainties and the influence felt from the global financial crisis as well as the paralysis of the Russian financial system. Thus, the action program proposed by the government of Prime Minister Sergei Stepashin was generally seen as difficult to realize and not likely to cause an economic upturn. Especially with the late 1999 Duma elections and the year 2000 presidential election, Russia will find it very hard to attend to its economy. Each party and political faction will be busy with political struggle and its own political fate, which will plunge the Russian economy into new instability.[9] My conclusion is that in the economic arena the new Russian government will be hard-pressed to accomplish much.[10]

Assessments of the next five to fifteen years are even more difficult. In 1996–1997, Russian government presentations to the State Duma, recommending three stages of development from 1997 to 2000, suggested an upturn, and Chinese forecasts were similarly hopeful. Many predicted that, if there was no shake-up in the Russian political environment and if economic reform policies continued, in 1997 the economy would reach its nadir and then start climbing into an unstable growth period for two or three years (1998–2000). Perhaps one year would bring slow growth, another high growth, and still another a return to decline. Only around 2000, according to these predictions, would the economy enter a comparatively stable stage of recovery, with growth in GDP of about 4 percent annually. After a certain foundation is set, the speed of economic recovery can accelerate. Only after 2010, however, can Russia recover to its level before the crisis.[11] Clearly, this forecast is not as optimistic as the development plan presented by the Russian government itself. Already the impact of the Asian and Russian financial crises has upset these predictions.

Chinese scholars also examine the impact of CIS (Commonwealth of Independent States) economic integration on the Russian economy. Calls for such integration have grown louder. These new states, after experiencing years of economic decline, are all thinking of integrating the CIS economic space in search of a way out. Integration reflects the common needs of the CIS economies; it also indicates that after independence these states have not shed their dependence on Russia. Moreover, these states are disappointed in their assistance and trade relations with the West. Russia regards the former Soviet territory as its sphere of influence and seeks to maintain its political, military, strategic, and economic interests in this region.

Although the states of the CIS objectively must pursue economic integration, they still must go through a transition. For some time, the Russian economy will remain unattractive to the newly independent states. CIS economic integration, moreover, will not become a stable and important element in Russian economic development for quite a while. These countries do not have one unified approach. Russia attempts to use political ties of geography, proclaiming that the CIS is the region of Russia's most important interests. Although Russia is considering economic interests in advocating economic integration, it has often been more interested in political control over this area.

The countries of the CIS intend to use integration to maintain former energy, capital, trade, credit, and debt privileges. They are extremely sensitive to influences on their sovereignty from economic integration. Thus, integration will be hard to achieve. The countries of the CIS have signed hundreds of multilateral agreements. In 1995 alone, leading government councils made close to fifty agreements, but the number actually put into effect was small. Russia does not plan to make concessions in the process of economic integration: Russia will not offer cheap prices for energy and raw materials and is eager to resolve inequalities in payments and trade. Russia stresses trade based on international prices. CIS economic integration also will not necessarily give Russia large economic benefits; on the contrary, Russia will pay a price for economic integration. As of the mid-1990s, CIS countries had received $5.8 billion in credits from Russia, a large part of which was for energy.[12]

In the social and political arenas, there are also a great many unstable elements, which will hinder a healthier economy. In the aftermath of the presidential election, the Russian political environment stabilized, but the struggle for power among various factions continued. As a result, it was difficult to form a consensus of political forces on economic reform. Social factors, in my opinion, limit Russia's economic stability. If one overlooks these problems, one cannot

draw a correct estimation of the future of Russian economic development. The main problems existing now are as follows:

- *Official Corruption.* Russia has become a state of extreme official
  corruption. Foreign businesspeople, economists, and Russian
  analysts all recognize that this is the biggest obstacle to investment and the development of a market economy.[13]

- *Crime.* Mafia organizations have penetrated into every sphere;
  their activities are rampant and cannot be resolved in a short time
  span. In the estimation of Russian specialists, criminal groups
  control two-thirds of Russian markets.[14]

- *Declining Living Standards.* The gap between rich and poor is
  widening. Serious sociopolitical disorder will continue to
  develop and will be a significant cause of pessimism toward
  economic reform.

- *The Weakness of the State.* Top Kremlin officials have emphasized
  that the most important problem facing Russia is repairing political order, a key requirement for advancement and for solving
  pressing issues.

Some Chinese scholars are more optimistic. They believe that
in the first decade of the next century, Russian development will
accelerate and past economic capacity will not only be restored
but also will achieve new heights. They give four reasons for this
prognosis. First, Russia's historical burden is not large, because of
a comparatively small population and low birthrate, unlike China's
large population and high birthrate. Although the former Soviet
Union left many problems for Russia, it also built important industrial and social structures, such as machine manufacturing, the petroleum industry, energy, metallurgy, communications and transportation infrastructure, and health and educational institutions.
Although agriculture is a weaker component of the economy, its
weakness is only relative. I can make a simple comparison: in the
Soviet period, grain per capita reached 800 kilograms, while China
estimates that for the year 2000 there will be 490 billion kilograms
for 1.3 billion Chinese, an average of about 390 kilograms per capita.

Second, resources are plentiful. The territory of Russia is 17,075,000
square kilometers, which is 76.3 percent of the former Soviet Union.
Its mineral, forest, water, and marine resources are vast, especially
oil, natural gas, coal, and other energy reserves. Siberia's reserves

alone constitute about one-third of the world's supply. Although in the near term resources will not necessarily speed economic development, over the long term their presence or absence will be an important factor in determining the speed of economic development.

Third, Russia retains impressive scientific and technological strength. Russia's civilian industry is backward, but its military industry is advanced. This contrast demonstrates that Russia has advanced science and technology, but that it has been confined to a narrow sphere and has not achieved widespread application. This serious problem nevertheless provided a legacy of tremendous potential. I expect that as Russia deepens its shift from a planned economy to a market economy, it will form a system for broadening the application of its scientific and technological legacy.

Finally, there is hope in market expansion. A striking feature of the post–Cold War era is the struggle for markets of various countries, which has become ever more intense. This struggle exists because international competition is increasingly concentrated in the economic sphere. Whoever has a big market will have more room for economic development. In this competition, Russia will not relent. In the near future, I predict that Russia's strategic focus will be the CIS and the states of Eastern Europe where it has already gained some success.[15]

Some scholars who analyze Russia's current socioeconomic prospects from the developmental history of the Russian nation point out that "from the character, geography and development potential of this young Russian nation the current disorder and weakness is nothing more than the prelude to its restrengthening. Of course, this restrengthening will be of a different nature, a different appearance, but we definitely cannot underestimate her might and influence."[16] How many years will be needed for this restrengthening, which indicates a restoration of the former Soviet Union's national strength? Analysts state:

> The time it will need to spend will at least be no less than the shortest time historically to overcome all previous disorder or about 15 years. If we start counting from 1991, this requires at least until 2005. And that is the most conservative estimate. But from Russia's history of development and her resources (including human resources), it positively can complete this transformation. On this there should be no doubt. Therefore,

we should neither believe the theories of current Russian authorities nor the theories of various people who consider that Russia has failed. We should start from China's own interest to watch Russian changes more deeply, more closely, and more broadly.[17]

CAN RUSSIA BECOME A GREAT ECONOMIC POWER IN A MULTIPOLAR WORLD?

After Yevgeniy Primakov was appointed Russian foreign minister on January 9, 1996, he repeatedly stressed the idea of moving toward a multipolar world. In his assessment, Russia fills the great-power position as one of the poles of this new world. He repeatedly emphasized that the United States is not the main global actor and that Russia is not a subordinate of the United States. Russia will continue to promote a strategy of restoring its great power status, and securing its sphere of influence. It wants to demonstrate its influence in the multipolar international framework that is forming. Both when Primakov served as Prime Minister in 1998–1999 and afterwards, that outlook has guided Russian policy.

The international system has begun a transition from bipolar to multipolar, which is an irreversible tendency. The post–Cold War international struggle and the battle for hegemony between two superpowers during the Cold War are different. No longer is the military used as the main instrument. As a Russian scholar, V. Lukov, has said, "Economic power has become the most important [and] decisive element in the international struggle."[18] He also noted correctly that the tendency toward economic mutual dependency in international relations is growing, and he stated that the "scale and effectiveness of Russia's participation in the important international multilateral management systems will be the foremost determinant of the speed of my country's economic and scientific and technological development."[19]

At present, Russia's role as one pole in a multipolar world mainly depends on its military power, second only to that of the United States. In addition, Russia also has abundant scientific and technological potential, a large territory, rich natural resources, and a comparatively developed foundation in heavy industry. But these traits do not equate to economic power. Therefore, based on economic power, whether today or in the future, it will be difficult for Russia to be called one pole in a multipolar world. Observers recognize that Russia's economic troubles complicate its becoming one such pole. According to the International Development Bank's estimates, twenty-five years from 1995, Russia will not be among the ten strongest economic great powers.[20] But Russia can raise its world economic rank and strengthen its position in the center of the international system, and to do this it must now stabilize its economy and induce growth.

Chinese scholars have also analyzed the restoration of Russia's economic great-power status. They "estimate that around the year 2000, Russia still will not be able to gain an advantageous position in the multipolar framework, and at the very least only in 2010 or even around 2020 will it be able to develop into an economic great power."[21] Another viewpoint similar to the above is that in GDP, Russia will not surpass England or Italy, Europe's second and third strongest countries, until the 2020s.[22]

Some Russian scholars draw an even harsher conclusion, declaring: "No matter how much supporters of world multipolar and unipolar concepts debate at present, this world is entirely a unipolar world regardless of how painful this is for our consciousness."[23] They cite some extremely disappointing figures to explain Russia's current world position:

> Now the GDP of NATO countries comprises 45 percent of the world GDP, but Russia's only comprises 2.4 percent. In 1995 the military expenses of NATO states comprise 46 percent of world military expenses, at least nine times the Russian figure. NATO has 7.3 million armed forces, but Russia only has 1.7 million . . . Russia now has no realistic possibility of changing this ratio. . . .[24]

This analysis is correct if seen from a purely economic angle, but as I discussed above, whether Russia is a pole in a multipolar world also requires looking at other factors.[25] Chinese scholars observe that, based on Russia's comprehensive national power, Russia has an arena to display its role as one pole in a multipolar world. At the same time, as economic factors become increasingly important in international relations, Russia's function as such a pole becomes significantly limited; its weaknesses are patently clear.

China considers the development of the world toward multipolarity an irreversible force. It is also willing to see Russia play a greater role in the multipolar international framework, which would be beneficial to China and the formation of the new international order. Therefore, China hopes that Russia will continue to increase its economic strength and gradually overcome existing weaknesses limiting its role as a world pole. I believe that for Russia to reach that point, it must carry out internal reform policies that correspond to its own national circumstances, rapidly shed its crisis, and improve its economy. In foreign trade, it should create conditions to participate positively in the Asia-Pacific region, especially in economic cooperation in Northeast Asia. In recent years, Russia's increasingly positive attitude toward participating in the Asia-Pacific region and in Northeast Asian regional economy and security cooperation is an important element supporting equilibrium in Northeast Asia.

Russia's positive attitude toward the Asia-Pacific region also has important significance for the development of the Russian Far East and Siberia. If Russia wants to become a pole in a multipolar world, then in addition to reviving its economy, it also should maintain a balance between East and West by stressing the Asia-Pacific region and intensifying cooperation with this region. In the next century, Asia will increasingly become the center of the world economy. The focal point of international trade will shift to this region. Russia is a great power in the Asia-Pacific region, but it was originally left out of the high-speed development of this region. If it wants to enter this process, it must open and develop its eastern areas.

Russia's center of gravity in economic development inevitably must advance from West to East. The objective necessity due to the exhaustion of European natural resources requires using even more resources of the East. Thus, accelerating the development and opening of the Far East and Siberia must be Russia's unchangeable long-term policy. Russia's development of this region will be difficult, but strengthening cooperation with countries of Northeast Asia, such as China, Japan, and Korea, will ease the strain.

When it comes to quadrangular relations, the United States and Japan want to maintain and expand their influence in the region and are not likely to adopt positive measures to cooperate with Russia in raising its role in this region. China hopes that Russia will positively participate in Asia-Pacific and Northeast Asian regional economic cooperation. In these circumstances, the outburst of "China threat" and "yellow peril" talk in the Russian Far East is extremely disadvantageous for this region's economic development.

WHERE IS RUSSIA HEADING?

What is the direction of Russia's social development? This question is of great interest for Chinese scholars, and it is a very complex question. A widely held view is that the direction is not yet set and that the present, visible social characteristics are a mixture of capitalism and democratic socialism.[26] Prospects for political development are particularly difficult to predict.[27] Chinese scholars agree that "a return to Stalin's old path is already completely impossible. This is because from Stalin to Brezhnev the old Russian tradition was already raised to its highest peak or its lowest valley, reaching the end of its historical road, and no longer has any life in it."[28]

Chinese analysts believe the main factor causing the dramatic transformation of the Soviet Union is its system (*tizhi*), which had so many shortcomings that it could not be renewed.[29] They also argue that, for a considerable period, it will be hard for Russia to realize Western-style political democracy and "complete Westernization." After independence, Russia attempted to adopt democratic political thought immediately, but in the process Russia encountered great difficulties. Perhaps most important, Russia discovered the contradiction between reduced government interference in the economy and the need for a degree of government involvement to establish conditions for a stable society as a precondition for a stable economy. Russia also lacked a developed market and the institutions, interests, classes, and political parties necessary for democratic politics. Swift or massive Westernization will be impossible because Russia's old traditions still possess considerable influence. In order to seek stability, Russia must compromise, maintaining a degree of tradition while advancing a degree of liberalization.[30] Although it is too early to draw conclusions about the social character and development of Russia, the main directions of the political and economic systems are already set, and they will produce something different from the typical Western model.

Chinese scholarly circles fiercely debate the influence of neo-authoritarianism in Russia or the possibility of a purely authoritarian political model in Russia. One scholar has argued that "although the democratic political system is already basically established in Russia, neo-authoritarianism still is comparatively influential."[31] He argues that Russia has a history of more than 300 years of feudal control. In its long historical development, a traditional political culture formed with feudalism and authoritarianism at the core. This historical legacy was followed by seventy years of Soviet socialism. The Stalin model, to a certain degree, fit this kind of traditional political culture. Finally, at the beginning of Russian independence, economic and political problems emerged that threatened to create social unrest. Naturally there were calls for the appearance of an "iron man," a role that Yeltsin filled to a large degree.[32]

Some scholars note that a "pure authoritarian political model can be the first idea for saving a democratic political model fallen into difficulty, and on the eve of the breakup of the Soviet Union, Soviet scholars examining developing countries raised this question. Now more than ever, this can become a development model with political influence."[33] But other Chinese scholars think that neo-authoritarianism does not fit in Russia. The time is different; now is not the 1930s or the 1950s. Today's trend is democracy. The reliance of the Asian "four little dragons" on a dictatorial system to realize their economic takeoff was a product of the Cold War era. With political change, there has also been economic change. The ownership system is different. The "four little dragons" used private property as the foundation for their economic takeoff. Originally, socialist states used public ownership as their foundation, and the government's use of administrative methods to induce enterprise activity was a very easy matter. But if a country does not reform the political system, enterprises will have no life. In addition, if a state wants enterprises to become independent commercial producers and no longer serve as appendages of the government, then it must transform the functions of government. This task includes reform of the economic system and the political system, the two of which cannot go forward separately.[34]

In summary, no matter which direction Russia heads, either to realize democratic government or to realize an autocratic governmental system, China hopes that Russia can gradually stabilize, which will be good for China and the world. Apart from this, China must closely monitor Russia's social development for the following two reasons. First, China has always stressed that if there is no democracy there is no socialism, and that one of the fatal weaknesses of the Stalin system is the high concentration of power. This problem must be solved through reform, but how? China is still in an experimental state; therefore, it needs to absorb lessons from various directions. From the start, Russia attempted complete Westernization, but reality proved this system was difficult to copy. Russia eliminated the one-party system of the Communist Party, but a mature multiparty system was difficult to establish in a short time, which forced the society into a disorderly state. China's democratization process ought to start from its own conditions and advance gradually, not radically. This is not to say that China can relax reform of the political system and slow the democratization process.

Second, sound management of relations between economic and political reform is also an important issue for China. In the Gorbachev period and in present Russia, reform of the political system was too radical, construction of a new system was not carried to completion, and the state lost control of society and the political environment, which hindered reform of the economic system. In China, reform of the political system has been held back, impeding the solution of many social and economic problems. The problem of corruption, for example, has long been impossible to resolve, and in some localities it is still growing and spreading. A solution to this problem must pass through reform of the political system to be guaranteed. Based on the history of reforms in China, Russia, and other countries, I consider the two sides of reform in the economic and political systems to be intimately linked; they should be simultaneously carried out so that they can function mutually to propel each other forward. Of course, throughout the process of reform, priorities will sometimes have to favor either political or economic reform, at the expense of the other. These priorities should be decided by looking at the actual conditions of the time and the main objectives that one wants to achieve.

NOTES

[1]Yan Yiteng, "Dui Eluosi jijin jingji gaige de pingjie" (Evaluation of the Russian Economic Reform), in Lu Nanquan, et al., eds., *Eluosi, Dongou, Zhongya jingji zhuangui de jueze* (Beijing: CASS, 1994), pp. 111–17.

[2]Ibid.

[3]Li Chuifa, "Dui Eluosi sannian jingji gaige de jiben guji" (Basic Estimates of Russia's Three-Year Economic Reform), *Xiandai guoji guanxi*, no. 11 (1994).

[4]Lu Nanquan, "Eluosi jingji de huigu yu zhanwang" (Looking Backward and Forward on the Russian Economy), *Xiboliya yanjiu*, no. 4 (1996).

[5]Chen Minhua, "Eluosi siyouzhe jieceng keneng chengwei minzhu de zhizhu ma?" (Can the Russian Capitalist Stratum Become a Pillar of Democracy?), *Guoji guancha*, no. 4 (1994).

[6]Lu Nanquan, "Xiang shichang jingji zhuangui guojia ziyouhua de ruogan wenti" (Some Questions on State Privatization in Changing Tracks toward a Market Economy), *Taipingyang xuebao*, no. 1 (1999).

[7]Xu Xin, "Cong weiji xiang wending zhuanzhe de Eluosi jingji" (The Russian Economy Changing Course from Crisis to Stability), *Dongou Zhongya yanjiu*, no. 1 (1996).

[8]Lu Nanquan, "Dui Eluosi jingji fazhan qianjing de yuce" (Estimation of the Future Development of the Russian Economy), *Ouya shehui fazhan yanjiu*, no. 1 (1996).

[9]Lu Nanquan, "Sijiepashen jinru xuanwo" (Stepashin Enters a Whirlpool), *Shijie zhishi*, no. 12 (1999); Lu Nanquan, "Jinrong weiji weikun Eluosi" (A Financial Crisis Besieges Russia), *Ziben shichang*, no. 8, (1998).

[10]Xu Xin, "Nanyou da zuowei" (It Will Be Hard Pressed to Accomplish Much), *Guoji jingmao xiaoxi*, June 2, 1999.

[11]Lu Nanquan, "Eluosi jingji de huigu yu zhanwang" (Looking Backward and Forward on the Russian Economy), *Xiboliya yanjiu*, no. 4 (1996).

[12]Ibid.

[13]*Moskovskaya pravda*, September 1, 1995.

[14]*Finansovaya Izvestiya*, January 23, 1997.

[15]Cheng Wei, "Eluosi jingji zhuangui chengxiao shenshi" (Scrutinizing the Effects of the Russian Economic Changing Track), *Shijie jingji yu zhengzhi*, no. 7 (1996).

[16]Jiang Changbin, "Eluosi: cong lishi zouxiang weilai" (Russia: Heading from History toward the Future), *Dongou Zhongya yanjiu*, no. 3 (1996).

[17]Ibid., p. 86.

[18]Li Cong, "Sulian jieti liangnianlai shijie xingshi de huigu" (Looking Back on the World Situation Two Years after the Breakup of the Soviet Union), *Shijie jingji yu zhengzhi*, no. 11 (1993), pp. 1–6.

[19]*Mezhdunarodnaya zhizn'*, November-December, 1996.

[20]Ibid.

[21]Wang Boyang, "Shijie jingji duoji gezhu zhong de qian SuDong jingji" (The Economies of the Former Soviet Union and Eastern Europe in the Framework of World Economic Multipolarity), *Shijie jingji yanjiu*, no. 3 (1994).

[22]Gao Zhongyi, "Eluosi jingji shili ji qi zai shijie de diwei" (Russia's Economic Strength and Its Position in the World), *Dongou Zhongya yanjiu*, no. 1 (1995).

[23]*SShA*, no. 11 (1996).

[24]Ibid.

[25]Li Cong, "Sulian jieti liangnianlai shijie xingshi de huigu."

[26]Zhang Jianhua, "Dui dangqian Eluosi zhengju tedian de yixie fenxi" (Some Analysis of Features of the Current Russian Political Situation), *Ouya shehui fazhan yanjiu*, no. 34 (1996).

[27]Jiang Yi, "Shehui zhuanxing yu Eluosi zhengzhi fazhan moshi de xuanze" (The Social Transformation and Selection of the Russian Political Development Model), *Dongou Zhongya yanjiu*, no. 4 (1996), pp. 28–34.

[28]Jiang Changbin, "Eluosi: cong lishi zou xiang weilai", p. 85.

[29]Lu Nanquan, "Sulian jubian de genben yuanin" (Fundamental Reasons for the Huge Changes in the Soviet Union), *Shijie jingji*, no. 9 (1996).

[30]Jiang Yi, "Shehui zhuanxing yu Eluosi zhengzhi fazhan moshi de xuanze."

[31]Zhang, "Dui dangqian Eluosi zhengju tedian de yixie fenxi".

[32]Ibid.

[33]Jiang Yi, "Shehui zhuanxing yu Eluosi zhengzhi fazhan moshi de xuanze."

[34]"Guanyu qian SuDong diqu guojia zhengju he xiang shichang jingji guodu wenti de yantaohui guandian congxu" (A Summary of the Viewpoints Expressed in the Symposium on the Political Situation and the Transition to a Market Economy in the Area of the Former Soviet Union and Eastern Europe), *Dongou Zhongya yanjiu*, no. 4 (1993), pp. 23–29.

5
Russia's Evolving Grand Strategy toward China

Alexei D. Voskressenski

Russian and Chinese officials may be premature in their remarks when they describe the current state of the relationship between the People's Republic of China and Russia as "a new kind of strategic partnership aimed to the next century." Indeed, this new "constructive partnership" (*konstruktivnoye partnerstvo*), or "equal partnership based on trust and aimed at strategic cooperation in the 21st century" (*ravnopravnoye doveritel'noye partnerstvo, napravlennoye na strategicheskoye vzaimodeistviye v 21 veke*), as it is also called, does not mean much more in practice than the changing forms of partnership between Russia and the United States—the early "wonderful partnership" (Bill Clinton's words), the later "pragmatic partnership,"[1] and the current "troubled partnership"—or the "partnership" between the PRC and the United States to which both U.S. President Bill Clinton and PRC Chairman Jiang Zemin referred in 1997–1998. But how wide is the gap between rhetoric and reality? And how might a stable and friendly relationship among the former participants of the so-called strategic triangle be created—one that will be constructive and will contribute to a new, just, and peaceful world order while not infringing upon the interests of each nation-state or effecting a "cold peace"?

Unfortunately, many Russian analysts judge today's China, like today's United States, almost exclusively from the point of view of their political interests and prejudices. Most pragmatists see China only as a market for the Russian military-industrial complex and, to a lesser extent, for state-subsidized heavy industries. Russian analysts of the procommunist persuasion insist on the necessity of learning from the Chinese experience, accentuating their vision of the Communist Party of China as the guarantor of stability in the process of reform and nostalgically projecting Chinese reality onto the Russian situation. They also believe that Russia and China, especially in the wake of the Kosovo crisis, can help each other in "rebuffing American hegemonism" and constructing a world without "leaders and followers," a euphemism that denies even a benign hegemonic role to the United States in the post–Cold War era.[2] The liberals in Russia reject Chinese experience merely because it is associated first and foremost with communists. Many Russian policy makers are characterized by an extreme evaluation of Russian-Chinese relations: if it is friendship, then it must be as close as in the 1950s; if it is hostility, then it must be as dangerous as the old armed conflicts between Soviet and Chinese border guards on the Island of Damansky. Today, however, when Russia's position in the whole system of global international relations is uncertain, Russia must be as careful in acquiring its friends as in acquiring its enemies.

In this paper, I shall identify the factors that, I believe, will influence the evolving Russian-Chinese partnership and examine different scenarios of possible interaction. In doing so, I will examine the historical heritage, that is, issues connected with past relations and the border controversy that implicitly influence the border demarcation process between Russia and China today; current geopolitical, economic, and demographic challenges; and mutual perceptions. In addition, I shall touch briefly upon how external factors might influence the relationship.[3]

THE HERITAGE OF THE PAST

For about three centuries, starting in the seventeenth century, Czarist Russia and China were engaged in the process of establishing contacts primarily to deal with trade and border issues. In principle, the unequal elements in their historical relations, now emphasized mainly by Chinese scholarship, could be seen on both sides.[4] Those elements alone, however, did not determine relations between the two states. External factors, mainly the attitudes and policies of other states toward Russia and China, were as important as, and sometimes even more important than, what went on between Russia and China. By the mid-1890s, Russian-Chinese relations entered a new period defined by the rise of imperialism in Russia. During this period, the center of gravity in the relationship shifted to Russia, which pursued a policy of de facto colonial political and economic infiltration into China.

Despite the ups and downs of more than 300 years of ties between Czarist Russia and China, there was never an openly declared war between Russia and China. Most of the time, the two neighbors managed to solve their bilateral problems through diplomatic negotiations. In large measure, the absence of major conflict was the result of an understanding on the part of the two ruling elites that large-scale military conflict between two neighboring giants would be a disaster for both.

The 1917 Russian Revolution marked the beginning of a new and complicated phase in Sino-Russian relations. The first decree of the Soviet government—the Decree of Peace—formally annulled the secret treaties that had determined Russia's preferential rights in the countries of the Far East, including China. Seeing the reluctance of the Chinese authorities (following the Western powers) to recognize Lenin's government and realizing that China was trying to benefit from Soviet Russia's difficulties, the Soviet government decided not to abrogate the Russian-Chinese treaties as a whole, but rather only those provisions that placed China in an obviously unfair position. This principle provided a basis for the Soviet approval, and later for that of the Russian Federation, of the former Russian-Chinese treaties. This approach was unique, because the provisions of the old border treaties were referred to in modern documents (for example, border treaties and Joint Communiqués). These provisions not only contradicted the utopian goals of communism and socialism but also were quite at odds with the prevailing views of the Chinese elite, which continued to harbor strong feelings about the weakness of the nineteenth-century Chinese state and its loss of sovereignty over territories of the Russian Far East and Central Asia.

Japanese aggression and the civil war in China made the 1930s and 1940s especially uneasy years for Sino-Soviet relations. The important issues for this period—to which there are still no adequate resolutions—are the Comintern's and Stalin's policies toward the Kuomintang (KMT) government and the communists in China, and the role of external factors on the formation of such policies. At first, Stalin seemed to orient his official policy toward the KMT. Subsequently, his ideological sympathies and, more important, geopolitical calculations led him to shift his attention to supporting the communists against the KMT, if not to "dividing" China. He also used both at the same time as a buffer against Japan and, later, against the United States; he created deep suspicions of Soviet policy among both Chinese communists and Guomindang. Stalin's policy toward China is not a matter of scholarly interest alone but is an issue with current geopolitical implications. Studying it gives clues to the origins of the Cold War in Asia and to Russian behavior in these years of uncertainty, which in turn can help Russia and China understand how to avoid such a situation in the future. The archives, however, are still closed, so no final judgment can yet be given on this issue.

For some time after the creation of the PRC in 1949, the Sino-Soviet relationship blossomed. There were no publicly proclaimed disputes between the PRC and the Soviet Union. The reality, however, is that during these years, the ideological proximity of the two governing Communist parties forced the leaders to present an environment where the state interests of the two countries coincided. Both the PRC and the USSR viewed the outside world as "capitalist and hostile," thus providing another incentive for this period of forced cooperation. China, in particular, faced the threat of invasion from Chiang Kai-shek's army on Taiwan and the possibility of an economic blockade and political isolation from the United States. As soon as the newly born PRC started to realize that its national interests did not coincide with those of the Soviet Union, however, controversies between the two states began to emerge.

The beginning of ideological polemics between the Communist Party of the Soviet Union and the Communist Party of China strained interstate relations. Little by little, the confrontation between the USSR and China acquired a global character, owing to the uncompromising nature of the strategic bipolarity of the Cold War. During Chairman Leonid Brezhnev's era, the militarization of the Sino-Soviet conflict occurred.[5] Increased tensions resulted from failed Sino-Soviet border negotiations in 1964 and Mao Zedong's July 1964 statement, considered by the Soviet side as a claim on 1.5 million square kilometers of Soviet territory. The lack of coincidence between the boundary lines—largely following rivers and other physical features—and the historic borders of the ethnic communities further aggravated relations. Even today, this Russian-Chinese border could become a zone for potential tension during periods of confrontation or instability, as has happened in the past when border changes have occurred either by expansion or by the arbitrariness of the authorities. Examples can be taken from any period, from the early days of Sino-Russian relations through Sino-Soviet relations to the present.

Only in 1969, during a meeting in Beijing between the Chairman of the USSR's Council of Ministers, Aleksey Kosygin, and the Premier of the State Council of the PRC, Zhou Enlai, did the two sides conclude that they both had to act to thwart the escalation of the conflict. Unfortunately, such a decision was made only after bloody clashes between Soviet and Chinese border guards near the Island of Damansky on the Ussuri River and the small town of Zhalanashkol (in Central Asia). These clashes created powerful obstacles to future reconciliation.

A NEW EPOCH AND NEW CHALLENGES

Economic and political instability, the political crisis, the collapse of the Soviet Union, and the creation of the Commonwealth of Independent States (CIS) have reduced the political and strategic weight of the Russian Federation as the successor of the Soviet Union.[6] For years, the bipolar world system of international relations had ensured the stability of geopolitical structures in international relations. Now that system is gone.

The Russian Federation differs considerably from the former Soviet Union. With the exception of military capability and total area, the status of Russia has been reduced to that of a regional power. Russia is still struggling to find an adequate niche in the international system. Owing to the current success of its reforms and its stable economic growth, the PRC is moving to the forefront of the developing world in terms of GNP (gross national product) and prospects for future development.[7] The PRC is concerned with changes on the perimeter of its borders. In view of separatist sentiments in Tibet, Xinjiang, Inner Mongolia, and Guandong, the Chinese government undoubtedly fears that a process similar to the one that led to the collapse of the Soviet Union could be started within its borders. Therefore, the PRC is doing more than merely attempting to develop pragmatic approaches for dealing with the "ideologically hostile" regimes of China's neighbors to the north and west. The PRC wishes also to emphasize its economic and social success in the hopes of filling the power vacuum in Asia, left after the collapse of the Soviet Union.

No clear system of alliances exists in Asia, such as the one that exists in Europe.[8] Although countries in Asia have economic reasons for avoiding conflicts, they lack the basic set of agreements and diplomatic structure for regulating confrontation and heading off future confrontations. They still do not have an elaborate mechanism for addressing military and security issues in Asia on a multilateral level. For this reason, U.S., Japanese, Russian, and Chinese policy may conflict in Northeast Asia, which will only increase the amount of tension in the Asia-Pacific region.

Many Russian analysts of what may be called the optimistic school consider China the only country upon which Russia can rely as Moscow attempts to strengthen its position in the Asia-Pacific region.[9] These analysts point to the shared interest of creating an external environment beneficial to domestic economic reforms as a basis for broader Russian-Chinese cooperation in resolving regional conflicts and other troublesome issues like nuclear disarmament. For China, cooperation with Russia could help Beijing preserve the balance of power in the region. Russia serves, in part, as a counterbalance to U.S. and Japanese influence. In addition, analysts in both countries see Russian and Chinese interests coinciding on many global issues.[10]

Whatever the achievements of Russian-Chinese summits, bilateral relations must still undergo significant changes to meet the needs of both countries in the new global environment. For two categories of Russian analysts—pragmatists and pessimists about China—the alarming factor in current Russian-Chinese relations is the sharp decrease in the economic and military potential of Russia, especially in the underpopulated and underdeveloped territories of Siberia and the Russian Far East. The Russian population between Lake Baikal in Siberia and the Pacific Coast is only 8 million and is steadily declining as a result of the migration of the Russian population to the central and western part of the country. In contrast, the neighboring Chinese provinces have a population of more than 300 million.

According to some Russian demographic prognostications, the Chinese could be the second largest minority in Russia as early as the first half of the next century.[11]

This issue is more complicated than the one-dimensional myth of Chinese demographic "expansion" or "infiltration." It is a problem of the constructive incorporation of Chinese and other nationals (including Russians from the "near abroad") who are settling or have already settled in Russia and want to live a Russian life. It is also a problem of creating an order in the Russian border areas that will be benign to trade, economics, and tourism but will establish a basic order and deter illegal activities, including illegal immigration.[12] Finally, it is a problem for the Russian government to devise sophisticated policies toward regions and border territories that can boost their economic activities, as well as manage labor and other migrations, in a way that preserves Russia's integrity and stability.

The growing economic gap between Russia and China is another important issue. According to some estimates, China already is the second largest economy in the world, outdistancing even Japan.[13] The expanding economy is matched by military modernization and an assertive regional policy that troubles some of China's neighbors. Using the 1996 United States–China face-off over Taiwan as an example, some analysts argue that more run-ins between the two states are inevitable. The May 1999 bombing of the Chinese embassy in Belgrade provoked a strong reaction from the Chinese government and angry demonstrations in Beijing. These developments, as well as U.S. public support for Tibet and U.S. concern over the future of Hong Kong, are increasingly seen by the PRC as a U.S. challenge to communist China. Some analysts in the United States see the PRC as the main challenger to U.S. leadership in the next century.[14]

These destabilizing trends in U.S.-Chinese relations could, under certain circumstances, overshadow the current contradictions between Russia and the United States. As a strong and assertive China emerges, the United States and the West as a whole may come to realize that a weakened Russia is not beneficial for stability in the long run. The structure that creates geostrategic competition between Russia and China, and China and the United States, within the framework of the post–Cold War system of international relations, continues to exist. It will likely become even more problematic after the enlargement of NATO; U.S. analysts generally deny the existence of this competition, but many in Russia and an increasing number of Chinese analysts see it as an inevitable consequence of NATO enlargement.[15] This view is not a "catastrophic scenario." It simply reflects the idea that this competition, if not properly analyzed and addressed, can be unexpectedly transformed from benign to malign and, consequently, can constitute a basis for possible future conflicts with global consequences. This view is why, in the uncertainties of today, Russia has no choice but to be very careful before embracing alliances and partnerships, especially if they are not of a purely economic nature.

A Russian-Chinese alliance of an anti-U.S., and hence an anti-Western, character will certainly call forth a U.S. and Western response. At the same time, a consensus is evolving in Russia that Russian-Chinese "pragmatic" partnership not aimed at any third country can be an important tool for strengthening the positions of both countries in the world system. Reasons for this perception are very simple: the enlargement of NATO; the alienation of Russia from the West; and the perception that the West is taking advantage of Russia, in its significantly weaker military condition, on a number of economic, political, and security issues. This perceived U.S. and Western policy contrasts sharply with the West's more benign approach to China,[16] and even with Western policies toward Germany after its defeat during World War II. In light of the above factors and the glacial emergence of any true "new world order," the developing Russian-Chinese relationship will be shaped not only by the proclaimed goals and strategies of the two countries concerned but also by the West, both its policy communities and general publics.

CHINESE AND RUSSIAN MUTUAL PERCEPTIONS

Let us begin with Chinese views of Russia and the CIS. After initial methodological difficulties in explaining the disintegration of the USSR, Chinese researchers started to publish a range of works on the fall of the USSR and subsequent developments. For the Chinese, the main problem is not to explain the collapse of the socialist superpower itself, but to explain the continued relevance of Chinese strategies of constructing "socialism with Chinese specifics" in a world where the majority of the states choose market-oriented models without "ideological labels." Most Chinese commentators, contrary to mainstream Russian and Western analysts, still regard the October Revolution, Lenin's theoretical and practical innovations, and Soviet-type industrialization in a positive light.[17] They stress the positive role the system played in the initial stages of industrialization in Russia, largely ignoring the costs to the Soviet people and the system's impact at a later stage as a brake on the modernization and development of the USSR. Generally speaking, Chinese researchers also believe that Gorbachev is personally guilty for the collapse of the socialist superpower.[18]

Yet the collapse of the USSR was also a dramatic and beneficial event, from the point of view of Chinese researchers, because it heightened China's status in world affairs, eliminated the threat to China from the North, and created circumstances beneficial to Chinese economic development.[19] From the Chinese point of view, the collapse of the USSR and the "dubious successes" of the Western-led reforms in Russia contrasted sharply with the "cautious and mostly indigenous" Chinese approach to reforming the economy. This analysis of the Soviet collapse has also played a consolidating role for China, because it shows what might happen to China should it take the Soviet Union's road.

Chinese researcher Lin Cun believes that the pro-Western period of Russian foreign policy has ended because "Russians have understood that the target of the West is to weaken Russia by all means and to transform it into the second-class state."[20] This new stage, according to Yao Wenbin, has laid good foundations for the deepening of bilateral relations and the formation of a Russian-Chinese partnership.[21] According to other Chinese researchers, these foundations have been strengthened by a degree of political stabilization in Russia. These researchers believe future political developments in Russia will be influenced by the balance of power between competing political forces carried out through multiparty competition, parliamentary maneuvers, and elections, not military confrontation.[22]

Chinese political scientists see the CIS as a quasi-union that was born under specific circumstances when the USSR collapsed and its former parts proclaimed independence individually. During the first years of the existence of the CIS, the newly independent states could freely choose their trade partners, which created centrifugal trends exploited by wealthy Western countries. But because the promises of economic support from the West have not been fulfilled, the CIS countries have already started the process of reintegration.[23] Chinese researchers understand that reintegration will not be an easy process, given that at least some of the CIS countries are afraid that reintegration could re-create a Soviet-style state devised by Russia and to Russia's benefit. Chinese researchers, contrary to many Westerners who regard the CIS with skepticism, admit the objective necessity of the reintegration of the post-Soviet territories and the heavy burden of this process for Russia.

The Central Asian region of the former USSR is clearly a zone of interest to both Russia and China. In this region, Russia is in retreat economically and still holds some of its positions by armed force plus diplomacy; China, however, is expanding there economically, demographically, and diplomatically. Consequently, Kazakhstan, Uzbekistan, Kyrgyzstan, Tajikistan, and Turkmenistan receive more attention from China than other parts of the CIS. Chinese researchers have praised Central Asian countries for achieving relative political stability by their attempts to create national harmony through dual citizenship with Russia, enhanced presidential governance, and the suppression of religious fundamentalism.[24] Chinese analysis of economic policy in these countries is, however, much different from mainstream Russian analysis. The Chinese show more sympathy to Uzbekistan and Turkmenistan and less to what they considered the "shock therapy" of Kyrgyzstan and even Kazakhstan.[25] It is more or less clear that this appraisal is tied directly to the Chinese model of reforms.

Chinese researchers have also stressed that if, during the early years of independence, Central Asian countries focused on establishing ties with the Asia-Pacific region, Europe, the United States, and the Muslim world, then at a later stage they have realized that they cannot distance themselves completely from Russia. They are still dependent on Russia in the security sphere and, to a lesser extent, in economic matters. Chinese writings stress, however, that the skillful diplomacy of these countries has managed to find freedom by maneuvering between the West, Russia, and China.

Some researchers (Wang Weizhou, for example) stress that the collapse of the USSR and the creation of the independent Kazakhstan, Uzbekistan, Kyrgyzstan, Tajikistan, Turkmenistan, and Azerbaijan are beneficial for China. These new states reduce the size of the

Sino-Russia border and create a buffer zone.[26] According to this analysis, the presence of a buffer zone has reduced Russian and therefore Western pressure on China from the Northwest. The controversies between these countries and Russia have created opportunities for China to develop a relationship with both sides. China can take advantage of this situation by enhancing its position in Central Asian markets, where Russia is in eclipse and other possible competitors, such as Turkey, are not major economic factors. At the same time, most of the researchers insist—in a reflection of China's official position—that China will not be Russia's competitor (or anybody's competitor) in Central Asia. China's researchers are also worried by the desire of some of the Central Asian states to create a World Kazakh Center, an International Union of Uighurs, a Central Asian Commonwealth, or other attempts to reanimate the so-called Eastern Turkestan Republic as a base of a possible pan-Turkish movement that could destabilize China's borders.[27]

Generally, two current trends among Chinese analysts in assessing Russia can be delineated. One—the official line—stresses the necessity of creating a Russian-Chinese partnership, especially in the buffer zone, for the purpose of mutual assistance on sensitive issues. These sensitive issues include the Taliban in an unstable Afghanistan.[28] A second, minor trend has emerged that sees Russian policies in the Transcaucasus and elsewhere as a continuation of Czarist and Soviet imperialist approaches. As for Russia's internal condition, the main approach of Chinese analysts corresponds closely to that taken by the Left in Russia, focusing critically on the sequence and Western flavor of the reforms.

THE CHINA DEBATE IN RUSSIA

Russian analysts of China fall into three main camps: optimists, pessimists, and pragmatists. For all three, the China question comes down to whether Russia can trust China as a genuine and reliable ally. Is China a constructive partner or an eternal geopolitical challenger? If current trends in China's economic growth can be extrapolated into the future, then early next century Russia will have as its neighbor a state with economic capabilities comparable to those of the United States. The current China debate in Russia centers on how to calculate the consequences of a new economic (and probably also military) superpower emerging on Russia's border and how past developments might influence future ones.

Russian optimists see the emergence of the new economic superpower as a smooth, nonconflictual process.[29] They believe that China is objectively moving along the road to "democracy of the Chinese type," that is, an Asian type of semiauthoritarian democracy seen in Singapore. This political regime is closer to the Russian type of democracy than to the classical Western model. The end result of this process, for left-wing optimists, is a construction of "socialism with specific Chinese characteristics." For optimists, it produces a less authoritarian China.

For Russian pragmatists and pessimists, the future of China is seen as a conflictual process dominated by a domestic struggle for power. Center-periphery ties in China will become looser than they are today. For Russian pessimists, the domestic political struggle in China can lead to the disintegration of China or the emergence of a military regime that will attempt to resolve internal problems by more radical policies, including external expansion.[30] This view is influenced by Russia's declining economic and military potential, especially in the less populated and less developed territories of Siberia and the Russian Far East. Pessimists also note with concern a Russian retreat from Central Asia. The pessimists argue that Russian weakness alone can lead to the separation of the Russian Far East from Central Russia and the destabilization of the eastern part of the continent. Such destabilization, together with the destabilization in the former Yugoslavia and Tajikistan, will be enough to cast the whole of Eurasia into long-term instability.[31]

For pragmatists, the most important question is whether the emergence of the new, economic superpower means the modernization of its armed forces to a level that accords with China's new status. If the answer to this question is yes, then Russia should not be so eager to provide sophisticated weapons to China.[32] At the same time, the pragmatists understand that the enlargement of China's economic ties with its neighbors (including military and technical ones) decreases the probability of a military confrontation, because a confrontation would impose real costs. Nor do the pragmatists doubt that Russia's alienation from the Western world, the emergence of the Taliban in Afghanistan, and China's preoccupation—for the short term at least—with the South give a new impulse to

Russian-Chinese cooperation. The main difference between Russian pragmatists and pessimists lies in the pragmatists' call for a carefully measured policy somewhere between containment and binding partnership.

THE OLD STRATEGIC TRIANGLE THROUGH RUSSIAN EYES

Russian optimists, pessimists, and pragmatists also have their views on the evolution of the old Sino-Russian-U.S. strategic triangle, relating these views to broad foreign policy strategies envisaged by different parts (left, center, and right) of the Russian political spectrum. Left-wing strategists in Russia believe that the former socialist countries are more dependent on the West than they were on the USSR in the past.[33] The disappearance of the USSR has, from their point of view, weakened the positions of most third-world countries in the international arena, turning them into objects of the global "offensive" policies of the West. For Russian communists, the social bipolarity of the world still constitutes the principal character of international relations. Accordingly, the final struggle with those who believe in capitalism as the last stage of the social development of humankind will objectively lead to the fierce global struggle for the establishment of the new world order. For Russian left-wing strategists, the parameters of industrial civilization and the critical condition of the biosphere make the West an adversary of the whole world. Because Russia is not considered an equal partner by the West, it must restructure as quickly as possible the economic and technical base of its military and try to find allies in opposing the West.

Because China, for Russian communists, has become the central object of the hatred of the world's anticommunist forces and is the only country that can lead the struggle of the "underdeveloped periphery" against the "overdeveloped center," Russia must enter a strategic partnership with China and build a Russian-Chinese military political alliance aimed against the West. This partnership will be the key to gaining victory in the "final battle" for a future world order that would be different from the one envisaged by the West and its leader, the United States. Because it is clear that, militarily, China is weaker in comparison with the potentially anti-Chinese "global coalition," China will be interested in establishing a military alliance with Russia, the one country that can adequately arm China. According to this logic, Russia can even be the subordinate party in this alliance, because Russia and China both are underdogs in the current international system. A growing sense of inequality will not undermine the China card for those who see it as an alternative to subordination to the West, simply because, in their logic, Russia will then have a greater chance to play a global role and to defend its national interests in the international arena in the future. The difference between Russian left-wing radicals and left-wing moderates lies in their attitude toward the military-political alliance with China. Moderates talk about strategic partnership but do not define it in a concrete form because of its openly confrontational character.

Liberals (including liberal nationalists) in Russia generally agree on the current multipolarity of the world, notwithstanding their attitude toward the theories of hegemonic stability. The Russian liberal vision employs the theory of a "ringlike" structure of the world. According to this theory, the bipolar system after the Cold War was transformed into a ring where the core comprised the developed countries and the underdeveloped countries were the external part of the ring. An interim zone between the core and the external part comprises the former socialist countries of Europe, the former USSR, and the new industrializing countries (NIC). According to this theoretical model, the formation of the new world order is seen as a differentiation of the interim zone countries from the external part of the ring and the core (the "crystallization" of the core) and at the same time as a greater equalization of the whole system.[34] Following this analysis, Russian strategy can be seen as an attempt to tie the country to the external part of the core and resist the drift to the external part of the ring.[35]

Departing from this theory, liberal analysts in Russia stress that the level of China's cooperation with the West and Japan is higher than the level of China's relations with Russia. They think that the only advantage that Russia has today in the sphere of international relations, compared with China, is its close political ties with the West. It would be unreasonable to lose this advantage merely to demonstrate that Russia is dissatisfied by the decision to enlarge NATO. For Russian liberals, an economically too strong, overpopulated, and authoritarian China is a challenge first to Russia and only in the second instance to the United States and the NATO countries. A future Russian-Chinese alliance would change Russia's dependency on the "overdeveloped" and "indulgent" West to dependency on a comparatively underdeveloped China that is eager to peacefully "colonize" the Russian Far East.[36]

Radical liberals even talk of testing the waters on coalitions to offset China's growing influence, while moderate liberals stress the need to keep the Russian-Western partnership intact.[37] Although they see this partnership as an uneasy one, they consider it to be based on certain privileges for Russia. From their point of view, a Russian-Western partnership would be more beneficial for Russia (and the West) than a "cold peace" in which Russia would play the role of a malign and weakening challenger to the West and, on this basis, form a military-political alliance with China.

For centrists and pragmatists, Russia must be very careful about long-term strategic and geopolitical partnerships in the present political environment. The only basis for these ties is pragmatism.[38] Thus, the pragmatists (especially liberally minded pragmatists) believe that the only guarantee against strains on political relations is a certain level of economic interdependency. The PRC is Russia's largest Asian neighbor, a fact that the pragmatists see as being, and continuing to be, the main geostrategic reality, not withstanding all variants of the relations between the two states. Russia's friendly relationship with the PRC thus establishes a reliable rear area in relations with the West, just as friendly Chinese-Russian relations are a guarantee of the reliable rear for the PRC. For Russia, there is no alternative to the growth of technological, economic, and cultural cooperation with China, but this cooperation must by no means jeopardize Russia's relationships with Western countries, including Western allies in Asia.

Liberal views, which became official policy under Foreign Minister Kozyrev, at least in the early months of his tenure, have evaporated with the turn of Russian internal politics toward a more nationalist direction. Russia's current China policy is mostly within a pragmatic framework drifting slightly to the Left, but a further drift leftwards or toward a more nationalist agenda in Russian foreign policy will depend on domestic developments in Russia as well as the ability of the West to help Russia find a worthy place in the international system. The drift of Russian politics leftward within the framework of mild nationalism will strengthen the foundations of Russian-Chinese cooperation, since this cooperation will be strengthened by a shared Russian-Chinese vision of the world.

CONSTRAINTS ON A SINO-RUSSIAN PARTNERSHIP

While Sino-Russian cooperation is a reality, a number of objective constraints limit how far the relationship is likely to go.[39] These constraints include economic, demographic, and strategic factors.

Economics play the largest role. Russia cannot provide China with what it needs for the modernization of its economy. It cannot provide large-scale investment, because such investment is desperately needed inside Russia itself. With a booming Chinese economy, coming on the heels of a more assertive foreign policy and a growing Chinese diaspora within Russia, Russia may become increasingly reluctant to provide China with the "dual-use" military technologies and know-how that China wants. China, which has had a great influx of foreign investment, is itself reluctant to invest in Russia. China is eager to provide Russia with cheap, everyday goods, food, and an uneducated labor force, saving its more sophisticated exports for the West. Cheap consumer goods and food have largely saturated the Russian market already. The increasingly sophisticated Russian consumer wants to buy expensive and sophisticated luxury goods from Asia, Europe, or the United States. Financially, economically, and technologically, both countries still depend more on the West than on each other. This consideration alone will limit Russian-Chinese strategic cooperation.

The ability of China to provide an uneducated labor force is also reaching its limits because of rising unemployment in Russia itself, the influx of Russians from the "near abroad," and the fears generated by large-scale Chinese migration. The new trend of unofficial Chinese immigration to Russia, including an increase in those engaged in illegal activities, is widely estimated at several times official figures and is seen as a profoundly unfavorable trend in Russia. The only remaining niche in Russian markets where a Chinese labor force can still be of widespread use is in private (or semiprivate), small-scale catering enterprises. In contrast, highly educated Russian specialists provide a real alternative to Western advisers and specialists for the Chinese.

Despite China's success in obtaining formidable economic growth, it has faced, and will face in the future, acute problems of a social, demographic, and ecological nature. To resolve these problems, China will need an economy open to the world, not only to Russia. There are no doubts about this within the Chinese leadership, and any ties with Russia will be judged by their benefit or harm to this larger economic program. Chinese-U.S. relations are more important for China than Chinese-Russian relations, mostly because of the volume of China's trade with the United States ($60 billion in 1998, compared with $5.8 billion with Russia). Any rapprochement with Russia that would risk the loss of U.S. dollars for the Chinese economy will not be seen favorably by the Chinese leadership. Within the symbolic strategic partnership, without further rapprochement with Russia, China could obtain what it needs at present: a limited amount of sophisticated weapons and military technology; an educated labor force to develop the technological base of the Chinese economy, particularly its military potential; and resources from the Russian Far East.

Whatever the terminology might be that describes Russian relations with China, it is doubtful that Russia, at present, will seek a further rapprochement with China that could endanger its relationship with the West, unless certain parameters in the Russian-Western relations are changed. Russian-Chinese military cooperation cannot go beyond certain levels, because, whoever is in the Kremlin, it is unlikely that the government would respond favorably to China's interest in obtaining Russian offensive weapons and military technology on a large scale. For such a trend to develop, Russia must be completely alienated from the Western world. NATO enlargement and other developments have clearly estranged Russia from the West, especially from the United States, but even this unwanted policy has not created the kind of separation that would generate large-scale and sustained Russian-Chinese strategic cooperation.

Moreover, Russians still remember the 1969 border clashes and Chinese claims to Russian territories.[40] China's ability to be a natural counterweight to an enlarged NATO seems limited at present, unless a new disposition of forces takes place after the extension of NATO. Russia needs China as a trade partner and as an ally in the political and economic struggle for the new world order—to ensure that Russia's place will not be too limited—but Russia does not want to create a bilateral relationship that would do serious damage to its relations with the West and the United States. At best, for Russia, friendly, equal, and balanced relations with the People's Republic of China must be placed on as solid a foundation as its "pragmatic" relationship with the West. The relationships with both will have certain limitations.

SCENARIOS FOR RUSSIAN-CHINESE INTERACTION

In keeping with the optimistic, pessimistic, and pragmatic approaches outlined above, what follows are three options for Russian-Chinese relations as they develop between now and early next century. The first is an optimistic scenario, generating a strong and stable Sino-Russian partnership in a stable Asia. The second is a pessimistic one, leading to serious stress upon Russia and especially the Russian Far East. Neither of these are as likely as the range of possibilities I have grouped under the category "realistic scenarios."

The Optimistic Scenario

This scenario is the official one of the Russian and Chinese governments. It sees Russia and China as able to implement an "equal partnership, based on trust and aimed at strategic cooperation in the 21st century." A regular and intensive dialogue—starting at the very top—will produce strategic cooperation in building a safer world, the parameters of which will be similarly interpreted by Moscow, Beijing, and even Washington and Brussels. U.S. aspirations to play a benign hegemonic role in the posthegemonic world will not be rebuffed by Moscow and Beijing, and China and even Russia (if later) will peacefully join the club of economic great powers that will form the foundation for a safer and more stable world.

The level of balanced commercial ties between Russia and China will be equal to that of the United States and China. Exchanging "rockets for coats" will be eliminated from Russian-Chinese trade.[41] Capital will be evenly invested on both sides of the Russian-Chinese border to create an economic buffer zone that can absorb any possible strains in the Russian-Chinese relationship. The border will be demarcated and will be considered permanently fixed by both sides. Polemics about historical ownership of the Far Eastern territories will be left to historians, not politicians or the populace on both sides of the border. This optimistic scenario, while possible, will be difficult to implement owing to the challenges and constraints envisaged in previous sections of this paper.

The Pessimistic Scenario

The second scenario grows out of a worsening of economic conditions, creating political instability in both Russia and China.[42] The combination of political instability and short-sighted economic policies that produce stagnation could, over time, lead to the loss of central control in the regions, resulting eventually in the loss of Russian control in the Maritime Territory. If illegal Chinese immigration in the area increases and separatist tendencies in the regions grow, these changes will produce a declining standard of living, political instability, and a sharpening of ethnic and cultural tensions between Russians and the enlarged Chinese minority. At its worst, this scenario could produce the loss of Russian control over the Far Eastern regions. Such a loss could take different forms; for example, nominal control might remain with Russian authorities in Moscow or with a semi-independent regional center, like the Far Eastern Republic of the 1920s.

If this scenario occurs, the central authorities in the Russian Federation will have only a limited possibility of influencing the evolution of this new state formation. Such an outcome will spur Russian measures to prevent its development, including, I believe, policies similar to those of the Stalin period: support of secessionist movements in neighboring countries, more emphasis on power politics, or even the use of military force (including nuclear force under certain circumstances). The evolution of Russian policies in this direction will be extremely serious for China, because it will mean renewed conflict on its longest border. It will create, in addition, long-lasting negative consequences for Russia because it will further weaken Russia's economy.

Five "Realistic" Scenarios

A Partnership Driven by Economics. The most benign for Russia, Asia, and the world is a Sino-Russian relationship driven by economic forces, with only limited political ties. This scenario is probably the most realistic of all, because it is a relatively conservative and benign form of Russian-Chinese interaction that will not be detrimental to Russian statehood. It will give benefits to Russian industries and thus be seen as beneficial by the Russian population. It will provide various interactions between Russian industries, the Chinese labor force, and international know-how and capital. It could well provide conditions similar to those that have led to growth in other parts of the Asia-Pacific region. This scenario is dependent on the advent of skillful reformers and political and economic managers of a new generation in the top and middle echelons of power in the Kremlin. This scenario will also open the region to other outside countries, including the United States and Japan, possibly South Korea, and probably Taiwan.

This scenario, however, is not without its stress on the territorial status quo. Sponsoring large-scale economic projects involving sizable amounts of foreign labor or opening the region to extensive foreign ownership will alter both demographics and political and economic power in the region. Granting concessions or long-term leases to foreign entities will generate needed financial resources to boost the development of the Far Eastern territories and to create the so-called points of growth. It could be a Russian answer to Chinese special economic zones. The effect of these zones, however, will undoubtedly be to stimulate greater regional autonomy and even serious political links between Russian regions and the foreign countries most responsible for their economic development.

A Partnership Driven by Shared Political Aims. A Sino-Russian relationship defined by common political aims could, for a time, produce anti-Western strategic cooperation. Under this scenario, the various political factors discussed above—the coincidence of Sino-Russian interests at a global level, the number of similar regional problems that must be resolved both by Russia and China, a certain complementarity of economic structure of the Russian Far East and Chinese northern regions, and the potential for Chinese-style economic reforms to pull the Russian Far East out of economic stagnation—will deepen the present partnership. Yet several factors will likely constrain and even transform such an alliance into a rivalry. In the first place, Russia is the weaker party. It will get less out of such a partnership, perhaps only some small economic benefits and ideological support. China, however, will gain not only these symbolic benefits but also substantial real goods: the purchase of energy, raw materials, fuel, modern arms, and military technology; the sale of consumer goods; the reduction of demographic pressure inside the country; and the reduction of social pressure, to name a few. The lack of symmetry will erode the foundations for cooperation, leading either to Russia's loss of real influence or to the reemergence of Russian-Chinese controversies, similar to the controversies of the 1960s. This scenario will be a double blow to Russia, creating initially increased friction with the West and leaving Russia isolated and confronted with a strong China.

Deepening Mistrust. Another possible scenario envisions a growing mistrust between the two states. Such mistrust could take "soft" and "hard" forms. As the experience of Czarist Russia and the USSR has shown, the "hard" confrontation is possible but can resolve problems only temporarily at a very high price to both countries. Former Soviet foreign minister Eduard Shevardnadze once calculated that a "hard" confrontation with China cost the USSR 200–300 billion rubles, based on 1970s prices.[43] Moreover, both Czarist Russia and the USSR, pursuing a "hard" policy toward China, could not avoid the direct physical destruction of people, which caused the emergence of a human rights problem and thus the complication of relations with the Western countries. Throughout history, including the successful, military Kanxi period and the policies envisaged by Zuo Zongtang and Zhang Zhidong, Chinese "hard" policies toward Russia never brought any considerable benefits, in the long run, to China. The "hard" forms seem unrealistic at the new stage of international development, both for economic reasons and because of uncertain gains on both sides. In its "soft" form, however, increasing mistrust between the two states could produce confrontation.

Using Russia for Geopolitical Leverage. This scenario posits growing Chinese political and economic power and increased anxiety about that power in Asia. The U.S. policy-making community focuses largely on the economic growth of the PRC, combined with concerns about a more assertive Chinese foreign policy. Japan and even South Korea cannot regard benevolently the emergence of China as a new economic giant if this will mean the strengthening of the Chinese military machine, externally oriented authoritarian trends, and assertive foreign policy toward its neighbors.[44] Hegemonic trends in China's foreign policy cause anxiety in the Asia-Pacific region. More and more countries that have their own differences with China will come to see China as a competitor, if not an adversary, using Russian resources for its own geopolitical interests. This scenario will increase the role of Russia in the new system of international relations but will also expose it to possible fallout from conflicts involving China and its neighbors and rivals.

A Mixed Scenario. A combination of elements from the above categories is a very realistic, if confusing, possibility. The consensus evolving among the Russian political elite and the public is that Russia must skillfully navigate between the Scylla of "idealistic Atlanticism" and the Charybdis of a Russian-Chinese, anti-Western, military-political alliance; this understanding shows that Russia has finally begun to clearly see its national interests.[45] Thus, Russian-Chinese cooperation, unless the status quo is altered, must be multi-dimensional and mostly economic, so that neither country will be further alienated from the Western world or considered a malign challenger to the West. Individual elements of the relationship, however, could appear to challenge the West or even produce serious disagreement between the two countries themselves. President Yeltsin's second term of office and (even more important) the development of Russian politics after the Yeltsin era, together with Chinese political development in the post-Deng period, will show which combination of different theoretical subscenarios will be reshaped in concrete foreign policy configurations.

CONCLUSION

For Russia, friendly, equal, balanced, and pragmatic relations with the PRC must be as solid a foundation of its external policy as are its pragmatic relations with the West. The main components of the national and state interests of Russia and China are not polar, although some seem to contradict each other. Both Russia and the PRC are interested in the development of peace and the economic prosperity of their peoples. That is why both countries can, at least in the short term, use each other's economic base for the modernization and reform of their economic systems. In order to navigate between "idealistic Atlanticism" and a Russian-Chinese, anti-Western alliance, Russia needs to fill niches in the global division of markets, labor, and international investments different from those of the PRC. The complementarity of the economic systems of the two countries, especially in their borderlands, will ensure the peaceful development of their economic and interstate relations. At the same time, Russia should adequately prepare to answer China's possible challenge to the weakening Russian Far East and reorient Russian exports toward selling industrial technologies, instead of mainly military ones, especially since Russia has failed in its attempts to sell them to Western markets. Thus, Russia may remain close to a united Europe and become a geopolitical bridge that can bring Europe and the Asia-Pacific region closer, ensuring the relative stability of the new multipolar system of international relations. This possibility will also limit the fears of Russian "expansionism," because Russia can then look inward without risking a new isolation.

Russian policy makers are hard-pressed to find adequate answers to the challenge of China and to the enlargement of NATO and the alliance's 1999 strategic doctrine. It is equally difficult to devise a foreign policy toward China and the West that will be beneficial to Russia first. The constrained policy of China during the breakup of the Soviet Union and the time of political turmoil in Russia—which contrasted sharply in the minds of Russian society with the "mercantilist" policies of the Western countries toward Russia—will force the Russian Federation to have carefully measured relations with China that will be more complex than the one-dimensional interaction evolved in the early stages of the Russian-Chinese, post-Soviet relationship and idealistically envisaged by the officialdom of both countries.

There is no doubt that this relationship must and will be carefully monitored by both countries to eliminate negative trends and malign consequences that under certain circumstances can lead to the politics of hostility and distrust of the past. Because of this, the relationship will also be closely monitored by the international community. Clearly mutual perceptions, still contaminated by ideological preferences and the burden of the past, are also factors that will influence the Russian-Chinese relationship. The enlargement of NATO is a negative factor that will cut off or at least constrain some of the scenarios and will make the strategic configuration of the West, Russia, and China a different one, compared with that of the early post-bipolar scene. Although the ability of Russia and China to separately influence the global character of events has been significantly reduced, their combined ability to influence it (especially if realigned with other countries of the so-called third world to which

Russia now belongs because of the common problems those countries face) is probably equal to that of the Western bloc. Russia is not a part of the Western bloc; this fact is already a fait accompli. This fact is the fault of both fragile Russian and solid Western democracies. For the future of the world system, however, it matters greatly where Russia—proclaimed by many Western analysts as a "third-class state"—will be and with whom it will ally, if Russia will be a European country in Asia, or an Asian country in Europe.

Western policy has become a major factor, together with the internal political developments in both Russia and China, influencing the future course of the Russian-Chinese strategic partnership. This relationship can be a benign one for the international community and Russia and China, but it still has the power to become malign. Understanding the latest possibilities in this relationship can help to overcome the existing contradictions and difficulties. Both countries have shared interests and can derive benefits from each other's economic base for the modernization and reform of their economic systems. Both countries can contribute to long-term stability in Asia and beyond. This development of the Russia-China relationship will be of substantial benefit to the world as a whole, because the two giants, Russia and China, will be involved in improving the lives of their people and not in conflict with each other or in attempts to upset the international system.

NOTES

[1]William Perry, who was then U.S. secretary of defense, described the Russian-U.S. partnership as "pragmatic" during a trip to Moscow on October 17, 1996. See Gerald B. Solomon, "Prizes and Pitfalls of NATO Enlargement," *Orbis*, vol. 41, no. 2 (Spring 1997), p. 219. A Russian view of cooperation as the "coincidence of pragmatic interests" is put forth by Sergey Kortunov in "Rossiya i SSchA: Put' k Partnerstvu" (Russia and the USA: The Path to Partnership), *Mirovaya Yekonomika i Mezhdunarodniye Otnosheniya*, no. 7 (1996), pp. 72, 77. In "Rossiiskaya Diplomatiya v Godu Minuvshem i Nastoyaschem" (Russian Diplomacy in the Preceding and the Coming Year), *Mezhdunarodnaya Zhizn'*, no. 1 (1997), pp. 108–10, the Russian Ministry of Foreign Affairs described the Russian-U.S. relationship as "aimed at creating the stable foundation for developing international relations" (*yest' stremleniye k sozdaniyu stabil'noi osnovi dlia razvitiya mezhdunarodnikh otnoshenii*). The relationship with China was upgraded from "creating the foundations for

the formation of the equal, confident partnership, aimed at the strategic cooperation in the 21st century" (*sozdana osnova dlia formirovaniya otnoshenii ravnopravnogo doveritel'nogo partnerstva, orientirovannogo na strategicheskoye vzaimodeiistviye v 21 veke*) to "strategic partnership." The formula of "equal, confident partnership, aimed at the strategic cooperation in the 21st century," however, was put only in the Russian-Chinese Declaration; see *Problemy Dalnego Vostoka*, no. 3 (1997), pp. 5–7. See also Li Jingjie, "Xin Shidaide Zhong-E Guanxi" (Russian-Chinese Relations in the New Era) (unpublished paper presented at the Princeton Seminar on the Evolution of Sino-Russian Relations in the 1990s, April 24–May 4, 1997), p. 5.

[2]See, for example, Vsevolod Ovchinnikov, "Mir bez Veduschikh i Vedomikh" (A World without Leaders and Followers), *Rossiiskaya gazeta*, January 15, 1997, p. 7.

[3]The disposition of internal political forces in each country and how this disposition influences bilateral relations is not considered in detail in this paper. For information on these issues, see my article "China in the Perception of Russian Foreign-Policy Elite," *Issues and Studies*, no. 5 (March 1997) and "Kitai Vo Vneshnepoliticheskikh Strategiyakh Politicheskikh Sil Rossii" (China in the Foreign Policy Strategies of Russian Political Forces) (unpublished paper presented by Professor Gelbras at the Seminar on Sino-Russian Relations held in the Carnegie Endowment's Washington Center, May 5, 1997).

[4]See, in English, Alexei D. Voskressenski, *The Difficult Border: Current Russian and Chinese Concepts of Sino-Russian Relations and Frontier Problems* (New York: Nova Science Publishers, 1996) and, in Russian and Chinese, Alexei D. Voskressenski, *Tsarskaya Rossiya i Kitai v Issledovaniyakh Poslednikh Let* (Tsarist Russia and China in the Historiography of the Past Ten Years in Russia and China) (Moscow: Institute of Far Eastern Studies, 1994); "Eluosi Xuezhe Dui E-Zhong Guanxi Ji Bianjie Lingtu Wentide Lijie" (Russian Scholar's Understanding of Russian-Chinese Relations and Territorial Problems), in Xing Yuling, ed., *Zhongguo Bianjiang Yanjiu Tongbao* (Research on China's Borderlands) (Beijing-Urumqi: Xinjiang Renmin Chubanshe, 1995).

[5]Sherman Garnett, "The Russian-Far East in Sino-Russian Relations," *SAIS Review*, vol. XVI, no. 2 (Summer-Fall 1996), p. 4.

[6]For the impact of geopolitical changes on the old Sino-Soviet-U.S. triangle, see Alexei D. Voskressenski, ed., *Russia-China-USA: Redefining the Triangle* (New York: Nova Science Publishers, 1996).

[7]On the comparison of Russian and Chinese economic might, see L. Kondrashova and A. Anisimov, "Sovremenniye Otsenki Ekonomicheskogo Potentsiala Kitaya" (Modern Appraisals of Chinese Economic Potential), *Problemi Dal'nego Vostoka*, no. 6 (1993), pp. 57–65, and Dmitri Trenin, "Rossiya i Kitai: Voyennii Aspekt Otnoshenii" (Russia and China: The Military

Aspect of Relationships) (unpublished paper delivered at the Carnegie Endowment's Moscow Center, March 19, 1997).

[8]See, for example, Gerald Segal, "How Insecure is Pacific Asia?" *International Affairs*, vol. 73, no. 2 (April 1997), pp. 245–46.

[9]Proceedings of the 6th International Conference "China and the Chinese Civilization," *Kitai i Rossiya v Vostochnoi Azii i ATR v 21 Veke* (China and Russia in Eastern Asia and the Asia-Pacific Region in the 21st Century) (Moscow: Institute of Far Eastern Studies, 1995), part 1, sec. 2 (Foreign Policy).

[10]*Sotrudnichestvo Kitaya i Rossii po Mezhdunarodnim Problemam* (Russian-Chinese Cooperation on International Issues), from the series "International Relations of the Countries of Northeast Asia" (Moscow: Institute of Far Eastern Studies, 1996); Xia Yishan, "Sino-Russian Partnership Marching into the 21st Century," *Beijing Review*, vol. 40, no. 18 (May 5–11, 1997), pp. 9–12.

[11]Yuri Kobishchanov, "Can Russia Deal with Major Influx from 'South'?" *Current Digest of the Post-Soviet Press*, vol. XLVII, no. 6 (March 8, 1995), pp. 1–2. Article originally published in *Nezavisimaya gazeta*, February 10, 1995, pp. 1–2.

[12]Alexandr Platkovsky, "Kitai Zavalil Rossiyu Narkotikami" (China Filled Russia up with Narcotics), *Izvestiya*, April 3, 1997, p. 3; Yuri Savenkov, "Khodoki iz Podnebesnoi" (People from the Celestial), *Izvestiya*, February 1, 1997, p. 4.

[13]P. Vlasov and T. Gurova, "Nasledniki Diadi Sema: Zakonniye i Samozvanniye" (Successors of Uncle Sam: True Heirs and Pretenders), *Ekspert*, no. 22 (1996), pp. 36–40; Alexei Voskressenski, "Veter s Zapada ili Veter s Vostoka?" (The Wind from the East or the Wind from the West?), *Svobodnaya Misl'*, no. 10 (1996), pp. 89–100.

[14]*Economist*, March 29, 1997, p. 79; William Norman Grigg, "Red China's Ocean Invasion," *New American*, vol. 13, no. 10 (May 12, 1997), pp. 4–8; Richard Bernstein and Ross H. Munro, *The Coming Conflict with China* (New York: Alfred A. Knopf, 1997).

[15]Shen Dingli, "U.S.-Russian Strategic Balance Fragile," *Beijing Review*, vol. 40, no. 18 (May 5–11, 1997), pp. 12–13; Xia Yishan, "Sino-Russian Partnership Marching into the 21st Century," *Beijing Review*, vol. 40, no. 18 (May 5–11, 1997), pp. 9–12.

[16]Regarding the perceptions of anti-Russian tariffs and quotas, see, for example, Sergey Kortunov, "Rossiya i SSchA: Put' k Partnerstvu" (Russia and the USA: The Path to Partnership), *Mirovaya Yekonomika i Mezhdunarodniye Otnosheniya*, no. 7 (1996), p. 77, and Richard Layard and John Parker, *The Coming Russian Boom* (New York: The Free Press, 1996), p. 98.

[17]Jiang Lu and Chen Zhihua, ed., "Istoricheskii Vzgliad na Evolutsiyu v SSSR" (An Historical View of the Evolution of the USSR), in *Kitaiskiye*

Politology o Polozhenii v Rossii i o Rossiisko-Kitaiskih Otnosheniyakh (Chinese Political Scientists on the Russian Situation and Russian-Chinese Relations) (Moscow: Institute of the Far Eastern Studies, Express-Information, 1996), no. 2, pp. 48–58.

[18]Ye. Gaidar, "Anomalii Ekonomicheskogo Rosta" (Anomalies of the Economic Growth), *Voprosi Ekonomiki*, no. 12 (1996), pp. 20–39, especially 25–28.

[19]Huang Zongliang, "Politicheskaya Situatsiya v Rossii i Razvitiye Otnoshenii Rossii so Stranami Severo-Vostochnoi Azii" (Russian Political Situation and the Development of Her Relations with Northeastern Asia) (trans. from Chinese), in *Kitaiskiye Politology o Polozhenii v Rossii i o Rossiisko-Kitaiskih Otnosheniyakh*, (Chinese Political Scientists on the Russian Situation and Russian-Chinese Relations) (Moscow: Institute of Far Eastern Studies, Express-Information, 1996), no. 2, pp. 69–76. The original Chinese text published in *Guoji Zhenzhi Yanjiu*, no. 2 (1994), pp. 1–7.

[20]Lin Cun, "Soiuz, Protivoborstvo i Partnerstvo. 45 Let Kitaisko-Sovetskikh i Kitaisko-Rossiiskikh Otnoshenii" (Union, Hostility and Partnership. 45 years of Chinese-Soviet and Chinese-Russian Relations), in *Kitaiskiye Politology o Polozhenii v Rossii i o Rossiisko-Kitaiskih Otnosheniyakh*, p. 37. The original Chinese text appeared in *Guoji Guancha*, no. 5 (1994), pp. 5–13, 13–16.

[21]Yao Wenbin, "Politika i Interesi Bezopasnosti KNR i Rossii v Regione ATR" (Politics and Security Interests of the PRC and Russia in the Asia-Pacific Region), in *Kitaiskiye Politology o Polozhenii v Rossii i o Rossiisko-Kitaiskih Otnosheniyakh*, pp. 339–47. The original Chinese text appeared in *Dongou Zhongya Yanjiu*, no. 4 (1994), pp. 28–30.

[22]Pan Dezha, "Retrospektivnii Vzgliad na Politicheskuiu Situatsiu v Rossii i Analiz yeye Razvitiya" (Retrospective View of the Russian Political Situation and the Analysis of Its Development), in *Kitaiskiye Politilogy o Polozhenii v Rossii i o Rossiisko-Kitaiskih Otnosheniyakh*, pp. 59–68. The original Chinese text appeared in *Dongou Zhongya Yanjiu*, no. 1 (1995), pp. 152–87.

[23]Jiang Lu and Chen Zhihua, "Istoricheskii Vzgliad na Evolutsiyu v SSSR" (Historical View on the Evolution of the USSR), in *Kitaiskiye Politilogy o Polozhenii v Rossii i o Rossiisko-Kitaiskih Otnosheniyakh*, pp. 48–58.

[24]Chen Minshan and He Xiquan, "Tsentralnaya Aziya Segodniya i Zavtra" (Central Asia Today and Tomorrow), in *Kitaiskiye Politologi o Polozhenii v Stranakh SNG* (Chinese Political Scientists on the Situation in the CIS Countries) (Moscow: Institute of Far Eastern Studies, Express-Information, 1996), no. 2, pp. 59–64. The original Chinese text appeared in *Contemporary International Relations*, vol. 5, no. 8 (1995), pp. 1–16.

[25]Ibid. For the Russian understanding see, among others, Irina Zviagelskaia, *The Russian Policy Debate on Central Asia* (London: The Royal Institute of International Affairs, 1995).

[26]Wang Weizhou, "Razvitiye Situatsii v Srednei i Zapadnoi Azii i yeye Vliyaniye na KNR" (The Development of the Situation in Middle and Western Asia and Its Implications for the PRC), in *Kitaiskiye Politologi o Polozhenii v Stranakh SNG*, pp. 65–76. The original Chinese text appeared in *SIIS Journal*, no. 1 (1994), pp. 2, 4–9.

[27]Song Yimin, "Interesi Bezopasnosti KNR i Sredneaziatskikh Stran" (The PRC and the Central Asia Countries' Security Interests), in *Kitaiskiye Politologi o Polozhenii v Stranakh SNG*, pp. 77–82. The original Chinese text appeared in *Dongou Zhongya Yanjiu*, no. 4 (1994), pp. 48–50.

[28]Wang Zongjie, "Spheri i Metodi Mezhdonarodnogo Sotrudnichestva Kitaya i Rossii" (The Spheres and the Methods of the International Cooperation between Russia and China), in *Kitaiskiye Politilogi o Polozhenii v Stranakh SNG*, pp. 29–32. The original Chinese text appeared in *Guoji Zhengzhi Yanjiu*, no. 4 (1994), pp. 7–9.

[29]Ye. Afanasiyev and G. Logvinov, "Rossiya i Kitai Na Poroge Tretiego Tisiacheletiya" (Russia and China on the Threshold of the Third Millennium), *Mezhdunarodnaya Zhizn'*, no. 11–12 (1995), pp. 33–38; M. Titarenko, "Kitai v Postdenovskuyu Epokhu i Rossiisko-Kitaiskiye Otnosheniya" (China in the Post-Deng Era and Russian-Chinese Relations), *Mezhdunarodnaya Zhizn'*, no. 8 (1995), pp. 27–36.

[30]Alexandr Vengerovskii, *Khochu i Mogu* (I Want and I Can) (Moscow: AO NII Zentrprogramsystem, 1995).

[31]Alexei Bogaturov, "Pluralisticheskaya Odnopoliarnost' i Interesi Rossii" (Pluralistic Unipolarity and Russia's Interests), *Svobodnaya Misl'*, no. 2 (1996), pp. 25–36.

[32]Sergei Trusch, "Prodazha Rossiiskogo Oruzhiya Pekinu: Rezoni i Opaseniya" (Russian Arms Sales to Beijing: Reasons and Doubts), *NG — Nezavisimoye Voennoye Obozreniye*, a supplement to *Nezavisimaya gazeta*, April 25, 1996, p. 6. See also the writings by the Western analysts, for example, Stephen Blank, *The Dynamics of Russian Weapon Sales to China* (Carlisle Barracks, Pa.: U.S. Army War College, 1997) and Gaye Christoffersen, "China and the Asia-Pacific Need for a Grand Strategy," *Asian Survey*, vol. XXXVI, no. 11 (November 1996), p. 1077.

[33]Alexandr G. Yakovlev, "Rossiya i Kitai kak Sub'ekti Mirovoi Politiki" (Russia and China as Subjects of the World Politics), *Obozrevatel'*, no. 19–20 (1994), pp. 57–69.

[34]Bogaturov, "Pluralisticheskaya Odnopoliarnost' i Interesi Rossii."

[35]Ibid.

[36]Ibid.

[37]Yegor Gaidar, "Rossiya XXI veka: Nye mirovoi zhandarm, a forpost demokratii v Evrazii" (Russia of the 21st Century: Not the World's Gendarme, but an Outpost of Democracy in Eurasia), *Izvestiya*, May 18, 1995;

Alexei Bogaturov, "Pluralisticheskaya Odnopoliarnost' i Interesi Rossii" (Pluralistic Unipolarity and Russia's Interests), *Svobodnaya Misl'*, no. 2 (1996).

[38]Alexei Voskressenski, "Kitai vo Vneshepoliticeskoi Strategii Rossii" (China in the Strategy of Russia's Foreign Policy), *Svobodnaya Misl'*, no. 1 (1996), pp. 94–105; Alexei Voskressenski, "Veter s Zapada ili Veter s Vostoka?" (The Wind from the East or the Wind from the West?), *Svobodnaya Misl'*, no. 10 (1996).

[39]On this theme, see Gerald Segal, "At Present, There's Not Much for Russia to Gain in East Asia," *International Herald Tribune*, April 24, 1996, p. 8; Alexei K. Pushkov, "A Russian-Chinese Alliance Doesn't Look Likely," *International Herald Tribune*, April 24, 1996, p. 8.

[40]Garnett, "The Russian-Far East in Sino-Russian Relations," p. 2.

[41]Alexandr Platkovsky, "Oruzheinii Biznes Na Grani Miasnoi Voini" (Arms Trade on the Edge of the Meat War), *Izvestiya*, March 15, 1997, p. 3.

[42]This scenario does not include the rapid disintegration of either the Russian Federation or China. Such disintegration would have such enormous implications for the international foreign policy agenda that it would entail a complete reevaluation of basic assumptions about the future of Central Eurasia and East Asia as a whole. While serious problems continue to challenge both the Russian and Chinese governments, the disintegration scenario is far less likely at the end of the 1990s than—in Russia at least— in the earliest days of Russian independence.

[43]*Pravda*, July 5, 1990, p. 1; *Izvestiya*, October 17, 1990, p. 3.

[44]On the complexity of Sino-Japanese relations, see Robert S. Ross, *Managing a Changing Relationship: China's Japan Policy in the 1990s* (Carlisle Barracks, Pa.: U.S. Army War College, 1996).

[45]See, for example, Alexei Arbatov, "Vneshnepoliticheskii Konsensus v Rossii" (Foreign Policy Consensus in Russia), *Nezavisimaya gazeta*, March 14, 1997, p. 5.

6
Sino-Russian Relations: Mutual Assessments and Predictions

Gilbert Rozman

With rhetorical flourishes aimed at domestic and global audiences, China and Russia between 1992 and 1999 repeatedly turned to each other to upgrade relations. They established a strategic partnership with world-shaking pretensions. Controversy swirls over how significant and enduring this partnership will become. Is it a strong bond between two angry opponents of the United States, as it appeared to be in May 1999 in joint statements against the NATO campaign against Yugoslavia? Or is it a weak link of two countries increasingly dependent on the United States, protesting futilely? To predict these relations we should consider the reasoning driving the two countries together, what each side has found important about the other—its internal prospects and changing national strength, its commitment to the partnership and the compatibility of its objectives, its emerging place in the world order. Such assessments matter more than usual, because the Sino-Russian partnership has developed unexpectedly and could change in ways not yet well incorporated into projections of great-power relations.[1]

To explain what Sino-Russian relations will accomplish, we must understand what they mean to the two parties themselves. China's and Russia's assessments of each other clarify why they have been building a special relationship marked already by at least four sequences of eye-catching sloganeering, symbolism, and summitry. The assessments reveal many of the doubts and objections to extending the partnership, ones never mentioned at state occasions but much debated in internal discussions. Where great-power identities are in flux, "objective" measures of interests that overlook assessments may miss some forces driving international relations. Failure to predict the course of Sino-Russian relations to date testifies to the need to explore the domestic roots in each country of views of the other and its global role.

From the summer of 1992 through the spring of 1999, Sino-Russian relations developed quickly and without interruption, apart from some wavering in 1994. Leaders of the two countries project sustained momentum well into the next century. Although they insist that the result will not be an alliance, the all-around strategic partnership they predict appears virtually synonymous with a peacetime alliance. Indeed, through coordination of arms supplies and joint efforts to shape the global strategic environment, what is promised could be one of the significant collaborations of modern times. Rhetorically, it is nothing less than a counterthrust against a new world order led by the United States.

Many are tempted to minimize the possibility of a lasting partnership of this sort. After all, the historical record reveals more discord than coordination between these two countries. Moreover, the economic interests of both countries—underlined by markets and investments for China and, for the present, loans for Russia—lie elsewhere. Significantly, the domestic roots of a close partnership remain weak. Indifferent and skeptical public opinion, hesitation or resistance in important areas of each country, weak interest-group support, and the potential of explosive nationalistic disputes all raise doubts about the durability of this still minimally substantive relationship.[2] Both countries have resorted to bombast before and have reason to do so now.

Before us is a discrepancy between alarmists who warn of a virtual Cold War ahead and rejectionists who deny that the rhetoric of partnership is backed by substance. On the one side are those who foresee a bloc of Eurasian continentalism solidifying versus the outside world. On the other are those who anticipate the two countries facing outward while largely turning their backs to each other. Such extreme interpretations, which downplay the middle ground, should not distract us from centering on the competing pressures that will buffet the partnership and the forces that will likely decide the outcome. These pressures and forces emerge from the writings in each country on the other. They point to a struggling relationship, but one with a good chance to have staying power.

Examination of the relevant articles in each country (several hundred were singled out for scrutiny); interviews with diverse experts in Beijing and Moscow; and intense discussions with specialists all point to a multigraded approach to assessments. At the top level are the views of the foreign policy establishments in Beijing and Moscow, advocating upgraded relations but in stages and with attention to balance in other bilateral relations. At the next level are moderately dissenting views, pushing from both directions to give new meaning to the partnership—either to strengthen it faster or to downplay its significance. Finally, at the bottom level in importance but not in visibility are opposing views to transform the partnership abruptly. In Russia both dissenting and opposing views stand out, while in China censorship and reliance on the center to set the parameters of discourse keep such views in the background. To rely only on carefully controlled sources representing the center would obscure the debates that at each stage of relations have influenced policy; to concentrate on opposing views would downplay the mainstream consensus that has been forming and gaining strength.

A review of Chinese and Russian assessments over seven years leads to the conclusion that the strategic partnership is likely to endure and even to strengthen, but not to advance in the manner or to the degree envisioned. Over the next five years, the partnership will face difficult hurdles. With cautious and committed leadership on each side, it should weather them. Over the next twenty years, efforts to realize the partnership's vision will pose an even steeper test of each side's commitment. Its realization is less likely. This potential limitation does not mean a return to confrontation. Although the threat of a reversal of relations is not trivial, more likely is a high degree of forbearance that will sustain the partnership as a global and regional force.

THE IMPORTANCE OF ASSESSMENTS

In the 1990s, Chinese and Russian assessments of each other are among the most important perceptions in one country of another. This importance can be traced to four factors:

- the continued attention of the two giants in the history of socialism to measuring the prospects of their own system and its reform against the realities of their alter ego in the second half of this century[3]

- an intense desire by the victims of the most vitriolic great-power rivalry of our times not to repeat the mistakes of their counter-productive schism when each country was shattered by astronomical expenses, ideological rigidity, and a weakened international position[4]

- the image of the other country in a period where each sits astride some of the world's most earthshaking regional realignments as the great-power neighbor of greatest future relevance[5]

- the search in each country for a counterweight to U.S. superpower dominance and to the spread of Western civilization, which has led to the other country as the number one force for achieving such balance.[6]

Assessing one another and the future of bilateral relations, China and Russia are measuring the potential for their own rise domestically, regionally, and internationally. China and Russia watch each other intently, because they recognize that in the transitional decades of the 1990s and 2000s their bilateral relationship is likely to be decisive in shaping the world order each is to face in the twenty-first century. They watch the United States, too, the number one concern of each country.

Yet, while they claim to understand the United States and its long-term objectives as leader of alliances from Europe to Japan, they are struggling to know what the other regional giant will do. Will it join the United States in a crippling alliance, as China briefly feared Russia would do at the end of 1991 and the beginning of 1992?[7] Will it bide its time and build its national power until it can assert recidivist claims and become a regional hegemonic leader, as many in the Russian Far East warn China is plotting?[8] Or will it become the most trustworthy great power and an indispensable partner in shaping a new regional and world order, as the foreign policy elites in each country have contended for several years?[9] The answers to these questions reflect not only the intentions of current leaders, but also changing capabilities and shifting political and economic forces. Moved by multiple objectives, officials and experts in the two countries may get some of these answers wrong, even as their assessments are guiding the two countries' policies.

The foundation of the strategic partnership forged between the two countries is a shared worldview. Bilateral relations are energized more by the two countries' wariness of the emerging global environment than by their approval of it. They rise and fall more in anticipation of the intentions of their partner than on the basis of hard evidence about cooperation or conflict. Consequently, the partnership depends on aspects of worldview that are more changeable than national interest, such as the psychological underpinnings of national identity that guide policy.

China and Russia are searching for a position in the emerging world order commensurate with their putative national interests. But in Beijing, the Communist Party defines these interests to preserve its power more, perhaps, than to ensure China's most successful place in the world.[10] In Russia, the psychology of national humiliation is so intense in opposition circles and even within the coalition in power that awareness of interests may be skewed to assuage worries more than to maximize opportunities. In such confused times, they have turned to each other. Domestically, official and elite circles have battled to define new identities and interests, debating as well which countries can best serve them. The debate over each other arguably has been the most intriguing. Regionally and globally, the two countries have calculated the national strength of rival great powers and searched for ways to establish an equilibrium that augments their own strengths. This effort, too, has led to scrutiny of the other great regional power as an unsettled force in global equations.

Beginning in the late 1970s, China's post-Mao reassessment of the Soviet Union reached a culmination in 1982. It not only cast aside in 1979 the notion of Soviet "revisionism," but it also downgraded Soviet "hegemonism" as a global and bilateral danger that required China to side with the United States and its ally Japan. Achieving a global equilibrium became a centerpiece of official thinking as Beijing indicated its interest in balancing the United States and the Soviet Union. Afterwards, attention shifted to calculating two important factors: (1) the continuing decline of Soviet power relative to that of the United States and Japan and the prospects of reform that would revive it, and (2) the overextension of Soviet expansionism and the potential for a pullback that would alter the global environment. Essential to these determinations were predictions of Soviet politics, particularly after Mikhail Gorbachev took office. Assessments from afar abstractly searching for answers to grand questions soon gave way to detailed investigations of year-by-year developments.[11]

In the Soviet Union, China-watching developed as a specialized field in the 1970s, but it was slow to adjust to the reform era under Deng Xiaoping. Authorities stifled debate as late as the summer of 1982 with the slogan "Maoism without Mao." Indeed, the deputy head of the department for liaison with socialist countries, O. B. Rakhmanin, in combination with Foreign Minister Andrei Gromyko, may have slowed normalization by as many as ten years by rejecting incrementalism and insisting on, at one stroke, one dramatic breakthrough. When the USSR finally showed an interest in compromise, it came at a time when the Chinese refused to go far owing to the three military obstacles of Cambodia, Afghanistan, and the Soviet troops ringing China in the North. Normalization was delayed further. With the start of serious negotiations in 1982, however, a concealed, if far-reaching, debate spread in Russian circles. This debate treated the impact of China's reforms on its national strength, the potential for normalization of Sino-Russian relations, and the effect of these relations on the global balance of power.

Of course, glasnost in 1986–1987 stimulated broader public discussion. With the ouster of Rakhmanin along with Gromyko, on-site observations highlighted recent achievements such as the prosperity of special economic zones. Throughout the decade and even more after the Tiananmen brutality of 1989, references to China were most significant for their meaning in the Soviet reform struggle. Yet, increasingly they also played a role in setting Soviet foreign policy and preparing for a new world order.

In the 1960s to 1980s, Soviets writing about China and Chinese writing about the Soviet Union usually had one eye turned to domestic considerations. The other country became a surrogate for debates about reform in one's own country. From 1978 to 1987, China signified the reform alternative to Soviet stagnation.[12] Subsequently, from 1987 through at least 1992, reform in the Soviet Union and Russia served as stimulus to Chinese, both those anxious to accelerate change at home and conservatives who warned of a fate that could befall their own system.[13]

The situation has not altogether changed in recent years. Chinese censorship warns still of incorrect interpretations of Russia that could encourage destabilizing change in China, while Russians have been so traumatized by their country's transformation that they find it hard to look beyond the most telling yardsticks when analyzing China. In China, the initial condemnation of "shock therapy" fit this pattern; failure of the Russian departure from socialism was anticipated and greeted as proof that China had made the correct choice.[14] Domestic calculations still matter. Despite high growth rates, China's reform of state-owned enterprises has been unsuccessful, and many sensitive areas of economic policy could still be cast in a negative light if comparisons with Russia were left uncontrolled. In Russia, superficial treatment of China's economic achievements also has much to do with a domestic political agenda. For critics of the Yeltsin leadership, the fact of rapid economic growth under socialist or anti-Western leadership suffices to justify an abrupt change of course. For Westernizing reformers, the association of the Chinese model with discredited socialism is enough to deny any need to examine it closely.

Although domestic factors still matter greatly, the accelerating enthusiasm since the summer of 1992 for close relations and the positive assessments needed to support them derive also from international factors. At the end of 1991, bilateral relations reached a low point. To be sure, Beijing had been disappointed by Moscow many times in the previous decade—the abortive nature of Andropov-era reforms, Moscow's slowness to address its expansionism in Asia, and Gorbachev's shift to glasnost and "new thinking" rather than the kind of reform course followed in China. But this time it feared a scenario of capitalism, Westernization, and alliance that would leave China utterly isolated amid the great powers. With mounting satisfaction in 1992–1993, China saw that its worst-case scenario did not materialize; Russia did not succumb to any of these temptations. Instead, Beijing led the way, in stages, in anticipating how a bilateral partnership can make a mark on the world. While Moscow remains fuzzier about its details, the vision of future relations is now at the center of intense joint deliberations. Because this is a vision in support of each country's "rightful place" as a great power, the fact that it is far removed from the reality of today may be less important than the degree to which it corresponds to a compulsion for a great-power identity in the emerging world order.

Between 1992 and 1999, the immediate interests pulling China and Russia together were weak, while elite perceptions of their need for each other steadily strengthened. The foundation of the strategic partnership is a shared worldview. This foundation needs to be undergirded by interest groups or it will remain fragile. A vision of the future suggests that when Russian economic growth begins in earnest and China's political transition stabilizes, both sides may find benefits to prove that the partnership delivers. But these benefits are unlikely to solidify a close, exclusive partnership that would pose a serious threat to other great powers.

A VISION OF THE STRATEGIC PARTNERSHIP TWENTY YEARS HENCE

In 1996–1997, behind the surface of improving relations, an optimistic image of a shared future was detectable. Although this vision changed in 1998–1999, it is worth bringing into the open. In that way, we can identify the hopes that underlined relations as the new partnership took root.

Beijing and Moscow call the Sino-Russian strategic partnership a new kind of relationship between great powers for the twenty-first century. For a world in transition from a bipolar order to a still uncertain order, in which one superpower remains prominent and global economic integration is occurring rapidly, the Sino-Russian gambit constitutes nothing less than a wedge in support of another direction of development. Together the two countries seek to limit the spillover of geoeconomic integration into the geopolitical arena, to accelerate the decline of the lone superpower's preeminence in favor of multipolarity, and to block the spread of Western civilization.[15] As non-Western countries with large and unsatisfied great-power egos, China and Russia feed on the legacy of .communist ideology in rekindling their struggle against a world order led by the United States, Japan, and the West European great powers.

To understand the intensity of the commitment of Beijing and Moscow to each other, focusing on the state of their current partnership is less important than grasping the reasoning that drives them together. Their present relationship is more a promise for the twenty-first century than an existing solid foundation for cooperation. Total trade of $5–8 billion over the past seven years, cross-border relations marred by deep suspicions, and popular indifference to each other do not constitute signs of solidarity. Yet commitments by national leaders, on balance supported by political and academic elites and backed by converging assessments of the world order and by great-power identities, make the Sino-Russian strategic partnership a more serious phenomenon than many other bilateral linkages. In broad strokes, they share a vision for the future, say, twenty years ahead. Even if this vision conveys only a vague notion of the emerging world order and the way the two countries will work together in it, the idea is present for bolstering current assessments with interests that could solidify the partnership.

China and Russia stress that they are preparing for a long-term relationship, one all-around in scope. The first determining force, which was already in place by 1997, is summitry. A close bond between the two countries is beginning from the top down. Top officials will meet regularly, and ministers and deputy ministers will be in close touch through committees and consultations. No matter what problems exist, the two sides pledge a warm atmosphere in their frequent meetings. In contrast to the first decade of relations, when leaders' egos set relations on a downward spiral, leaders' conviviality and frequent attention to each other will steer relations ever forward. Of course, the discrepancy must be overcome between a top-down relationship guided by frequent summits and regular consultations of interministerial committees, and a dearth of sub-stance on which the two sides can work on a bilateral basis. The warm atmosphere of a leadership generation educated together in the 1950s will not be passed along to the next generation unless subcommissions on energy, transportation, and a host of other sub-jects make important decisions binding the countries together.

The second key to this relationship is its strategic nature. Russia is economically too weak to sustain its military-industrial complex. China proclaims itself a great power politically but not fully so economically or militarily. Rapid escalation in Russian arms sales from 1992 to 1997 is a harbinger of closer cooperation ahead. Russia will continue for many years to fall further behind the United States, but with China's cooperation, Russia may at least be able to produce the weapons it regards as vital. Meanwhile, cooperation will grow in research and development of advanced arms technology. Russians have some qualms about this vision of strategic collaboration. They prefer to transfer older technology. Many recognize China less as a savior of an endangered arms industry than as a potential threat.

But the momentum for cooperation has been accelerating, and Russia is not likely to receive a better offer. If Beijing and Moscow had pushed to achieve a trade volume of $20 billion by the year 2000, as agreed, or soon thereafter, then arms exports from Russia could have reached as high as $4 billion, or a fifth of total trade.[16] In 1996–1997, they were roughly one-fifth to one-quarter of a still small trade total, but the percentage has been rising. More likely, the economic dimension will lose priority as they fall further and further behind the target.

Security cooperation is not limited to armaments. In Northeast Asia and Central Asia, the two countries pledge to redouble their efforts to work together. They agree on the goals of limiting the rise of Japan as a military power, ensuring a soft landing in Korea that reduces U.S. influence, and preventing the spread of Islamic fundamentalism. China promises to support Moscow's sphere of influence in Central Asia, while Moscow promises to back Beijing's reunification with Taiwan and buildup of Greater China, focusing on Southeast Asia. Both sides will staunchly support the territorial integrity of the other. Territorial integrity is a worry for Russia because of newly tenuous economic ties with its Far East and separatist intrigues in some of its republics, and it is a worry for China because of ethnic separatism in Xinjiang and Tibet as well as the threat of Taiwan independence. Particularly if the two countries succeed in security cooperation in Central Asia and Korea, the complementarity of their military requirements will be likely to prevail. The declining superpower anxious to maintain one element of its superiority and the aspiring superpower worried about military weakness will see one another as meeting each other's needs.

In 1998, relations with Asian powers began to expose a split in national interests. Accelerated negotiations between Moscow and Tokyo showed that Russia was ready to back the U.S.-Japanese security alliance to an extent that far exceeded China's cautious tolerance. Then in May, the sudden explosion of the Indian-Pakistani nuclear rivalry left Russia and China on opposite sides. Doubts were rising about Russian and Chinese claims of a common worldview, doubts that remain in many quarters, but the two countries continue to brush them aside. In 1999, especially at the time of the Yugoslav bombing, Russia and China seemed to draw closer together again. They stressed their shared worldview.[17] As anger against the United

States mounted, they recommitted themselves to a special relationship.

In addition, strategic cooperation includes confidence-building measures along China's borders with Russia and Kazakhstan as well as along the shorter borders with Kyrgyzstan and Tajikistan. Both Russia and China need to reduce their troop deployments, in part to facilitate transfers to areas of greater immediate priority and in part to reduce the military's size and budgetary weight. Agreement in April 1997 on measures to reduce troops along the borders sets in motion cooperation that is likely to continue. Strategic cooperation also aims at global coordination on hot spots, peacekeeping forces, and other security matters. China and Russia will consult each other and try to work out a common position. With two vetoes in the UN Security Council, they expect to shape global security decisions in opposition to unipolarity.

The third decisive element in the Sino-Russian partnership is economic relations. The Chinese, in particular, recognize that current economic ties fall far short of what is expected for a close partnership and that, given the way the world is becoming integrated, close economic ties will be essential to sustain the partnership. From China's perspective, there are at least four ways to achieve economic integration:

- Russian industry should rebuild using its strong, if aging, physical base and its advanced science and technology, but also drawing on Chinese human resources, entrepreneurship, and markets. Joint development zones in Russian cities and along the Far Eastern border, discussed at the April 1997 summit, would spearhead this cooperation.[18]

- Exploitation of energy resources in Siberia and the northern Russian Far East should become the locomotive for regional cooperation, fueling China's rapid economic growth and Russia's entry into the Northeast Asian division of labor.[19] Of course, other countries must provide most of the financing, but the Chinese market and Chinese labor provide two indispensable ingredients for successful projects on an enormous scale.

- Cross-border cooperation between Northeast China and the southern Russian Far East offers the best hope for both areas to meet the high hopes for regionalism voiced widely early in the

1990s. Together China and Russia should proceed with the long-proposed bridges, transit corridors, and other infrastructure projects to achieve regionwide prosperity.[20]

- Chinese exports of foodstuffs, clothes, and other consumer goods will naturally become part of the economic integration between the two countries. Chinese exports of light industrial goods have skyrocketed around the world in the 1990s, and Russia, too, will benefit from them.

Based on the above calculations, the Chinese have no trouble envisioning a huge volume of trade and economic integration ahead and, correspondingly, an all-around partnership. If $20 billion was viewed as a reasonable target for trade in 2000, then by 2015, after Russia's economy has recovered, in part through integration with China, a figure of $50 billion would not be beyond reach. After all, Chinese trade with the United States and Japan climbed to about $65–70 billion in 1997. By 1999, the bubble of optimism had burst; even the target of $20 billion had slipped from sight.

As Chinese are all too aware, Russians did not share this vision of economic ties. Yet if Russia swears its adherence to a strategic partnership, how can it continue to be blinded by what in the Far East at least appears to be a revived fortress mentality? China intends to convince Russians by controlling Chinese behavior that has bothered them—shoddy goods, illegal immigration, and so on.[21] Although Russians may not yet be ready to focus on the advantages of economic integration, after completion of the eastern border demarcation in November 1997 and with the visa system imposed in 1994 working effectively, Chinese are still counting on Russian psychology to change. If Moscow has so far pushed harder for upgraded partnership in the abstract, it will gradually accept China's advocacy of a more substantive partnership as suspicions recede.

Russia has operated what might be called a dual-track leadership since at least the beginning of 1993. On the one side, the security apparatus distrusts the United States and the West and strives for global balance, which for Foreign Minister Yevgeny Primakov and others in this group leads to China. On the other side, the economic apparatus, whether guided by Anatoliy Chubais, Boris Nemtsov, or Sergei Kiriyenko, works closely with international organizations and shows little interest in China. If the security elite squeezes out the internationally minded economists, it is hard to imagine Russia getting on track for global integration economically. Dependence on China without such balance would frighten Russians and would be unlikely to provide the capital, technology, and markets foremost in economic thinking. To squeeze out the others, the economic elite would require economic success and a sense of identity with the West and Japan that scarcely seems imaginable at present. It follows that we can expect a continuation of the dual track, of interest in working with China to enhance multipolarity while relying on the United States to enhance economic integration. Only a direct conflict between Beijing and Moscow would be likely to challenge this duality.

The appointment of Boris Nemtsov in April 1997 to take charge of economic policy toward China and Japan and of the presidential program for the Russian Far East and Trans-Baikal temporarily tilted the balance somewhat in the dual-track leadership. After all, with strong representation from local governors, the presidential program anticipates multilateralism and even Japanese leadership in regional cooperation.[22] The program may reduce China to a secondary role, which may, in fact, be the only way for China to get an economic foothold in Russia in the near future. Without such balance, Russians would remain frightened of Chinese dominance, and required foreign sources of capital and technology would not be forthcoming. Even if a Nemtsov-led multilateral strategy prevailed, we may still have expected a continuation of the dual-track approach, as Foreign Minister Primakov pressed forward with close ties to China to enhance multipolarity while Nemtsov turned to Japan and the United States, including a secondary role for China, to enhance economic integration. The surprise selection of Sergei Kiriyenko one year later as prime minister further shifted the balance toward the economists. But then came the Russian financial collapse, the rise and fall of Primakov as prime minister, and economic drift without tackling serious problems. For China, this change meant an ever weaker Russia. It also shifted the bilateral partnership even further away from economics.

ASSESSMENTS OF NATIONAL STRENGTH

In 1992, Russians did not have great appreciation for China's economic prowess, but Chinese still respected Russia's prowess despite condemnations of first perestroika and then shock therapy as self-destructive. For Russians, the next years did not bring a slew of analyses on the Chinese "economic miracle" of double-digit growth, but the impression spread without such analysis of a juggernaut taking shape. Two contradictory conclusions followed: (1) China's internal strength would be huge as the next superpower was born, and (2) China's internal problems would become overriding as the country's needs spilled over national borders.[23] In China, the mid-1990s brought intense scrutiny of Russian economic prospects and a mixed evaluation. Despite disagreements over how long it would take for the decline to bottom out and the growth to begin in earnest, the prospects for long-term recovery were seen as good.

Russian views of China are superficial, contradictory, and somewhat dismissive. They are superficial because little of a scholarly nature is published and what research there is on internal conditions in China is shockingly thin. Arguments for and against the relevance of the Chinese model for Russia take for granted one or a few basic premises. They do not delve deeply into China's success in attracting foreign investment into special economic zones, incentives for rural entrepreneurs in farming and nonfarming pursuits, and responses to overpopulation. Russian views are contradictory because they divorce China's strength as a positive force for political partnership from fears of the impact of its strength on unwelcome economic integration. Finally, Russians dismiss the Chinese experience as unique, sometimes by crediting overseas Chinese and assuming further success without regarding this experience as relevant, at other times by seeing this experience as a short-term phenomenon that will self-implode because of problems with overpopulation, food, energy, environment, and so on, and as a phenomenon that needs to be taken seriously only when it comes apart.

The foreign policy mainstream in Russia credits China as a rapidly rising great power with the potential of becoming a superpower, meaning that its national strength will be augmented by sustained economic growth, strong and focused national leadership, and military catch-up. Russia cannot prevent this, but it can cooperate with China in influencing the rise of one of the next world leaders.

Chinese may not be sophisticated in their analysis of the Russian economy, but no one could accuse them of neglecting the subject. Since 1993, Chinese have intensely debated the prospects of Russian reforms, above all the timing and extent of economic growth. The prevailing position remains that Russia started on the wrong foot by weakening administrative control before taking economic reform seriously and then compounded the problem by applying shock therapy without the necessary conditions, such as competitive producers able to replace existing monopolies. It has dug itself a hole, needlessly setting back production by more than a decade. Yet, while bemoaning past mistakes, Chinese well understand that there is no turning back.

For some time, a centrist position has dominated in Chinese publications on the Russian economy. This position does not actually embrace the economic policies of Yeltsin's ministers, but it also does not recognize a superior alternative of the Left opposition. With Yegor Gaidar gone and shock therapy a thing of the past, it accepts that Russia is not simply copying a Western model. Yes, more is needed and Russia is having trouble, but with clear direction from the top, it will pull through this historical trough. The debate gravitates around identifying when the bottom will be reached and how fast the recovery will proceed.[24] It has become almost a matter of faith that the recovery will pick up steam and Russia will resume its rightful place as a great power with a suitable economy.

Comparisons highlight advantageous conditions for Russia: its small population relative to land and resources; its educated labor force; its social welfare system mostly divorced from enterprise obligations for housing, pensions, and other social services; its world-class science and technology in not a few areas. Coupled with continued military prowess, these conditions mean that Russia's future as a pole in a multipolar world is all but assured.[25]

Lately, however, Chinese have not been able to overlook the threat that continued economic weakness will leave Russia vulnerable and an unstable partner for China. Because economic strength is now recognized as the most fundamental basis of national power, Russia is in danger of remaining a very weak pole in the global system.[26] Low in strength and confidence, Russia may swing more against the West and, under a new leadership, try to entice China into an alliance. Or it may turn desperately against China as a threat because of the growing disparity in national strength, especially on the two sides of the border. China is not looking for such flailing about; it wants Russia as a partner, integrating, to a degree, into the global economy and open to China's economic advances.

Chinese do not directly address the contradiction between their warning that Russia must avoid dependency on the West, which wants to keep Russia weak, and their recognition that Russia must become hospitable to foreign capital. There is a lack of candor in explaining how nationalism, fearful of foreign penetration into the Russian economy, hinders Russia's recovery. Somehow, Moscow's firm resistance to the West's political designs is expected to make no difference, as in China, in attracting assistance and investment.

Die-hard socialists in China do not conceal the fact that one of their goals is to prove that socialism can outperform capitalism in the global competition. If China's high rate of economic development persists, they may reach the point of claiming a socialist model not just for "Chinese characteristics." Even if Russia did not revive its claim to socialism, its proud assertion once development accelerated that it had found a path different from that of the West could serve Chinese ideological needs. But for the time being, Russia is not successful and Chinese do not mention ideology in discussions of economic results. Russia's prospects for economic recovery depend on pragmatism plus understanding national specifics, not on following an ideology of socialism or, of course, capitalism.

A balance of national strength serves the strategic partnership best. As long as Russians do not assess Chinese national strength as rising rapidly for long into the future and Chinese do not become concerned that Russian strength will continue to decline indefinitely, the prospect for keeping relations in balance will likely be in the forefront. This prospect is essential for a fragile partnership based more on assessments than on interest groups.

Mutual assessments show a lack of confidence in each other's internal development and in the balance between development in the two states: Russians fear a stronger China; Chinese wonder if Russia will be too weak to serve as a pole. The policy mainstream, however, expects a suitable match as both strengthen. A balance in national strength serves the strategic partnership best. Assessments show that if either country lands in trouble, the other will fear the consequences. A still fragile partnership cannot easily cope with imbalances.

ASSESSMENTS OF PARTNERSHIP

Russian sources are still struggling with doubts about China's commitment to the partnership. A strong nationalistic orientation perceives the border demarcation agreement that will transfer several plots of land to China as a one-sided advantage not befitting genuine partnership. Many go further in their concern about "quiet expansionism," projecting hidden motives to gain large tracts of Russian land from past territorial claims still evident in some maps and texts and from illegal immigration. Chaotic conditions of 1992–1993 especially fueled charges of conspiratorial intentions in Heilongjiang or even Beijing that have been slow to disappear.

Little is written in Russia to suggest Chinese appreciation for Russian culture or Chinese respect for Russia's role in the world. On the contrary, two factors suggest the opposite. The first is Russian memories of three decades of the Sino-Soviet split and the intense propaganda accusing China of ingratitude for Soviet assistance of the 1950s and of hurling invectives against everything sacred in the Soviet Union. The second is personal encounters with Chinese in recent years that leave Russians complaining of arrogance. Chinese authorities do not easily conceal an attitude of condescension at what their country is accomplishing while Russia has been falling apart. Even ordinary Chinese, who long ago were told a mistake had been made in treating Russia as "big brother," may give the appearance of talking to "little brother" when they impatiently seek to transfer lessons from their own country. Concerned that cultural tensions are serious already, Beijing warns authors and travelers of the need to treat Russians with respect. It wants there to be no doubt about China's commitment to an equal partnership.

The long Cold War era has left a residue of zero-sum reasoning in Russians. Rather than anticipate how China and Russia can cooperate to the benefit of both, officials and media warn repeatedly of China gaining an advantage. Through the building of a multilateral city in Tumen on the border, as many Chinese in the Northeast advocate, Russians charge that China will gain an outlet to the sea, and the ports of the Russian Far East will atrophy. Russia's top admiral warned in 1997 that this project was something far more than an issue of navigation rights, suggesting that the Chinese were intent on deepening the river and building up a fleet that would alter the balance of naval power in the Sea of Japan. As long as Russians view their country as losing out even from joint projects with abundant Chinese labor, an inferiority complex will make any signs of rising Chinese national strength suspect.

Chinese also hesitate to trust Russia's commitment to the partnership. Although they have welcomed shifts in the balance of Russian foreign policy at each stage since the summer of 1992, Chinese sources eventually reveal when the next stage comes along that they still perceived Russia as leaning to the West. In other words, China keeps wishing that Russia would do more to prove it is truly balanced. Even in the pairing of Russian opposition to NATO expansion and Chinese insistence on reunification with Taiwan, Chinese fear asymmetry. As much as they approve of Russia's resistance to NATO, they observe enough wavering and compromise to suspect that it is not the moral equivalent of Taiwan. Moreover, Chinese keep complaining that Russian local officials are traveling to Taiwan and are too cozy with the Taiwanese government, in contrast to China's steadfast support for Russia against NATO.

Although Chinese sources were instructed not to criticize Russian leaders, this barrier was relaxed a little when indirect criticisms of local leaders, especially Governor Yevgeniy Nazdratenko of Primorskii Krai, started in 1995. Chinese protest anti-Chinese demagoguery and have difficulty understanding why officials and publications in a partner country are so hostile. In 1997, there was talk of a public relations campaign to boost China's image. Such a campaign would showcase high-quality products, demonstrate appreciation for Russian culture as well as the allures of China's great civilization, clarify Beijing's good intentions on sensitive territorial and immigration matters, and introduce models of partners at work. Public relations, however, have not been China's strong suit in recent years. Apart from Jiang Zemin's daylong visit to Yasnaya Polyana where Leo Tolstoy had lived, redolent with allusions to this writer's deep impact on China's president and other Chinese, the campaign had trouble getting started.

What gives Chinese confidence that a close bond with Russia will last is the straightforward assumption that a great power will act in accord with its national interest. Such a power will build up its national strength as fast as possible and maneuver for maximum balance and minimum dependency in foreign relations. China sees Russia striving to consolidate a sphere of influence in the space of the former Soviet Union, struggling against the West's planned hegemony in Eastern Europe, seeking a voice in regional affairs such as the Korean conflict, and generally grasping to be taken seriously as a global political and military power.

On one issue after another, Chinese contrast their country's firm support for Russia's aspirations with Western and Japanese opposition. They do not seem to notice that Chinese support has been cheap; it is little more than words of encouragement at virtually no cost in resources. Furthermore, Chinese conveniently overlook the economic side to national interests, compartmentalizing competitive great-power relations from the need for cozy arrangements to achieve integration into the global economy. Realism, however, is not altogether absent. Chinese recognize that unless economic ties soon bolster the strategic partnership, it will be on fragile footing. Trust in the other side's commitment to the partnership will continue to waver, especially among Russians who see China seeking an advantage but also among Chinese who find Russia only weakly focused on Asia.

ASSESSMENTS OF WORLD ORDER

Assessments of the emerging world order in Russia and China point to some differences but also to a fundamental similarity. Whereas Russian reactions to the shifting post–Cold War environment appear rooted in short-term calculations and a sense of humiliation, Chinese responses reflect a more stable, long-term strategy. Russians are flailing about after their palpable disappointment at the enormous loss in stature resulting from the collapse of the Soviet Union, the dismemberment of the economy it left behind, and the weak state capacity available to Moscow. They are displeased with the world order they see emerging but react less with a strategy to transform that order over a long period than with sharp gestures to land some blows now.

This contrasts with Chinese expectations that the balance of global power is shifting to the Asia-Pacific region, where the PRC can position itself with the most rapid economic development and a series of subregional groupings to become the prime beneficiary. Moscow does not have a clear image of an alternative world order except for the vague notion of multipolarity and preventing U.S. hegemony. Beijing, meanwhile, wants to entice Russia into a world parceled into regions as well as poles that buys time for the East and China to rise and shape a world order replacing some current Western principles with supposedly Eastern ones.

Russia and China do share some convictions about the world order. They oppose a unipolar world under U.S. hegemony. To limit the alliance grouping North America, the European Union, and Japan, they want to build at least a loose coalition of rival non-Western powers. Correspondingly, they regard each other as the first and foremost partner in this coalition. Without the steadfastness of the other, they could be isolated with what the West regards as rogue states and be ineffective in countering attempts to build a new world order that would hem them in. Unable to forget the dire consequences of their falling out at the end of the 1950s, Russia and China expect to cling to each other for leverage in shaping the new order.

Russians are divided in how seriously they regard such matters as the expansion of NATO, the U.S.-Japanese security alliance, and the threat of Western civilization. Lashing out against what happened to the superpower that they controlled only recently, they do not know where to turn. One group of experts on China views Beijing as the best hope, calling for an alliance against the West.[27] In their view, the goal of the United States is a weak and fragmented Russia. World economic integration is a misnomer for neo-imperialist economic designs to convert Russia into a raw-material base locked into a division of labor favoring only the rich capitalist powers. By cooperating with China to organize global resistance, Russia has a chance to escape this fate. This rallying cry, however, was too radical in 1997–1998 for the Chinese, who for the most part had become hooked on the advantages of world economic integration. It was also too radical for the reform-oriented Russian business community and those Russians who, in the face of China, deemed themselves to be defenders of Western civilization. By 1999, however, the Chinese had become more nationalistic and focused on opposing U.S. hegemonism, while Russian resistance to nationalistic appeals had declined.

What rivets attention to the Sino-Russian partnership is not the normalization of what was once a conflict situation nor even the good-neighbor cooperation to solve regional problems and contribute to Northeast Asian regionalism, but the exclusive nature of a nexus in which geopolitics are at the core and opposition to the emerging world order is the raison d'être. Whatever their misgivings about each other, China and Russia expect these reasons driving the strategic partnership to continue. As great powers, they need each other. It does not hurt either that as countries long steeped in socialist reasoning they recognize one another's worldview. Their mutual assessments weigh the world order above everything else.[28] Above all, shared convictions about the world order raise each country's hopes for the other. In late 1997 and much of 1998, the degree of agreement between Moscow and Beijing was tested by improved U.S.-Chinese relations, improved Russo-Japanese relations, a nuclear arms race in South Asia, and the spillover from the Asian economic crisis. The strategic partnership appeared narrower in scope. But in late 1998 and 1999, this partnership widened as both countries condemned U.S. displays of power. The spring 1999 war in Yugoslavia showcased the partnership as never before.

PREDICTIONS OF SINO-RUSSIAN RELATIONS

Beijing and Moscow officially take care to qualify their strategic partnership with the words that it is for the twenty-first century. In other words, it has not reached its mature form. Discourse on the partnership has remained noticeably silent on how to advance from the current limitations in bilateral relations to the vision of a mature partnership. In Russia, this silence has to do with the priority of coping with immediate manifestations of nationalism for political advantage rather than weighing controversial choices that recognize Russian weakness. But one fundamental truth is not neglected: Russia will remain weak relative to the United States and will see itself as an outsider in a Western-dominated world; therefore, it will benefit from the leverage of a close partnership with China. China uses the same reasoning in response to its own weakness.

Chinese and Russian leaders concede that the partnership must be solidified before it can be accepted as a stable and balanced force in world affairs. Policy makers have decided that this can be accomplished, but only with lots of effort. They have yet to settle on a joint strategy to achieve this goal largely because Russia is confused about what it wants, but also because China is hesitant about symbolism that could damage its economic interests with other countries without gaining much in substance. To the extent that the strategy for a close partnership is not clearly articulated, Sino-Russian ties are not likely to advance dramatically.

Moscow policy makers recognize that intense nationalism is a double-edged sword. Nationalism focuses on the West, thus demanding a response that shows the Russian government can stand up for its own interests. At the same time, it worries about China, allowing for no more than cautious compromises to boost the partnership. In the elections of 1996, Yeltsin neutralized some of the nationalistic criticism by showcasing his close relations with China's leadership and their joint rhetoric in opposition to U.S. hegemony. But Yeltsin's two compelling needs in 1997–1998 were to back an economic development strategy oriented toward the West and Japan so that his choice for successor would have a record on which to run, and to sell the May agreement with NATO as the best deal Russia could achieve so that nationalistic opposition to his leadership would not mobilize around this issue. In 1997–1998, there was no need to prove his mettle as a friend of China.

Another deadline in 1997 cast Yeltsin's role in a different light. He had promised to deliver on border demarcation in the face of an inevitable nationalistic outcry against China, led from the Russian Far East. If the strategic partnership was not to sink into oblivion, Yeltsin had to stick to his 1996 commitment that the demarcation agreement was sacred. The resulting transfers of land reinforced Russia's commitment, and the remaining three islands were set aside for the future after a strategic partnership for the twenty-first century congeals.

Policy-making circles face with trepidation the tough choices needed to solidify the foundation for bilateral relations. Assessments generally are silent about these choices for fear of arousing Russian nationalism. After the demarcation, how will the problem of an outlet for China to the Sea of Japan be resolved: A multinational city at Tumen? A transit corridor through Russian territory? A Herculean dredging operation combined with Chinese requests for Russian and North Korean approval for navigation authorization over the 10 miles to the sea? How will negotiations commence to resolve the other border demarcation problems along the Amur River, especially the island below Khabarovsk city, set aside in 1991? Will Moscow oppose any such talks? Will it offer a territorial trade, giving up a less sensitive plot of land? If the issue of access to the sea demands this time that the Yeltsin administration face its frequent nemesis in Vladivostok, Governor Nazdratenko, then another stage of demarcation could pit it several years from now against Governor Viktor

Ishaev in Khabarovsk, who is the regional leader working with Nemtsov on development.

In the coming five years, two domestic political challenges, two bilateral economic challenges, and two bilateral political challenges will test Sino-Russian ties. Some of these may be difficult hurdles, but chances are Beijing and Moscow will keep the partnership intact. China can expect a challenge from the Left to Jiang Zemin, anxious to push Hong Kong's integration, to pressure Taiwan more aggressively, and to regain the domestic initiative that many believe was lost to Deng Xiaoping. But just as China's moral support in August 1991 could do little for Russia's Left, there is no reason to expect a weak Russia under Boris Yeltsin to give comfort to the Chinese Left. On the Russian side, the presidential elections of 2000 will most likely turn on domestic policy, not foreign policy, but opposition to NATO's expansion could persuade some Russians to edge closer to China. Simultaneous shifts to the Left in each country could temporarily intensify the partnership. Much less likely is that either country will shift sharply to the Right and opt for the West at the expense of its strategic partner.

Bilateral economic ties have been tested by the goal of $20 billion in trade. With little progress achieved, the frailty of the partnership has been exposed. If agreements are to come, the choice between bilateralism and multilateralism will become clearer. Implementation of the presidential program for the Russian Far East and Trans-Baikal beginning in 1997 has also clarified China's place in Russia's development strategy. The program has failed. For it to be revived in any form, gradual increases in economic ties as part of a multilateral approach by Russia would tend to diminish the special or exclusive nature of the partnership.

In bilateral politics, 1997 was the year of border demarcation. If the strategic partnership was not to sink into oblivion, Yeltsin had to stick to the 1991–1992 commitment and to his 1996 declaration that the demarcation agreement is sacred. The resulting transfers of land would reinforce Russia's ties to China, but the terms of the agreement have not been fully disclosed. More steps must follow, perhaps after a prudently arranged delay by China. But however long the delay, China will not be satisfied with a halt to the full resolution of the demarcation problem and access to the sea. Another stiff test for bilateral relations will come unexpectedly when the situation in Korea changes. If China and Russia can work together on this transition, their political ties will become stronger. If not, the partnership will be exposed as hollow.

After seven years, none of these hurdles is likely to unsettle Sino-Russian relations. At the same time, the frequency of problems and the only partial success in handling them will limit advances in the partnership. Given the unbalanced and still quite fragile state of the partnership, tough choices and strong support from above will be needed to keep it on course.

One such choice was faced in June 1997 when Yeltsin at last declared his intention to oust Nazdratenko as governor of Primorskii Krai.[29] As the biggest thorn in the side of Sino-Russian relations, especially the completion of the border demarcation of 1997, the local governor symbolizes the very nationalism that has cast doubt on the future of the partnership. At the same time, he also symbolizes the maverick and criminal localism that obstructs foreign investment and Moscow's direct role in integrating the Russian Far East and Siberia into regional development in Northeast Asia. If China appears to gain in the short run, the long-term result may actually be a spur to multilateralism. But a year later, Nazdratenko had survived, toning down his rhetoric on China in return for a continued lease on power. Yeltsin's power to oust an elected governor had been found wanting.

Over the next twenty years, at least four paradoxes so far largely overlooked will likely make the Sino-Russian partnership self-limiting. The first paradox is the acute Russian nationalism that draws Russians to China and, simultaneously, repels Russians from China. Such fleeting emotionalism is not a sound basis for a partnership, especially when Russian public opinion generally lacks deep understanding or sympathy for China.

The second paradox is that close economic ties are necessary to develop a firm partnership, but the projects likely to produce such ties depend on multilateralism that will diminish the exclusive nature of the partnership. Economic circumstances allow for long-term complementarity only if short-term reliance increases precisely on those great powers most adverse to an exclusive partnership.

The third paradox is that the regions best positioned to benefit from close economic ties are the ones most difficult to persuade to trust the other side. Historical animosities, recent tensions resulting from the anarchic trade of 1992–1993, and a narrow sense of national interests all turn the Russian Far East away from Northeast China and leave the Chinese across the border troubled about their dealings with Russians, too.

The fourth paradox is that the closer Sino-Russian relations develop at this stage, the more troublesome they are likely to become for the two sides. Neither side is capable of managing these relations on the basis of modern principles without lingering barter elements, traditional state enterprise practices, rampant corruption, criminal groups in the fore, and incompetent local administrations wreaking havoc. The least modern forces in each country have a stake in the other country—a problem that will take a long time to overcome.

Having recognized the fragile state of economic, cross-border, cultural, and nationalistic ties and having noted various paradoxes that make the Sino-Russian partnership self-limiting, I still want to conclude with the prediction that the most likely outcome over the next five years and even the next twenty years is some strengthening in the relationship. This conclusion is based on several underlying assumptions. Most important, the Sino-U.S. rivalry will remain the central great-power opposition, as it has been in the 1990s. Also important, Russian integration into the European community will proceed slowly, and nationalism wary of the West will persist as one of the defining elements in Russian great-power identity. Deeply conscious of their decades of schism, Beijing and Moscow will take extra care to prevent a new deterioration in relations. They will be reminded of the danger of digging themselves into a deeper geopolitical hole than they are already in. Finally, military-industrial cooperation is likely to advance as the most solid boost for mutual dependency. Unable to realize their vision of partnership, the two countries will still be keen to maintain a partnership with some global influence.

The United States and its two military alliances in Europe and Northeast Asia will be a powerful force in shaping the Sino-Russian partnership. Overreaction and threats of sanctions, mindless of the national psychologies in each country, will drive the countries closer together. A careful combination of engagement toward Moscow and Beijing and strengthening bonds that could most effectively restrain the military and geopolitical ambitions of the two offers the best promise of success, but such tactics will pose a test to the patience and consistency of U.S. leadership.

Many are tempted to define U.S. interests negatively, stressing what should be prevented, but generally acknowledge that U.S. interests are best served by discouraging a swing in China's leadership to the Left and a shift in Russian power to extreme nationalists. Such negative goals may not seem within reach by U.S. pressure alone. Indeed, there is a danger that one negative goal would spiral into another, accelerating a confrontational atmosphere. More attention should turn to positive goals capable of eliciting cooperative behavior and improving public attitudes. Limitations on Sino-Russian relations offer reassurance that there is room for positive approaches. Because China and Russia are unlikely to achieve their vision of partnership on their own, essential multilateral partners can combine rewards and restrictions to help shape the outcome. When internal assessments in both China and Russia begin to stress the promise of multilateral cooperation and its limitations on certain types of bilateralism, these results will be evidence that the United States is asserting leadership with forethought of the consequences and feedback on the impact.

NOTES

[1] This paper, along with that of Lu Nanquan, is a product of research supported by the National Council on the Soviet Union and Eastern Europe in 1996–1997. A large compilation of Chinese and Russian sources were used in preparing these papers, thanks to the efforts of Vilya Gelbras and Lu Nanquan. The Chinese articles come largely from journals, which convey a consistent position on the principal issues. Russian views are scattered in newspaper articles as well as journals and reflect the diversity of the current political spectrum. In 1996–1997, the consensus against NATO expansion helped to narrow the range of views on great-power relations.

[2] Gilbert Rozman, "Sino-Russian Relations in the 1990s: A Balance Sheet," *Post-Soviet Affairs*, vol. 14, no. 2 (April-June 1998), pp. 93–113.

[3] Gilbert Rozman, *A Mirror for Socialism: Soviet Criticisms of China* (Princeton: Princeton University Press, 1985); Gilbert Rozman, *The Chinese Debate about Soviet Socialism* (Princeton: Princeton University Press, 1987).

[4] This historical cost-benefit analysis has been invoked by Russia when responding to pressure to criticize China after the bloodshed of June 4, 1989, and by China when resisting temptation in 1992 to criticize Russia after the collapse of the Soviet Union and its communist leadership. See the principal journals in each country on the other: *Problemy Dal'nego Vostoka* and *Zhongya Dongou yanjiu* (formerly *Sulian Dongou yanjiu*).

[5] Although Russia faces Germany across Eastern Europe and China sees Japan as a rival in Southeast Asia, the two countries recognize each other

as bordering states and as determining forces in Central Asia and Northeast Asia. Reconciliation as neighbors presaged cooperation on a global scale.

[6]Alexei Voskressenski, "Kitai vo vneshnepoliticheskoi strategii Rossii" (China in the Foreign Policy Strategy of Russia), *Svobodnaia mysl'*, no. 1 (1996), pp. 94–105; Shi Ze, "Lun xin shiqi de ZhongE guanxi" (Discussing Sino-Russian Relations in the New Period), *Guoji wenti yanjiu*, no. 2 (1996), pp. 1–6.

[7]Intense internal discussions in China at this time were poorly reflected in publications; bluster about what was going right soon blotted out fear of what might go wrong.

[8]V. Larin, "Rossiia i Kitai na poroge tret'ego tychiacheletiia: kto zhe budet otstaivat'nashi national'nye interesy?" (Russia and China on the Threshold of the Third Millennium: Who Will Insist on Our National Interests?), *Problemy Dal'nego Vostoka*, no. 1 (1997), pp. 15–26.

[9]V. Rakhmanin, "Rossiia I Kitai: na puti k strategicheskomu vzaimodeistviiu" (Russia and China: On the Path to Strategic Cooperation), *Problemy Dal'nego Vostoka*, no. 1 (1997), pp. 10–14.

[10]Chinese publications fail to differentiate Chinese Communist Party interests from national interests, taking for granted that the interests defined by the party are precisely China's national interest. In contrast, Russian publications long attacked Foreign Minister Kozyrev for failing to define and defend Russia's national interests but lately have taken for granted that Foreign Minister Yevgeniy Primakov is doing this job well.

[11]In pre-Gorbachev years, Chinese sources on the Soviet Union took a broad historical and comparative perspective; by 1987, they switched to a narrow approach to current reform initiatives.

[12]Gilbert Rozman, "Chinese Studies in Russia and Their Impact, 1985–1992," *Asian Research Trends*, no. 5 (1994), pp. 143–60.

[13]Yan Sun, *The Chinese Reassessment of Socialism, 1976–1992* (Princeton: Princeton University Press, 1995).

[14]The debate centered on which choice by China had been correct: opposition to Western ideological penetration and political reform, as stressed by conservatives in journals such as *Waiguo wenti yanjiu*, or acceleration of market reforms and economic openness, as Deng Xiaoping directed be placed in the forefront after he interceded in his Southern talk in late January 1992.

[15]"Russia: Sino-Russian Cooperation Tends to Strategic Partnership," *FBIS-SOV-97-107*, April 17, 1997.

[16]"Russia: Energy, Military Links May Triple Trade with China," *FBIS-SOV-97-106*, April 16, 1997.

[17]Gu Guan Fu, "ZhongE zhanlue xiezuo guanxi de xin Fazhan," *Heping yu Fazhan*, no. 1 (1999), pp. 42–44.

[18]Xu Xin, "Lun Eluosi de jingji jiegou" (On Russia's Economic Structure), *Dongou Zhongya yanjiu*, no. 6 (1996), pp. 24–33. This source stresses what

Russia can do to revive its industry, high technology, and arms exports without noting China's potential role, which emerges from the planning of joint committees.

[19]Specialized journals such as *Dongbeiya yanjiu* (Northeast Asian Studies) and *Xiboliya yanjiu* (Siberian Studies) have long raised hopes of a regional takeoff based on a sharp division of labor in which Russia provides primarily natural resources, including energy.

[20]Lin Heming and Jin Yan, "Jianli Zhongguo Heihe—Eluosi Bushi ciquyi ziyou maoyi qu de xianshi moshi" (Set Up a Chinese Heihe—Russia's Blagoveshchensk City Subregional Free Trade Zone's Realistic Model), *Eluosi yanjiu*, no. 3 (1995), pp. 47–50.

[21]Numerous Chinese articles on cross-border trade and relations point to steps China has taken since 1994 to control the chaos along the border.

[22]As of April 1997, no full text of the presidential program had been issued. It has been interpreted differently to various audiences at home and abroad. See, for example, M. Titarenko, "S novymi podkhodami navstrechu XX1 veku (Rossiia, Kitai, Iaponiia i SSHA v ATR)" (With New Approaches for Meeting the 21st Century [Russia, China, Japan and the USA in the Asia-Pacific Region]), *Problemy Dal'nego Vostoka*, no. 1 (1997), pp. 5–6; Alexander G. Granberg, "Development of the Russian Far East and Trans-Baikal Region and Activization of Russia's Participation in Pacific Economic Cooperation (On Main Propositions of the Presidential Program)," *ERINA Report*, vol. 13 (1996), pp. 32–37.

[23]Vilya Gelbras has examined the diversity of Russian thinking most closely.

[24]Lu Nanquan is one of the most prominent analysts in this debate over the Russian economy, and his paper in this collection reflects the diversity of Chinese thinking.

[25]Jiang Changbin, "Eluosi: cong lishi zou xiang weilai" (Russia: From History Goes toward the Future), *Dongou Zhongya yanjiu*, no. 3 (1996), pp. 81–86.

[26] Guo Zhenguan, "1998 nian shijie zhengzhi anquan xingshi huigu" (A Look Back at the 1998 World Political and Security Situation), *Heping yu Fazhan*, no. 1 (1999), pp. 7–10.

[27] Alexander Lukin, "Russia's Image of China and Russian-Chinese Relations," *East Asia: An International Quarterly*, vol. 17, no. 1 (Spring 1999), pp. 5–39.

[28]Liu Shitian and Zhu Xinyan, "Shixi EMei maodun de yuanyin he shizhi" (Trial Explanation of the Causes and Substance of Russian-American Contradictions), *Dongou Zhongya yanjiu*, no. 6 (1995), pp. 69–72.

[29]Michael Specter, "Yeltsin to Oust a Foe as Governor in Russia's Far East," *New York Times*, June 11, 1997, p. A3.

PART THREE

The Russian Far East

7
Turning Fortresses into Free Trade Zones

Gilbert Rozman

Cross-border relations share a high level of geopolitical, geoeconomic, and geocultural significance with cross-national relations between China and Russia. Yet, by involving a different set of actors with their own mix of local and national interests, cross-border relations alter the dynamics and even the balance of power in Sino-Russian relations. The timetable of transformations in these border relations is distinctive, as is the challenge of setting ties back on a promising course. In 1992–1993, cross-border relations led the way to improved bilateral ties; in 1994–1995, they spoiled the mood of the emerging "constructive partnership" with bad economic news; and in 1996–1998, they put a brake on efforts to undergird the newly touted "strategic partnership" with substance. Without synchronization of the two levels of relations, China and Russia can never be confident that their stormy bilateral history will not be repeated.

This chapter contrasts local and national factors over three periods: 1991–1993, 1993–1995, and 1995–1998. It looks simultaneously at both sides of the 4,300-kilometer border, asking how relations have changed and why, as well as at the linkages between local and national levels. By collating information from local media and periodic interviews on both sides of the border, the analysis below provides clues about how cross-border relations will continue to develop.[1] If the local level has complicated national relations since late 1993, what can we expect over the next five to ten years?

On the Chinese side, primary attention goes to Heilongjiang Province, which includes roughly three-quarters of the borderline and official border crossings. Heilongjiang looms as the centerpiece in cross-border relations, even though Xinjiang Province is important for Central Asian multilateral and multiethnic relations, Inner Mongolia draws attention for the principal rail line between Beijing and Moscow, and Jilin receives notice for multinational cooperation involving the Koreas. Indeed, the large crossings at Manzhouli in Inner Mongolia and at Hunchun in Jilin may be seen as two wings closely connected to the huge head of Heilongjiang that juts into Russia. Although it does not border on Russia, Liaoning also merits consideration as the third province of Northeast China (NEC) next to Jilin, especially for the Russian consulate in Shenyang and the region's foremost port in Dalian.

On the Russian side, the hierarchy of border territories must begin with Primorskii Krai, which links Heilongjiang and Jilin to the Sea of Japan. Next comes Khabarovskii Krai, the other populous and powerful territory of the Russian Far East (RFE). It is followed by Amurskaya Oblast, inland and agricultural but most dependent on China. Finally, the Jewish Autonomous Oblast, a small area dependent on Khabarovskii Krai. Other border territories, such as Chitinskaya Oblast further inland, rank low on the hierarchy, known for their transit functions between China and more notable administrative units of eastern or western Siberia.

Geopolitically, if the Beijing-Moscow connection largely concerns great-power relations on a global scale, relations between NEC and the RFE represent a potentially significant force in Northeast Asia (NEA) and the larger Asia-Pacific region (APR). Sino-Russian cross-border relations play an essential role in determining the degree to which regionalism (involving also the Koreas, Mongolia, and Japan) will develop in NEA and the extent to which Russia will be able to balance its status as a European power with a much anticipated status as an Asian power. Russia's role in Central Asia and possible link to India in South Asia alone do not realize this goal; Russia has set its sights on a premier status in Northeast Asia, bringing as well broad access to East Asia and full membership rights in the APR. Recognizing that it could gain no more than a junior partner's standing in the well-institutionalized structures of Europe and the West, Moscow by the fall of 1992 opted for a balancing role in more chaotic Asia, turning increasingly to China as an equal partner but also requiring orchestration through the RFE. Yet, the prickly issue of border demarcation with China came to symbolize for some, especially in the RFE, entrance into the region on the basis of weakness. After the completion of demarcation in November 1997, the issue slipped into the background, but it could return.

For China, the stakes along the border are also large. In its proportion of the country's population, industrial complex, and military clout, as well as in the strength of traditional expectations about its rightful place in a resurgent country, NEC exceeds the RFE. Chinese goals to remake the world and especially the regional order rest on a geopolitical reordering in NEA as well as on the consolidation of Greater China at the gateway to Southeast Asia. Sino-Russian cooperation across their border creates a united front capable of shaping the outcome on the Korean peninsula, limiting Japan's regional power, and keeping the United States at arm's length.

Geoeconomically, Sino-Russian border relations hold considerable meaning for the development of Russia's natural resources and any strategy to escape from Russia's current malaise. Talk of new or revitalized Eurasian land bridges, vast networks of energy pipelines, and Pacific port expansion invariably is premised on projects to exploit the treasure-house of raw materials and energy deposits of Siberia and the RFE. Loss of territory due to the breakup of the Soviet Union has left Russia much more of an Asian country in its distribution of land area, access to warm water ports, and potential economic prowess. Even if, from the vantage point of Moscow, Asian areas of Russia are weakly developed and sparsely populated, many in and out of Russia argue for their advantages. To achieve rapid growth, Moscow is strongly tempted to attach itself to the dynamic engine of NEA development, hitching its Far East to the neighboring provinces of China as well as Japan in the process. The goal seems obvious; the means and the priority are sharply disputed. Indeed, the combination of geostrategic alarm and geocultural clashes in the Far East has cast doubt on economic ties as well. What looks promising in the long run is floundering at present.

Many in NEC became mesmerized by the prospect of an economic juggernaut emerging once the Tumen River area project (Tumen) is launched at the juncture of Jilin, Primorskii Krai, and North Korea, and economic ties expand in NEA. In managing Sino-Russian cross-border relations, they have searched for a breakthrough project as a step to extend coastal dynamism to what is considered an inland region; as a means to revitalize the region that still symbolizes the albatross of debt-ridden, large, state-owned industries; and as a necessity for overcoming national inequities in setting reform and openness on an irreversible course.

Geoculturally, the struggle for a "national idea" in Russia is magnified by the identity crisis in the RFE, which exists as an outpost amid Asian civilizations. Here contacts with Asians are most intense, and fears abound of living in a sparsely settled and little-subsidized periphery 6,000 kilometers from Moscow while neighbors amass resources capable of overwhelming a dwindling residue of citizens. For Russians, it did not take a book by Samuel Huntington to demonstrate that the RFE stands as the frontline in a clash of civilizations.[2]

The slogan "Eurasianism" helped to rally support for Russia's search for Asian partners to lessen its dependence on the West. But this is a broad concept that leads to diverse interpretations. From the standpoint of the RFE, where Asia means East Asia rather than Central Asia, the goal of giving higher priority to Asiatic Russia does not stand in the way of an intense self-identification as Europeans in need of backup before an onslaught of Asian culture and economic practices.

With pride in their own civilization and efforts to bask in the successes attributed broadly to Eastern civilization, Chinese are not blind to the cultural differences faced on their northern border. Allusions to special bonds of historic friendship to Russia hardly mask the real tensions observed in recent years, which can ignite suspicions left from a quarter century of vitriolic accusations by both sides. The complexities of regionalism lead some to question the meaning of cultural identity. Is what matters most a common Confucian heritage? A shared experience in the modern struggle against imperialism? The background of a communist model of development? Untangling civilization from ideology remains an illusive target.

THE EUPHORIA OF "BORDERLESSNESS": 1991–1993

In the heyday of Sino-Soviet friendship, cross-border relations started slowly, depended on strict controls in Beijing and Moscow, and proved vulnerable to rapid decline after Soviet advisers were withdrawn in 1960. When negotiations for normalization resumed in 1982, local trade revived. It began as barter under tight control in the old bureaucratized manner, but in the 1980s, three forces began to enliven it.

First, the model of special or free economic zones already developed in Southeast China gave an impulse to this area. In 1984, the State Council extended precedents in the Southeast to Dalian, on the coast at the southern tip of Liaoning Province, and this city sought to become the "dragon's head," or leading force, for all NEC. Also that year, Hu Yaobang visited Heihe on the Heilongjiang border with Amurskaya Oblast, where he proposed the slogan "in the South there is Shenzhen, in the North there is Heihe" (*nanyouShen, beiyouHei*).[3] Growing envious of the economic growth in coastal China, Heilongjiang Province in 1987 announced its own strategy of "link to the South and open to the North" (*nanlian, beikai*). By this strategy, Heilongjiang indicated that it could transfer the advantages of China's dynamic coastal areas for opening its borders to trade with the Soviet Union.[4]

Second, Mikhail Gorbachev's perestroika set in motion a succession of changes in Russian foreign trade, increasing the authority of territories in the RFE and of enterprises. Opportunities for decentralized trade accelerated after Gorbachev's summer 1986 Vladivostok speech, and a follow-up development proposal for the RFE gave the green light to regional cooperation. If at first crude barter trade took the form of a boatload of Chinese watermelons exchanged for a boatload of Russian fertilizer, in 1988 an agreement opened the way to less restricted border trade.[5]

Third, at the end of the decade regionalism emerged as a hot topic, driven by Japanese images of the Sea of Japan economic rim, South Korea's northern strategy of isolating North Korea by luring its neighbors, and Jilin's excitement over proposals for the Tumen River project. Judging from the frequency of international conferences, meetings to discuss regionalism reached a high pitch by 1990. Both sides of the Sino-Russian border took satisfaction from the steadily increasing trade from 1986 to 1990 and expected better things to come.

After two years of rapidly expanding border trade, Chinese labor exports, and the creation of joint-venture enterprises, the mood along the border in 1992 grew much more upbeat. Terms such as "border fever" and "hot spots" captured the frenzy of cross-border relations.

In China, Deng Xiaoping's go-ahead in January for a sharp shift to a market economy and openness was followed in March by State Council approval for Hunchun, Suifenhe, Heihe, and Manzhouli to become open border cities on a par with many southern coastal ports. Companies from the South rushed to open branch offices there. Major enterprises in Harbin and other large NEC cities extended their networks to the border. And, most visibly, thousands of "suitcase peddlers" gathered wares to sell along the border or inside the RFE.

Once Beijing had transferred the authority to license trading companies to Heilongjiang Province, virtually any fly-by-night operator could obtain a license through forming the right connections (*guanxi*) with a larger firm or by bribing officials. Starting even from a one-room office in China, a "firm" needed only a tiny amount of cash to buy goods and cross the border to sell or barter its wares or, with more ambitious acquisitions in mind, to establish a joint venture in a room on the Russian side. A depressed area of China with high underemployment saw its salvation in supplying an RFE market troubled by acute consumer shortages with foodstuffs, clothing, and other daily necessities, however suspect their origin. One popular slogan asserted "if you want to think of getting rich, quickly come to Heihe."[6] Larger operators could make a quick killing by purchasing fertilizer, steel, cement, and lumber—the four staples— at a fraction of world prices, at a time when the Soviet planned economy was collapsing and industrial enterprises either could not find a market for their goods or sought to evade artificially low Russian internal prices.

As their borders opened, Russian consumers and producers turned to Chinese for obvious reasons. The Chinese were closest, arrived first, offered the cheapest goods, bought items of marginal quality, and did not require hard currency. Before the Chinese, Vietnamese brought to Russia as workers had been slipping away from their jobs, turning to illicit trade, and forming criminal gangs. At the end of the 1980s, the Chinese arrived, sometimes occupying another wing of the same second-rate hotel, quickly overwhelming the Vietnamese in numbers while winning turf battles by resorting to similar methods. The Chinese had no compunctions about barter trade and seemed to know how to cut deals with minimal formality and paperwork. As government contracts declined rapidly in

1990–1992 while local and border trade flourished, the role of these unregulated traders became decisive. The model for bilateral economic relations was abruptly changing without forethought or oversight into the possible consequences.

While NEC media proudly proclaimed that border trade had become the locomotive for economic development, announcing month-by-month advances as signs of prosperity to come, RFE media and public opinion quickly turned sour on what was happening. Even as border trade continued to increase through the first half of 1993 and then remained on a high plateau (despite failing to expand during the "golden season" of July through October), voices of exasperation and anger turned on the Chinese and toward Moscow for relief. Charges of secret plots and infiltration warned of a conspiracy organized in China that endangered Russia.[7]

In the early phase of expanding border relations, trade predominated over other ties. Although both sides were eager, the Chinese were more enthusiastic. They viewed Sino-Russian relations in a regional context, arguing that the end of the Cold War meant the rise of regionalism. Analysts advised local governments to press Beijing for the transfer of more power and rights and then to seize the moment before others had captured Russian markets. In their view, ignoring the primacy of Japan and other providers of the massive capital investments required, long-term prospects would be tremendous because of extraordinary regional economic complementarity. If some problems remained in the region in 1991–1992, as a result of stark differences in economic systems and levels of economic development or even as a result of the absence of formal or normalized diplomatic relations, they did not apply to Sino-Russian relations.[8] Although many central officials feared a partnership between Russia and the West, other Chinese exuberantly viewed the breakup of the Soviet Union as the key to the accelerated integration of Siberia and the RFE into NEA.[9]

China's perspective proved to be flawed in at least five respects: (1) Beijing and the NEC provinces looked at NEA and Russia from different angles; (2) the Chinese seriously misjudged Russia's transition, failing to anticipate how fast it would decline economically; (3) narrow economic thinking blurred the geopolitical realities; (4) geoeconomic thinking overweighed the goal of equality in opposition to the reality of a vertical division of labor among countries;

and (5) Chinese writings viewed geocultural problems primarily through the lens of socialism or differences with the West. In its "blind spontaneity" to integrate the region, China provoked an intense counterreaction in Russia.[10]

Beijing did not give cross-border ties the attention it might have. It conceived of NEA in broad terms inclusive of the Yellow and Bohai seas, seeing Beijing itself, Tianjin, and Shandong Province as core areas and leaving the Russian border as a secondary economic concern to be handled locally. By 1994, it was to regret its inattention, yet it lowered the priority of the border further because of the lack of an economic payoff. Observers in China further misjudged Russia's economic frailty, while taking too seriously both Russia's intention to develop Siberia and the RFE and its early calculation of labor shortages that would range in excess of 5 million, requiring imported foreign workers.[11]

Until late 1991, Chinese thinking was also rooted in the assumption that the Soviet Union was socialist, even to the point that some Chinese identified Soviet, North Korean, and Chinese cooperation as one option for NEA development.[12] There was too much extrapolation of the Chinese reform experience, such as expecting Russia to welcome and receive large foreign investment. Influenced by China's own narrowing of theory after June 1989, analysts were not skeptical enough either of the role of government in the economy or of the prospect of grand projects such as a new Eurasian land bridge or Tumen. Above all, there was an absence of comparative socialist scholarship able to expose how seriously ailing Russia and especially the RFE was and how negatively Chinese actions were perceived. Even after analysts had become convinced of the failure of "shock therapy" and the great difficulties in privatization, a Harbin conference in August 1992 proved typical in reexamining causes of the Soviet collapse and supposed implications of current conditions for bilateral relations but failing to draw lessons for readjusting border ties.[13]

Sino-Russian trade took a primitive form of barter mixed with direct administrative interference under weak market conditions and little institutionalized oversight, which meant freewheeling disregard for contracts without corrective punishment. As a transitional form of economic relations, it gave rise to countless disputes. What Russia exported did not reflect real transport costs or international prices and also was so limited in variety that it proved vulnerable to a change in the market of NEC once a temporary construction boom had passed. What China exported was of inferior quality, filling a large niche in the market only when goods from the center suddenly became prohibitively expensive and foreign competitors were slow to enter the Russian market. The trade boom of 1992–1993 had to reach a dead end, but not necessarily with such abrupt and negative consequences.

Companies could not find creditworthy partners and could not cope with fluctuating prices and policies for goods sought in exchange. On the Russian side, people began to believe that their country lost badly from barter; estimates ranged as high as $1 billion. New limits were imposed on the types of goods that could be traded in this way.[14] Tightened control on Chinese imports came just as illegalities and economic deterioration were reducing purchases and contract fulfillment. On the Chinese side, tightened monetary policies in June 1993 left companies without funds even for barter trade. If for a time there was a tendency to gloss over the causes of declining border trade, for example to overemphasize that success had caused transportation bottlenecks at border points, the reality did not escape both local residents and officials who read internal reports.

Already at a November 1992 bilateral conference on Sino-Russian relations, Russian analysts warned their counterparts that the poor quality of Chinese goods was damaging the image of the Chinese people and that the monopoly of NEC provinces over trade was driving up the costs of trading with coastal China.[15] At least a few experts heeded such warnings. They alerted others that the speed of trade expansion should not be allowed to conceal that the amount of bilateral trade remained low, barter arrangements left little room for investments and advanced technology, and conditions along the border remained fragile. The notion that a "time gap" (*shijian cha*) existed that allowed China only a brief window of opportunity spurred short-term behavior. Whether this gap was measured at three to five years or two to three years, implications that complementarity between the two economies would soon decrease or that other countries would otherwise capture the RFE markets led Chinese firms not only to rush to buy Russian exports before prices were raised to international market levels and to sell foodstuffs and light industrial products before severe shortages eased, but also to care little about their reputation. In 1992, Chinese debated how to seize the moment, but by year's end analyst Lu Nanquan warned that Beijing should intercede because the results were actually interfering with putting trade on a stable foundation.[16]

Whereas local interests in NEC required that Russo-Japanese relations progress and Japan invest heavily in the RFE and in projects such as Tumen, in essence providing a political and financial foundation for regionalism, Beijing gave more weight to geopolitics and the balance of power. China shifted its position on the disputed Kurile Islands, discouraging Russia from compromising with Japan and then concluding that Japan was wrongly pressuring Russia by not separating economics from politics. While insisting that military and political factors had receded and national strength depended on getting the economics right, Beijing did not get the politics right in the complex arena of North Korean isolationism, Russian fall from power, and Japanese interest in reentering Asia while remaining part of the West.

Warning against the purported Japanese "flying geese" strategy of regional economic development—that is, countries with advanced technologies stayed in the lead as the formation advanced together—China insisted on more equal development based on a rapid transfer of technology to those in the rear. An exaggerated view of Russia's ability to reequip Chinese enterprises with higher technology, civilian as well as military, figured into regional planning. Moreover, by vigorously pressing for development of a growth triangle in Tumen as the ideal for stimulating regional cooperation, Chinese oversimplified the economic effects for the RFE.[17] On the other side, Russians also oversimplified the impact of a port open to Chinese migration and entrepreneurship, warning that RFE ports would wither away.

Although events proved Chinese expectations to be misguided, rarely did the many multinational conferences supposedly aimed at understanding the actual prospects and problems of regionalism directly confront China's optimistic proposals. An exception occurred in July 1993 when Viktor Larin, a Vladivostok scholar, charged at a Jilin meeting that Chinese were overlooking political and social psychological factors by viewing an extremely complex region solely from an economic angle. Treating Russia as a single entity, optimists in China were ignoring the diversity of Russian interests and perceptions. Specifically, Larin pointed to public opinion surveys in the

RFE, implying that against this negative backdrop the Chinese could not rely on Moscow to achieve their goals at Tumen and in the RFE.[18] Yet, other Russians from the comfortable distance of Moscow, citing recently signed agreements, booming trade statistics, theoretical compatibilities, and the deepening economic separation of the RFE from central Russia, encouraged Chinese to expect more forward momentum in cross-border economic ties even as the collapse was nearing.

The sentiment for changing course to boost relations with China in the summer and fall of 1992 came from Moscow without any enthusiasm from the RFE. While sympathetic to conspiracy theories accusing the West and Japan of evil designs on Russia, voices in the RFE did not welcome Eurasianism as a new worldview nor embrace close ties with China as a geopolitical advantage. On the contrary, even in the first half of 1993, they were objecting to Russia's weakness in dealing with China. Arguing that Beijing reinforced its local interests in cross-border dealings rather than ignoring them, they warned that Moscow had no strategic vision and no program for the RFE and, thus, was no match for a cohesive China guided by a long-term strategy. According to this reasoning, China was taking the lead in cross-border relations for geopolitical advantages that Russia in its disorder failed to counteract. Reflecting Moscow's own geopolitical position, Ambassador Igor Rogachev in October 1993 said that trade was far from its full potential.[19]

The geoeconomics of border trade drew criticism in the RFE, too. If in the view of these local analysts Russia was selling its natural resources for peanuts and letting its industries slide irreversibly, the RFE was in danger of slipping from an exploited outpost of central Russia to a true colonial-style supplier to China at the bottom of the regional division of labor. The terms of trade brought harsh warnings.

For many in the RFE, the geocultural implications of cross-border relations proved even more bothersome. Believing that they represented European civilization, they found the Chinese with whom they came into contact to be uncouth standard-bearers of a threatening way of life. In particular, the intelligentsia of Vladivostok and Khabarovsk conceived of themselves as cosmopolitans. While acknowledging the hardworking character of the Chinese, they accused them of deception and criminality and of threatening the moral climate of an area already degenerating from within. Cossacks, who are important factors in the Jewish Autonomous Oblast, Primorskii Krai, and so on, have been in the forefront of a xenophobic reassertion of Slavic civilization. Battles over turf between Russian and Chinese criminal groups, and increasingly among the Chinese themselves, aggravated the impression that uncontrolled migration was bringing a "yellow peril" into the RFE cities.

Until October 1993, Moscow was too preoccupied with its own power struggle between the executive and legislative branches of government to pay much heed to the warnings about Chinese in the RFE. To be sure, many Chinese were making their way to other regions of the country and to Moscow itself, and the RFE was not alone in its reaction. Yet, on a national scale, the geoeconomic and geocultural dangers did not appear to be major threats. Just as Boris Yeltsin was preparing to turn to China in January 1994 with a geopolitical initiative potentially worrisome to the RFE, he faced a groundswell of hostility to cross-border forces that he could hardly ignore.

THE COLLAPSE OF CROSS-BORDER COOPERATIONS 1993–1995

By October 1993, the RFE was in an uproar over cross-border relations with China. In May, Yevgeniy Nazdratenko was appointed by Yeltsin, at the strong urging of the local industrial establishment and an overwhelming vote of the Krai Soviet, as governor of Primorskii Krai. In contrast with his predecessor, the more cosmopolitan Vladimir Kuznetsov, Nazdratenko presented himself as protective of local elite interests, which many observers equated with criminal interests. Before long, he also pressured Moscow with threats of local separatism and fanned the flames of nationalism by charging China with concealed expansionism. Controls increased over Chinese as trade was more tightly confined in outlying markets. With central politics stalemated, the local leadership grew bolder over the summer. After Yeltsin broke the stalemate with his assault on the Supreme Soviet, Nazdratenko swung his support behind Yeltsin, while the center recognized the need to foster a reconciliation with leaders in the RFE by addressing problems with China. Before long, however, Nazdratenko would again provoke Moscow reformers and rattle Sino-Russian relations.

In 1994, a border-guard mentality peaked in the RFE. Operation "Foreigner" was launched, leading to roundups of aliens in a search for Chinese who were present illegally. Most had overstayed their visas in order to trade. If through 1993 the media grew increasingly alarmed over a "China threat," in 1994 there was a steady drumbeat of warnings about the danger to national security. Not relief but heightened wariness could be seen.[20] Catering to the angry mood, leaders closed Chinese joint ventures, which were seen as pumping resources out of the RFE rather than investing in it. In some cases, Chinese investors with serious long-term intentions were also stripped of their properties. If the most alarming danger was China colonizing the RFE through immigration, then strict controls adding greatly to the costs and complexity of obtaining travel documents sharply reduced movement by Chinese. It left most Russian imports in the hands of Russians who could cross more easily and contributed to a sharp decline in trade. Nearly completely dependent on trade with China, Amurskaya Oblast was the lone holdout against these changes and perhaps the biggest loser in Russia.

In late April 1994, the legislative branches of the Russian Federation held joint hearings on the topic "On Problems of Russo-Chinese Relations and Perspectives of Their Development." A report from the Far East and Trans-Baikal regional association warned that an uncontrolled situation had aroused anti-Chinese and anti-Russian tendencies, which demanded a shift to regulated relations.

By 1995, the pain of contraction was continuing to hurt the Russian side, while the most flagrant abuses by Chinese were receding. So-called Chinatowns or Chinese villages, if any had existed, disappeared, and few Chinese traders could be seen except in controlled markets. China took care to inspect exports, although Russian traders aware that only the poorest of their compatriots would still buy Chinese goods continued to bring back goods of marginal quality.

Heilongjiang and border points in nearby provinces suffered badly from the about-face in border trade. If a decline of 7.2 percent was indicated in the second half of 1993, the province still registered a record of $2 billion in trade with Russia; however, the first half of 1994 saw a drop of 56.7 percent from the corresponding period of 1993, which helped bring the annual total back below $1 billion.[21] In Heihe and other cities, stores were boarded up, streets deserted, and thousands of firms driven out of business. The brain drain to South China from Harbin and other intellectual and industrial centers accelerated.

Some Chinese consoled themselves with wishful thinking. For instance, it was common to assert that the RFE still needed what NEC produced—agricultural products and light industrial goods; therefore, as soon as China got rid of the lingering influence of uncontrolled exports, cheap local goods would again dominate the Russian market and, in return, NEC would receive raw materials and other needed items.[22] Countering the view that Russian industry had little to offer, some who predicted that trade could soon be directed onto new rails argued that Russia had many areas of science and technology where it was in the forefront and China could benefit greatly.[23] Others insisted that Russia would soon emerge from its slump and if China was not well established it would lose to Japan or South Korea. Sometimes the tactics were reversed. For instance, Chinese attempted to win Russian support in Primorskii Krai for a transit route through the Tumen area to the Russian port of Zarubino by pointing to North Korean steps toward giving Jilin Province an alternate route from Hunchun to its ports.

Eager to revive economic dynamism along the border, official sources in NEC adopted the slogan of starting trade with the RFE all over again. They called for a new strategy, a fundamental change in the forms of trade, its content, and its pace. But the past could not be wiped away, especially in the minds of RFE residents. Calls for replacing barter trade, conducting financial transactions according to international standards, relying on mid- or large-sized firms, diversifying trade, building on new developmental zones in major cities, and so on failed to address many fundamental problems. In fact, for all the mea culpas coming from China and demanded by Beijing of Heilongjiang, there was a strange silence in available publications about how and why matters had failed so badly and who was responsible. The Chinese, like the Russians, were slow to make the border less dangerous, corrupt, expensive, and complicated. Tighter controls reduced some frictions without stimulating cooperation oriented toward development.

In 1994, as Beijing and Moscow were strengthening their ties, Moscow's supporters of closer relations sought to reverse the downturn in cross-border relations. While blaming local forces in the RFE for not developing suitable new policies, they also requested Chinese cooperation in reassuring Russians that their national interests were met. In regard to Tumen, Mikhail Titarenko, director of the Institute of the Far East, proposed five steps that should be considered before Jiang Zemin's visit to Moscow in September 1994 to assuage the doubts of Russians opposed to Tumen's realization: (1) reconceptualizing the division of labor so that the RFE would not be a raw-material base in the emerging industrial system, as the Chinese portion of the zone became the nucleus of industry and the international economy; (2) addressing immigration concerns so that a huge number of foreign workers would not flock into the RFE, rapidly changing the racial mix of the population and leading to conflicts, by ensuring that a main part of the immigration would be refugees from former Soviet republics, for example; (3) protecting the natural environment and the great economic potential of Primorskii Krai's marine resources; (4) not allowing great investment here at the expense of Nakhodka and Greater Vladivostok; and (5) not funneling cargo away from the Trans-Siberian and BAM railroads.[24]

Beijing's advocates of closer ties accepted much of Moscow's reasoning. When leaders met with their Russian counterparts, they stressed what Beijing was doing to control immigration, limit improper trade practices, and encourage cooperation between local governments on both sides of the border. Beijing blamed local authorities in Heilongjiang, replacing the party leader in the spring of 1994 and leaving border trade with weak central backing. Although it continued to discuss Tumen with Moscow and even seemingly made progress in 1995 on a scaled-down version, to the chagrin of Jilin, its commitment waned. And Liaoning Province, which had sought to take advantage of Shenyang's role as the nearest consulate for now-essential visas and its larger industrial base in the planned switch to more substantial firms and science and technology rather than trade in simpler goods, discovered that financial institutions on both sides were adverse to such partnership and to the rampant corruption present in the state sector of NEC and the RFE. The so-called new regime for economic relations was long on controls and short on modern institutions and trust.

Trade from 1994 to 1996 hovered at a much lower plateau than in 1993. For Russia, it meant a substantial trade surplus, generated by exports of raw materials under stricter central control and an underreported surplus from smuggling, which was more profitable to local interests. For China, it meant a shift away from high-value-added products such as electronics and clothing to less profitable exports of watermelons and vegetables. What was reported as barter trade included cash payments hidden from tax inspectors.

If in 1990–1991 regionalism in NEA was closely identified with megaprojects in the RFE or along borders, and in 1992–1993 the greatest momentum came from Sino-Russian border trade, then in 1994–1995 new partnership ties between Moscow and Beijing came to be seen as the best hope to break the logjam. But despite some attention to border trade at summits and other high-level meetings, the centers did little to revive commerce. Periodic showdowns still underway between Nazdratenko and Moscow added to the unresolved tensions over decentralization in Russia. Although Nazdratenko returned from a fall 1994 visit to Moscow with a seemingly improved attitude toward China, his willingness to offer private assurances to Chinese officials or to cut deals for coal and other products urgently needed in the RFE did not signify cooperation for large-scale development.

For a time, Chinese sources tried to ignore regional issues as if they mattered little in bilateral relations or it would only take a strong hand in Moscow to set matters right. In 1996–1997, however, they had begun to recognize the gravity of local tensions that were disturbing economic ties and reverberating throughout the country in a national mood of suspicion. Future disgruntlement where ties were most intense made it difficult to turn what was still mostly a rhetorical strategic partnership into close ties likely to endure.

Beijing seemed little concerned over the geopolitical consequences of the drop-off in cross-border trade. No competitor was gaining a real foothold, while Moscow was pushing Beijing to upgrade bilateral relations to give both countries additional geopolitical clout. Actually, in September 1994, the visit of a Russian official to North Korea brought a breakthrough in a different direction, postponing debt repayment in favor of further cooperation that Beijing saw in its interest. Recognizing that Moscow's fear of decentralization was so extreme that it abandoned plans to allow free economic zones vital to cross-border economic prospects, Beijing suppressed any criticisms.[25] It resorted to quiet diplomacy such as Jiang Zemin's visit to Russia in September 1994 where he urged more border trade, although little in fact later materialized.

Various Chinese sources suggested geopolitical reasoning of a reassuring nature. In essence, they argued that Russia placed its hopes on the West and on leaning to Europe, but it was betrayed by the unwise choice of shock therapy and by countries that had no interest in nurturing a rival. Instead, Russia decided to turn to the East, above all China, to reassert its great-power standing. To realize this goal, it urgently needed to develop Siberia and the RFE with Chinese cooperation.[26] It follows that with the other supports for its great-power status weakening, natural resources ought to become the pillar in Russia's new rise in the world. Recognizing 1994 as Russia's China year (*Zhongguo nian*), some Chinese analysts argued that such a year was just what was needed as a dependable guarantee for economic cooperation, that is, "first become friends, later do business" (*xian jiao pengyou, hou zuo maimai*).[27]

Even before cross-border trade deteriorated, governors in the RFE began to cast problems with China in a geopolitical light. A letter from Governor Victor Ishaev to Prime Minister Chernomyrdin on September 14, 1993, charged that the central government had allowed a sharp worsening of the situation on the border opposite Khabarovsk. His letter warned of several disturbing trends: After the 1991 demarcation agreement, ships of all types, including military vessels, could sail along the Amur River, opening up the possibility of a free, uncontrolled passing of masses of Chinese into the city of Khabarovsk. Since the spring of 1992, Chinese ships had been photographing objects in Russia, ignoring warning signals of Russian border guards, violating Russian space to fish in waters near the Russian shore, and even attacking Russian boats in an attempt to steal their load. At bilateral meetings of border guards, the Chinese side had refused to listen to Russian complaints, charging that they constitute interference in China's internal affairs. Unofficially, Chinese participants indicated that the Chinese side had to put up with the presence of Russian citizens on the islands of Bol'shoi Ussuriiskiy and Tarabarov, the status of which was deferred in the demarcation agreements of the 1990s. Ishaev ended his letter by appealing for Moscow to reject the demarcation accord signed by the former Soviet leadership in 1991, to forbid the Foreign Ministry to examine any territorial questions connected to Khabarovskii Krai without the krai's agreement, and to work out a new order for Chinese ships on the Amur.[28]

Opposition to carrying out the border demarcation became a symbol in Primorskii Krai and the Jewish Autonomous Oblast of dissatisfaction with the new relationship with China. Not only were those who had approved it charged with failing to defend Russia's national interests, but also they were accused of weakening Russia's geostrategic position and inviting further encroachments. Local voices refused to recognize that this was the best deal Russia could get or, in the reasoning of Moscow, that it turned the border from being the most contentious dispute poisoning bilateral relations into a belt of friendship and cooperation.

To alleviate concern, Moscow had delayed the start of the demarcation until May 1993 and then had begun it in the least controversial areas. In January 1994, it also had proposed that after islands belonging to Russia were turned over to China joint economic use be permitted.[29] But Moscow's plans for public relations to reduce negative reactions palled before the fiery rhetoric of demagogic governors and the media in the RFE. Although the Yeltsin administration had assured Beijing that 1997 would see the completion of the demarcation process, the debate in Russia continued to draw attention until the very eve of the November 1997 summit with Jiang Zemin, even in the capital.[30] Finally, Nazdratenko quieted down, perhaps as part of a deal whereby Yeltsin would stop trying to oust him.

For the RFE, holding China at bay averted a geoeconomic failure, although there was no confidence that the Russian side of the border could soon end its economic slide. The next challenge centered on Moscow, gaining its policy and financial support for a development program. Only then would the RFE be in a position to balance Japan, South Korea, the United States, and China in a regional program it could accept.

Many local observers on both sides of the border described the breakdown in cross-border relations in geocultural terms. When they tried to couch the loss of trust in less strident tones, they complained that the Chinese had chosen Russian partners poorly or that an unusual group of criminal elements had rushed across the border from China to fill a vacuum. But especially on the Russian side, the accusations extended to alleged plots of the Heilongjiang government working closely with Chinese mafia groups or even to a conspiracy hatched in Beijing intended to subvert the RFE. The media charged that Chinese customs officials had become shockingly coarse (*bezobrazno gruby*) with Russian tourists.[31] From the Chinese side came the view that earlier the Russians had given as much as they had received, but because many Russians did not understand that, they felt that they had earned a right to cheat Chinese business-men in order to get back at them. Chinese also worried that RFE administrators were catering to such forces and not encouraging local businessmen to work with serious Chinese business.[32] Russians charged that Chinese ignored hygiene and even endangered the health of others, while Chinese accused Russian managers of failing to deliver on promised pay or other conditions.[33] In conditions where customs barriers are regarded as the only hope for preventing enor-mous economic losses and damage to a way of life, for example through the worrisome flow of narcotics into the RFE, trust is not easily achieved.[34]

At their worst, economic linkages have generated hostages rather than trust. Russian media report on kidnappings of Russian busi-nessmen who are lured into China and held sometimes for months in an attempt by Chinese enterprises to recover debts owed to them. They imply that local communities in NEC, Chinese authorities, and at times even the Chinese army are working together to resolve trade disputes in any way they can. On the Russian side, it became common when one or more members of a Chinese tourist group did not appear at the rendezvous point on time to hold the rest of the group. Left no other recourse, traders join tourist groups for a specified number of days, often paying large deposits and leaving their passports with their Russian hosts to ensure their return. Host Russian tourist firms lose their licenses if they cannot guarantee the same result. Actual visas for commerce are reserved for tiny num-bers, and even tourists must prove no criminal record and appro-priate employment in addition to a letter of introduction from the Russian side. The Russians and Chinese do not trust each other enough to open nearby consulates in Vladivostok and Harbin, as was earlier discussed. Fortunately, the cellular phone offers one way to address high levels of suspicion: word is passed of goods and money simultaneously changing hands as representatives of both sides look on. Neither side has to assume the risk of acting first without certainty of reciprocity.

THE SEARCH FOR A NEW PATH: 1995–1998

Since late 1993, the balance has shifted sharply from open to con-trolled borders. Using a typology of national, local, and border trade,

Chinese officials have narrowed the definition of border trade, allaying Russian concerns and addressing World Trade Organization requirements. Privileges along the border, such as the right of localities to keep half of all customs payments, were lost. In place of a broad belt leading to major cities, the border zone as a legal entity entitled to privileges was reduced by the Chinese in 1996 to points within 20 kilometers of the border. Despite plans to supplement the island market between Heihe and Blagoveshchensk with other markets for mass trade and the recent temporary revival of trade in some Chinese towns within the border zone, existing privileges are not supposed to outlast the decade. Meanwhile, local trade in cities such as Harbin is faring worse than border trade. Controls may serve other purposes, but so far they are not succeeding in stimulating economic ties.

Both Beijing and Moscow need each other's help to find a balance between localism and recentralization. Existing localism is a drain on central resources, deceives the center with false documents in order to reduce taxes, encourages criminality, and threatens to lead to political instability as local discontent continues to rise. Recentralization, as attempted since 1994, in turn denies incentives to local areas, shifts blame to the center, and does little to resolve fundamental problems. The presidential program of 1996 recognizes the need to integrate the RFE into NEA, stressing the need to create an investment climate not less attractive than that in the neighboring APR countries. The thrust of the report, however, favors Japanese multinational corporations, not Chinese "suitcase" traders or cash-starved state enterprises. The powerful financial cliques in Moscow and the local administrations in the RFE share this pro-Japanese outlook on economic cooperation.[35] Negotiations in 1997–1998 suggested that bilateral economic ties with Japan would soon advance, but in fact prospects were not favorable. After the Russian financial crisis of 1998, it was once again the Chinese traders who could fill the void with barter goods.

In China, the principle that NEC must be economically integrated into NEA is well established, but local provinces doubt that they can find a strategy to succeed without more help from Beijing. Meanwhile, in Beijing the focus is now on all-around trade, not border trade. Motivated by the goal of boosting the strategic partnership, some analysts accuse China's economic ministries of exerting a negative influence through their one-sided conceptions of the Russian economy as burdened by old equipment, backward technology, and coarse goods that cannot be delivered on time. In place of this thinking, they propose that Russia is a big market, has a huge influence on other CIS (Commonwealth of Independent States) markets, and, most important, is a science and technology great power. If Russia has failed to find a way to apply its technological inventions in production, China can do so. Working together, the two governments can also establish a united bank, offering guarantees for commerce; improve transport infrastructure; and strengthen order and inspections on the border. While noting that the 1996 summit adds momentum to these efforts, one article warned that China faces fierce competition for the Russian market and may be left behind.[36]

A minority of Chinese analysts started warning Beijing of troubles in cross-border relations before their sudden downturn; they insisted in 1994–1995 that the problems were more than temporary and required radical surgery. These analysts hoped in 1997–1999 for new approaches to great-power relations as a force for transforming cross-border relations and regionalism in NEA more generally. If multipolarity accompanied by strict balance-of-power politics led to valuing the Sino-Russian partnership highly despite its negligible economic benefits, then multilateralism associated with economic integration placed Sino-Russian relations in a broader strategy for developing NEA.

According to multilateralism, China on its own had little chance to revive Russian interest in cross-border dynamism. A different strategy to attract Japanese, U.S., and South Korean investment would be required. This strategy would not arise from a narrow economic approach. Rather, it would result only from a far-reaching reassessment of a combination of geopolitical, geoeconomic, and geocultural factors. Unfortunately, censored academic and media publications had trouble directly discussing these matters. Only indirect evidence of internal discussions that ranged far beyond the hints in these writings suggested what was under consideration.[37] Such sources agree that the key problem in the RFE and NEC is a capital famine exacerbated by an uninviting environment for international investors. Only nonthreatening geopolitics and a civilized commercial environment will entice such investors and thus permit the region to get the geoeconomics right. Indeed, as early as March 1994, a conference in Harbin called for "civilized commerce" (*wenming jingmao*). Although a majority optimistically predicted that the low tide would last only one to two years, some participants warned that with both China and Russia in transition to a market economy the solution demanded financial practices beyond the resources of either.[38]

The Sino-Russian strategic partnership is premised on geopolitical priorities. Forces behind planning for economic development show little sign of sharing those priorities. Local areas along the border also have a different set of priorities, which in the RFE lead away from China and in NEC continue to focus on Russia.

The crux of the Sino-Russian strategic partnership is an equal relationship intended to balance great-power relations in the region and the world. Cross-border relations are problematic because they reflect an asymmetry in power and potential. The RFE regards China as seeking geopolitical dominance, beginning with the demarcation; as bound to achieve geoeconomic superiority, initially through labor migration and commerce; and as a foreign civilization that surrounds its European outpost. Integration with NEC threatens to bring inequality and a loss of great-power status, not any kind of balance to the environment they know best.

Champions of economic development in both countries also look at cross-border relations differently from great-power strategists. To develop NEC, they recognize the importance of multilateralism, which means dimming the strategic elements of partnership in order to become more inviting to Japan, South Korea, and the United States, as well as other potential economic partners. To develop the RFE, they must direct attention more to Japan than to China. The logic of cross-border economic development and the emotions of cross-border contacts in recent years are propelling China and Russia in a different direction than their leading proponents of strategic partnership favor.

In 1997, China could only watch and wait. Yeltsin moved to oust Nazdratenko, but he was thwarted. Although First Deputy Premier Boris Nemtsov took charge of coordinating the development program for the RFE as well as economic relations with Japan and China, the State Duma hesitated to approve the necessary legislation. China's proposals for new bilateral economic ties continued to receive a hearing even if commitments were few. Russia must break the impasse of recent years before the border area has any hope of development. The Asian financial crisis of 1997–1998 made both countries more vulnerable, especially adding to Chinese wariness about risks of conducting business in Russia.

As long as no end is in sight for Russia's economic troubles, political conditions are likely to be unstable, and tensions between the RFE and Moscow, difficult to resolve. Improving Sino-Russian relations are a product of recent instability and could advance further as a result of future instability, for example through the election of a more nationalistic president in Russia. But in the RFE, economic troubles provide fertile ground for suspecting China as well as for blaming Moscow. A program for regionalism centered on the RFE could change this mood, suggesting both to the local population and to the nation as a whole that the country was on the way to emerging from its decade of troubles.

Virtually any plan for large-scale development of the Far East would call, above all, for heavy foreign investment, much of it from Japan and the United States. While such investments would likely quiet local concern about Chinese domination, they would draw localities into broad integration with the global community rather than into a bilateral linkup with China. If regionalism gains momentum, China is likely to benefit, too, economically, but without building a foothold for a strategic partnership that separates its ties to Russia from the wider international community. Northeast Asia does have a remarkable degree of complementarity, including vast Russian natural resources and a large Chinese population with a growing need for them. But the indispensable force of international capital and technology means that multilateralism focused on economic cooperation, not bilateralism centered on strategic partnership, is the logical path to regional development. In the summer of 1999, however, great-power tensions stymied multilateralism.

NOTES

[1] I want to thank the United States Institute of Peace for supporting my research on regionalism in Northeast Asia, including trips to both sides of the Sino-Russian border and regular access to local publications. Interviews proved that Russian local officials were playing on discontent to encourage negative images of China, while China's continued censorship meant underreporting of problems and artificially induced optimism.

[2] Samuel P. Huntington, *The Clash of Civilizations and the Remaking of World Order* (New York: Simon & Schuster, 1996), p. 132.

[3]Wang Lizhun, "Beijiang ZhongE bianmao fazhan shixi" (An Attempt to Explain the Development of Northern Border Sino-Russian Border Trade), *Eluosi yanjiu*, no. 3 (1995), p. 45.

[4]"Heilongjiang sheng duiSu maoyi he jingji zhixu hezuo de zhanlue gouxiang" (The Strategic Framework of Heilongjiang Province's Trade and Economic and Technological Cooperation with the Soviet Union), in Zhang Haosheng, ed., *Heilongjiang sheng duiSu jingmao zhanlue he celueh yanjiu* (Haerbin: Heilongjiang renmin chubanshe, 1991), p. 101.

[5]Xu Taojie, "Eluosi yuandong diqu tong Zhongguo dongbei diqu be bianmao hezuo" (Border Trade Cooperation of the Russian Far Eastern Region with the Northeast China Region), *Xiboliya yanjiu*, no. 4 (1994), p. 2.

[6]"Redian wenti: bianmao, zheli he yizai paihuai?" (Hot Points: Here and Always Hesitant), *Yuandong jingmao xinxi*, no. 5 (1996), p. 17.

[7]"Velikii brat' k nam tianet ruki: Kitaiskaya ekspansiia v Primorskom krae Rossii" (Great Brother Extends His Hand to Us: Chinese Expansion in Primorskii Krai, Russia), *Vladivostok*, September 1, 1993, p. 5.

[8]Ma Hong, "Zhongguo de duiwai kaifang zhengce yu Dongbeiya diqu de jingji hezuo" (China's Open Door Policy and Economic Cooperation with the Northeast Asian Region), in *Dongbeiya jingji quan de meili* (Dalian: Dalian ligong daxue chubanshe, 1992), pp. 1–8.

[9]Zheng Biao, "Sulian jieti dui Dongbeiya de yingxiang" (The Influence of the Soviet Union's Breakup on Northeast Asia), *Dongbeiya luntan*, no. 2 (1992), pp. 84–87.

[10]Zuo Changqing and Sui Shaonan, "Eluosi duiwai jingji guanxi de tiaozheng yu ZhongE jingji hezuo" (Readjustment of Russian Foreign Economic Relations and Sino-Russian Economic Cooperation), *Dongou Zhongya yanjiu*, no. 5 (1994), p. 70.

[11]Shan Rong, "Eluosi de dongfang zhengce ji Dongbeiya de jingji hezuo" (Russia's Eastern Policy and Northeast Asian Economic Cooperation), *Xiboliya yanjiu*, no. 4 (1995), p. 15.

[12]Xiao Xiangqian, "Dongbeiya diqu ge quyi kaifa yu hezuo qianjing" (Projects for Opening up and Cooperation of Various Districts of the Northeast Asian Region), in *Dongbeiya jingji quan de meili* (Dalian: Dalian ligong daxue chubanshe, 1992), p. 16.

[13]Wang Yonggui, "Qian Sulian wenti Haerbin yantaohui zongxu" (A General Description of the Harbin Conference on Questions of the Former Soviet Union), *Longjiang shehui kexue*, no. 5 (1992), p. 50.

[14]Xu Jingxue, "ZhongE maoyi he Dongbeiya quyi hezuo" (Sino-Russian Trade and Northeast Asian Regional Cooperation), *Dongou Zhongya yanjiu*, no. 1 (1994), p. 22.

[15]"Xin xingshi xia de ZhongE guanxi—guoji xuexu yantaohui jiyao" (Sino-Russian Relations under the New Situation), *Xiandai guoji guanxi*, no. 1 (1993), p. 30.

[16]Lu Nanquan, "Jinyibu fazhan ZhongE jingmao guanxi de ruogan wenti" (Some Questions on Advancing the Development of Sino-Russian Economic and Trade Relations), *Dongou Zhongya yanjiu*, no. 1 (1993), pp. 68–69; Lu Nanquan, "Dui dangqian fazhan ZhongE jingmao guanxi ruogan wenti de kanfa," *Guoji maoyi*, no. 4 (1993), p. 17.

[17]Chi Yuanji and Li Xiao, "Dongbeiya quyi jingji hezuo yu Tumenjiang 'chengzhang sanjiao'" (The Northeast Asian Region Economic Cooperation on the Tumen River "Growth Triangle"), *Dongbeiya luntan*, no. 4 (1992), pp. 7–12.

[18]Viktor Larin, "Shishi Tumenjiang hezuoqu fangan zhong de minzu, renkou, he zhengzhi wenti" (Ethnic, Demographic and Urban Questions in the Actual Implementation of the Plan for the Tumen River Cooperative Area), in *Dongbeiya jingji kaifa zhanlue yanjiu* (Changchun: Jilin renmin chubanshe, 1993), vol. 2, pp. 51–54.

[19]Hou Baoquan, "ZhongE bianjing maoyi de xin wenti he xin quxiang" (New Questions and New Tendencies in Sino-Russian Border Trade), *Dongou Zhongya yanjiu*, no. 3 (1994), p. 60.

[20]Marina Iashina, "Raz Kitaets, dva Kitaets" (One Chinese, Two Chinese), *Vladivostok*, July 8, 1994, p. 2.

[21]Zhao Lizhi, "Heilongjiang sheng bianjing maoyi xingshi, duice he qianjing" (Heilongjiang Province Border Trade Situation, Countermeasures and Prospects), *Xiboliya yanjiu*, no. 3 (1995), p. 1.

[22]Liu Xiuyun, "Tumenjiang diqu kaifa de qianjing ji qi zhiyue insu" (Prospects for Opening up the Tumen River Area and Restraining Elements), *Dongou Zhongya yanjiu*, no. 3 (1995), pp. 22–31.

[23]Li Jingyu, "ZhongE liangguo jingji hezuo lingyu wenti tantao" (A Study of the Territorial Questions in Sino-Russian Bilateral Economic Cooperation), *Dongbeiya yanjiu*, no. 2 (1995), p. 28.

[24]M. Titarenko, "Dongbeiya yitihua ji Eluosi de liyi" (Northeast Asian Integration and Russian Interests), in Li Shaokang, ed., *Dongbeiya jingji kaifa zhanlue yanjiu* (Changchun: Jilin chubanshe, 1994), vol. 3, pp. 63–70.

[25]Lin Heming and Jin Yan, "Jianli Zhongguo Heihe—Eluosi Bushi ciquyi ziyou maoyi qu de xianshi moshi," *Elousi yanjiu*, no. 3 (1995), p. 48.

[26]Shan Rong, "Eluosi de dongfang zhengce ji Dongbeiya de jingji hezuo" (Russia's Eastern Policy and Northeast Asian Economic Cooperation), *Xiboliya yanjiu*, no. 4 (1995), p. 15.

[27]Luo Hongyi and Li Kangliang, "Haerbin shi duiE jingmao fazhan de qianjing ji duice" (Prospects and Countermeasures of Harbin City's Economic and Trade Development with Russia), *Xiboliya yanjiu*, no. 1 (1995), pp. 18–21.

[28]V. I. Ishaev, "K voprosu o granitse s KNR na territorii Khabarovskogo kraya" (On the Question of the Border with the PRC on the Territory of

Khabarovskii Krai), unpublished letter to V. S. Chernomyrdin, September 14, 1993.

[29]"Rossiisko-Kitaiskie otnosheniia" (Russo-Chinese Relations), unpublished materials for the joint legislative hearings of April 1994, sections "O pogranichnykh peregovorakh s KNR" and "O demarkatsii vostochnoi chasti Rossiisko-Kitaiskoi granitsy."

[30]*Nekotorye problemy demarkatsii Rossiisko-Kitaiskoi granitsy. 1991–1997 g.g.: sbornik statei i dokumentov* (Some Problems of the Demarcation of the Russian-Chinese Border, 1991–1997: A Collection of Articles and Documents) (Moscow: Nezavisimaya gazeta, 1997).

[31]Georgii Konstantinov, "V zhizni kitaiskikh 'nelegalov' poiavitsia 'polosa prepiatstvii'" (In the Life of Chinese "Illegals" a "Belt of Criminality" Appears), *Novosti*, July 22, 1994, p. 2.

[32]Andrei Kholenko, "Kharbinskaya iarmarka" (The Harbin Fair), *Vladivostok*, June 29, 1994, p. 5.

[33]"Heilongjiang sheng bianmao ju laowu gongzuo kaochaduan fuE fangwen" (Heilongjiang Province Border Trade Office Labor Working Inspection Team Visits Russia), *Yuandong jingmao daobao*, nos. 7–8 (1996), p. 4.

[34]Tatiana Baulina, "'Goriachaya tochka' Grodekovskoi tamozhni" ("Hot Point" at Grodekovskaya Customs), *Vladivostok*, September 1, 1995, p. 9.

[35]Alexander G. Granberg, "Development of the Russian Far East and Trans-Baikal Region and Activization of Russia's Participation in Pacific Economic Cooperation (On Main Propositions of the Presidential Program)" (unpublished manuscript for the 29th International General Meeting of the Pacific Basin Economic Council, Washington, D.C., May 21, 1996).

[36]Wen Huan, "ZhongE maoyi: ji dai shuangfang dazhong qiye de canyu" (Sino-Russian Trade), *Guoji maoyi*, no. 7 (1996), p. 19.

[37]Lu Nanquan, et al., "Dongbeiya quyi jingji hezuo yanjiu xianzhuang he redian" (Study of the Northeast Asian Region Economic Cooperation Current Situation and Hot Points) (manuscript offprint, Harbin, 1995); Xu Jingxue, "Mianxiang 21 shiji: Heilongjiang sheng kuobu xouxiang shijie" (Facing the 21st Century: Heilongjiang Province Takes Big Strides Going to the World), *Xiboliya yanjiu*, no. 5 (1995), pp. 1–3.

[38]Wang Shaozhu, "Eluosi jingji xingshi ji ZhongE bianmao wenti taolunhui lundian zhaiyao" (Digest of Discussion Points at the Conference on the Russian Economic Situation and Sino-Russian Border Trade Questions), *Xiboliya yanjiu*, no. 4 (1994), pp. 6–9.

8

A View from the Russian Far East

Tamara Troyakova

Long-term economic development of the Russian Far East depends on the ability of the federal and regional leaders to come to a power-sharing agreement with the center. Such an agreement would allow Moscow to retain control over defense, security, and foreign policy issues while providing local leaders with the authority to deal with their own economic problems. There are several potential scenarios for the region's development. They range from the preservation of its current role as an exporter of raw materials to the radical restructuring of the regional economy and its integration into the larger East Asian economy. In the absence of a real federalism in Russia, the country's territorial integrity can only be preserved if the existing state mechanism is improved.

The current Russian system of center-regional relations is based on several important agreements and documents, including the Declaration of the Sovereignty of the Russian Federation, the Federation Treaty, and the 1993 Russian Constitution. In 1994, various regional entities—technically referred to as "subjects of the Russian Federation"—within Russia began to sign power-sharing agreements with the central government. By 1999, such agreements were in place with about half of Russia's eighty-nine regions, including the Republic of Sakha (Yakutia), Khabarovskii Krai, and Sakhalin Oblast. In April 1997, the State Duma adopted the law On the Principles and the Manner of Power Sharing Between the Government of the Russian Federation and the Subjects of the Russian Federation. This new law establishes that the constitution and the federal laws supersede individual agreements with the regions.

Formal equality of the regions before the center has not produced equal outcomes. The Republic of Sakha (Yakutia) gained a special position in the region. Sakha has many attributes of a state: a well-defined territory, an independent and viable government headed by a president, and even its own Ministry of Foreign Affairs. In April 1996, Moscow signed a power-sharing agreement with Khabarovskii Krai. The administration of Primorskii Krai did not manage to negotiate such an agreement and continues to bargain with the center, actively using "the Chinese factor." Its relations with the center are more conflictual than those of Khabarovskii Krai, offering yet another model of center-regional relations in this part of Russia.

The goal of this essay is to analyze how the evolving and contrasting models of center-regional relations in Primorskii and Khabarovskii Krais shape and are shaped in turn by Russian-Chinese relations. In particular, I will concentrate on the cooperation between these two key Russian regions and neighboring Northeast Chinese provinces. Since 1992, two tendencies dominated at the regional level. The first was the local authorities' desire for greater independence, which has led to a strengthening of ties with the neighboring Chinese provinces and could lead to deeper integration with them and Asia as a whole. This was a leading tendency from 1992 until 1994. The second, which has become dominant since 1995, is the strengthening of local authoritarian regimes combined with an increase in xenophobia and anti-Chinese sentiments. This article is based on analysis of local data, including statistics published by Primorskii and Khabarovskii Krais, articles by local politicians in local newspapers, regional laws and decrees, interviews with experts, and the results of regional public opinion polls.

THE REGIONAL ECONOMIC CRISIS

The devastating economic crisis that still shapes the Russian Far East and the policy responses—or lack thereof—to this crisis by both the center and the regions provide the context for considering regional views of Sino-Russian relations. In the first half of the 1990s, the decline of state subsidies and uncontrolled growth of prices had catastrophic consequences for the region's economy. In order to solve the crisis, local authorities increased exports of natural resources, but most of the measures to expand foreign economic relations did not bring lasting success. Among those attempted were free economic zones, interregional cooperation councils, and the tried-and-true method of attempting to win additional concessions or subsidies from the center.

The Role of the Central Government

Federal aid is provided to the region through both normal and backdoor channels. The normal channel is represented by federal transfer payments. Backdoor channels provide some regions with preferential treatment and benefits despite the constitutional provisions for the equality of rights of all Federation subjects. This structure of "unjustified privileges" clashes with interests of individual territories and thus impedes successful cooperation within the Far East and neighboring Russian regions.

The federal government has also adopted a comprehensive program for the region. The Federal Program on Economic and Social Development of the Far Eastern and the Trans-Baikal Regions in 1996–2005, adopted in June 1995, discusses measures for structurally adjusting the economy, preventing outward migration, and prompting highly trained specialists to stay in the region. It also envisions the region's inclusion in the world economy through economic cooperation with the countries of the Asia-Pacific region, protection of the environment, and rational use of natural resources.[1] Successful implementation of this program should undermine separatist tendencies and oust the ghost of the Far East republic. It seems, however, that the program was adopted only to increase Yeltsin's chances for garnering votes from the region in the 1996 reelection, since its financing dried up soon thereafter.

For a number of years, Moscow demonstrated its inability to provide socioeconomic incentives for the increase, or at least the stabilization, of the Far East's population. The law On State Guarantees and Compensation for People Living and Working in the Far North Regions and Other Regions of Similar Status, adopted in February 1993, is not being implemented because an already constrained budget must finance its guarantees and compensations. The situation is a catch-22: On the one hand, it is impossible to attract new people to the region because of the harsh living conditions. On the other hand, it is almost impossible to use the funds provided for various kinds of additional compensation, because the region lacks the human resources to develop industrial infrastructure as a base for self-financing. The program of development for 1996–2005 proposes to solve this problem with foreign investments.

Free Economic Zones

The regions' initial response to the economic crisis was the establishment of free economic zones. Inconsistency of reforms, however, dashed any hopes of attracting foreign capital to special economic zones such as Nakhodka, Sakhalin, and the Jewish Autonomous Republic (JAR). The federal government's desire to use a universal method of transition to a market economy, without taking into account local peculiarities, led to a degradation of the North Economic Zone (NEZ).

The example of Nakhodka and the NEZ is instructive. Only 10 percent of the krai's population live in the NEZ. In 1995, foreign trade accounted for nearly 9 percent of the total volume in the NEZ. Japan, China, and South Korea were the largest trade partners. Before 1995, Britain was the leading foreign investor ($5,465,000). It was followed by the United States with $5,102,000 and China with $4,768,000.[2] In 1995, however, foreign involvement declined. The United States became the leading foreign partner, but with a total of less than half its previous levels ($2,100,000). The Netherlands stood in second place with $1,050,000; the next three places found South Korea with $935,100, the United Kingdom with $405,000, and China with $376,700.[3] In March 1997, a hearing was held on the creation of a special economic zone on the territory of the Sakhalin Oblast. The result was a decision to speed up the preparation of basic documents for establishing such a zone. In April 1997, the State Duma adopted a law on free economic zones that will possibly revive this idea in the region.

Interregional Cooperation

A leading example of attempted regional cooperation is the Transbaikal Association, headed by V. Ishaev, the governor of Khabarovskii Krai. Most of the meetings on foreign economic cooperation are held in Khabarovsk. At the 29th Session of the Pacific Economic Council in Washington, D.C., Ishaev spoke on the prospects for the Far East's cooperation with foreign countries.[4] Economic prosperity and political governability are the prerequisites for the region's stability. The strategic task is to formulate a program to promote economic development and political stability, and to attract residents to the area. Only then should the region forge its economic and political ties with foreign countries.[5]

Khabarovsk is the region's recognized leader in forging foreign economic ties. Meetings devoted to economic problems are regularly held in the city, and in April 1996 Boris Yeltsin stopped there on his way to China. In the spring of 1996, representatives of the region's krais and oblasts discussed investment projects and possibilities for their financing by foreigners. Most of them dealt with the creation and modernization of the communications infrastructure in the Russian Far East, particularly in the Khasan commercial port and the ports of Vanino and Sovetskaya Gavan, and also in the building of a bridge between Blagoveshchensk and Heihe.

SINO-RUSSIAN ECONOMIC UPS AND DOWNS

With the collapse of the Soviet Union, a decline in state subsidies, and a breakdown of the all-union production chain, the Russian Far East was forced to forge economic ties with foreign partners. In the late 1980s, a system of tariff licenses and currency regulation was introduced that fostered the revitalization of trade relations on the regional level. In 1992, local producers received the right to export their production, which led to an additional increase in foreign trade. By 1994, however, with the introduction of export tariffs and obligatory registration of the strategic-resources exports, the Ministry of Foreign Economic Relations had again strengthened the center's hold over the region's foreign trade. This tension between central regulation and regional autonomy has remained dominant in foreign trade throughout the 1990s.

The Boom of the Early 1990s

Improvements in Russian-Chinese relations in the beginning of the 1990s led to the rapid increase in the Far Eastern territories' border trade with the Chinese provinces. In 1992, in the Amur region,

Table 8.1
Trade Turnover with China (in millions of dollars)

	1992	1993	1994
Primorskii Krai	426.8	302.0	83.0
Khabarovskii Krai	114.3	391.4	53.4
Amur Oblast	382.6	374.4	69.3

Source: *Delovoi Vostok*, April 30–May 6, 1995.

Primorskii and Khabarovskii Krais were "invaded" by Chinese traders who came to Russia via twenty border checkpoints in Heilongjiang Province. In 1993, about 2.5 million people were registered at the border checkpoints. (Before 1986, Grodekovo-Suifenhe was the only checkpoint on this part of the border.) Russian shuttle travelers moved back and forth across the border with cheap clothing, shoes, Chinese food products, metal dishes, and electrical appliances. The number of joint companies specializing in barter trade increased. China was importing construction materials, ferrous and nonferrous scrap metal, mineral fertilizers, and fish and other products of the sea from Russia. Russia was importing cheap consumer goods and food products from China.

Development of Russian-Chinese relations during this period was accompanied by the creation of numerous committees, commissions, and working groups on economic cooperation in the border regions. The customs services of both countries exchanged experience. Russian entrepreneurs participated in the work of the Harbin international show. Russian and Chinese airlines both scheduled charter flights from Khabarovsk and Vladivostok to Harbin and Beijing. In 1994, construction of the fiber-optic cable between Harbin and Khabarovsk began, and in 1997 direct communications between the two countries was established.

The Bust

In the first half of the 1990s, Primorskii and Khabarovskii Krais' and Amur Oblast's trade with China did not develop evenly, experiencing a sharp drop from 1993 to 1994, as table 8.1 illustrates.

Primorskii Krai has the largest share of foreign trade in the Russian Far East: 34.2 percent in 1992, 26.5 percent in 1993, and 26.1 percent in 1994.[6] China's share in the total volume of Primorskii Krai foreign trade was 58 percent in 1992, 45 percent in 1993, 19 percent in 1994, 15 percent in 1995, and 20 percent in 1996. Despite fast growth in the beginning of the 1990s, which was fueled by a general revitalization of foreign economic relations, a decline has occurred. The decline in trade is a natural result of Moscow's policies, as well as other economic, political, and cultural factors, six of which are listed below.

First, the center's customs and taxation policies are a principal source of constraint on commercial activity. An increase in customs duties and a tightening of the border regime played a decisive role in the decline of commercial activity. The high level of taxes (forty-four kinds, taking more than 85 percent of profits) discouraged trade or drove it into illegal or corrupt structures. Second, barter, important in the early boom of Sino-Russian trade, could not sustain long-term and stable growth of commerce. It had to give way to a cash payment system. Yet many regional businesspeople in Russia do not have the necessary cash.

Third, high interest rates and inflation, especially in energy and transportation costs, made some forms of commerce unprofitable. Fourth, the legislative and administrative structure was not stable and predictable enough to facilitate commerce. The government was often the source of overregulation and underperformance. In the first half of 1994, the volume of freight and passenger transit over highway checkpoints decreased because of stricter rules for obtaining business passports and regular visas for both Russian and Chinese citizens.

Fifth, poor and unethical business practices, corruption, and distrust were also serious factors in the slowdown. Sixth, the low quality of Chinese goods had a negative impact on trade development. Russian middlemen bought very cheap Chinese goods at wholesale markets. But because of the low handling costs, shuttle traders and Chinese tourists sold their products on markets for approximately twice as cheap, making the quality irrelevant.

Although Sino-Russian trade has recovered from 1994 lows, these factors continue to constrain interregional trade.

Back from Decline

In 1995, Primorskii Krai's cooperation with China was rejuvenated. In June, Governor Nazdratenko participated in the opening of the

Primorskii Krai pavilion at an exhibition in Harbin. In July, the Committee on Foreign Economic and Regional Relations of the Primorskii Krai's administration and the Institute on Foreign Economic Cooperation on Jilin Province signed an agreement. More than sixty representatives of business circles of Heilongjiang, Guangdong, Yunnan, and other provinces participated in Vladivostok's conference on the development of economic relations. In July 1995, the Russian government approved the country's participation in the Tumen River project and the creation of a transport junction based around the Khasan commercial port. The administration of Primorskii Krai, however, looks suspiciously upon the realization of this project, afraid of possible competition from Chinese entrepreneurs. One of the plausible excuses used to slow the project down is a potential threat to the environment in the Tumangan River and Lake Khasan regions.

A historic pattern and inclination toward increased foreign trade exists. In 1996, total exports were $111 million and imports were $90 million. China was importing timber, ferrous and nonferrous scrap metal and metal products, and frozen fish. Russia was importing primarily foods (rice, grain, wheat flour, frozen meat, raw sugar) but also ships and other floating devices. Exports of fish and other sea products allow Primorskii Krai to be the region's leader in foreign trade.

Regional authorities have tried to address the decline in trade and the factors constraining it. Authorities of Primorskii Krai and the Chinese provinces of Jilin and Heilongjiang, for example, have concluded an agreement on bilateral efforts to solve the arrears crisis. In 1995, the local administration paid $72,000 from its own funds to Harbin's Department of Foreign Trade for the shipments of food in 1991–1992 to the Primorie flood victims. Primorskii Krai and Jilin Province hold negotiations to repay the krai's $4-million debt through state mutual payments. They plan to open branches of banks on the krai's territory and on the territories of the neighboring provinces, creating a system of payments among them.

In the summer of 1996, the Russian government restricted the weight and the monetary value of goods allowed into the country by tourists in order to increase control over traders' incomes. It also limited the number of companies that organize "tourist" trips to China. With widespread unemployment and payments arrears, for some people trips to China were the only source of income. So far, it is difficult to talk about the magnitude of the decline in trade, because official statistics do not account for trade by private individuals. The number of trips to China, however, has declined.

Starting in the fall 1996, the main bulk of cheap goods was brought into the region by private Russian companies and by Chinese who came to the Far East on tourist visas. In 1997, with local authorities' assistance, big wholesale markets in Blagoveshchensk, Khabarovsk, Vladivostok, Ussuriisk, and Pogranichnyi were created in an attempt to better control Chinese commercial activity in the area. Moreover, shuttle traders satisfy the local population's demand for cheap clothing and shoes by delivering goods from Poland and Turkey.

These measures led to some increase in the quality of Chinese goods and to a decline in the number of Chinese trading illegally in the Russian Far East. At the same time, the decrease in trade negatively affected the local budget revenues. Customs duties from barter operations were mostly used by the local budgets, while revenues from wholesale trade and visa fees were usually transferred to the central budget.

Regional Differentiation

Primorskii Krai not only leads the Far Eastern region by the volume of imports and exports, but it also has the highest number of foreign participants in its economy. In 1995, Japan accounted for 30 percent of the turnover, South Korea for 20 percent, China for 15 percent, and the United States for 14 percent. As of 1997, South Korea had the highest level of investments ($59,987,000). It was followed by the United Kingdom with $56,637,900; the United States with $44,608,400; China with $27,467,300; Singapore with $23,897,600; Austria with $22,648,000; and Japan with $19,151,500. One-fifth of this capital is invested in joint enterprises and the rest goes to loans.[7]

Khabarovskii Krai is in second place. The leading export industry is lumber, most of which is exported to Japan in accordance with the November 1991 global agreement on lumber. In 1992 and 1993, China was the second largest trade partner after Japan. The region exported to China machinery and equipment, goods made from ferrous and nonferrous metals, and consumer goods. The future of Russian-Chinese relations depends on the regulation of commercial relations, a solution to the arrears crisis, and improvement in quality and assortment of exports and imports.

The area's relations with the countries of the Asia-Pacific community were discussed at the meeting of representatives of the Far Eastern and Trans-Baikal regions held in March 1997 in Khabarovsk. Gennady Karasin, deputy minister of Foreign Affairs, and V. Matvienko, who was then the director of the Department of Relations with the Subjects of the Federation, Parliament and Socio-Political Organizations of the Ministry of Foreign Affairs, helped the sides accept mutual obligations on further development of foreign economic relations. The final protocol of the regional meeting helped define the center's and regional authorities' jurisdictions. Federal authorities were asked to discuss with krai and oblast administrations drafts of international treaties, agreements, and other documents that affect the interests of the Far East.

In order to further develop foreign economic relations with China, "Chinese and Russian local governments would be allowed to make mutual payments on foreign deals in the border regions not only in fully convertible currencies but also in Chinese yuan. Russia enterprises would also be allowed to hold accounts in yuans in the authorized banks."[8] The activities of the working group on interregional and border cooperation of the interparliamentary Russian-Chinese commission on economic and scientific technical cooperation were renewed. The group also suggested a discussion on signing the intergovernmental agreement on trade zones on the Russian-Chinese border, including the Zabaikalsk-Manzhouli, Blagoveshchensk-Heihe, and Grodekovo-Hunchun regions.[9]

Implementation of these recommendations will demand much responsibility from regional leaders. Some of the problems result from the government's steadfast actions but many of them arise from disorganization. Help from the center alone will not cure the decline in production; the chronic payment, wage, and pension arrears; or the decline in the population's real incomes. The degradation of the economy taking place in the absence of an effective regional policy makes local leaders resort to ideas of independence, particularly in foreign policy.

A HALF-OPEN BORDER

An additional major problem hampering Sino-Russian commerce is the lack of an efficient border regime and transportation infrastructure to support expanded trade between the Far East and Northeast

China. Currently there are six border checkpoints in Primorskii Krai: five on highways (Poltavka, Kraskino, Turii Rog, Markovo, and Pogranichnyi) and one on the railroad (Grodekovo). None of them correspond to modern standards in their transit capacity, the quality of service, or the work of border guards. Only Pogranichnyi and Poltavka checkpoints have improved conditions for expediting transit loads and tourist groups traveling from Pogranichnyi to Suifenhe.

Construction of highway border checkpoints Kraskino, Markovo, and Turii Rog was postponed because of the fund scarcity in the Far Eastern customs department. In order to supply inhabitants of the northern parts of Primorie and a part of Khabarovskii Krai with fruits and vegetables from China, local authorities were forced to start construction of a car passage over the Ussuri River near the cities of Bikin and Zhaokhe. Joint-stock company Samur, with the help of authorities from Pozharskiy raion and four regions of Khabarovskii Krai, carried out the main construction. In 1995, however, the federal government suddenly stopped financing the project and would not respond to requests by the Far Eastern customs department to continue it. Half-completed buildings are falling apart and loads are being delayed because navigational routes freeze during the winter. Attempts to attract Chinese investors have not been successful so far.

In 1996, local authorities asked for the federal government's permission to begin using 30 percent of the collected customs duties to finance the adopted resolutions, an increase from the current 10 percent, which the region is entitled to in accordance with a previous November 1992 decree. Moscow, however, has abolished these sources of revenue in recent years, citing the rise of federal budget deficits.

The result has been a growing contrast between the Chinese and Russian sides. Since the early 1990s, the Chinese city of Suifenhe has turned from a shabby village into a prosperous trading town. On the Russian side, however, Pogranichnyi remains a small town with dusty unpaved roads and half-built buildings. In 1992–1993, crime increased along with trade. Local authorities could not deal with the conditions and thus closed the market. Only in 1997 did the market for Chinese traders reopen and start to bring revenue to the local budget. The quota for Chinese traders, however, is currently set at 300 people and the duration of visas is thirty days.[10] Local customs transfer funds to the nonbudgetary accounts of the administration of Pogranichnyi for the town's modernization, providing work for local inhabitants.

Customs and border officials initially were not able to deal with the increased flow of goods and people. In June 1994, an interministerial commission on setting up border checkpoints was created. It then began to implement the program on normalizing border crossing. In essence, the implementation of this program not only brought order to the border but also seriously decreased the number of crossings. By the end of 1994, after the Agreement on the Regulation of the Rules of the Russian-Chinese Border Crossing took effect, the flow of traders slowed considerably.

Concern with regulating the border and financial constraints also affected efforts to improve the transportation links between the Russian Far East and Northeast China. In the early 1990s, the joint-stock company Rodok started construction of the Zarubino-Kraskino-Hunchun highway. In 1992, the Far Eastern property fund; the Far Eastern railroad management and its Vladivostok, Ussuriisk, and Khabarovsk branches; the Khasanskii region property committee; and the Transsvyaz joint-stock company created the joint-stock company Zolotoe Zveno to build the Kamyshovaya-Hunchun railroad.

Russian-Chinese working groups were set up in 1994 to develop the checkpoint Hunchun-Kraskino, which would facilitate mutual visits of Primorie and Jilin leaders. They had hoped to open the checkpoint to passenger traffic by December 1996, but in late 1997 it still did not work to full capacity. The building is ready on Hunchun's side of the border but work still continues on the Russian side. The Head of Administration of the Khasan region and Primorskii Krai Duma Deputy A. Melnichenko's efforts to find additional funds are so far in vain. The joint-stock company Zolotoe Zveno has finished construction of the railroad but still needs to create a corresponding structure to make the road functional. On the Chinese side, work was scheduled to be completed in 1997. Hunchun-Kraskino will become a transit point for Chinese goods on the way to Europe and will help make the ports of Posyet and Zarubino prosperous.

CHINA'S DEMOGRAPHIC SHADOW

Demography is the largest noncommercial factor in the Far East's relations with China. Over the past five years, the situation has been exacerbated by the existence of the Russian region's small population right next to the large population of Northeast China. In 1991, the Russian Far East's population reached its peak at 8,057,000. By 1998, however, it had decreased to 7,400,000.[11] In 1992, the population of Primorskii Krai stood at 2,309,200, but in 1996 it had fallen to 2,241,300. In Khabarovskii Krai, the figures are 1,855,400 and 1,555,500, respectively.[12] Over the past five years, a rapid decline in the number of inhabitants (about 1 percent annually) was also registered in the Republic of Sakha (Yakutia) and the Kamchatka, Magadan, Sakhalin, and Chita Oblasts.

Two-thirds of the population live in the southern zone of the Russian Far East, which covers about one-fifth of the general territory of the region. In 1996, population density in Amur Oblast and Khabarovskii and Primorskii Krais was 3.7 people per square kilometer, while in the neighboring three Chinese provinces it was 127 people per kilometer.[13] This stark contrast gives a potential international dimension to the Russian Far East's internal demographic problem and is the source of much anxiety in the Russian Far East itself.

The region's population is 87 percent ethnic Russian and Ukrainian, with all other nationalities accounting for no more than a few percentages each. As a result of Stalin's 1937 deportation of ethnic Koreans and Chinese, for several ensuing decades there were more Gypsies in the Far East than there were Chinese. According to the 1989 Soviet census, 1,742 Chinese lived in the region, primarily in Primorskii and Khabarovskii Krais and the Amur Oblast. A loosening of the border-control regime and trade development in the early 1990s led to a large Chinese influx in the region. According to some estimates, in 1990 the number of Chinese was 15,000, but in 1993 it was no less than 100,000.[14] In September 1995, China's ambassador to Russia stated at a press conference in Khabarovsk that only 170 Chinese permanently lived in Khabarovskii Krai and 87 lived in Amur Oblast.[15] In 1996, Boris Yeltsin noted during his speech in Khabarovsk that "180,000 people live illegally in this region. Most of them are Chinese citizens."[16]

In September 1993, the government of the Russian Federation issued the new decree On the Prevention and Decree of Uncontrolled Foreign Migration. Chinese account for most of the foreign migration in the Russian Far East. In order to end illegal fishing, raids were held in Primorskii Krai under the code name "Foreigner" and in

Khabarovskii Krai under the code names "Regime" and "Fishing-Amur." On the Ussuri and Amur rivers, border guards inspect not only military but also civilian Chinese ships and motorboats.

In November 1993, the decree Introduction of a Temporary Regime for Foreign Citizens Present on the Territory of Khabarovskii Krai was adopted. In January 1994, local authorities in Khabarovsk and Vladivostok announced their determination to patrol the Russian-Chinese border rigorously. As a result, several months later, the number of Chinese in the region had sharply declined. In 1994, in Khabarovskii Krai 1,580 violators (primarily Chinese) were registered. In the first half of 1996, this number was 508.[17]

In 1994, in accordance with the decree On the Further Regulation of the Presence of Foreign Citizens on the Krai's Territory, 1,657 people were arrested in Primorskii Krai. Most of them were Chinese. In 1995, 5,974 foreigners were deported from Primorie, of which 4,973 were Chinese. During the first half of 1996, 1,175 foreigners were deported, including 680 Chinese whose tourist visas had expired.[18] In April 1997, according to the press service of the Ministry of Foreign Affairs of Primorskii Krai, 60 foreigners were arrested for the violation of the passport-visa regime. Only twelve of them were Chinese and the rest were CIS (Commonwealth of Independent States) citizens from the Caucasus.[19] A decline in illegal Chinese immigration means that the adopted measures have been, in part, successful. A seasoned observer from the region must also suspect that the precipitous drop reflects payoffs and other forms of corruption.

Authorities of the Far Eastern and Pacific districts regularly meet with their Chinese colleagues from Heilongjiang Province in order to facilitate border cooperation in Khabarovskii and Primorskii Krais. Special committees of border guard representatives exchange operative information and implement intergovernmental agreements between the Federal Border Control Service of Russia and the Ministry of Defense of China, as well as the memorandum on the coordination of the customs control.

In 1993, Primorskii and Khabarovskii Krai branches of the Federal Migration Service were opened, and in September 1995 they became independent structures of the Federal Migration Service of Russia. These structures deal with issues of forced migration, containment of illegal migration, and control of the employment of foreigners.

Cooperation on employment of the Chinese labor force is actively developing.

THE BENEFITS OF CHINESE LABOR MIGRATION

Although the regional press usually focuses on the dangers of mass Chinese migration, there is another, more positive, side of the picture. Since the end of the 1980s, Primorskii Krai annually attracted about 7,000 foreign workers in accordance with intergovernmental agreements with China and Vietnam. In the beginning of the 1990s, direct barter links started to develop among local enterprises and Chinese companies. Fishing industry enterprises, for example, which invested funds in the building of housing for their workers, started to attract Chinese labor because there were no qualified Russian workers for their construction. Their services were paid for by shipments to China of fish products, mineral fertilizers, and timber, which was a mutually beneficial arrangement. An increase in the customs duties for the export of raw materials has made payments possible over the past two years. Chinese workers are employed for low wages and the quality of their work is good, so their numbers continue to increase. In 1995, 4,985 foreigners worked in construction, most of whom were Chinese.

With the introduction of market relations, local authorities lost their ability to use the free labor of high school and college students and researchers in agriculture. Thus, foreign manual labor was called to fill in a considerable hole. State and collective farms and individual farmers were forced to employ Chinese workers and lease some of the lands in the Pogranichnyi, Ussuriisk, and Khankaisk raions.

Over the past several years, business contacts between Primorskaya Hydro-Electric Power Station and Heilongjiang Province's Fortuna company have developed. About 100 Chinese experts participate in a seasonal repair of the station's energy blocks. It costs two times less to hire a Chinese installer over a Russian counterpart. In return, Russian experts assist Chinese enterprises that use Russian equipment. In the agricultural cooperative Luchegorskoe, which is a structural unit of Primorskii Hydro-Electric Power Station, Chinese workers grew vegetables, built a vegetable depository, and helped with the produce processing.[20]

In the beginning of the 1990s, Primorskii Krai developed plans to supply the Primorskii Hydro-Electric Power Station with coal from

Heilongjiang Province's deposits. Some electrical energy was supposed to be sold through the energy bridge in the Pokrovka-Zhaokhe region.[21] In October 1994, a contract with Heilongjiang Province was signed for a shipment of 250,000 tons of coal from mines in the 12-kilometer radius from the border checkpoint Poltavka. Chinese coal helped the Primorskii Krai authorities to solve the problems of the 1994–1995 heating season.

B. Poleshchuk, general manager of Dal'nergo, thinks that "coal from China is considerably cheaper than Russian coal. For one ton of Chinese coal we pay 132,000 rubles, including customs duties and taxes. At the same time, we would have to pay 300,000 rubles for a ton of coal mined in Suchan. Chinese coal also has higher heat-conductivity."[22] Primorie miners, however, categorically oppose regular imports of Chinese coal. The problem is that Primorskugol needs considerable investments to develop its own production. The Russian government is not in a hurry to finance and the local budget does not have the funds to modernize coal deposits in the region.

In December 1993, the presidential decree On Attracting and Using Foreign Labor in Russia came into effect. During the past several years, Primorskii Krai led the region in the number of foreign workers and led the country in the number of Chinese and North Korean workers. In 1995, 12,848 people worked in Primorie, including 8,349 Chinese and 3,956 North Koreans. In 1996, more than 13,500 people from twenty-nine countries worked in the region. Foreigners were involved in joint and foreign enterprises, education, and religious organizations, but the majority of them were involved in construction and agriculture.

Vladivostok attracted the majority of foreign workers. In 1994, 2,227 foreigners lived in the city. In 1995, this number increased to 3,154. It included 2,146 Chinese, 842 North Koreans, 60 Vietnamese, and 45 South Koreans.[23] In 1996, their number dropped to 2,500, including 1,250 workers from China, 800 from North Korea, and 226 from South Korea. The majority of foreigners worked in construction.[24] In 1996, 1,341 foreigners worked in Ussuriisk, 276 in Partizansk, and 206 in Artem. Most of them were Chinese.

During their stay in Russia, Chinese workers actively participate in commerce. According to the polls, in the second half of the 1990s, 75 percent of the Chinese aliens who worked in construction and agriculture also traded on Vladivostok markets.[25] Such activities cannot be controlled, and they frustrate both the Chinese traders, who have to compete with illegal traders, and Russian consumers, who are not always satisfied with the quality of goods.

RUSSIAN FEARS AND ANXIETIES REGARDING CHINA

Cultural factors play an important role in shaping Sino-Russian relations at the regional level. There are doubtless such factors on the Chinese side, but in the following sections, I want to concentrate on those on the Russian side. It is not surprising to find that Vladivostok and Khabarovsk have a different perspective on Sino-Russian relations than Moscow. In the regions, Russian-Chinese relations are not driven by geopolitical calculations and strategic considerations. People are preoccupied with pedestrian issues, such as emergency purchases of fuel, regular shipments of meat for local sausage factories, or crime. As a result, relations at the local level quite often contradict the direction and tone set in Moscow and Beijing.

While there is a growing pragmatic and mutually beneficial relationship between individual Russians and Chinese and between the businesses of both countries, national-patriotic slogans of local politicians find support among a part of the population and help fuel anti-Chinese sentiments in the border regions. According to some politicians, Moscow's pro-Chinese positions encourage the growth of Chinese migration into the Russian Far East. Claims of the number of illegal Chinese immigrants living in the region vary from tens of thousands to millions of people, depending on the sources and their political views.[26]

One could well conclude that the anti-Chinese sentiment is maintained from the top of the region down. Governor Nazdratenko actively plays the "Chinese card" in relations with the center. He has taken a vocal stand against border demarcation, speaking several times at the Federation Council and initiating resolutions by the Krai Duma, Cossacks, and other public organizations against the transfer to China of land in Ussuriisk and Khasansk regions of Primorskii Krai, as stipulated by state treaty.

On February 22, 1995, the Primorskii Krai Duma, after discussing the presentation of the krai administration, adopted the resolution On Banning the Violation of the Territorial Integrity of the Russian Federation During the Demarcation of the Russian-Chinese Border in Primorskii Krai.[27] In March 1996, the Duma decided "to consider unconstitutional the decision by the Supreme Soviet of the Russian Federation from February 13, 1992, on the ratification of the agreement from May 16, 1991, between the USSR and China on the Eastern Soviet-Chinese border."[28]

The Cossack regional union demanded a transfer of land along the eastern part of the Russian-Chinese border to the Cossack communities.[29] In April 1997, citizens of the Khasan region asked the Federal Assembly not to give away any Russian territory during the demarcation of the Russian-Chinese border in the delta of the Tumen River. The deputies claimed the transfer would harm Russia's economic interests, create geopolitical problems in the Asia-Pacific region, and cause a sharp economic decline in the Russian Far East. They adopted a resolution to collect signatures from the citizens of Primorskii Krai to support their position.[30]

The sociological service of the Department of World Politics of the Far Eastern Technical University polled 291 people. According to the result, only 7 percent approve of the demarcation process; nearly 17 percent suggest resignations of the Ministry of Foreign Affairs officials who oppose Governor Nazdratenko.[31] Nazdratenko has thus successfully incorporated xenophobia and anti-Chinese sentiments into his political toolbox, using them as frequently as he has used more traditional authoritarian methods of control.[32]

The result has been orchestrated waves of anti-Chinese sentiment, playing on the fears of the local population. One such anti-Chinese campaign in 1996 saw the publication of *The Yellow Peril*. It is, of course, not difficult to guess the book's contents from the title. It included a variety of anti-Chinese materials, including Spiridon Merkulov's 1912 speech "Russia's Business in the Far East," Vladimir Arsenyev's 1928 speech to the Far Eastern Committee of the Communist Party of Russia, a selection of articles and photographs from the newspaper *Vladivostok*, and "a brief chronology of Russia's relations with the neighboring countries of the yellow world." B. Dyachenko, editor of the book, emphasizes that—as the historical and contemporary materials show—"a yellow peril" has a long history and "is not at all outdated."[33] Nazdratenko has himself made use of this text, citing Merkulov's and Arsenyev's speeches in his own article "We Need a Culture of National Rebirth."[34] It is hard to prove that Nazdratenko himself has initiated reprinting of these materials, but it is clear that *The Yellow Peril* is his manual.

Local newspapers, such as *Vladivostok* and *Forpost Rossii* (an organ of the local branch of the Liberal Democratic Party), frequently publish anti-Chinese materials. The sensationalist newspaper *Novosti* published an article in March 1997 entitled "Will There be a War Tomorrow? Just Wait. Very Soon Primorskii Krai Could Be Dragged into a Military Conflict on the Chinese Border."[35] There is simply no shortage of official and media stimuli for nationalist and anti-Chinese popular feelings.

These feelings are showing up in public opinion polls. In 1994, the Laboratory for the Study of Public Opinion polled 869 citizens of Primorskii Krai on the issue of Russian-Chinese relations. Only 5 percent of respondents had positive feelings about the Chinese presence in Russia. More than a third expressed negative attitudes toward the Chinese presence. Half approved of Chinese as workers.[36]

In March 1997, I conducted a survey of a small group of citizens of Vladivostok—fifty people—for the Carnegie Moscow Center's project "Chinese Migration in the Russian Far East and Siberia." Half of the respondents thought that there were a lot of Chinese in the city, a third disagreed, and the rest found it difficult to respond. A total of 66 percent agreed with the notion that the region needed to attract more Chinese laborers. Only a quarter, however, thought that Chinese citizens should be allowed to buy apartments or build their own houses in the region. A large minority supported the activity of Chinese enterprises in the city and nearly all approved of Chinese trade. While 14 percent regularly buy goods from Chinese traders, 70 percent buy them sometimes and 16 percent never do. Moreover, 70 percent mentioned Chinese industriousness and 14 percent mentioned politeness among their leading positive national qualities. The existing border-control regime was approved by half, a third preferred an even stricter regime, and 16 percent wanted to close the border. Only 5 percent thought no visas would be needed. Though a very small sample, the results square with observations I have made of public attitudes throughout the region since the early 1990s.

In March 1997, the Primorskii Party was founded. According to Oleg Logunov, one of the organizers of the movement, it is a

> union of like-minded people, which includes military person-
> nel, workers, peasants, bureaucrats, businessmen, members
> of political parties and social movements, representatives of

the intelligentsia and of the Cossack movement, intellectuals, and state and municipal officials, who are all united by only one desire—to protect the interests of Primorie, and interests of the whole country as far as border demarcation is concerned.[37]

Nazdratenko's antidemarcation campaign has support in Moscow. In March 1997, a special issue of the journal *Politika* was issued in Moscow supporting Nazdratenko's approach. The editor-in-chief of *Politika* wrote, "It boils down to the fact that the Governor of Primorskii Krai, Yevgeniy Ivanovich Nazdratenko, and his supporters in Primorie are the only ones who create Russia's outpost on the Pacific ocean shores. Nobody in the center wants to help him or even make his task a little easier."[38]

Other regional voices have joined the campaign. Major General Rozov, retired, attacked the Ministry of Foreign Affairs in his article "Demarcation—One More Pain of Primorie." A. Polusmak, chairman of the Committee on the Defense Industry of Primorskii Krai, and V. Orlvov, the committee's leading expert, insist that "the Russian Far East is an object of constant foreign expansion from the neighboring states, China in particular."[39] The demarcation process became grounds for the regional elite's insistence on the supremacy of its opinion in finding solutions to territorial disputes, thereby attempting to redistribute power in its favor. Despite the strength of this orchestrated campaign, it could not disrupt demarcation, which was virtually completed at the end of 1997. The remaining disagreements over islands near Khabarovsk have been left for the future by both parties. But if local political pressure could not alter the official course of Russian-Chinese relations, it could still make the practical realization of that course in the region quite difficult.

KEEPING THE DOOR CLOSED

One final factor deserves note: the region's predisposition to shutting out the outside world. For several decades, Vladivostok and other cities of Primorskii Krai were closed to foreign citizens. The entire region was not a window to Asia but the first line of defense against the outside world. Restrictions eased up under Gorbachev. In September 1988, the USSR Council of Ministers issued a decree that allowed foreigners to visit the closed cities and regions with the permission of the Ministry of Defense as well as from the Committee on National Security. In 1987, sixty foreign delegations visited Vladivostok. By 1989, there were 1,150 such delegations. The city was officially "opened" in January 1992, but the region still has some closed zones (Fokino, Putyatin, and Dunai) in accordance with the law of the Russian Federation from June 14, 1992, On Closed Territorial-Administrative Entities.

Yet, to date, the dominant impulse in Primorskii Krai is to restrict access, not to open up. In October 1994 and May 1995, the Primorskii Krai administration adopted the decree On Further Regulation of the Foreign Citizens' Stay on the Territory of the Region, Including Citizens of the Former Republics of the USSR, People without Citizenship, and People without a Permanent Place of Residence, Who Are Temporarily Present in Primorskii Krai. In October 1995, the Primorskii Krai Duma passed the rules for foreign citizens who stay on the region's territory.[40]

Given the difficult economic times, many regional authorities believe that retaining a closed status is the best way to preserve economic prosperity and keep subsidies flowing from the government. In July 1996, the formerly closed city of Bol'shoy Kamen' returned to closed status. Arsen'ev very much wants to be a closed city again. Under this special arrangement, entry is restricted, the local budget is formed from taxes collected on its territory, and the deficit is covered by different subsidies from the federal budget.

CONCLUSION

This essay has focused on several factors shaping Sino-Russian relations at the regional level: economic trends, structural impediments at the border and in the transportation system, demographic imbalances and the related anxieties they cause, Russian cultural and social attitudes toward the Chinese, and a continuing predisposition toward keeping the doors closed to the outside world. One could also cite the debilitating effects of Russian economic decline, the political competition between center and regions and between various factions in both, and a host of other factors. In the late 1990s, the "Chinese theme" is still used by regional elites to fight with Moscow for the redistribution of power. Local authorities, especially in Primorskii Krai, are not interested in the expansion of relations with China, demanding instead greater independence in political, economic, and foreign policy. The result is the crisis that deeply afflicts the Russian Far East, my home region. I fear that until the center and region reach a stable and enduring understanding on political and economic policy, we will not be able to get the region moving again, take advantage of the opportunities offered by our Chinese neighbors, or work together to manage the potential challenges these same neighbors present to Russia and the world.

NOTES

[1]*Zavtra Rossii*, May 17–24, 1996, p. 19.

[2]Primorskii Krai Committee on State Statistics, *Sotsial'no-ekonomicheskoe razvitie svobodnoy ekonomicheskoy zony v 1995 godu* (Socioeconomic Development of the Free Economic Zone in 1995) (Vladivostok: Primorskii Krai Committee on State Statistics, 1996), p. 12.

[3]Ibid., p. 13.

[4]*Izvestiya Tikhookeanskoi Rossii*, August 1996, p. 5.

[5]See Pavel Minakic, "Integratsia Rossiyskogo Dalnego Vostoka v ATR i SVA: vozmozhnosti i realnosti," and Pyotr Baklanov, "Kontaktnye Struktury i funktsii vrazvitii integratsionnykh processor v basseyne Yaponskovo morya," in Galina Vitkovskaya and Dmitri Trenin, eds., *Perspektivy Dalnevostochnogo Regiona Rossii. Mezhstranovye vzaimodeystvia*, Carnegie Moscow Center (Moscow: Gendalf, 1999), pp. 11–22, 23–42.

[6]P. A. Minakir, *Dal'niy vostok Rossii: ekonomicheskoe obozrenie* (Russian Far East: Economic Review) (Khabarovsk: Institute for Economic Research, Far Eastern Branch, Russian Academy of Sciences, 1995), p. 220.

[7]*Utro Rossii*, February 5, 1997, p. 3.

[8]*Tikhookeanskaya zvezda*, March 29, 1997, p. 2.

[9]Ibid.

[10]*Vestnik Prigranichya*, March 28, 1997, p. 3.

[11]Gomkomstat (Russian State Committee on Statistics) figures. Quoted in "Perspektivy Dalnevostochnogo regiona: naselenie, migratsia, rynki truda" working paper (Carnegie Moscow Center Working Papers, Moscow), issue 2, 1999, p. 19.

[12]Minakir, pp. 350–52.

[13]Institute of Economy and Population Forecast, Center for Demography and Ecology of Population, *Naselenie Rossii 1996* (Russia's Population 1996) (Moscow: Institute of Economy and Population Forecast, Center for Demography and Ecology of Population, 1997), p. 141.

[14]L. L. Rybakovskii, O. D. Zakharova, and V. V. Mindrogulov, *Nelegal'naya migratsiya v prigranichnykh rayonakh Dal'nego Vostoka: istoriya, sovremennost' i posledstviya* (Illegal Migration in Border Regions of the Far East: History,

Present Day, and Consequences) (Moscow: Institute of Socio-Political Research, 1994), pp. 15, 19.

[15]*Dalniy Vostok*, September 17–23, 1995, p. 1.

[16]*Tikhookeanskaya zvezda*, April 25, 1996, p. 3.

[17]Ibid., June 12, 1996, p. 2.

[18]*Krasnoe znamya*, July 25, 1996, p. 2.

[19]*Vladivostok*, April 29, 1997, p. 3.

[20]*Krasnoe znamya*, June 24, 1995, p. 1.

[21]*Utro Rossii*, March 19, 1996, p. 1.

[22]*Vladivostok*, November 30, 1996, p. 3.

[23]Yu. Kazakov, "Vladivostok Labor Market," *Sociological Research*, no. 7 (1996), p. 113.

[24]*Utro Rossii*, December 15, 1996, p. 11.

[25]E. Plaksen, "Whom Do Chinese Pay for Their Safety in Primorie?" *Izvestiya Tikhookeanskoi Rossii*, April 23–May 23, 1997, p. 12.

[26]For a reliable estimate on numbers of Chinese migrants to the region, see the article by Vitkovskaya, Zayonchkovskaya, and Newland in this volume.

[27]*Vedomosti Dumy Primorskogo Kraya* (Vladivostok), no. 5 (1995), pp. 66–67.

[28]Ibid., no. 18 (1996), p. 18.

[29]*Ussuriiskii Kazchii Vestnik*, April 1997, p. 4.

[30]*Vedomosti Dumy Primorskogo Kraya* (Vladivostok), no. 45 (1997), p. 31.

[31]*Ussuriiskii Kazchii Vestnik*, April 1997, p. 4.

[32]P. Kirkow, "Regional Warlordism in Russia: The Case of Primorskii Krai," *Europe-Asia Studies*, no. 6 (1995), pp. 923–47; Tamara Troyakova, "Regional Policy in the Russian Far East and the Rise of Localism in Primorie," *The Journal of East Asian Affairs* (Seoul), no. 2 (Summer-Fall 1995), pp. 428–61; Tamara Troyakova, "Formirovanie pravyashchey gruppirovki v Primor'e" (The Formation of the Ruling Elite in Primorie), *Rossia i ATR* (Vladivostok), no. 3 (1996), pp. 65–72.

[33]*Zheltaya opasnost'* (The Yellow Threat) (Vladivostok: Voron, 1996), pp. 119–24.

[34]*Vladivostok*, April 15, 1997, p. 7.

[35]*Novosti*, March 18, 1997, p. 2.

[36]E. A. Plaksen, "Otchet rezul'tatakh oprosa, provedennogo v 1994 g" (Results of a 1994 Poll), author's manuscript. Only 6 percent responded that they were not sure, and 3 percent gave no answer.

[37]*Vladivostok*, March 13, 1997, p. 5.

[38]T. Grosmani, "Primorie—a Part of Greater Russia," *Politika* (March 1997), p. 3.

[39]Ibid., p. 29.

[40]*Vedomosti Dumy Primorskogo Kraya* (Vladivostok), no. 12 (1995), pp. 14–15.

9
Chinese Perspectives on Cross-Border Relations

Elizabeth Wishnick

Despite the development of a much-hailed strategic partnership between Russia and China in the mid-1990s, regional issues have introduced new irritants in Sino-Russian relations. With the rapid opening of border trade in the early 1990s, numerous problems surfaced in Sino-Russian regional relations, among them difficulties with border trade and controversies over border demarcation and illegal immigration. Because of the importance of stable regional relations for the continued development of the bilateral relationship, regional relations now occupy a prominent position on the bilateral agenda.

As in Russia, economic liberalization in China has enabled provincial elites to take greater initiative in formulating a foreign economic policy agenda serving regional interests. Greater autonomy in economic policy making at the provincial level has made it more difficult for the authorities at the national level to implement consistent foreign economic policies, however.

More and more, in cases ranging from intellectual property rights to foreign trade, national leaders in Beijing have had to deal with regional officials with differing priorities.[1] In the case of cross-border relations with Russia, the measures taken by Heilongjiang provincial leaders focusing on regional development needs often ran at cross-purposes with national interests in standardizing foreign trade practices in preparation for China's entry into the WTO as well as in reducing irritants in Sino-Russian bilateral relations.

Because of the importance of regional politics in the Russian Federation in general and the publicity accorded to problems in Sino-Russian regional relations in the Russian media in particular, Russian concerns over regional problems in relations with China are better known. Russian residents in the border regions complain about the poor quality of goods sold by Chinese traders and the crime associated with the markets that cater to them. Journalists and politicians in Moscow and the border regions have come up with conspiracy theories about China's intentions in the Russian Far East. Armed with few facts, they have claimed that millions of Chinese intend to immigrate to Russia, according to a policy allegedly planned by officials in Beijing. Regional officials in the Russian Far East have called for the renunciation of the 1991 Border Demarcation Treaty and have warned against cooperating with Beijing in the Tumen River area development plan.

The Chinese have their share of complaints as well, although they have not aired them as vocally as their Russian counterparts. Officials and scholars lament the dwindling supply of Russian goods for export, as well as the changing trade rules in Russia. They point to difficulties caused by a shift to hard currency in cross-border trade and problems in enforcing contracts because of the lack of interbank and arbitration agreements. Chinese observers, especially in Beijing, have been extremely critical of the chaos resulting from the heating up of border trade in the early 1990s. Because these problems have damaged the reputation of Chinese goods and introduced new complications into Sino-Russian relations, Chinese central government officials have sharply criticized the management of cross-border trade at the provincial level and imposed new administrative measures to regulate it.

This chapter will explore Chinese perspectives on problems in Sino-Russian regional relations, focusing on relations between Heilongjiang Province, the Chinese region with the longest border with Russia, and its neighbors in the Russian Far East. I argue here that many of the problems afflicting Sino-Russian border trade are economic in nature. The chapter shows that Heilongjiang's attempts to resolve its economic problems by expanding border trade with Russia have led to unintended economic and political consequences, which have introduced complications in Sino-Russian bilateral relations as well as in relations between Heilongjiang and Beijing. With the exception of cooperation in military technology, space, and nuclear power, most of the planned joint economic projects and a significant proportion of trade and investment have been targeted in the border regions. As a result, unresolved problems in regional relations may limit the future development of Sino-Russian economic relations as well as sow distrust in political and military ties.

Misperceptions on both sides have made it more difficult for Russia and China to resolve their regional problems. Cross-border issues with political ramifications, such as Russian complaints about alleged Chinese illegal immigration and the inequities of the 1991 Border Demarcation Treaty, tend to be minimized in the Chinese press. While censorship may be partly responsible for this, there is also a tendency, most pronounced in Beijing, to downplay the importance of regional problems for bilateral relations and to overestimate the prospects for regional cooperation.

If Russian observers often underestimate the influence of economic problems on China's handling of border trade, many Chinese analysts pay insufficient attention to the foreign policy consequences of regional politics in the Russian Far East. To a large extent, Chinese and Russians are talking past each other, ultimately limiting the ability of both sides to resolve outstanding problems in cross-border relations. Contiguous territories are not automatically "natural" trading partners, and, while there are many potential areas of economic cooperation between the Russian and Chinese border regions, a solid foundation for economic relations is unlikely to be realized without greater willingness on both sides to confront areas of discord more dispassionately.

HEILONGJIANG PROVINCE AND THE OPENING OF CROSS-BORDER TRADE

The Chinese Northeast is China's earliest industrialized area and, in fact, many of its ailing industries were built with Soviet assistance in the 1950s. Heilongjiang alone has 22 of a total of 156 of these firms, including industrial giants in the machine-building sector such as the Harbin First Automobile Factory, and the province depends on cooperative projects with Russian aid for their renovation.[2]

In addition to having a preponderance of large factories in heavy industry, especially in the defense sector,[3] these regions are some of China's top resource producers. Many of these resource industries are part of China's planned economy, however, making it difficult for the Chinese border regions to raise revenue by boosting exports. Heilongjiang, for example, is rich in oil, timber, and coal, but much of these resources go directly to Beijing, where they are eventually parceled off to other provinces, only to return to Heilongjiang as finished products. The province loses in such exchanges because the state assigns oil an artificially low price in these transactions, while manufactured goods are overpriced.[4]

Although economic growth from 1978 to 1992 averaged 5.8 percent in Heilongjiang Province and 8.3 percent in neighboring Jilin Province (as opposed to 12 percent in China's southern coastal areas), central government support for these areas declined during this period.[5] While economic growth has climbed dramatically in Jilin in the 1990s, it has remained stagnant in Heilongjiang because of the province's continued dependence on noncompetitive resource-producing industries. Town and village enterprises are weakly developed in the province because of the lack of financial support from the central government and their inability to compete for raw materials with state-owned enterprises.[6] Throughout the Northeast, inadequate infrastructure and an undeveloped service sector have made it more difficult to diversify industry by developing joint ventures.[7]

As a consequence, underemployment is a significant problem in cities like Harbin, where ailing state enterprises struggle to pay idle workers. In the absence of a major commitment by Beijing to industrial restructuring, these factories can only hope for interim measures, such as the additional central government contracts promised by Prime Minister Li Peng to one ailing enterprise, the Harbin Turbine Works, during his high-profile visit to Heilongjiang in July 1996.[8] These are patchwork solutions, however, and in the meantime Harbin's surplus workers are left to their own devices. Many take their tools and congregate on the streets, where they wait for piecework or work as bicycle repairmen.[9]

Given the intractability of Heilongjiang's economic woes, provincial officials have experimented with foreign trade as a means of boosting the province's level of economic development. Like the Russian border regions, the border areas in the Chinese Northeast have sought the decentralization of foreign trade to achieve greater economic autonomy.[10] Heilongjiang Province officials, for example, took advantage of Beijing's Open Door policy to put forward a proposal to spur economic development through border trade with Russia. China's central government has welcomed these efforts as long as they have kept in step with China's Moscow policy.

THE OPENING OF HEILONGJIANG'S TRADE WITH THE NORTH

During an August 1982 visit to Heilongjiang, CCP General Secretary Hu Yaobang gave official sanction to provincial efforts to reopen Sino-Russian border crossing points.[11] Hu Yaobang's trip took place two years after Deng Xiaoping opened the first three special economic zones in Shenzhen, Xiamen, and Shantou in the southern coastal region in 1980. Hu traveled all along the Sino-Soviet border, stopping in Manzhouli in Inner Mongolia; then in Heihe, Tongjiang, Fuyuan, and Suifenhe in Heilongjiang Province; and finally in Hunchun and Tumen in Jilin Province.

In Heihe, Hu Yaobang gave a speech in which he noted that Shenzhen had already opened to the outside world and raised the issue of opening China's North, too. He stated that "Shenzhen in the South, Heihe in the North—they should take off side by side" (*nan shen, bei hei, biyi qifei*). Residents of Heihe were enthusiastic about Hu's visit and speech. During the 1983 Chinese New Year celebration, when they hung the traditional red streamers on their front doors, instead of a couplet about prosperity they wrote the words from Hu's speech referring to Heihe as the next Shenzhen.

After a sixteen-year suspension, Soviet-Chinese border trade resumed on April 10, 1983, when agreements were signed reestablishing economic links between Heilongjiang and the Soviet Far East, and Inner Mongolia and Siberia.[12] Subsequently, several leading economists, as well as representatives from the Ministry of Foreign Trade, were invited to visit the border regions and to participate in three-month study tours of the Sino-Soviet border in the winters of 1983 and 1984. They met with local officials and residents and discussed how to open border crossing points with the Soviet Union, how to reach out to their "Soviet friends," and how the Northeast should respond to the Open Door issue in general. In August 1984, Hu Yaobang returned to the province. During this second inspection tour, the Chinese leader offered his recommendations for the development of the border regions.[13]

The Heilongjiang government next put together a proposal about opening the northern border regions, which involved initially opening four border ports each on the Chinese and Russian sides, and then opening additional ports in stages. These four ports, which would face each other, would be opened to two types of trade: trade by the residents of the border regions and regional trade by regional governments and large enterprises.

Because Sino-Soviet relations had only just begun to improve in the early 1980s and many outstanding problems remained, the Heilongjiang government convened a meeting in Harbin about Sino-Soviet border trade. The economists and officials who had traveled to the border regions as a part of study groups in 1983 and 1984 attended, and other specialists from a wide variety of fields (economics, politics, transportation, and so on) joined them in a meeting on border trade in Heihe in 1985. The group agreed that the border areas should be opened to trade and suggested starting with Heihe and the city across the Amur River from it, Blagoveshchensk, the capital of Amurskaya Oblast. The first steps involved opening the two cities to border trade, permitting border trade to take place, and developing transportation links between the two cities. Because of the legacy of Sino-Soviet confrontation, at the time there were no flights between Heihe and Blagoveshchensk, and the rail line from Harbin only went as far as Beian, a 200-kilometer drive to Heihe along a dirt road.

As a result of this meeting, the group came up with the concept that would become Heilongjiang's foreign trade strategy: "link with the South, open to the North, open up to development in all directions" (*nan lian bei kai, quan fangwei kaifang*).[14] The idea behind it was to open border trade with the Soviet Union and create new transportation and trade links within China so that goods produced in the South could be finished and then sold in the North.

After the specialists in Heilongjiang Province were in agreement about the goals and means of opening the border, provincial officials met in Beijing to discuss the matter further. More than 200 specialists were invited, including officials from the State Council, the Foreign Ministry, and the Ministries of Foreign Trade and Customs. After the Beijing conference, the State Council asked the Heilongjiang government to write a formal proposal. This report was sent to First Deputy Prime Minister Yao Yilin, who signed it with the notation "completely approve."

Once the Heilongjiang proposal was accepted, the issue was handed over to the State Council, and Yao Yilin began negotiating with his Soviet counterparts. As the Heilongjiang experts had proposed, initially four pairs of cities were opened in August 1985: Heihe/Blagoveshchensk; Suifenhe/Grodekovo; Tongjiang/Nizhneleninskoe; and Manzhouli/Zabaikalsk.[15]

This case shows a serious provincial effort under the most favorable circumstances. The Chinese government had already approved a general policy of opening foreign trade and was cautiously moving toward improved relations with the Soviet Union. Under these conditions, Heilongjiang officials worked to make the best case possible for reopening regional economic relations. Calling on a wide range of experts and striving for consensus both in the province and in policy circles in Beijing, provincial officials were able to succeed in convincing the central leadership of the benefits of developing border trade by opening border crossing points in the Northeast. As cross-border trade flourished, the number of frontier trading ports in Heilongjiang grew to eighteen, and Harbin, Jiamusi, and Fujin were designated inland ports—a total of twenty-one ports.[16]

THERE IS NO LIMIT TO BORDER TRADE

While Sino-Russian border trade has had a palpable impact on the development of bilateral relations, its expansion had more to do with efforts to resolve pressing economic problems on both sides of the border than with regional attempts to participate in foreign policy. Heilongjiang's foreign trade strategy, for example, initially was designed to redress two types of disparities: (1) the lag in the rate of growth between China's border provinces and coastal areas, and (2) the gap in the standard of living between Heilongjiang's border districts and the rest of the province.

Just as Hu Yaobang made an explicit connection between China's Open Door policy for southern coastal areas and the opening of border trade with the Soviet Union, so have Heilongjiang provincial officials and scholars compared the conditions and prospects for foreign trade in coastal and border areas. They noted the coastal areas' advantages, including a higher technological level, more competitive market, and export orientation of coastal areas, which have enabled them to attract investment. They argued that while the border areas lacked these advantages, provinces such as Heilongjiang had other strengths: abundant natural resources, a strong agricultural base, and a large labor supply. While the province worked on making its market more competitive, it could focus on cooperative projects, especially with the Soviet Union, which would involve contracts for exports of labor and technology and would highlight barter trade.[17] As cross-border trade has flourished, the number of frontier trading ports in Heilongjiang has grown to a current total of twenty-five, with Harbin, Jiamusi, and Fujin designated as inland ports.

The assumption behind this policy is that the economic complementarity between the Chinese Northeast and the Russian Far East fosters favorable conditions for cross-border trade and economic cooperation between them. Because the Russian border regions have a labor shortage and depend on imports of agricultural products, Heilongjiang, for example, could fulfill these needs and receive in return needed products such as machinery, chemical fertilizer, and steel. Such exchanges would be mutually beneficial, but in practice they have proved difficult to do.

Indeed, the complementary nature of the economies of the Russian Far East and the Chinese Northeast has often been overstated. These regions share many of the same economic problems and conditions—both facing the need to restructure ailing enterprises, especially in the defense sector, with little hope of attracting necessary investment either from within their respective countries or from abroad. Moreover, as the final section will show, cross-border economic cooperation has been complicated by differing perceptions of the costs and benefits of cooperation in the Russian Far East and the Chinese Northeast.

Nonetheless, initially the Chinese border regions, especially Heilongjiang Province, were very enthusiastic about the potential for developing Sino-Russian cross-border trade on a mutually beneficial basis. According to the "link with the South, open to the North" strategy devised in the mid-1980s, Heilongjiang opened its borders to trade with Russia, its northern neighbor, while also fostering transportation and trade links with the southern coastal areas. Expanding economic connections with the South is crucial to the province's trade strategy, since, according to an official in the Heilongjiang provincial government, only some 20 percent of goods exported to Russia are produced in the province. Typically, Heilong-jiang imports unfinished goods, such as clothing, toys, and electronic goods, from southern provinces, which are then finished and packed in the border regions for export to Russia.[18]

In the early 1990s, Heilongjiang Governor Du Xianzong high-lighted the importance of border trade. "Borders are limits, but there's no limit to border trade" (*bianjing you bian, bianmao wu bian*) became his rallying cry. Although officials originally hoped that border trade would boost the province's economy as a whole, its main impact has been on its nineteen border districts.[19] As a conse-quence of these new economic ties with the South and the opening of border trade, the standard of living has greatly improved in the border regions. These had been some of the province's poorest counties because, during the twenty years of Sino-Soviet tensions, they suffered from a lack of investment and infrastructure.[20] From 1988 to 1995, however, average income in these areas increased from 400 yuan to 2,000 yuan.[21] Now the standard of living in some areas of the border districts reportedly is higher than in Harbin, and border cities like Suifenhe, previously the recipient of large subsidies from Beijing, are now net contributors to the central government budget.[22]

The boom in border trade in the early 1990s not only reinvigorated the economies in the border areas but also began to have a significant impact on the Sino-Russian trade balance. In 1993, for example, Heilongjiang Province's border trade with Russia accounted for one-third of the Sino-Russian trade balance of $7.68 billion.[23] In 1994, however, trade plummeted to $5.1 billion, a 34 percent drop overall and a 22 percent drop in Heilongjiang Province.

Trade regained some of its earlier momentum, reaching $5.5 billion in 1995 and $7.2 billion in 1996, but it has yet to reach its 1993 record high. Although Jiang Zemin and Boris Yeltsin pledged at their April 1996 summit to achieve $20 billion in trade by the year 2000, this appears to be a remote possibility. Sino-Russian trade actually fell by 20 percent in the first eight months of 1997 and, by the end of the year, reached $6.12 billion, still short of the 1996 level. In 1998, trade between Russia and China continued its decline to $5.48 billion, a 10 percent drop from 1997, reflective of crises in Russia and Asia.[24]

Since the precipitous fall in border trade, Chinese economists and officials have been trying to understand the causes of its rapid development and decline.[25] They have noted that the boom in border trade was unsustainable because it was sparked by a very specific set of circumstances: the acute need in the Russian border regions for consumer goods and food products produced in Heilongjiang and the other Chinese border regions, due to the collapse of the Soviet economic system in 1990–1991.

The Soviet economy was highly centralized and specialized, and, as a result, when the central planning and economic distribution system collapsed in 1990–1991, the Russian Far East faced desperate economic conditions. Economic links with other areas of the former USSR were disrupted and the Russian Far East experienced particularly severe shortages of food products and consumer goods. Central investment funds were cut off and the regions were unable to raise sufficient tax revenues to compensate. Even promised central funds did not come—in 1991, for example, the Russian Far East received only 30 percent of promised subsidies from Moscow.[26]

The rapid devolution of economic responsibility to the regions did not achieve the desired end—self-supporting regions—because this strategy assumed that they would maintain economic stability.[27] Changes in relative prices, however, especially due to the dramatic rise in transportation costs, drove up the cost of primary inputs and production in the Russian Far East. The region's defense, machine-building, and resource industries fell dramatically and more sharply than in other areas of Russia. In the early 1990s, as the economic situation deteriorated, separatist trends began to develop in the Russian Far East.[28] Some more radical political leaders proposed the creation of an independent Far Eastern republic. Most political leaders, however, favored compensating for the central government's neglect with increased economic autonomy. They developed the slogan "There's no money, give us freedom" (*net deneg, daete svobodu*).[29] If Moscow was unable or unwilling to provide sufficient revenue for the regions, then the regional leaders sought the freedom to seek funds elsewhere, as they saw fit.

The rapid development of border trade with China was one the most dramatic consequences of this new regional policy. In 1992–1993, Sino-Russian border trade began to boom and relieved many of the shortages in consumer goods and food products in the Russian border regions. This boom had a big impact on the volume of Sino-Russian trade, which jumped from U.S.$3.9 billion in 1991 to U.S.$5.8 billion in 1992 and then to U.S.$7.68 billion in 1993. In the early 1990s, border trade, carried out through barter, represented an increasingly large share of the total volume.[30]

THE LIMITATIONS OF CROSS-BORDER TRADE

By 1993, however, the structure of exports and imports in the Russian border regions began to change. While in the early 1990s the Russian border regions exported machinery and equipment, by 1993–1994 raw materials accounted for the bulk of exports to China. In the early 1990s, much of the machinery and equipment exports from the Russian border regions were reexports from elsewhere in Russia. In 1993–1994, tariffs on rail transportation increased at the same time as industrial production continued to fall in the Russian Far East, which led to a diminished supply of machinery and equipment in the border regions for export.[31]

By 1993, low-cost and often low-quality Chinese goods saturated the consumer goods market in the Russian Far East. Higher priced Korean and Japanese goods became more attractive to the increasingly differentiated consumers in the Russian border regions. Consequently, demand for Chinese consumer goods fell. This trend coincided with complaints in the Russian border regions that their exports of raw materials were underpriced in barter trade. The shift to hard currency dealings in border trade, at the same time as the PRC was carrying out currency reform, caused additional dislocations.

Moreover, in 1993–1994, the Chinese government implemented tighter controls on the economy, resulting in decreased investment and reduced capital construction. Because construction materials were an important source of Chinese imports from the Russian border regions, the change in Chinese economic policy also adversely affected Sino-Russian border trade.[32] The Chinese government reimposed quotas on other key Chinese imports from the Russian Far East, such as vehicles, chemical fertilizer, and steel.[33] According to one Chinese specialist, these economic measures not only made border trade less attractive but also made it difficult for firms to fulfill existing contracts.[34]

Chinese observers in Beijing and the border regions optimistically refer to the current stage in Sino-Russian border trade as one of transition (*guodu*) and adjustment (*tiaozheng*).[35] In their view, the main problems that have prevented border trade from fulfilling its promised potential are economic and administrative and, therefore, potentially resolvable.

Economic Problems

Complaints about the quality of Chinese goods are of greatest concern to both Heilongjiang provincial officials and policy makers in Beijing. China's Ministry of Foreign Trade, in particular, has contended that the poor-quality goods traded in the Russian Far East and brought into Moscow and other Russian cities by shuttle traders have undermined the reputation of Chinese goods in general, as well as China's value as a trading partner.[36] In fact, officials in Beijing have echoed many of the complaints heard in the Russian Far East about the inadequate sanitary standards for Chinese foodstuffs, as well as their contamination by pesticides and other pollutants, and the poor quality of Chinese exports of clothing and children's toys.[37]

While there is widespread agreement in the border regions and in Beijing about the need to improve quality controls and inspections, observers in Heilongjiang note that the problem is not just on the Chinese side. They admit that Chinese merchants may be guilty of producing and selling shoddy and counterfeit goods but argue that Russian shuttle traders at times seek out the cheapest goods for resale in Russia. Policing the border for shipments of low-quality goods will require efforts by both sides. Some analysts in Heilongjiang argue that it is the Russian side that should be faulted for its lack of thoroughness in customs and quality-control inspections, usually done by hand, while Chinese border controls use X-ray equipment.[38]

Although the production of low-quality goods in Northeast China may have deep-seated causes, some of the financial problems with border trade are truly transitional and reflect a lag between institutional development and the expansion of foreign trade.[39] In June 1995, at the regular meeting of the Sino-Russian Committee on Economic and Scientific-Technical Cooperation, Russia and China decided that bilateral trade should use hard currency rather than barter.[40] The share of barter trade has been diminishing: while it accounted for almost 60 percent of Sino-Russian trade in 1993, barter transactions dropped to 49 percent of the trade volume in 1994 and to just 28 percent in 1995.[41]

Although the switch to hard currency resolved some Russian complaints about the undervaluing of their resources in barter trade, a range of new problems soon emerged. The dearth of interbank agreements on credit between the Russian Far East and the Chinese Northeast forced trading companies either to complete transactions by sending their representatives with large amounts of cash—thereby putting them at risk of crime—or to resort to cumbersome methods such as using banks in third countries. So far, few interbank agreements have been signed. Among the first were agreements between the Nongye Bank in Heihe and the Amur Commercial Bank in Blagoveshchensk and between the Harbin branch of the China Investment Bank and Regiobank in Khabarovsk. The Russian banks involved are very small, however, and many Chinese businesspeople have continued to prefer more established banks in third countries.[42] Two larger Russian banks, Rossiyskiy Kredit and Inkombank, opened branches in China to improve the conditions for mutual payment, but these went bankrupt after the August 1998 financial crisis. In December, however, a Primorskii Krai bank, Dalrybank, opened a ruble-based correspondent account with China Investment Bank in Harbin to facilitate trade.[43]

The lack of arbitration mechanisms has made it difficult to resolve claims from both the Russian and Chinese sides about nonfulfillment of contracts and nonpayment. With no legal recourse available, Chinese and Russian businesspeople at times have resorted to criminal means, such as hiring the Russian mafia to enforce contracts or hiring Chinese criminals to kidnap Russian traders who refused to pay their Chinese partners. In July 1996, China's Committee for the Promotion on International Trade and Russia's Industry and Trade Committee signed an arbitration agreement, but, according to a senior Chinese specialist, it lacks the enforcement power that a bilateral agreement would have.[44]

Administrative Issues

Apart from undermining the reputation of Chinese goods, border trade has been criticized equally sharply, especially in Beijing, for creating chaos on China's borders. Throughout the 1980s, the liberalization of foreign trade was a controlled process, but in the early 1990s in Heilongjiang and other border provinces it turned into a mad rush to the Russian border. Established trading companies found themselves competing with small-scale, often inexperienced (and sometimes shady) businesspeople who undercut their prices. These small companies often had difficulty meeting the terms of contracts and sometimes sold counterfeit or poor-quality goods.

Officials and scholars in Beijing and Harbin have described the environment on their northern border in the early 1990s as chaotic (*hunluan*). China's Foreign Ministry has criticized Heilongjiang Province, in particular, for indiscriminately handing out thousands of passports allocated to the province for use in foreign trade.[45]

Many Chinese specialists on Sino-Russian trade noted that the authorities became concerned about a loss of government control to what one Beijing scholar referred to as anarchistic (*wuzhengfu*) elements in the border regions.[46] Moreover, Chinese officials, fearing that these small-scale traders were harming the reputation of Chinese goods, reportedly criticized the border provinces for inadequately administering border trade.[47]

Much to the frustration of people in Heilongjiang, the province's border trade with Russia has come under particular scrutiny from Beijing, although Inner Mongolia and Jilin Province have been involved as well and experienced similar problems. According to a *Heilongjiang Ribao* journalist's account of border trade in Suifenhe, the problem of shuttle trade has been perceived unfairly as a "Heilongjiang phenomenon," since more than 80 percent of the traders at the market there were from areas outside Heilongjiang.[48]

Lapses in Political Leadership

Problems with border trade coincided with a period of economic disarray and social instability in Heilongjiang. Reform of the province's state industries proved intractable and increasingly workers took to the streets to protest against low pay and poor working conditions.[49] The central leadership in Beijing became very concerned about the problems in the province and sent high-level delegations to evaluate the situation. In September 1993, a delegation from the National Committee of the People's Congress traveled to Heilongjiang on an inspection tour.[50] Later that year, as problems with cross-border trade became more apparent, Du Xianzong, the deputy governor and the official most connected to the province's policy of expanding trade with Russia, retired.

In January 1994, Politburo members Li Ruihan and Hu Jintao arrived in Harbin for an inspection tour, and in March provincial leaders were asked to make a report to Jiang Zemin on the province's problems.[51] More leadership changes were to follow, and, in April 1995, Zhu Rongji headed an inspection tour that culminated in the removal of the province's party secretary and governor.[52] Yue Qifeng, the former governor of Heilongjiang's more prosperous neighbor, Liaoning Province, was made party secretary and soon announced a new reform program.[53]

THE CONTRASTING VIEWS OF BEIJING AND HARBIN

Like Moscow, Beijing became concerned when problems in regional economic relations began to surface as topics in bilateral meetings. Although the Chinese authorities kept silent on the initial spate of articles in the Russian press in 1993 that complained about the poor quality of Chinese goods, illegal immigration, and the controversy over border demarcation, by 1994 Chinese officials began to speak out.

One of the problems stemming from the decision by Deng Xiaoping and Mikhail Gorbachev in May 1989 to put the past behind them and look to the future of their relations is that the context for problems has been pushed to the background. Although Russian scholars recently have reexamined the history of the "yellow peril," for example, few Chinese scholars note the continuity in regional tensions.[54] Given the continued sensitivity of coverage of Sino-Russian relations, in published articles most Chinese specialists shy away from direct discussion of problems with political overtones.

Problems with Expanded Cross-Border Exchanges

During a visit to Moscow in late June 1994, for example, Foreign Minister Qian Qichen blamed problems in border trade on the activities of a small number of criminals and affirmed that China has never condoned illegal immigration across the border. Qian stated that "what the Chinese Government wants to support and protect are legal and orderly economic and trade activities and the legitimate rights and interests of citizens engaged in this kind of proper trade."[55]

In 1994, the Chinese undertook two surveys of problems in the border regions. One was a joint Sino-Russian mission and the other was a study tour of border crossing points, including Heihe and Manzhouli, by members of the Institute of Contemporary International Relations, the Foreign Ministry, and the Ministry of Foreign Trade. As a result of these surveys, the Chinese side concluded that Sino-Russian border trade lacked order (*wuxu*) and that the main problem was its inadequate administration.[56]

For the most part, Chinese officials and scholars in Beijing and Harbin minimize the problem of illegal immigration and accuse the Russian press of exaggerating it.[57] Some leading scholars also attribute these sentiments to efforts by pro-West political actors in Russia to reorient Russian foreign policy toward the West.[58]

Nonetheless, specialists who are more familiar with Russian regional politics note the connection between the allegations of Chinese immigration to the Russian Far East and center-regional tensions within Russia.[59] Others relate the criticism of Chinese traders in the Russian Far East and of the border demarcation treaty to rising nationalist sentiment that coincided with Russian election campaigns.[60] According to an official at China's Moscow Embassy, agreement on the demarcation of the border was important to support orderly border trade—"unlimited border trade" should not be encouraged.[61] Indeed, Chinese scholars and officials generally argue that inadequate governmental regulation of border trade is responsible for existing problems.[62]

Obstacles to Regional Development

Some observers from Harbin, however, speak of political obstacles to improved regional economic relations, especially the competition with China perceived by some Russian regional leaders that has driven them to raise concerns about the population imbalance on both sides of the border.[63] Other specialists note that fears of being overshadowed by China initially led Primorskii Krai Governor Yevgeniy Nazdratenko to object to giving back to China 330 hectares of land near the Tumen River. The governor complained that this territory would give the Chinese an outlet to the Sea of Japan and enable Chinese ports to compete with Russian ports for cargo.[64]

Indeed, efforts by Chinese and Russian officials to highlight the economic complementarities existing between the Russian Far East and the Chinese Far East appear to have been counterproductive.

Russians on all sides of the political spectrum have decried economic policies that turn their country into a "Third World resource supplier," and the dominance of resource exports in trade with China has rankled in particular.[65] Some scholars, outside the mainstream of Russian opinion, have even argued that it is exactly China's need for the resources located in the Russian Far East and the space within which to relieve mounting demographic pressures that may lead to a threat of Chinese expansion into the region in the future.[66]

If regional political problems are minimized today in China, to some extent, a lack of familiarity with regional politics in the Russian Far East is to blame. Some Chinese observers, for example, view the inflamed rhetoric on the Chinese illegal immigration issue as a negative consequence of a free press.[67] The problem is exactly the contrary in Vladivostok, however, the locus of the most vocal anti-Chinese campaign, which largely has been manufactured by the governor and his supporters, who control most of the newspapers in the region.[68]

Despite the confusion in China about the sources of anti-Chinese sentiment in the Russian Far East, many Chinese analysts feel confident that the Yeltsin government, at least, has not overreacted.[69] Apparently, Yeltsin has been able to sufficiently reassure his Chinese counterparts that allegations regarding Chinese illegal immigration were not being taken seriously and to concentrate instead on resolving the main issue: introducing more effective administration of the lengthy Russian-Chinese border. Indeed, most officials and scholars in Beijing and Harbin tend to focus on the administrative and economic aspects of problems in border trade, rather than analyzing the political factors responsible for present difficulties.

While they underestimate the political problems in Sino-Russian regional relations, conversely many Russians fail to consider the economic and administrative sources of difficulties in cross-border trade. The lack of coverage of these issues fuels anti-Chinese sentiment, especially in the Russian border regions, where political leaders such as Nazdratenko have been able to make use of the "China threat" in Primorskii Krai's struggles with Moscow. In attributing the chaos in border trade to a Chinese strategy for expansion in the Russian Far East,[70] for example, Russian observers neglect some of the more important factors that led to the problem, especially the conflicts of interest over economic development between Beijing and Heilongjiang Province.

BEIJING'S ADMINISTRATIVE SOLUTIONS FOR PROBLEMS IN CROSS-BORDER TRADE

To rein in some of the enthusiasm in the border regions and reestablish order there, the authorities in Beijing decided on two sets of regulations governing border trade. In late December 1995, the State Council passed a statute that narrowed the definition of the border region to an area within 20 kilometers of the border and limited preferential policies to these areas. Thus, while previously an entire border province was able to pay 50 percent of customs duties, after the statute passed just border counties were eligible, and only through 1998. The rest of the areas in a border province had to pay full customs duties. The new rules also reduced import taxes on unprocessed goods by 50 percent in the border counties. The rules, however, set limits on the volume of each barter transaction that border residents could carry out tax free, to provide the greatest tax relief to small businesses in the border counties.

Furthermore, in a move to discourage fly-by-night firms from participating in border trade, as of 1995 only firms earning more than U.S.$2,000,000 were given export permits. Previously small firms paid a fee to larger trade firms to export their goods, but this system is no longer possible under the new rules. The only exceptions are small-volume firms in the border regions themselves. Such firms can apply for a license to engage in border trade.[71] The Chinese government also attempted to stem the flow of people involved in trade by restricting the issuance of passports. As a consequence, Heilongjiang now allots a maximum of ten passports to each trading company, regardless of the number of people who need to travel for business reasons.[72]

Although the new State Council measures did not take effect until April 1, 1996, the other rules mentioned above, as well as new visa requirements and Russian duties and taxes, had a dampening impact on trade in 1994–1995. Sino-Russian trade fell by 34 percent in 1994— the year new visa rules took effect. In Heilongjiang Province, border trade with Russia fell by 26 percent from its peak level of U.S.$2.2 billion in 1993 to U.S.$1.6 billion in 1994. In Jilin Province, Sino-Russian border trade fell by 46 percent in 1994 to U.S.$1.5 billion. In 1995, the volume of Sino-Russian border trade continued to fall in the Chinese border regions, although the rate of its decline lessened. In 1995, for example, Heilongjiang reported U.S.$1.4 billion in border trade with Russia, more than a 30 percent drop from its 1993 high, but only a 14 percent decrease from 1994.[73] Although Sino-Russian bilateral trade has been recovering some of its past momentum, albeit slowly, Russia's share in Heilongjiang's trade has continued to decline from 52.6 percent of total exports in 1993 to 25.1 percent in 1994 and then to 18.9 percent in 1995.[74]

Moreover, many firms in the Chinese border regions lost interest in border trade when they realized they would have to pay full customs duties. The drop in trade has also hit the border trading posts hard, because many of the hotels that were built there to accommodate all the traders who were flocking to Russia in the early 1990s now stand empty.

In 1994–1995, central and provincial government officials and scholars examined the causes of the drop in Sino-Russian border trade and discussed ways to address it. In Heilongjiang, for example, scholars saw the need to tighten quality controls and improve the management of border trade but made a case for continued preferential customs policies for the entire province.[75] Similarly, at a 1995 conference in Harbin, Heilongjiang Vice Governor Wang Zongzhang noted that problems had arisen because of new restrictions on passports and licensing of contract laborers and pressed for continued preferential customs and licensing policies for barter trade in the border provinces.[76]

While officials in Heilongjiang Province see the need to end the chaos in the border regions as well as to end preferential policies that might impede China's entry into GATT and the WTO, they admit that the new Chinese rules are not advantageous for the province. According to the director of the Heilongjiang Planning Commission, some problems with border trade can be attributed to policy changes, such as China's 1994 licensing requirements, which affected the province's top imports from Russia (chemical fertilizer, steel, and oil) as well as increased Russian prices, customs duties, and licensing requirements.[77] Scholars in Heilongjiang have also noted that Chinese licensing requirements on exports of food, one of Heilongjiang's primary exports to Russia, have also affected the volume of the province's trade.[78]

In the wake of the rule defining the border region as a 20-kilometer zone, cities in border provinces like Harbin find themselves competing on equal footing with the southern cities Shanghai and Guangzhou for a share of the Russian market. This change has complicated

Heilongjiang's strategy of linking with the South in that the southern provinces can easily bypass Heilongjiang and sell higher quality (and often less expensive) goods directly to the Russian border regions.[79]

In response to such complaints, officials in Beijing argue that the regions try to defend their own interests, especially when policies such as the licensing requirement for food exports—developed to safeguard future food supplies for an extremely populous country—have a negative impact on regional trade. Nonetheless, officials in Beijing contend that the new rules restricting border trade were not inevitable and resulted from inadequate management of border trade in the provinces.[80]

Discussions continue between the regions and the central government regarding the future of border trade. According to one account, the province understated its border trade figures for 1995 to show a continued decline in trade (although trade actually may have increased slightly to $1.7 billion) in an effort to press its case that the province has been hit hard by the new visa rules and still needs preferential policies.[81] While the overall trade balance began to rebound in 1995, in Heilongjiang it continued to fall, albeit at a slower rate, 14 percent.[82] By 1995, Sino-Russian trade had recovered to $5.5 billion, reaching $6.8 billion in 1996 but still falling short of the 1993 record high of $7.68 billion.[83] Before the onset of the August 1998 financial crisis, Heilongjiang's cross-border trade with Russia had been recovering slowly but steadily—climbing from $153 million in 1995 to $701 million in 1996 and reaching $1 billion in 1997, about half of its 1993 peak figure.[84]

The recovery in border trade demonstrates that both Russian and Chinese businesspeople have adapted to the new measures regulating border trade. Some have found ways to circumvent new policies such as the 1994 rule requiring visas for business travel. Given the cost and time involved in traveling to the consulates general in Khabarovsk and Shenyang, some businesspeople find it less cumbersome to purchase a one-week tourist package, for which a visa is unnecessary.[85] Tour companies have sprung up on both sides of the border to cater to such travelers.

In addition, firms located outside the 20-kilometer zone have taken to registering a subsidiary in the border region and then claiming it is the main office in order to take advantage of 50 percent customs duties. There is also some anecdotal evidence that small-scale barter traders in the Russian and Chinese border regions work together to circumvent central government licensing requirements, for example, by hiding such items in truckloads of goods that can be legally exported.[86]

Although the Chinese government was especially concerned about the adverse impact of chaotic border trade on Sino-Russian relations, all the new policies apply across-the-board to all nine of China's border provinces. Even southern border provinces, such as the Guangxi Autonomous Region, have experienced setbacks in border trade in the mid-1990s.[87] China's border regions have proved more difficult to develop than originally anticipated, because they started off at a disadvantage without the history of integration into the world economy and the policies to attract investment from East Asia's more dynamic areas, qualities that were present in the southern coastal regions.

Although officials in Beijing and Harbin recite like a mantra that the complementarities between the Russian Far East and the Chinese Northeast inevitably will spur rapid development on both sides of the border, actually the similarities in their economic predicament have created barriers to economic relations. Just as Russian hopes for large infusions of capital from the West and Japan to finance reform have proved unrealistic, the much vaunted Chinese strategy of linking with the South (nanlian) also has exaggerated the interest of investors in Hong Kong, Taiwan, Thailand, and other Asian countries in investing in Heilongjiang. While there are some Taiwanese shoe stores and Hong Kong–owned hotels in Harbin, these kinds of investments cannot turn around the province's economy. Some investment is developing in the electronics sector, but the province is far from becoming a source of quality high-tech equipment (or even clothing) for export. Transit trade may be a promising area for cooperation. In June 1999, officials from Heilongjiang, Primorskii Krai, and Washington State signed a protocol to create a trade corridor connecting Harbin by rail to ports in Primorskii Krai and then to Seattle and Tacoma. If implemented, this corridor could stimulate trade between the Northwest of the United States and Northeast China and enhance transportation links between Heilongjiang and Primorskii Krai.

The Chinese central government has decided to bank on market forces, rather than targeted economic privileges, as a way of spurring development in flourishing and underdeveloped regions alike. Preferential policies for the border regions came under attack at the same time that a debate emerged in the Chinese government over special privileges for the special economic zones (SEZ) in the southern coastal areas. Ultimately Beijing decided to phase out investment and tax privileges granted to the SEZs and to equalize tax policies between these areas and other parts of China in an effort to reduce income disparities in the country. While policies governing the southern SEZs and northern cross-border trade are carried out by different offices in Beijing, the retraction of privileges in both areas had similar purposes—to strengthen free trade and recentralize economic authority over regional foreign economic relations.[88] Preferential trade policies within the 20-kilometer border zone with Russia were extended in the fall of 1998, however, because of the negative impact of the Russian financial crisis on Chinese border cities and cross-border trade as a whole.

CONSEQUENCES FOR SINO-RUSSIAN RELATIONS

According to scholars and officials in Beijing, a healthy economic relationship is crucial to the continued development of friendly Sino-Russian relations.[89] This sentiment is echoed in the border regions, where one scholar asserted that regional economic ties are "the barometer of bilateral relations."[90] Indeed, in 1993 the dramatic boom in border trade was one example of the great progress in Sino-Russian relations. It soon, however, became an indicator of underlying political and economic limitations of the new partnership between Russia and China, especially in regional relations. Today, leading scholars in Beijing remark that Sino-Russian political relations have outpaced economic ties and argue that the imbalance must be redressed for the emerging partnership between Russia and China to continue to develop.[91] In an effort to address some of the impediments to regional economic relations, in late 1998 a coordinating committee for Sino-Russian border and regional economic cooperation was established to facilitate dialogue among Russian and Chinese regional leaders.

Although the vaunted strategic partnership between Beijing and Moscow may provide political respite against perceived U.S. pressures, the Sino-Russian trade relationship remains anemic, especially in comparison with the $50–60 billion in trade achieved in the prick-lier but economically more robust Sino-Japanese and Sino-U.S. rela-tionships. Yeltsin's prediction that Sino-Russian trade will reach $20 billion by the year 2000 seems likely to remain an empty promise unless both the Russian and Chinese border regions are able to attract the large influx of capital needed to make their dreams of pipelines and other joint infrastructure projects a reality.

With a much weakened ruble in the aftermath of the August 1998 financial crisis, the Russian border regions were no longer able to afford many imports of food and consumer goods from preferred partners such as Japan, the United States, and, to a lesser extent, South Korea, and compensated by increasing purchases from China. Although the volume of Chinese imports to the Russian Far East in 1998 declined considerably relative to 1997, China still became the leading trading partner for Khabarovskii Krai and replaced the United States as Primorskii Krai's second highest source of imports.[92]

China's investment in the Russian Far East continues to be very low—just $0.2 million in the first nine months of 1998 compared to $133.7 million for the United States, the leading investor in the region.[93] Even if sufficient sources of investment were found, joint development projects are unlikely to find support in the Russian Far East unless the underlying misperceptions in Sino-Russian regional relations are addressed. Indeed, China seems to have a general prob-lem articulating its foreign policy intentions when its actions are perceived differently by other countries. And some Russian regional leaders, too, must decide between the short-term political capital to be gained from anti-Chinese campaigns and the potential benefits of participating in a more open trading regime in East Asia.

Some of the fundamental economic problems in cross-border trade, however, stem from problems in center-regional relations afflicting both China and Russia. The neglected peripheries initially turned to each other to resolve pressing economic problems, but long-term solutions will have to come from elsewhere. Together the Chinese and Russian border regions can achieve a degree of mutually beneficial economic cooperation, but for cross-border trade to flour-ish, development in the peripheries must reach its potential. If this development has not occurred, it is not the fault of cross-border trade, but one of regional policy in both countries.

NOTES

[1]On center-regional tensions in China, see David S. G. Goodman, ed., *China's Provinces in Reform* (London: Routledge, 1997).

[2]On Soviet assistance to Chinese industries in the Northeast, see Yuriy Kapelinskiy, et al., *Razvitie ekonomiki i vneshneekonomicheskikh svyazey kitayskoy narodnoy respubliki* (Moscow: Vneshtorgizdat, 1959), chap. 6.

[3]Harbin, for example, has ten factories with more than 10,000 workers, some of which produce weapons such as tanks. Interview with an institute director, Harbin, July 25, 1996.

[4]Interviews in Harbin with midlevel provincial government researchers, July 24, 1996, and an institute director, July 25, 1996. On this point, also see Yanzhong Huang and Dali. L. Yang, "The Northeast Phenomenon in China: Heilongjiang and the Dilemmas of Industrial Adjustment" (paper prepared for China's Provinces in Reform, 2nd Workshop sponsored by the Institute for International Studies, University of Technology (Sydney) at Zhejiang University, Hangzhou, October 2–24, 1996), p. 8.

[5]For average growth rates, see C. Goodhart and C. Xu, "The Rise of China as an Economic Power," *National Institute Economic Review* (February 1996), p. 63. For data on transfers from Beijing to the provinces, see Jun Ma, "Macroeconomic Management and Intergovernmental Relations in China," Policy Research Working Paper 1408, The World Bank, January 1995, pp. 28–29.

[6]Yanzhong Huang and Dali. L. Yang, "The Northeast Phenomenon in China," pp. 8, 9. Interviews in Harbin with midlevel provincial government researchers, July 24, 1996, and an institute director, July 25, 1996.

[7]"La Rue vers le Nord-Est?" *Perspectives Chinoises*, no. 25 (September–October 1994), pp. 18–20.

[8]Matt Forney, "The Workers' State," *Far Eastern Economic Review*, September 12, 1996, pp. 68–69.

[9]Personal observations, Harbin, July 1996.

[10]For a detailed analysis of the history of the decentralization of foreign trade in the PRC, see Zhang Amei and Zou Gang, "Foreign Trade Decentralization and Its Impact on Central-Local Relations," in Hao Jia and Zhimin Lin, eds., *Changing Central-Local Relations in China* (Boulder: Westview Press, 1994), pp. 154–77.

[11]Deng Liqun and Qi Wuheng, *Dangdai Zhongguo de Heilongjiang* (Beijing: Dangdai Zhongguo, 1988), vol. 2, p. 400. Interview with former high-ranking Heilongjiang party and government official, July 26, 1996. The details of the opening of border trade in 1982–1985 have not yet been published and are drawn from this interview.

[12]Deng Liqun and Qi Wuheng, *Dangdai Zhongguo de Heilongjiang*, p. 402; Alan J. Day, ed., *China and the Soviet Union, 1949–84* (New York: Facts on File Publications, 1985), p. 186.

[13]Deng Liqun and Qi Wuheng, *Dangdai Zhongguo de Heilongjiang*, pp. 402, 407; Day, *China and the Soviet Union*, p. 186; "Harbin Heilongjiang Provincial Service in Mandarin, August 18, 1984," *FBIS* (China), August 20, 1984, pp. K1–2.

[14]The Heilongjiang provincial government formally adopted this slogan as its foreign trade strategy in 1986. See Zhang Housheng, *Heilongjiang dui Su jingmao zhanlue he duilue yanjiu* (Harbin: Heilongjiang renmin chubanshe, 1991), p. 2. For a detailed discussion of this strategy, see Du Xianzong, *Bian mao molu* (Harbin: Heilongjiang renmin chubanshe, 1995), p. 540. Du Xianzong was governor of Heilongjiang Province until 1994 and was an active supporter of opening up border trade with Russia.

[15]Three of these cities are in Heilongjiang: Heihe, Suifenhe, and Tongjiang, while Manzhouli is in Inner Mongolia. On the opening of the border ports in Heilongjiang, see Yuan Qingshou, *Heilongjiang shen bianjing diqu: jingji shehui fazhan gaikuang* (Harbin: Heilongjiang shen chubanshe, 1990), pp. 54–55.

[16]Xu Jingxue, "Sino-Russian Trade Problems and Prospects—Concurrently the Economic Relations between Heilongjiang Province and the Russian Far East" (unpublished paper prepared for the international conference Russia on the Pacific: Past and Present, August 1995), p. 16. Xu Jingxue is the director of Heilongjiang's Siberian Studies Institute.

[17]For a comparison of economic conditions in border and coastal areas, see Sun Weiben, "Shixian yan bian kai fang tong yan hai kai fang de xietiao tuidong, wanquan wo guo dui wai kaifang quan qiu geju," in Zhang Housheng, *Heilongjiang dui Su jingmao zhanlue he celue yanjiu*, pp. 3–25.

[18]Interviews with midlevel provincial government researchers, Harbin, July 26, 1996.

[19]The Heilongjiang provincial government formally adopted this slogan as its foreign trade strategy in 1986. See Zhang Housheng, *Heilongjiang dui Su jingmao zhanlue he duilue yanjiu*, p. 2; Du Xianzong, *Bian mao molu*, pp. 514, 540.

[20]Interview, Heilongjiang provincial government researchers, Harbin, July 24, 1996.

[21]Wang Zongzhang, "Heilongjiang shen bianjing difang jingji maoyi shingshi yu duice yanjiu" (unpublished paper, June 11, 1995), p. 12. Wang Zongzhang is vice governor of Heilongjiang Province and his primary responsibility is the administration of border trade.

[22]Interview with an institute director, Harbin, June 27, 1996.

[23]Li Zhuanhai, "Bianmao, zheli keyi zai pai huai?" *Yuandong Jingmao Daobao Xinxi* (May 1996), p. 16.

[24]*RFE/RL Newsline,* February 8, 1999. Imports of Chinese food products and consumer goods fell by 50 percent in the fourth quarter of 1998. The collapse of banks and Russian firms involved in Sino-Russian trade, as well as the shortage of foreign currency in Russia further complicated an already difficult economic relationship. Xinhua, November 4, 1998, in *FBIS* (China), November 4, 1998 (electronic); Dmitriy Kosurev and Stanislav Petrov, "Spasti torgovlyu s Kitaem," *Nezavisimaya gazeta,* November 10, 1997, pp. 1–2.

[25]See, for example, Wang Zongzhang, "Heilongjiang shen bianjing difang jingji maoyi shingshi yu duice yanjiu."

[26]Pavel Minakir and Nadezhda Mikheeva, "Ekonomika Rossiyskogo Dal'-nego Vostoka: Mezhdu Tsentralizatsiey i Regionalizatsiey" (unpublished paper presented at the international conference Russia on the Pacific: Past and Present, Khabarovsk, August 1995), p. 5. Minakir, the former vice governor of Khabarovskii Krai, is the director of the Institute of Economic Research in Khabarovsk, where Mikheeva is a leading scholar.

[27]L. Vardomskiy and E. Samburova, "Rossiya i Kitay: sravnitel'niy analiz regional'nikh prosetsov," *Problemy Dal'nego Vostoka,* no. 3 (1994), p. 27.

[28]Viktor Pavlyatenko, "Rossiyskiy Dal'niy Vostok v sisteme otnosheniy Rossii so stranami CVA," *Problemy Dal'nego Vostoka,* no. 4 (1995), p. 11.

[29]Minakir and Mikheeva, "Ekonomika Rossiyskogo Dal'nego Vostoka," pp. 2–3, 5–6.

[30]Oleg Davydov, "Rossiya i Kitay-novyi shag navstrechu drug druga," *Segodnya,* April 23, 1996, p. 10.

[31]For an account of the impact of these economic changes on border trade between Amurskaya Oblast and China, see Yuriy Moskalenko, "Vneshne-ekonomicheskoe sotrudnichestvo Amurskoy oblasti so stranami Severo-Vostochnoy Azii," *Problemy Dal'nego Vostoka,* no. 1 (1996), p. 48. Moskalenko serves in Amurskaya Oblast's Department on Foreign Economic Relations.

[32]Ma Weixian, "Sino-Russian Border Trade" (unpublished paper, presented at the international conference on Russia on the Pacific: Past and Present, Khabarovsk, August 1995), p. 8.

[33]Interview with Wen Ke, head of the Heilongjiang Planning Commission, "Bian mao zou xiang chengshu 'jia kuai' shi zai bi xing," *Heilongjiang Jingji Ribao,* May 1, 1996, p. 1.

[34]Ma Weixian, "Sino-Russian Border Trade," p. 8.

[35]See, for example, Lu Nanquan, "Dui muqian ZhongE jingmao guangxi ruogan wenti de sikao," *Guoji Shangbao,* May 27, 1996, p. 2. Lu Nanquan is one of Beijing's top experts on the Russian economy. See, also, Wang Zongzhang, "Heilongjiang shen bianjing difang jingji maoyi shingshi yu duice yanjiu;" Xu Jingxue, "Sino-Russian Trade Problems and Prospects," p. 14.

[36]Interviews, Ministry of Foreign Trade Research Institute, Beijing, August 6, 1996.

[37]See, for example, Sun Xiufeng, "Zhengdun ZhongE bianjing maoyi zhixu, tuidong liangguo piling diqu jingmao hezuo," *Guoji Maoyi Wenti* (Beijing), no. 12 (1995), p. 51. The author is a commercial attaché at China's Moscow Embassy.

[38]Interviews with senior scholars, Harbin, July 2, 1996.

[39]The Chinese Ministry of Foreign Trade is concerned about these financial problems and is devoting attention to them. The June 20, 1996, issue of the ministry's newspaper, *International Trade News*, published a special section on financial problems in Sino-Russian border trade, which included articles on the lack of an arbitration mechanism and adequate insurance, the problems caused by the switch to hard currency, and transportation bottlenecks. *International Trade News*, June 20, 1996, p. 2.

[40]Ma Weixian, "Sino-Russian Border Trade," pp. 8, 13.

[41]Davydov, "Rossiya i Kitay-novy shag navstrechu drug druga," p. 10. Oleg Davydov is the Russian deputy premier and minister in charge of foreign economic relations.

[42]Interviews, Ministry of Foreign Trade Research Institute, Beijing, August 6, 1996; Davydov, "Rossiya i Kitay-novy shag navstrechu drug druga," p. 10.

[43]Igor Korkunov, "Rossiysko-kitayskie vneshneekonomicheskie svyzi: itogi i perspektivy," *Problemy Dal'nego Vostoka*, no. 6 (1996), p. 75.

[44]Lu Nanquan, "ZhongE jingmao guangxi" (unpublished paper, March 15, 1997), p. 9.

[45]Interview with a senior scholar, Beijing, June 3, 1996.

[46]Interview with a senior scholar, Beijing, June 3, 1996.

[47]Interviews with senior scholars, Beijing, June 3, 1996, and June 10, 1996.

[48]Fang Peien, "'Dao bao' zhe de qishi," *Heilongjiang Ribao*, April 10, 1996, p. 2.

[49]Yanzhong Huang and Dali. L. Yang, "The Northeast Phenomenon in China," pp. 8, 21. Interviews in Harbin with midlevel provincial government researchers, July 24, 1996, and an institute director, July 25, 1996.

[50]*Heilonjiang Ribao*, September 14, 1993, p. 1.

[51]Yanzhong Huang and Dali. L. Yang, "The Northeast Phenomenon in China," pp. 8, 21. Interviews in Harbin with midlevel provincial government researchers, July 24, 1996, and an institute director, July 25, 1996. This tour was Li Ruihan's second trip in five months. As chairman of the People's Consultative Congress, he had participated in the September 1993 inspection tour. See Xinhua, January 6, 1994, in *FBIS-CHI-94-006*, January 10, 1994, p. 26.

[52]Gaye Christofferson, "Nesting the Sino-Russian Border and the Tumen Project in the Asia-Pacific: Heilongjiang's Regional Relations," *Asian Perspective*, vol. 2, no. 2 (Fall-Winter 1996), p. 285; Hua Hsia, "Zhu Rongji Again

Shows the True Qualities of a Czar," *Hsin Pao,* April 28, 1994, p. 17, in *FBIS-CHI-94-082,* April 28, 1994, p. 33.

[53]Yanzhong Huang and Dali. L. Yang, "The Northeast Phenomenon in China," pp. 8, 22–23. Interviews in Harbin with midlevel provincial government researchers, July 24, 1996, and an institute director, July 25, 1996.

[54]Some Chinese scholars call attention to this problem. See, for example, Li Zhuanxun, "EYuandong diqu fandui ZhongE bianjie xieding he xuanchuan 'Zhongguo kuoda' xinlun shuyao" (unpublished paper, May 1996), p. 5. Interview with senior scholar, Beijing, August 21, 1996. For a discussion of the "yellow peril" by a Vladivostok scholar, see Viktor Larin, "Sindrom 'zheltoy opasnosti' v dal'nevostochnoy politike rossii v nachale i kontse XX v" (unpublished paper prepared for the international conference Russia on the Pacific: Past and Present, August 1995).

[55]Xinhua, June 28, 1994, in *FBIS-CHI-94-126,* June 30, 1994, p. 8.

[56]Interviews, Institute for Contemporary International Relations (ICIR), Beijing, August 22, 1996.

[57]Interviews with senior scholars, Beijing, June 13, 1996, and August 12, 1996.

[58]Li Jingjie, "Shi lun ZhongE zhanlue huoban guangxi" (unpublished paper, May 1996), p. 13.

[59]Li Zhuanxun, "EYuandong diqu fandui ZhongE bianjie xieding he xuanchuan 'Zhongguo kuoda' xinlun shuyao," p. 6. Also, see Li Jingjie, "Shi lun ZhongE zhanlue huoban guangxi.".

[60]Interviews, ICIR, Beijing, August 22, 1996.

[61]Sun Xiufeng, "Zhengdun ZhongE bianjing maoyi zhixu, tuidong liangguo piling diqu jingmao hezuo," p. 51.

[62]Li Jingjie, "Shi lun ZhongE zhanlue huoban guangxi," pp. 11, 13.

[63]Interviews with senior scholars, Harbin, July 8, 1996; June 27, 1996; and July 3, 1996.

[64]Li Zhuanxun, "EYuandong diqu fandui ZhongE bianjie xieding he xuanchuan 'Zhongguo kuoda' xinlun shuyao," pp. 2, 5. Interviews with an institute director, Harbin, July 9, 1996; senior scholars, Harbin, July 2, 1996; and provincial government researchers, Harbin, July 25, 1996. Interview with senior scholar, Beijing, August 21, 1996. Larin, "Sindrom 'zheltoy opasnosti' v dal'nevostochnoy politike rossii v nachale i kontse XX v".

[65]For an example of such criticism by Russian analysts, see Korkunov, "Rossiysko-kitayskie vneshneekonomicheskie svyzi," p. 74. Korkunov argues that the Chinese point of view denigrates Russia's role as a source of scientific-technical know-how. On China policy and the spectrum of Russian opinion, see Alexei D. Voskressenski, "The Perceptions of China by Russia's Foreign Policy Elite," *Issues & Studies* (March 1997), pp. 1–20.

[66]On this point, see Alexey Bogaturov, *Sovremennye teorii stabil'nosti i mezh-duranodnye otnosheniya rossii v vostochnoy azii v 1970–90e gg* (Moscow: Moskov-skiy obshchestvennyi fond, 1996), p. 199.

[67]Interviews with senior scholars, Beijing, August 12, 1996; June 6, 1996; and June 3, 1996.

[68]On the political uses of anti-Chinese rhetoric and a discussion of the "yellow peril" by a Vladivostok scholar, see Larin, "Sindrom 'zheltoy opasnosti' v dal'nevostochnoy politike rossii v nachale i kontse XX v."

[69]Interviews with a senior scholar, Beijing, June 10, 1996; interviews with specialists at the Foreign Trade Ministry Research Institute, August 6, 1996.

[70]For a typical example of this line of thinking, see Vladimir Shcherbakov, "'Velikiy brat' k nam tyanet ruki—Kitayskaya ekspansiay v Primor'skom Krae Rossii," *Vladivostok*, September 1, 1993, p. 5.

[71]"Guowuyuan guanyu bianjing maoyi you guan wenti de tongzhi," *Yuan Dong Jing Mao Xinxi* (May 1996), pp. 3–4. Interview, Harbin, June 30, 1996.

[72]Interview with a businessman, Harbin, June 30, 1996.

[73]Li Zhuanhai, "Bianmao, zheli keyi zai pai huai?", pp. 16–17. Interview, Heilongjiang provincial government, Harbin, July 24, 1996.

[74]Unsigned article, "Yi duoyuanhua shichang caijin heilongjiang wai mao chukou fazhan," *Guoji Shang Bao*, July 19, 1996, p. 2.

[75]Interviews with senior scholars, Harbin, July 31, 1996.

[76]Wang Zongzhang, "Heilongjiang shen bianjing difang jingji maoyi shishi yu duice yanjiu," pp. 12, 19–20. Wang Zongzhang is vice governor of Heilongjiang Province and his primary responsibility is the administration of border trade. Until recently, when the Russian and Chinese border regions have been trying to switch to cash transactions, almost all border trade was carried out on a barter basis. Given the continuing lack of hard currency experienced by small firms in these regions, even today transactions are often calculated in hard currency but then equivalently valued goods are exchanged.

[77]Interview with Wen Ke.

[78]Interview with an institute director, Harbin, July 9, 1996.

[79]Interview with a senior scholar, Harbin, July 16, 1996.

[80]Interviews with senior scholars, Beijing, August 5, 1996.

[81]Interviews with provincial government researchers, Harbin, July 25, 1996.

[82]For Heilongjiang figures, see Li Zhuanhai, "Bianmao, zheli keyi zai pai huai?" pp. 16–17.

[83]Lu Nanquan, "ZhongE jingmao guangxi," p. 3.

[84]Li Jianmin, "Heilongjiang shen de duiE bianjing maoyi," in Lu Nanquan and Xue Jundu, eds., *ZhongE maoyi guanxi* (Beijing: Chinese Academy of Social Sciences Press, 1999), p. 167.

[85]Interview with a businessman, Harbin, June 30, 1996.

[86]Interview with senior scholars, Beijing, August 5, 1996.

[87]See Li Zhuanhai, "Bianmao, zheli keyi zai pai huai?" pp. 16–17. The Guangxi Autonomous Region, for example, experienced a 25.5 percent drop in exports in the first four months of 1995.

[88]On the debate on privileges in the southern SEZs, see Michel Bonnin, "End of the Road for Special Economic Zones?" *China Perspectives*, no. 1 (September-October 1995), p. 19.

[89]Lu Nanquan, "Dui muqian ZhongE jingmao guangxi ruogan wenti de sikao," p. 2. See, also, Wang Zongzhang, "Heilongjiang shen bianjing difang jingji maoyi shingshi yu duice yanjiu." Interviews with senior scholars, Beijing, June 3, 1996; June 10, 1996; and June 13, 1996.

[90]Interviews with senior scholars, Harbin, June 28, 1996.

[91]Li Jingjie, "Shi lun ZhongE zhanlue huoban guangxi," p. 10; Lu Nanquan, "Dui muqian ZhongE jingmao guangxi ruogan wenti de sikao," p. 2.

[92]South Korea remains Primorskii Krai's leading source of imports, and Japan still ranks number one in terms of the region's exports. Because sales to China of SU-27 aircraft, produced in Khabarovskii Krai, are counted as exports of machinery in regional trade statistics, this region reported $636.9 million in exports to China in 1998, compared to $67.2 million in 1997. Elena Devaeva, "Vneshnyaya Torgovlya Dal'nego Vostoka Rossii" (unpublished paper prepared for JETRO Conference, Khabarovsk, March 1999), pp. 15, 19.

[93]The United States accounted for 40 percent of all investment in the region during the same period. Anatoliy Bouryi, "Interregional Association 'Far East and Transbaikal' and Perspectives for Integration" (unpublished comments for IREX Conference on "The Russian Far East on the Road to Openness: Regional Development and Prospects for Integration with the Pacific Rim," Vladivostok, June 1999).

10
Reform in the Russian Far East: Implications for Economic Cooperation

Judith Thornton

The Russian Far East, Russia's vast storehouse of resources and mineral wealth, lies at the center of Northeast Asia, bordering China, North Korea, Japan, and Alaska. Yet, until economic reform gave its producers direct access to the world market, it developed in nearly complete isolation from the dynamic markets of the Pacific. Historically, the region played the dual role of resource colony and military outpost. Most of its fish, timber, and minerals were railed westward to European Russia, which sent a return flow of food and consumer goods. Closed cities, such as Vladivostok and Tikheokeanskii, served the military and military industries. The region's ports were home to the Pacific Fleet.

Today, the region faces a dilemma. It must adjust to large cuts in its military production and personnel, reorient its economic activity toward its neighbors in the Pacific, and gain access to the investment, technology, and know-how that it needs to be competitive in the Pacific market. Such an opening of the Russian Far East (RFE) toward its neighbors in Asia raises concerns for policy makers in Moscow, however. Can the Russian Federation retain control of the Far East's natural wealth once regional producers establish links to the world market? Will resource rents that once flowed to Moscow be diverted from the center to the local regions or to the offshore affiliates of private firms? Will foreign investment give foreign owners control of Russia's wealth? Will economic development flood the region with foreign traders and foreign workers, leading to ethnic conflict or foreign claims on Russia's territory in the future?

The situation for the territories (krai, oblast, or autonomous okrug) in the RFE is no less difficult. Collapse of demand for military production and loss of federal subsidies leave many of the region's territories with drastically lower levels of production and income, and an outflow of unemployed population. Recent large purchases of military products by foreign customers, such as China, have propped up some military producers, but other military towns are destitute, seeking outside sources of support with central authorization or without. Still, regional leaders can do little to restructure their local economies, for the regions are hostages to policies set in Moscow.

The activities of firms and their access to markets are constrained by confiscatory taxes and contradictory, burdensome regulations. They must operate in a domestic environment that provides weak legal and financial infrastructure and an intrusive and sometimes corrupt governmental infrastructure. In this environment, newly privatized firms and regional political leaders face stark choices: they may operate within punitive, centrally determined rules of the game; they may seek an exemption, avoiding the centrally determined rules; or they may attempt to evade the rules, risking punishment or retaliation. When the rules of the game are expropriatory, local decision makers survive through one or another form of noncompliance.

In 1997, the prospects for reform looked better than at any time since 1992. With formal privatization nearly complete, Yeltsin's new government hoped to undertake further steps in what had been a partial and incomplete process of economic reform. The Russian Federation needed to collect additional tax revenue to bring its budget into better balance, reduce direct and indirect subsidies to industries and regional governments, and stem the growth of nonperforming bank credits and payments arrears. Policy makers sought to diminish the outflow of capital and, if possible, to address the political and economic risks that generated capital flight.

The future agenda of Russian reform, however, is bound to be a painful and contentious process because of the immense structural adjustment that must take place. It is rendered doubly difficult by the competition for control of Russian assets and wealth. With Russian political and economic life focused on who will own Russia's wealth, there are strong pressures to direct central policies to serve the ends of elites at the center and to focus regional policies, in response, on the protection of local interests. All too often, the policies of Russian Federation agencies–such as a policy requiring central government approval for the export of polymetallic metals–have the goal of reestablishing central control over RFE producers and resources at the expense of regional development. The result for the region, in turn, is likely to be either further decapitalization of regional assets and further capital flight or reimposition of centralized controls from Moscow.

The uncertainty created by a system in flux raises barriers to foreign participation in the Russian market, as well. Local owners of dominant firms and Moscow-based strategic investors agree on only one thing: direct competition from efficient, well-funded foreign multinationals is unwelcome, particularly when foreign links give small local producers alternative access to the foreign market and to foreign investment. Instead, the managers of large Russian enterprises and financial-industrial groups hope to create a closed capital market. They wish to attract funding from passive foreign investors, while acquiring and retaining full control rights over Russian assets themselves.

In late 1997, President Yeltsin rescinded earlier ceilings on foreign ownership in Russian oil and gas. Yet, high nominal interest rates on Russian treasury bills in the wake of weakness in Asian financial markets directed portfolio lending into government paper, crowding out demand for investment by industry.

How will these new developments affect the region? Can the region build a stable economy based on its resources, skilled labor force, and strategic location in Northeast Asia in an environment with weak infrastructure, high risk, and competition for ownership of wealth? In the short run, Moscow seems unwilling to allow the unregulated opening of its Pacific territories to the world market. Instead, trade and investment in Russia's Pacific region are likely to remain highly regulated by Moscow. If central regulation retards institutional change, then the continuing weakness of legal, financial, and governmental infrastructure and continuing costs of crime and corruption may hinder the expansion of international business activity and retard the supply of investment.

If an opening of the RFE to the Pacific presents Moscow with certain risks, then a failure to stem the economic decline of the region raises yet other risks. Contraction of the regional economy, out-migration of its Russian population, and a weakening of Russian military presence all raise fears of an influx of foreign population and eventual loss of control of the region. Despite these concerns, a fragmented central government seems unable to put the social and institutional infrastructure in place to rekindle regional recovery.

An inflow of foreign investment into the offshore oil and gas industry of Sakhalin is under way that could stimulate demand for local manufacturing and provide low-cost energy to stimulate future growth. The full-scale development of Sakhalin's energy resource is still uncertain, however, pending the resolution of inconsistencies between production sharing and other Russian legislation and regulatory practices.

Other important legislative changes are pending, as well. A long-awaited tax code is still stalled in the Duma. Russia has been unwilling to legalize full private ownership of agricultural land to allow new private farms in Amur or Primorsk, and it has been reluctant to give regional decision makers sufficient autonomy to chart their own futures. As a result, the region faces uncertain prospects. Without integration into the Pacific market, the region's resources may simply fund capital flight, while the prospects for long-term Russian economic cooperation with any of its neighbors in Asia will remain limited.

ECONOMIC REFORM AND ECONOMIC INTEGRATION

With its economic institutions in flux, patterns of international trade in the RFE have reflected short-run responses to risk rather than long-run opportunities. The years following the collapse of the former Soviet Union have seen contradictory trends in Russia's regions. The fundamental institutions of a market system are emerging. Most market prices are freely determined. A population of independent small businesses has emerged. The majority of large-scale firms has been privatized, their shares in the hands of a variety of stakehold-ers—managers and employees, pension funds, outside strategic investors, banks, and governmental bodies. In financial markets, after a period of wildcat banking, a small population of independent, specialized banks is emerging that can supply a growing array of financial services and survive without hidden subsidies from Russia's central bank, although the financial market remains weak and undercapitalized. In the regions, territorial and local authorities are gradually taking over the responsibility for delivery of local public services and social welfare. Yet, in resource extraction and in foreign trade markets, central administrative control has remained strong, enforced by government ownership of resources.

After the dissolution of the former Soviet Union, trade flows between the former republics collapsed to one-third of former levels. As inflation, currency inconvertibility, and high costs of transport impeded the establishment of market links with domestic markets, producers in the RFE turned their hopes to the Pacific. For RFE regional producers, however, access to world markets remained constrained. Export was restrained by a host of barriers. There were export licenses and quotas, export taxes, limited licensing of authorized exporters, monopsony purchases on the domestic market of exportable goods by state trading organizations, control by state trading organizations of external trade of key commodities, and surrender of foreign exchange at below market exchange rates.[1]

Initially, the cornerstones of Russian trade policy were export quotas and import subsidies, but, gradually, Russia moved to consistently protectionist policies–export taxes and restraints and import tariffs–combined with special exemptions for favored interests, such as Gasprom, the vertically integrated oil companies, and certain importers of food products. Not surprisingly, access to export quotas and tariff exemptions generated substantial rent-seeking activity.

Until 1994, export quotas applied to all the energy and raw materials traded by the RFE. Quotas were calculated by the Ministry of Economy from material balances projecting the difference between domestic production and estimated domestic use. The Ministry of Foreign Economic Relations allocated export quotas by formula: 50±55 percent to the government's centralized trading organization, Roskontrakt; 30 percent to firms; 10±12 percent to territorial administrations; and 3±5 percent for sale through auctions. Exports produced by joint ventures were not subject to quota.[2] After 1995, export quotas were eliminated and export restrictions reduced, but an elaborate ``passport" system was established to monitor financial transactions and transfer prices of exports and imports.

CHART 10.1
Russian Trade 1994±1998

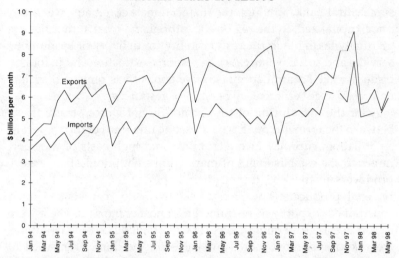

Source: Russian Economic Trends, data bank.

After reform, the export of energy and natural resource products was the only dynamic sector in Russia's declining economy. Still, Russia's large positive trade balance reflected capital flight and a rising informal economy rather than economic health (see chart 10.1).

The main trading partners of the RFE have been Japan, South Korea, the United States, and China. In 1995, Japan accounted for about one-third of the region's trade, buying fish, timber, and energy products. With the development of Sakhalin's offshore oil and gas going forward, Japan and the United States will be involved in large-scale investment in the region.

RFE trade with China surged in 1993 and then dropped sharply after restrictions were reimposed on visa-free access to the region. Russian trade with China comprises two parts: centrally determined trade and decentralized trade (of which border trade is a part). Centrally negotiated trade involves big-ticket items such as Chinese purchase of military hardware and nuclear power equipment, while decentralized trade involves exchange of Russian timber, fish, fertilizer, metals, and raw materials for Chinese food, textiles, and consumer products. In 1996, a partial recovery in Russian-Chinese trade reflected an increase in centrally negotiated trade activity, especially in military hardware. In 1997, Chinese provincial authorities reported that Russian timber and fertilizer were no longer available through decentralized sources.[3] Fishing vessels from the RFE also supply Northeast China with fish. Some of this trade remains unrecorded in Russian trade statistics but shows up in Chinese statistics.

The low level of their economic interaction shows that neither Pacific Russia nor Northeast China looks to integration with each other as an important source of regional development. Both regions view the attraction of foreign investment and technology from Japan, the United States, and Western Europe as their top priority. China's potential growing demand for energy and the considerable untapped RFE stock of oil, gas, and hydroelectric power offers the best prospect for future cooperation, but even that will depend, in part, on Western equipment and technology.

In the pages that follow, I look at the extent and direction of economic reform in the Russian Far East, investigating the impact of institutional change on the RFE region and forecasting the consequences for trade and investment in the region. As an example, I look specifically at the potential for economic cooperation between Russia and China in the light of their changing economic potential and emerging institutions. In the case of Russia and its largest neighbor, I identify significant hurdles to expanded trade resulting from the weak legal, financial, and institutional infrastructure of both countries, but I also recognize areas with significant future potential, such as energy and transport infrastructure.

THE STARTING POINT: INSTITUTIONS

Few Western observers understood before the reform era how dysfunctional or how brittle were the administrative institutions of the Soviet Union. The Soviet system was a highly centralized bureaucratic hierarchy that produced distorted incentives, biased information, and high levels of lobbying. Its structure protected bureaucratic monopolies and allowed party leaders to pursue political objectives at the expense of economic performance.

The RFE shared the costs of overcentralization. Seen from the viewpoint of the enterprise, the RFE was at the end of a long bureaucratic channel originating in Moscow. Almost everything of importance came down the hierarchy from the center–production plans, research designs, access to supplies, and approval of investment. Even enterprise directors were assigned directly from Moscow, their primary responsibility being the coordination of production between the region and the center.

According to official rules of the game, two firms in the same city but subordinate to different ministries were unable to trade with each other in input markets, but their directors were part of a local network of officials who formed a relationship system to break bottlenecks, resolve disputes, and lobby at the center. Among themselves, local officials and managers managed to provide some of the local infrastructure that went unfunded from the center.

Without horizontal market links, the production enterprise was like a feudal barony. In addition to mining, for example, the Magadan branch of the Ministry of Non-Ferrous Metals maintained apartments, built roads, distributed coal, imported food, repaired trucks, and ran medical facilities, a gas station, a hunting lodge, and a cleaning shop.

The poor information features of the administrative system were particularly harmful to performance. Good decision making requires accurate information about the options available—information that is best obtained from people on the spot. But opening a decision process to individuals with a stake in it increases the resources devoted to lobbying. Often, the center denied individuals in the hierarchy access to the information they would need to politic effectively, but this strategy reduced the accountability of top officials and reduced the information on which central decisions were made. In turn, production managers provided central allocators with biased information on their own performance.

It is easy to understand why the interaction between the center and the firm raised problems of opportunism (moral hazard and adverse selection) on every margin. The enterprise director faced a multitude of higher officials in the party, the industrial ministry, the central bank, and the regional government, each of whose instructions negated the others. These agencies claimed enterprise surpluses (if discovered) and bailed out losses, taking on much of the risk the enterprise faced.

While, in theory, factory directors had few control rights over resources, in practice, their control over information and their ability to trade off unmeasured dimensions of performance against measured criteria gave them considerable leeway. Despite heavy monitoring by the center, the enterprise overstated costs, concealed true capacity, diverted resources to local purposes, and avoided innovation.

The result was a static system with backward technology. A visitor arriving in the city of Khabarovsk in 1989 could have imagined that he or she had just been transported back to the 1950s. The wide streets of the provincial capital were devoid of traffic except for a few trucks and military jeeps. On the street, soldiers outnumbered civilians. The state grocery had only stale bread and Bulgarian pickles, and the water delivery system was closed for repairs. At the start of reform, the RFE was a down-at-the-heels colonial outpost whose subsidization imposed heavy costs on the center.

THE STARTING POINT: ECONOMIC STRUCTURE

As a result of the command system, the RFE entered the reform era with a distorted structure of costs and production. Its economy was linked to the Western Soviet Union in a pattern of forced integration. With a population of almost 8 million, its primary industries were fishing, military machine building, timber, nonferrous metals, and diamonds. It was the terminus of the Trans-Siberian and Baikal-Amur railroads connecting Europe and Asia. It supported a military establishment of some 300,000-plus troops and served as the home of the Soviet Pacific Fleet and its corresponding support industries.

The region was highly dependent on imports from outside for its subsistence, however. Value-added goods produced in the region accounted for only one-third of regional output. Transportation costs accounted for another third. More than half of the food, consumer goods, and energy used in the region were shipped in from elsewhere in the Soviet Union. Despite its high level of dependence on outside supply, little exchange took place in the foreign market: 80 percent of imports came from elsewhere in the Soviet Union, and 90 percent of exports were sent to other regions of the Soviet Union.

The structure of domestic prices was distorted relative to the world market, as well. The RFE bought energy and sold raw materials at low domestic prices, buying consumer goods and industrial equipment at high relative prices, much as if it faced implicit import tariffs on manufactures and implicit export taxes on its raw materials exports. Exporting firms received not world price, but the low domestic price, for their goods.

The prospect of opening its economy to the world market and adopting a structure of prices close to those on the world market confronted the region with a daunting situation. At world terms of trade, the region's raw materials had far greater value relative to manufactured goods outside than inside the country. With access to the world market, raw materials could be sold more profitably to Japan than to Moscow.

Many of the region's manufacturing firms faced a more difficult alternative, however. When valued at world prices, the value of the final products they produced would not cover the cost of raw materials needed to produce them, even if the charges for existing labor and capital stock were zero. These industries exhibited negative-value-added products at world market prices. They would be bankrupt once the regional economy opened to the world market unless they could improve their underlying technology.

Identifying which sectors of the regional economy would be noncompetitive at world prices was easy, relying on a detailed input-output table for the region (see table 10.1). In a 1996 publication, for example, the author estimated the impact of changing terms of trade on regional competitiveness by revaluing a 1987 input-output table for the RFE by price relatives between internal Soviet prices and world prices. These estimates measure apparent competitiveness of each industrial sector at world prices and identify four sectors of the Russian Far East–food processing (fishing), forest products, light industry, and the chemical industry–as negative-value-added sectors at world prices. Three additional sectors–agriculture, ferrous metals, and coal–were unprofitable (could not cover existing wages) at world prices.

The implications of these estimates were serious for the region, because two of the region's main export sectors, fishing and timber, would become unprofitable once they paid the full price of energy. Furthermore, the precipitous drop in domestic demand for military equipment after the collapse of the Soviet Union reduced regional machinery production to a fraction of its former levels. Without central subsidies, the region's traditional industries would have to downsize. What new economic activities could take up the slack?

Table 10.1
Russian Far East: Profitability at World Prices, 1987

Sector	Profit/ Capital	Capital/ Labor
Oil and Gas	2.151	296.403
Nonferrous Metals	1.789	18.983
Other Production Sectors	0.517	12.409
Machine Building	0.373	12.073
Other Industry	0.365	29.032
Construction	0.262	9.359
Construction Materials	0.218	25.025
Electricity	0.168	117.218
Trade and Supply	0.123	11.888
Transportations & Communications	0.086	50.464
Coal	−0.030	24.426
Other Energy	−0.040	36.636
Agriculture	−0.150	20.198
Ferrous Metals	−0.201	28.486
Food Processing	−0.266	33.468
Forest Products	−0.444	17.419
Light Industry	−0.530	4.739
Chemical Industry	−1.208	45.121
TOTAL	0.126	

Source: Judith Thornton, ``Structural Change in the Russian Far East: the Implications for Trade and Factor Markets,'' *Atlantic Economic Journal*, vol. 24, no. 3 (September 1996), pp. 208±28.

POLITICAL CAPITALISM

Eight years into the reform process, new economic activities are slow to appear and the economic future of Russia's Maritime Territory is still uncertain–a status that it shares with all but a few regions of Russia. Like other regions, the RFE does not control its own fate; it is hostage to policies that are in place or that have yet to be developed by Moscow. These policies define a partial and incomplete reform that has created a set of institutions best described as ``political capitalism.''

Since Russia began the task of building the framework for a new state, a market economy, and a civil society, its leaders have achieved much. Domestic markets are liberalized and regulatory barriers in the foreign market are much reduced. Since 1995, subsidies have been reduced and price inflation brought under control. Most small firms and the majority of large firms were privatized between 1992 and 1994. During this same period, almost a million new small businesses were created, a private banking sector emerged, and Russia's elected legislature drafted many laws that could provide the foundations of Russia's future legal system.

At the same time, however, Russia has experienced some daunting failures. Output has collapsed, perhaps to as little as 60 percent of former levels. Unemployment exceeds 14 percent of the labor force and many millions more are partially employed. Government tax revenues have collapsed amid rising wage and payments arrears. The government has maintained budgetary balance through large-scale borrowing that crowds out most private borrowing. In 1996, foreign direct investment in Russia reached just $2.2 billion (versus $2.3 billion for Poland). At the same time, Russia's capital outflow was $22.3 billion.[4]

The government itself is the source of most of the failures. Government at all levels–federal and territorial–is bloated and predatory. It is also corrupt, fragmented, and unable to supply the most basic public services. Most serious is the government's inability to provide the public with basic law and order. In a 1997 speech to the U.S. Russia Business Council, Deputy Secretary of the Treasury Lawrence H. Summers described Russia's problems:

> The enormously difficult job of fighting corruption is just as critical. The problem remains pervasive and fundamentally corrosive. Commercially motivated murders may have fallen but that may only indicate that corruption and criminal activity have become more organized. Three-quarters of Moscow shops pay private security firms for protection. Russian businesses routinely pay bribes to obtain export and import licenses, to lease commercial space, and to register their enterprises with local officials. Bribery, payments to overcome regulatory obstacles, and protection payments may total as much as 15% of wage costs, according to a small survey of private sector firms. Investment just will not happen with that kind of uncertainty or that kind of fear.[5]

What Russia has failed to do in the process of economic reform is to create the basic governmental infrastructure of a market economy:

Table 10.2
Russia's Reform Record

Agenda	Russia's Record	Problems
Stabilize macroeconomy		
Reduce government deficit	Progress	Tax shortfall, exemptions
Control money supply and credit	Progress	Debt and payments arrears
Liberalize markets		
Domestic markets	Yes	Regulation, exemptions
Foreign markets	Yes	Customs, certification
Privatize		
Housing	Progress	No specific problems discussed
Small-scale business	Private	Confiscatory taxes, crime
Large-scale business	Two-thirds private	Weak corporate governance
Land	Incomplete	Agricultural organization
Create market infrastructure		
Financial institutions	Improving	Undercapitalized, bad loans
Law and order	Improving	Crime and corruption
Legal infrastructure	Weak	Enforcement, bureaucratic law
Property rights	Incomplete	No specific problems discussed
Establish social safety net	Weak	No specific problems discussed
Attract investment, restructure	Slow	Economic, political uncertainty Weak legal framework Incomplete production-sharing laws Tax and regulatory Regime Weak financial markets Capital flight

a government that can provide law and order and basic public goods, define and enforce property rights, and provide legal and judicial institutions (see table 10.2).

A market economy requires fundamental institutions: property rights, rule of law, and financial institutions supporting payments flow and capital markets. Without law and order, actual property rights for Russia's citizens in Khabarovsk or Vladivostok are less secure than they were in the prereform era. Without legal infrastructure, businesses cannot enforce contracts, or they must turn to private enforcement, itself a source of risk. (One businessman in Vladivostok told the author, ``I pay 25 percent of the gross for protection, but at

Table 10.3
Political Capitalism

	Political Capitalism	Competitive Capitalism
Goal	Rent-seeking Capture of wealth	Productivity Growth
Government Role	Control access to resources, markets Subsidize, redistribute	Provide infrastructure, legal, financial, civil services Provide social insurance Provide public goods
Foreign Trade	Protectionist Antiforeign	Open
Foreign Investment	Passive foreign investment	Foreign direct investment Technology transfer
Domestic Investment	Closed capital market Capital flight	Open capital market Requires economic stability Requires secure property rights

least I get some services; I pay 28 percent of my gross to the government in taxes and get nothing.")[6] Without clear property rights, enforceable contracts, and mechanisms for dispute resolution, capital markets cannot develop. Without capital markets and ownership of land, new housing cannot be financed, and without housing, unemployed workers cannot leave the declining military cities, such as Komsomolsk-na-Amur or Petropavlosk, to find work elsewhere.

What has emerged in place of market-supporting institutions and an accountable government is a system that might be termed ``political capitalism." Joseph Blasi, Maya Kroumova, and Douglas Kruse depict in detail the closed capital markets and close ties between political influence and business success that characterize contemporary Russia in their book, *Kremlin Capitalism; Privatizing the Russian Economy.*[7] Political capitalism is focused on the capture and control of wealth rather than on growth and productivity (see table 10.3).

Because economic institutions and political jurisdictions are in flux, it is difficult to describe a stable set of rules of the game that characterize political capitalism. (``The first rule of the game is that there are no rules of the game," one specialist in business law in Vladivostok maintained in 1996.) The institutions, however, clearly serve a different set of goals than the textbook vision of competitive capitalism that motivated Russian reformers in 1992. With fuzzy property rights, the goals of productivity and growth are subordinate to the goals of capturing wealth and protecting wealth from capture. Instead of providing transparent legal and administrative infrastructure that is open to all, administrative authorities control access to resources and markets, distributing hidden subsidies to insiders at the expense of outsiders. The ability to do business depends on one's relationships. With bureaucratic authority changing rapidly, however, each firm faces the uncertainty of yet another source of economic risk–the risk of having the wrong friends.

Like executives anywhere, Russian managers are in no hurry to plunge into a competitive market. Thus, despite formal governmental initiatives to stimulate foreign direct investment and growth in Russia, Russia has received passive investment in Russian government debt rather than foreign direct investment or inflow of foreign-owned business, which have been the major source of transfer of know-how and technology in Eastern Europe.

Who will emerge as the eventual owners of Russia's productive assets? Seen from the vantage point of a port city such as Nakhodka, insiders and outsiders still battle for control rights over the governance of Russia's major industrial giants and other assets, such as ports. In one dimension, this conflict involves competition between established regional managers and Moscow-based banks and financial-industrial groups. In another dimension, it involves competition between former Soviet-era executives and a young, highly trained financial elite with considerable financial backing. In still another dimension, it involves competition between a military-industrial complex that controls uncompetitive, high-technology industrial assets and exporting sectors that control access to natural resources, foreign exchange revenues, and hard-currency balances. The energy and resource suppliers are often the major creditors of the manufacturing sector. Frequently, they are in a position to emerge as owners when the manufacturers are put into bankruptcy for their unpaid debts.

With legal rights of ownership to energy, minerals, timber, fish, diamonds, and other natural resources all in state hands, the ultimate asset is the state itself. Whether as owner or regulator, the state authorities determine who receives the control rights to Russia's resources and its wealth. Just as there are bitter corporate battles for control of Russia's largest exporting firms, there are also bitter bureaucratic battles between competing bureaucracies, such as the Federal Securities Commission and the Central Bank, and between the federal and territorial levels of government for administrative control over economic assets and outcomes.

The institutional arrangements for exercising ownership are still in flux, so the outcome of the competition for control of Russian assets is still uncertain. In the political battles ahead between the regions and the center, it is a matter of considerable importance that the political leaders who control Russia's government are in a position to determine the terms on which some will emerge as owners of Russia's wealth.

POLITICAL CAPITALISM AND TRADE

Capital flight is a predictable consequence of Russia's lack of legal, financial, and administrative support for capital markets and property rights–a consequence, too, of the unresolved competition for wealth that underlies political capitalism. In the period surrounding the collapse of the former Soviet Union, elites controlling Soviet wealth had an opportunity to capture state assets and move their value offshore. Yet, capital flight has continued even after privatization was largely complete in 1995. In an environment with high political and economic risk, asset owners have strong incentives to diversify their portfolios into lower-risk assets by increasing their holdings offshore. When the tax assessor has considerable ability to confiscate net income, then managers have strong incentives to leave income offshore. With weak financial markets at home, they turn to the world market to transact, borrow against collateral, and enter into enforceable contracts.

In addition, Russia's weak institutional infrastructure makes corporate governance difficult. Whoever holds control rights to assets is in a position to capture cash flow righ's, as well. In consequence, inside owners have a short-run outloo... Through underpricing of exports or a variety of other mechanisms, they sometimes transfer part of the value of current exports to offshore corporations. Even Gasprom and the major, vertically integrated oil companies invest their profits abroad and finance net domestic investment with foreign borrowing (sometimes from returning capital). Because of the

CHART 10.2
Russian Exports 1997

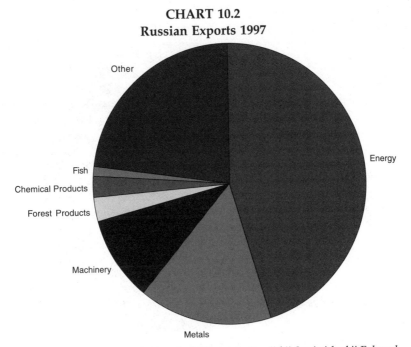

Other

Energy

Fish

Chemical Products

Forest Products

Machinery

Metals

Source: Russian Economic Trends 1998, no. 1; *Rossiiskii Statisticheskii Ezhegodnik, 1997* (Goskomstat, 1997).

important links between trade and investment, major reexporting countries such as Finland and major capital market centers such as Switzerland, Liechtenstein, Cyprus, Hong Kong, and Singapore have become significant trading partners.

As a result, Russian trade shows a steady export surplus. In 1996, Russia's officially reported exports rose 9 percent to $83.5 billion, while imports fell 4 percent to $44.3 billion. Most observers believe that the reported trade surplus of $39.2 billion is biased by the failure to report shuttle imports, which might total as much as $18 billion. In any case, in 1996, production for export was the chief dynamic component of a contracting economy.[8]

Oil and gas accounted for almost half of Russia's exports. Fertilizer, timber, ferrous and nonferrous metals, and ships were other top-ranking products (see chart 10.2). Food and consumer goods made up an estimated 41.3 percent of imports by value, including

CHART 10.3
Russian Imports 1997

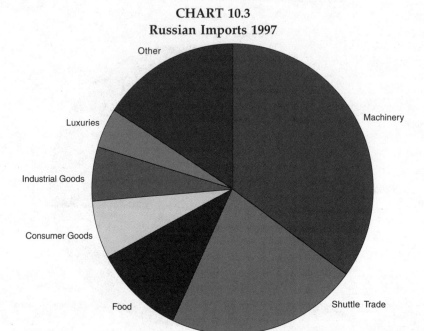

Source: Russian Economic Trends 1998, no. 1; *Rossiiskii Statisticheskii Ezhegodnik, 1997* (Goskomstat, 1997).

shuttle trade. Machinery and equipment accounted for one-quarter of imports (see chart 10.3).

In 1996, Ukraine was Russia's largest trading partner, followed by Germany, and the U.S. breakdown of trade by region for 1995 shows that Russia exchanged one-third of its exports and 39 percent of its imports with Western Europe. Other CIS (Commonwealth of Independent States) countries received 18 percent of Russia's exports and sent Russia 29 percent of its imports. Central and Eastern Europe ranked third with 6 percent of exports and 11 percent of imports (see table 10.4).[9]

China is another large trade partner for Russia. Russian customs data record Russia's 1996 exports to China at $4.7 billion and imports at $1 billion. Chinese customs data place the same values at $5.2 billion in Russian exports and $1.7 billion in Russian imports–a considerable difference.[10] Chinese government purchases of military hardware and nuclear power equipment were a large component

Table 10.4
Russian Trade by Partner, 1996
($ millions)

Region	Export	Import	Balance
Western Europe	31,370.9	16,582.3	14,788.6
CIS Europe and Baltic	13,908.5	10,335.4	3,573.1
Eastern Europe	9,909.7	3,318.3	6,591.4
Asia (excl. China)	6,217.5	2,467.4	3,750.1
United States	4,777.0	2,890.2	1,886.8
China	4,707.4	1,000.2	3,707.2
Middle East	4,505.9	1,589.6	2,916.3
CIS Asia	4,427.7	4,338.1	89.6
South America	2,862.4	1,033.2	1,829.2
Africa	708.5	134.7	573.8
Canada	91.0	338.8	−247.8
South Pacific	12.2	241.3	−229.1
TOTAL	83,498.7	44,269.5	39,229.2

Source: *Vneshneekonomicheskaia deiatel'nost' SNG* (Gosudarstvennyi komitet Rossiiskoi Federatsii po statistike, 1996).

in the total. In Northwest China, Russia has completed construction of the first phase of a uranium enrichment plant and is finishing details for the construction of two 1,000-megawatt nuclear reactors, according to Nuclear Energy Minister Viktor Mihailov. He placed the total value of these projects at $3±4 billion.[11]

Russia's sale of military hardware to China, such as SU-27 fighters and service support, submarines, destroyers, radar, missiles and missile technology, and related equipment, all contributes to the budget of Rosvooruzhenia, Russia's military export agency. Regional military producers, however, face long delays in payment from Moscow. In May 1997, B. Bregman, deputy general director for economics at the Aviation Production Association of Komsomolsk-na-Amur, in Khabarovskii Krai, complained that the aviation plant did not have enough operating capital to acquire materials and parts, because the government had paid only $4 million of the $108 million due. When China made an advance payment, for example, said Bregman, the federal government held back the entire 20 percent of the total contract value as a value-added tax.[12]

Table 10.5
Foreign Investment in Russia by Type, 1996±97
($ millions)

	1996	1997
Total Foreign Investment	6177.9	10498.0
Direct Investments	2090.0	3897.3
Portfolio	45.4	342.8
including		
Shares	11.4	
Other Securities	34.0	
Other Investments	4042.5	6257.9
including		
Trade Credits	384.9	
Other Credits	2714.8	
Bank Deposits	942.8	

Source: Russian Federation State Committee on Statistics. Current Statistical Survey 1997, no. 1, and Current Statistical Survey 1998, no. 1.

The important role of state-to-state trade relative to decentralized market-based trade is one indication of the cost that the administrative institutional framework of political capitalism imposes on market-based activity. I will look at the details of RFE regional trade in a later section of the paper.

POLITICAL CAPITALISM AND INVESTMENT

High levels of political and economic uncertainty, weaknesses of legal and financial infrastructure, and a predatory regulatory regime discourage Western investment in Russia. Moreover, short-term lending in Russia has been diverted to the government bills market by high real interest rates. (See table 10.5.)

Total Western investment in Russia in 1996 was estimated at $6.5 billion, of which only $2.2 billion was direct investment in industry and commerce (see chart 10.4). Of foreign direct investment, more than one-third went to import-related activities, especially food, consumer goods, and retail trade. Less than 10 percent of foreign direct investment was directed to Russia's main export sectors in energy. In energy, shortcomings of production-sharing laws, the Duma's unwillingness to extend production sharing to most resources, and other government barriers to foreign ownership limited investment. In natural resource and infrastructure sectors, Western companies maintain a small presence in Russia, attempting to

CHART 10.4
Foreign Direct Investment by Sector, 1997

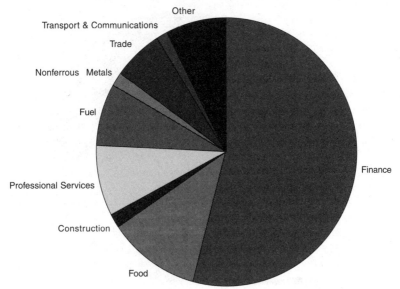

Source: *Statisticheskii biulleten, 1998,* no. 1. Gosudarstvennyi komitet Rossiiskoi Federatsii po statistike.

hold an option to invest in the future if market infrastructure improves.

Russia's largest sources of investment were the United States, Great Britain, Germany, and Switzerland (see chart 10.5). For the most part, U.S. investment is contingent on government political insurance and other guarantees. Switzerland presumably was a source of returning domestic capital, as was Liechtenstein. Western investment was concentrated in Moscow and Central Russia (see table 10.6). Although the RFE was ranked third among regions receiving foreign investment, it accounted for a mere $195 million of the total in 1996.

In 1997, the appointment to the government of proreform deputy prime ministers, Anatoliy Chubais and Boris Nemtsov, fueled rising optimism on the part of investors, leading to increased portfolio and short-term lending and to rising stock market prices. At the end of the year, however, the Russian Central Bank was forced to raise interest rates again when the Asian financial crisis caused a large

CHART 10.5
Total Foreign Investment in Russia by Partner, 1997

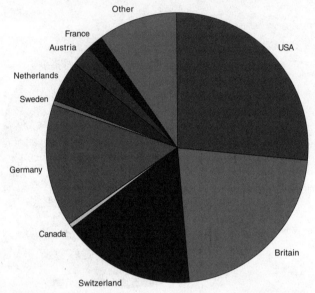

Other
France
Austria
Netherlands
Sweden
Germany
Canada
Switzerland
USA
Britain

Source: *Statisticheskii biulleten 1998,* no. 1. Gosudarstvennyi komitet Ross-iiskoi Federatsii po statistike.

outflow of capital from Russia. With Standard and Poors and Moody rating Russian borrowing as speculative at BB-, the Russian government still had much to do to make investment attractive to outsiders and its own population.

POLITICAL CAPITALISM AND REGIONAL ADMINISTRATION

The collapse of the Soviet Union dissolved the established system of administration, but what has emerged in the regions is an inconsistent mosaic of old and new laws and bureaucracies. Many new laws have been written, but old laws and regulations remain and the new regulations frequently contradict the laws they are supposed to implement.

In practice, the unraveling of the industrial ministries left control rights to natural resources less clear than they had been in the command system, when industrial enterprises had limited but clear-cut authority over the resources assigned to them. The Federation

Table 10.6
Foreign Investment in Russia by Region, 1997
($ millions)

Region	Total Foreign Investment	Direct Foreign Investment
Russia	17,574.7	6,953.7
Moscow City	7,076.7	3,056.4
Central (incl. Moscow)	7,283.6	3,191.5
Volga	839.9	113.5
Western Siberia	823.2	107.4
Eastern Siberia	430.8	28.6
Northwest	372.2	122.1
Russian Far East	215.1	140.2
Volga-Vytka	148.9	7.1
Central Black Earth	127.6	2.3
Urals	114.1	82.0
North Caucasus	69.9	57.9
North	63.5	36.3
Kaliningrad	9.2	8.6

Source: Russian State Statistics Committee. Interfax Statistical Report (March 7±13, 1998).

Treaty and Law on Subsoil Resources of 1992 and the Russian Constitution of December 1993 provided for government ownership of natural resources, but the delineation and exercise of ownership rights was less clear. In the Federation Treaty, the Russian Federation is given exclusive jurisdiction over the federal energy system, territorial waters, and the continental shelf. Utilization of natural resources and protection of the environment are subject to joint jurisdiction, as is protection of original areas of habitation and traditional ways of life of small ethnic communities (see table 10.7). The Russian mineral rights law, *Zakon O Nedrax*, establishes a State Minerals Fund, *Gosudarstvennyi Fond Nedr*, and describes procedures for licensing mining activities, surveying mineral resources, and paying for access to mineral rights.

Administration of the State Minerals Fund is under dual control of the central government and territorial officials. But, in fact, the procedures described in the legislation assign most of the rights to regulate resource use to the central authorities. All mineral stocks

Table 10.7
Legislation on Subsoil Resources

Federation Treaty	Delineates powers between the Russian Federation and the republics, initialed on March 13, 1992.
	Assigns many of the powers over land and natural resources to the joint jurisdiction of federal and republic authorities.
	Questions of utilization of natural resources and protection of the environment are subject to joint jurisdiction.
	Article III gives the republics power on their territory, other than those powers under federal authority.
Law on Mineral Rights	Adopted by the Russian Parliament, February 21, 1992; establishes a State Minerals Fund and describes procedures for licensing mining activities, surveying mineral resources, and paying for access to mineral rights.
	Fund administration is under dual control of the central government and territorial officials; however, most rights to regulate resource use remain in the hands of central authorities.
	Licensed organizations receive exclusive rights to the mineral wealth of a land parcel together with the right to manage the leased territory for a specified time period.
Production-Sharing Laws	Adopted by the State Duma on December 6, 1995.
	Passed by the Federal Council on December 19, 1995.
	Implements production-sharing agreements; provides simplified tax structure.
	The law on the list of fields eligible for development under production-sharing terms passed by the State Duma.
	Federal Law on Amendments and Additions to the Russian Federation Legislative Acts following from the Law on Production-Sharing Agreements contains amendments to twelve federal states.

are to be administered by the Committee on Geology and Use of Minerals. The Committee on Geology will then license rights to exploit mineral deposits to firms and organizations. (See table 10.8.)

Rights to use resources are subject to licensing, with payment set in money or as a share of output, with the revenues shared among levels of government according to the following scale:[13]

Table 10.8
Issues in Resource Ownership

Unclear Delineation of Federal and Local Control Joint control rights Rents shared Competition between levels of government for rents Government controls terms of private access
Legal Framework Federation Treaty, March 1992 Law on Sub-soil Resources, February 1992 Production-Sharing Law, December 1995
Central Government Rights Develop and update legislation Develop procedures for payment, together with other entities Develop a strategy for exploitation of mineral stocks Develop an integrated information database Enforce legislation regarding mineral resources Undertake exploration and valuation of mineral resources
Territorial and Autonomous Republics Rights Develop and use the territorial geological data base Value local resources Articulate the interests of national minority groups
Municipal and Local Rights Participate in the process of licensing in so far as it involves rights to lease land Develop a raw materials base for local firms in the building materials industry License and monitor the mining of scattered resources

- hydrocarbons: federal, 40 percent; territory, 30 percent; municipal or local, 30 percent
- minerals: federal, 25 percent; territory, 25 percent; municipal or local, 50 percent.

The actual delineation of federal, territorial, and district rights over resources is still in flux. When the Soviet Union collapsed, territorial and district officials began to exercise greater de facto control over local resources. Frequently, rights to resources were transferred from former state-owned firms to new organizations that were under the control of local or regional elites. Since then, during a period of conflict and confusion, federal agencies have been reasserting increasing federal authority.

During the same period, the political and administrative jurisdictions of central and local governments have also been in flux, leaving local firms subject to a multitude of overlapping authorities. In the Russian Constitution of 1993, Russia is a federal republic, with power divided between the federal government and the eighty-nine sub-units.[14] Since 1993, in the RFE, Moscow has signed power-sharing agreements with the Republic of Sakha, Khabarovsk, Amursk, and Sakhalin, granting them special privileges.

After the collapse of the Soviet Union, there was a period of confusion and conflict between executive and legislative authorities and between central and regional actors. In Siberia, regional legislative bodies attempted to claim jurisdiction over resources and assets on their territories, but President Yeltsin reasserted control, naming his own appointees as governors in more than half of the regions.

Today, all the territorial governors in the RFE are elected and exercise considerable authority. They are often former industrial managers who profited from the privatization of regional assets in 1992±1994 and who operate within a relationship system that provides some stability at a time when the formal rules of the system are changing and contradictory. Today, as earlier, the federal government manages to pit one region against another, discouraging their attempts to find a common cause. Moreover, it has given autonomous sub-units, called okrugs, quasi-independence from the territories to which they formerly belonged.

The territorial legislative body, or Duma, has a large number of members and meets infrequently. Its modest legislative authority is exercised by specific commissions of its members. Each territory has, in addition, an appointed president's representative who is responsible for coordinating the activities of the multitude of federal agencies in the territory. Relations between the governor and the president's representative are often uneasy, particularly in Primorskii Krai, where the president has transferred budgetary authority to the president's representative.

While regional authorities have uncertain rights, they have acquired heavy responsibilities. In the Soviet Union, the individual territorial administrative unit–the republic, krai, oblast, or okrug–merely implemented centrally determined policies. Moscow maintained its control, in part, through arrangements that set each region in competition with its neighbors for central allocations of resources. In practice, centralized funding for regional infrastructure was always inadequate, and local and municipal governmental agencies

CHART 10.6
Tax Share Retained in the Region, 1995

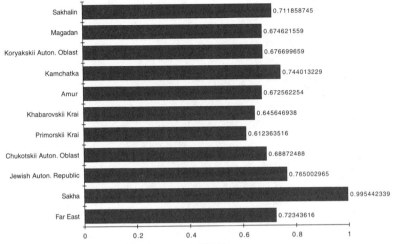

Sakhalin	0.711858745
Magadan	0.674621559
Koryakskii Auton. Oblast	0.676699659
Kamchatka	0.744013229
Amur	0.672562254
Khabarovskii Krai	0.645646938
Primorskii Krai	0.612363516
Chukotskii Auton. Oblast	0.68872488
Jewish Auton. Republic	0.765002965
Sakha	0.995442339
Far East	0.72343616

Source: *Regiony Rossii* (Goskomstati, 1998).

had insufficient authority to provide effective regional coordination. So, in practice, industrial ministries provided a share of local infrastructure, coordinating their activities through Communist Party channels.

With the collapse of the Soviet Union, the responsibility for providing many local public goods and services devolved to territorial and local units of government. Gradually, a division of tax revenues between the territories and the center has emerged to support decentralized supply of public services (see chart 10.6). As of January 1, 1995, the RFE region as a whole retained 72 percent of total tax receipts, a larger share than the all-Russian average of 59 percent. The shares of taxes retained in the region varied from a low of 61 percent in Primorsk and 65 percent in Khabarovsk to a high of 99.5 percent in the Republic of Sakha. Three units (designated autonomous okrugs) received significant federal subsidies as Northern territories–Yevreyskaia, Chukotskii, and Koryakskii autonomous okrugs.

The structure of local government expenditure reflects municipalities' and territories' growing responsibility in provision of local public goods, including subsidized housing and utilities. Using Khabarovsk government expenditure as an example (see chart 10.7), the three

CHART 10.7
Khabarovsk Government Expenditure, 1996

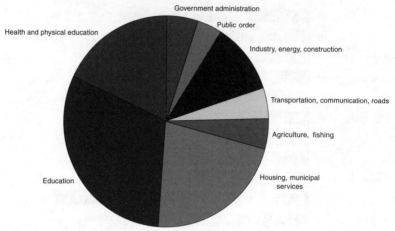

Source: Sotsial'no-ekonomicheskoe polozhenie Khabarovskogo kraia (Goskomstat, 1996).

main directions of expenditure were education (31 percent), housing and municipal services (22 percent), and health and physical education (18 percent). Subsidies to energy producers, industry, and construction accounted for 11 percent of expenditure, while government administration, public order, transportation and communication, and agriculture each received 4±5 percent.

Russia has not yet succeeded fully in establishing separate, tax-based governmental structures, so implicit charges and subsidies flow between Moscow and the territories through a multiplicity of vertical channels. (One region, Chukotskii Autonomous Okrug, supports itself largely through access to a fishing quota.) Moreover, a buildup of payment arrears affects both enterprises and territorial governments. In the RFE, federal government agencies and the military are the most remiss in failing to pay for delivery of electric power and wages in publicly owned firms; yet, they cannot be cut off.

Payments arrears and resulting nonpayment of wages led to strikes and a virtual shutdown of the electric power system in Primorskii Krai in spring 1997. The federal government intervened in the region in June, appointing Viktor Kondratov, head of the local office of the Federal Security Service, as president's representative and transferring all budget authority from the region's governor, Yevgeniy Nazdratenko, to Kondratov. President Yeltsin also transferred to Kondratov all authority to approve the allocation of quotas for the harvesting of commercial fish, seafood, and timber by organizations located in Primorskii Krai.[15] The Federation Council voted unanimously to oppose President Yeltsin's attempt to remove the governor, but the crisis in Primorskiy leaves the roles of central and territorial authorities in confusion.

TRADE IN THE RUSSIAN FAR EAST

The continuing confusion in establishing the legal and administrative framework for ownership and contracting means that trade relationships continue to be based on short-run interests. As Russian reform began, Western businesses were willing to commit resources to the RFE market in the hopes of acquiring access to resources or of gaining first-mover advantages in a market with the potential to serve all Northeast Asia. Russian decision makers turned initially to a world market that offered them exceptional profit opportunities to serve Russian markets that had been deprived of competitive consumer goods and services. Traders with the requisite licenses, quotas, and trading rights could arbitrage between the vast price differentials in world and Russian markets.

Russian firms, seeking security from domestic hyperinflation, moved their portfolios offshore to capital centers, often taking advantage of central bank credits at low rates of interest to privatize the benefits of trade and leave the costs socialized on the accounts of a state-owned firm. In this environment, a few large, Western multinational corporations in fields such as telecommunications and transportation were willing to commit investment to regional projects that, they hoped, would become nodes in their global system, but most Western firms entered into small projects that could provide short-run profit and generate information on the risks and costs of potential future investments.

Because neither Russia nor China could provide a framework of legal infrastructure to support contracts, property rights, and collateral, decentralized firms in these two countries had particular difficulties in entering into long-term relationships. Payments flow between Russian and Chinese firms was likely to require offshore affiliates in capital centers such as Hong Kong, Singapore, or Seattle. So, decentralized Russian-Chinese economic links focused on a short-run exchange of Russian timber, fertilizer, and fish for Chinese food and apparel. Even this short-run pattern of exchange was valuable to a region that had lost its European markets and its federal sources of support.

Foreign trade, particularly with the Pacific, has offset the precipitous fall in domestic purchase of RFE products. In the future, regional production will continue to depend on links to the Pacific market, because, while economic recovery in Russia and the Central Asian republics may again expand demand for some high-value products of the region, a permanent rise in energy and transport costs will make most of its raw materials uncompetitive in Europe. So, the region's turn to world markets will have to be a permanent one.

Shortcomings of Russian statistics complicate the task of following trade. Some important trade items are missing from regional data. These items include military products, some equipment for nuclear power, production of diamonds and gemstones, and production of gold and precious metals. Other categories are inaccurate because local traders have incentives to understate the value of shipments to avoid import tariffs, export taxes, and financial controls. Sales of timber are believed to be understated. Fishing vessels registered in Primorsk, Sakhalin, and Kamchatka frequently transfer catch to processors on the high seas, so it is difficult to monitor their total catch. In response to presumed understatement, government statistical offices attempt to make offsetting estimates (and to collect additional taxes), which are also likely to be inaccurate. Moreover, trade flows themselves have been volatile. Capital flight fueled exports in 1991±1992; border trade with China first surged and then collapsed in 1993±1994; and large one-time military purchases by the Chinese government increased exports in 1993 and 1996.

Published trade data that exclude gemstones, precious metals, and military hardware rank the fishing industry as the top trading sector followed by forest products, ferrous and nonferrous metals, energy, and machinery (see chart 10.8). These itemized products account for regional exports of approximately $2.2 billion annually. In 1996, the inclusion of military production, diamonds, precious metals, and offshore fishing would have added another $4-plus billion to total exports.

CHART 10.8
Russian Far East Foreign Trade by Commodity, 1995

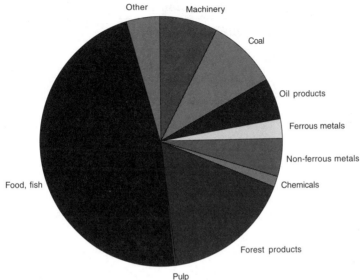

Source: Economic Cooperation between the Russian Far East and the U.S. West Coast and Alaska, white paper (American Chamber of Commerce in Russia, September 1996).

On the import side, the region is highly dependent on trade for its food and consumer goods–Chinese apparel, Korean TVs, Japanese cars, and U.S. meat and machinery (see table 10.9).

After years of reform, there is considerable evidence that Russian government institutions and policies put in place present a tremendous hindrance to regional adjustment and recovery as a genuine part of the Pacific market. The emerging official rules, centrally provided exceptions, and local evasions all reflect the incomplete competition for control of regional assets and wealth.

The beneficiaries of close political-commercial links are bureaucratic and commercial insiders at the center and in the regions who are increasingly in a position to dictate the terms on which small, newly privatized firms or new entrants can gain access to the foreign market. They are also in a position to determine the terms on which

Table 10.9
Russian Far East Foreign Trade Customs and State Statistics
($ millions)

Region	Exports			Imports		
	1995	1995	1996	1995	1995	1996
	Customs	State Statistics	Customs	Customs	State Statistics	Customs
Primorskii Krai	469.4	713.2	600.8	611.7	549.2	629.7
Khabarovskii Krai	585.6	559.7	829.4	289.4	288.6	246.4
Amurskaya Oblast	63.8	63.8	46.0	76.3	76.3	52.2
Sakhalinsk	181.2	475.9	346.7	272.4	292.6	213.7
Kamchatsk	69.8	393.3	172.5	133.5	147.1	150.5
Magadan	33.6	31.9	21.5	122.4	130.4	127.3
Sakha	244.1	244.1	227.8	220.8	220.8	197.4
Including Diamonds	1,644.1	1,644.1	1,627.8			
Jewish Autonomous Oblast	7.4	7.4	5.3	5.8	5.8	4.9
TOTAL*	3,299.0	4,133.4	3,877.8	1,732.3	1,710.8	1,622.1

* Includes diamonds, excludes military production and precious metals.
Source: International Technologies Laboratory, ``Economic Life in the Russian Far East'' (electronic subscription), March 1997.

foreign firms can participate in the Russian market. In some industries, competition for control of rents is still heated. In others, the rents have been divided–at least until new political developments change the balance of power. Unfortunately, political capitalism creates political and economic risk, discourages investment and technology transfer, and concentrates wealth in the hands of an elite who lack the ability to modernize.

INSTITUTIONAL BARRIERS TO DECENTRALIZED TRADE IN FOREST PRODUCTS

There should be a strong complementarity between Russian natural resource availability and China's rapid growth in production of labor intensive products. Yet, the RFE has had difficulty in building long-run, rather than short-run, decentralized trading relationships with

China. Weak financial markets and reliance on barter impedes Russian-Chinese trade. The most significant barrier, however, is an emerging recentralization of control over exportable resources from small, newly privatized firms to larger economic units linked to the regional, territorial, and central governments. In both fishery and forestry, the former Soviet industrial links are reemerging in a quasi-private form, based on control of access to resources, Russian government investment, and Western governmental or multinational investment.

A careful look at one sector that should enjoy strong markets in China, forest products, is instructive. In the case of forest products, China is a potentially strong market for wood products, including larch, that are not in high demand elsewhere in the Pacific, but trade has been short-run, with apparent underreporting on the Russian side. Russian-Chinese joint ventures have been small and relatively inactive.

In the forest products industry, competition for control of the resource has occurred in an environment of collapsing production. Foreign sales of timber, which averaged roughly 20 percent of output in the 1980s, accounted for almost two-thirds of production in 1994 and 1995, not because exports rose but because production dropped disastrously from 34.5 million cubic meters of total timber produced in 1985 to 10.5 million cubic meters in 1995 (see chart 10.9).

Although the Russian forest industry is largely privatized, the de facto control rights over resources have gone through a series of confusing changes. In the prereform era, the Soviet government earmarked most of its timber for domestic use, but it also turned to logs as a fungible commodity with which to pay for Japanese equipment. Soviet purchase of Japanese equipment was carried out through Russian-Japanese bilateral general agreements. There were five agreements in all—four on forest products and one on the construction of the first part of the port of Vostochnyi. Under these agreements, the Soviet government received credits from the Export-Import Bank of Japan for the purchase of Japanese machinery and equipment. Payment was made in kind by supplying raw materials to Japan. Three agreements were in force at the end of 1991: an agreement on wood chips, an agreement on the joint development of the Sakha coal fields, and a joint feasibility study of Sakhalin oil and gas.

Today, long-term agreements for forest products have lapsed because of continuing problems with terms of quality and delivery,

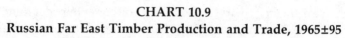

CHART 10.9
Russian Far East Timber Production and Trade, 1965±95

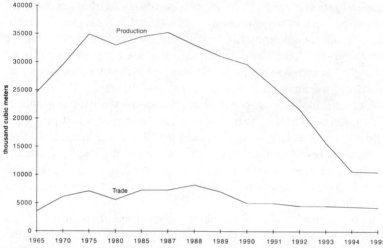

Source: Alexander Sheingauz et al., *Forest Sector of the Russian Far East: A Status Report* (Khabarovsk-Vladivostok: Economic Research Institute RAN, 1996).

but the RFE continues to send almost 90 percent of timber export to Japan. (In 1993, the combined exports of the Russian Far East's two major foreign trade companies went to Japan, 87.4 percent; South Korea, 9 percent; China, 3.5 percent; and Taiwan, 0.2 percent.)[16]

With the start of reform, a new law, the Fundamental Forestry Law of the Russian Federation, was passed in March 1993. The new law appeared to give territorial and district officials unprecedented authority over timberland management.[17] Districts were to have rights to sell timber, allocate rights to log, and monitor compliance—jurisdiction that was held earlier by federal and territorial officials. In practice, territorial governors were able to assert authority to control resource stocks, and an expanded multilevel bureaucracy emerged to allocate timberland assignments.

During the Soviet era, management of forests was coordinated by two government ministries, the Federal Forest Service (*Minleskhoz*) and the Ministry of Forest Products (*Minlesprom*); the former was responsible for protection of forest stocks, and the latter, for harvesting and production. In December 1992, the Russian Federation Property Committee created a partially state-owned commercial entity called Roslesprom. It was to be a joint-stock company responsible for investment services, research, and export of forest products. ``In reality,'' wrote scientists Alexander Sheingauz, Vladimir Karakin, and Vladimir Tyukalov, ``Roslesprom is attempting to gain control over the Russian Federation forest industry, including those in the RFE.''[18] In 1994, the State Property Committee delegated managerial authority of the state shares of all privatized enterprises in the industry (about 3,500 in number) to Roslesprom. The government issued 150 billion rubles in credit at 10 percent interest (when inflation was almost 1,000 percent), giving Roslesprom the right to distribute this credit.[19]

During 1994±1995, Roslesprom organized the former territorial branches of the Forest Products Ministry into fifty holding companies. A national forest products strategic exporter, called Rosexportles, was established, with 96 percent of its stock in the hands of Roslesprom. Roslesprom also became co-owner of the National Forest Bank and the Russian Forest Investment Company, incorporated in Boston.[20] Export licenses and access to export were managed through a few large former ministry units, now organized as regional associations.

At the same time as former ministerial units were attempting to reestablish control of the industry from above, a decentralized private sector was emerging in the regions, in the form of production cooperatives and small businesses. Many of these businesses, however, served to transfer revenues away from existing state-owned companies, leaving the state entity burdened with the production costs.

Privatization of the eighty-two timber-cutting firms, fourteen sawmills, twelve furniture factories, ten pulp and paper plants, and assorted machine repair and other shops in Khabarovskii Krai during 1992±1994 created about 150 private, mixed-forest sector enterprises controlling almost 90 percent of forest output. But state shares and, thus, control rights over these nominally private firms remained in government hands. After the first phase of privatization in Khabarovsk, controlling interest in some firms was in the hands of the territorial administration, and in other firms it was in the hands of a financial-industrial group (FIG) led by a regional association and marketing organization, Dallesprom. In an exchange of shares in

1995, Dallesprom gave the territorial administration shares representing a 51 percent controlling interest in its capital. In turn, Dallesprom received a controlling interest in forest harvesting companies managed by the state.[21] Similar territorial FIGs formed in other regions of the RFE.

In 1995, state shares in privatized firms were supposed to be sold on the stock market for rubles. But fearing loss of control to outside owners, territorial administrators devised a number of administrative strategies. The number of forest industry enterprises was increased and rights to harvest were redistributed in negotiations between territorial and local administrations and harvesting firms (although the Fundamental Forestry Law of 1993 requires open auctions for stock allocation).

Meanwhile, in Moscow, Roslesprom lost most of its control over forest product export when the federal system of export quotas and strategic exporters was abolished in 1995, but it retained the ability to control access to Russian governmental credits. It also gained the right to control access to U.S. Export-Import Bank guarantees when it signed a Memorandum of Understanding with the U.S. Export-Import Bank, under which the Export-Import Bank is providing up to $1 billion in credit guarantees for loans issued by U.S. commercial banks to forest industry enterprises in Russia for purchase of U.S. goods and services. Loan recipients are required to sell timber to foreign firms that will deposit revenues directly into an offshore escrow account. The 1996 state plan for Roslesprom included setting up a centralized system of equipment procurement, strengthening sanctions against enterprises violating tax laws, coordinating export trade, and representing the timber industry in tax agencies.[22] In 1996, Dallesprom, in Khabarovskii Krai, established a joint venture with U.S. Caterpillar Company to sell and service caterpillar equipment to the regional forest products industry.[23]

Although many joint ventures have been initiated with foreign partners, including Chinese firms, few of these projects have enjoyed medium-term success. By September 1995, 108 joint ventures were registered in the forest products sector, 71 in timber harvest, and 37 in wood processing and export. In Primorsk, out of seventeen joint ventures operating in forest products in 1995, seven had links with Chinese firms, two with Singapore, and one with Hong Kong.[24] In total, however, Russian-Japanese joint ventures accounted for 98.4

percent of production; Russian-South Korean, 0.7 percent; and all other countries, 0.9 percent.[25]

Several of the early joint ventures, such as Hyundai's project in Primorsk with the territorial and district forest associations at Svetlaya, employed Chinese labor. With an initial subscribed investment of $54 million, the Svetlaya project employed 400 Chinese loggers from Jilin Province and 200 local Russian workers in 1991. With the collapse of the Soviet Union, however, the project lost its export earnings, held in Russia's Vneshekonombank, and Chinese workers went unpaid for six months. Subsequent changes in domestic and export taxes, loss of logging rights, and environmental problems leave the project operating unprofitably at one-fifth capacity, currently employing about 150 Chinese workers and 280 Russian workers.[26]

In sum, then, despite its nominal privatization, the Russian forest products industry remains in the hands of governmental-commercial elites who control access to investment, credit, and links between domestic producers and foreign markets. The resulting political and economic risk complicates attempts to form long-term economic links and shifts trade toward short-run transactions. Decentralized trade in other industries in which China has potential long-run interest, such as fish and seafood, ferrous and nonferrous metals, fertilizer, and building materials, are similarly hindered by weak infrastructure on both sides, but especially in Russia. The postreform pattern of Russian-Chinese trade, then, presents a split-level economic relationship. On the one hand, there are a small number of large transactions and projects negotiated at the center that account for most of Russia's export surplus with China. On the other hand, there is a modest level of small, decentralized border trading and contracting. (Decentralized trade accounts for about $1 billion, or 17 percent, of total Russian-Chinese trade.) The disparity of Chinese and Russian data show that some portion of decentralized trade goes unreported in Russian data, but the fact remains that the level of Russian-Chinese economic activity is far below the potential value that might be expected if the legal, financial, and administrative infrastructure for business were stronger in both countries.

THE FUTURE OF RUSSIAN-CHINESE TRADE

In recent top-level meetings, Russia's and China's leaders gave top priority to an expansion of economic activity, promising to create a

Table 10.10
China's Trade by Country, 1996
($ millions)

Region	Exports	Imports
Hong Kong, Macau	33,478	7,949
Japan	30,874	29,184
United States	26,685	16,155
South Korea	7,511	12,481
Germany	5,845	7,324
Singapore	3,749	3,601
United Kingdom	3,200	1,881
Taiwan	2,803	16,132
France	1,907	2,240
Italy	1,838	3,246
Russia	1,693	5,153
Australia	1,673	3,434
Canada	1,616	2,570
Indonesia	1,428	2,280
Malaysia	1,371	2,243
Thailand	1,255	1,890
UAR	1,077	68
Belgium	1,043	1,023
Philippines	1,015	372
Brazil	763	1,484
North Korea	497	69
Sweden	392	1,380
European Community (subtotal)	**19,831**	**19,868**
Asia (subtotal)	**91,247**	**83,444**
TOTAL	**151,065**	**138,837**

Source: China's Customs Statistics, no. 88 (December 1996), pp. 32±49.

``strategic partnership.'' During visits by China's president, Jiang Zemin, to Russia in April 1997 and a return visit by President Yeltsin to Beijing in November 1997, both sides initialed ambitious plans for future projects. The reality of their trade flow, however, falls far short of their ambitious goals. In 1996, Russia ranked eighth in two-way trade with China, well below Japan, the United States, Taiwan, South Korea, Hong Kong, and Germany (see table 10.10). According

Table 10.11
China's Exports to Northeast Asia and Russia, 1996
($ millions)

Sector	Japan	South Korea	Russia	North Korea
Animals	1,549	265	233	5
Vegetables	1,470	320	129	141
Fats, Oils	11	6	1	11
Foods, Beverages	1,847	328	113	24
Minerals Fuels	2,583	1,133	45	174
Chemicals	1,240	529	38	29
Plastics, Rubber	380	64	14	24
Hides, Leather	759	160	375	1
Wood Products	881	144	1	1
Pulp, Paper	108	9	10	3
Textiles	9,607	1,619	324	31
Footwear	947	201	183	1
Stone, Cement, Glass	650	84	17	1
Gems	36	18	1	-
Metals	1,404	1,244	28	14
Machinery	4,810	983	105	19
Transport Equipment	356	218	4	13
Instruments	1,180	77	13	2
Arms	-	-	-	3
Misc. Manufactures	1,054	109	59	2
Artworks	5	-	-	-
Other	-	-	-	-
TOTAL	30,877	7,511	1,693	499

Source: China's Customs Statistics, no. 88 (December 1996), pp. 32±49.

to Chinese customs statistics, Chinese imports from Russia totaled $5.1 billion; exports to Russia were $1.7 billion. The top-ranked items in Russia's exports to China were ferrous and nonferrous metals, chemicals, energy, military products, and nuclear power equipment; Russia's top imports from China were food and consumer goods. (See tables 10.11 and 10.12.) Currently, China limits fertilizer and steel imports, two of Russia's top export products. Chinese sources

Table 10.12
China's Imports from Northeast Asia and Russia, 1996
($ millions)

Sector	Japan	South Korea	Russia	North Korea
Animals	87	42	185	7
Vegetables	25	8	13	3
Fats, Oils	3	1	5	-
Foods, Beverages	87	27	34	-
Minerals, Fuels	268	432	258	9
Chemicals	1,406	919	1,455	2
Plastics, Rubber	2,160	1,737	131	-
Hides, Leather	95	801	7	1
Wood Products	12	69	51	19
Pulp, Paper	365	480	268	-
Textiles	3,259	3,019	43	4
Footwear	23	131	-	-
Stone, Cement, Glass	289	51	1	-
Gems	23	1,253	-	-
Metals	3,521	3,086	1,703	16
Machinery	14,827	144	153	5
Transport Equipment	6,361	129	761	-
Instruments	1,863	-	17	-
Arms	-	143	69	-
Misc. Manufactures	247	71	-	-
Artworks	-	-	-	-
Other	-	-	-	-
TOTAL	**34,921**	**12,543**	**5,154**	**66**

Source: China's Customs Statistics, no. 88 (December 1996), pp. 50±70.

speculate that there is another $2 billion in unrecorded export of Chinese consumer goods to Russia.[27]

China has seized a target of opportunity in the collapse of Russia's military-industrial complex to upgrade its military hardware. The items on its list include Russia's SU-27 fighter aircraft–China purchased twenty-four in 1992 and forty-eight in 1996–and four TU-26 long-range bombers. With the aircraft comes improved *Zhuk* radar from Phazotron. Russia also agreed to sell China the licenses and technology to manufacture SU aircraft at a factory in Shenyang.

China is to receive four Kilo-class diesel electric submarines, worth about $200 million each, to be serviced in Russia, and is expected to acquire six other Kilo-class submarines, some with advanced quieting technology. China has purchased two Sovremenny-class guided-missile destroyers with SS-N-22 supersonic antiship missiles and surface-to-air missiles, and it has acquired key technological information about submarine noise reduction, missile guidance, and solid-fuel rocket motors.[28] In 1997, Rosvooruzhenia signed a protocol with the Chinese Ministry of Defense to service Russian-made Chinese diesel submarines at Bol'shoi Kamen, Primorskii Krai. Moreover, Russia has completed construction of the first phase of a uranium enrichment plant in Northwest China.[29] In making these military purchases, China has reportedly taken advantage of Russian disorganization to acquire technology from central-, territorial-, and firm-level sources.

A large-scale upgrading of China's air, sea, and missile technologies means a substantial change in the Asian security balance as well as a shift in the Sino-Russian security balance itself, but Russian producers of military hardware see foreign sales as the only way to maintain their remaining facilities and labor force. From the Western point of view, a buildup of Chinese military capacity is viewed with alarm by its neighbors; thus, proposed Sino-Russian economic cooperation in other areas such as energy would provide a double dividend if it diverted former military production capacity in Russia from military hardware to energy equipment.

Other large projects have been agreed to by political leaders, as well. These projects include:

- a nuclear power station in Jiangsu Province
- a project to lay a gas pipeline from Irkutsk through Mongolia and China to South Korea and possibly Japan
- possible Chinese purchase of $1.5 billion of Russian electric power
- cooperation in expanding rail transport across their common borders
- creation of a special Russian-Chinese trade zone near the town of Suifenhe, in Northeast China, bordering Primorskii Krai
- a framework agreement designed to increase trade to $20 billion.

The main barrier to immediate progress on these high-visibility projects is financing. Russia was one of the bidders to sell turbines and generators for China's $30-billion Three Gorges electric power project, but its inability to offer credit put it at a disadvantage relative to Japan, for example, which offered to provide Japanese Export-Import Bank funding.

Russia's weak financial markets and the lack of correspondent links between Russian and Chinese banks continue to be a serious barrier to growth of small-scale, decentralized trade. Russia complains that China has been unwilling to move Russian-Chinese trade away from barter to a currency basis, but payments flow between decentralized firms often is entrusted to Western banks.

PLANS FOR RUSSIAN-CHINESE COOPERATION IN ENERGY

How realistic are plans for a strategic economic partnership? Will the ambitious goals of top leaders be realized in the coming five years? There are genuine opportunities for expansion of trade and investment both at a decentralized, regional level and on a state-to-state basis. As China begins to close loss-making state-owned firms in its depressed Northeast, China's regions will be forced to seek new sources of employment.

The existing small-scale exchange of resource products, such as timber, fish, fertilizer, and metals, and the exchange of medium-technology equipment, such as agricultural equipment and vessels, for Chinese food and consumer goods would expand if customs administration, trade regulation, and financial infrastructure improved. Small-scale investment, such as Chinese financing of Russian fishing vessels and Russian financing of Chinese construction projects, would be possible with improved capital markets.

The most visible opportunities for state-to-state cooperation are in the energy and infrastructure sectors. In a highly publicized project to pipe natural gas from Russia's Kovyktinskoye field, U.S. gas producer Enron and the Japanese Pipeline Association are preparing a proposal to transport natural gas 1,300 kilometers across Mongolia to China. Tapping the Kovyktinskoye field appears more economical than alternative proposals to bring natural gas from Yakutia to Korea and Japan, because natural conditions would be considerably easier. Yet, even if technical problems of gaining access to Kovyktinskoye's

870 billion cubic meters of proven reserves are solved, formidable institutional obstacles remain in negotiating terms and financing.

A second prospective energy project is provision of natural gas by pipeline to Russia, China, North and South Korea, and Japan from the Republic of Sakha. Development of Sakha's natural gas would require a 3,200-kilometer pipeline to provide 25 billion cubic meters of gas annually to South Korea and other Northeast Asian markets. The pipeline alone is estimated to cost considerably more than development of gas in Sakhalin, not including the cost of specialized liquified natural gas ships, local Russian costs, or the cost of port terminal facilities. In autumn 1992, President Yeltsin proposed development of Sakha's natural gas during his visit to South Korea. The Korean side established an eight-company consortium, but this group has not moved ahead with specific proposals.

In the meantime, the Sakha Republic is seeking cooperation with Japan. Japanese companies have taken the position that Sakha's proven reserves would have to be doubled from about 1 trillion cubic meters to 2 trillion cubic meters before development would be feasible. Japan has formed a group of electric power and gas companies, engineering firms, and steel pipe producers to study development of Sakha's resources. Geographically, Sakha's resources are more accessible to China than to other countries, but only Japan appears to have the capital resources to fund such a sizable project. (See table 10.13.) •

Meanwhile, progress in developing the offshore energy resources of Sakhalin Island is serving as a barometer of the prospects for dozens of other large energy projects currently stalled in Russia. In 1996, oil consortiums Sakhalin-1 and Sakhalin-2 stepped up their exploratory work on Sakhalin's shelf. The resources of the Sakhalin shelf had been under exploration since 1976 when the Japan National Oil Company and the Japanese government created a consortium of eighteen Japanese companies, the Sakhalin Oil Development Cooperation Company, Sodeco. Between 1976 and 1983, exploration led to the discovery of two fields, Odoptu and Chayvo, with total reserves of 67 million tons of oil and 172 billion cubic meters of gas.[30] Under terms of their compensation agreement, the Japanese partners provided credits, which totaled $276.6 million by 1987, which were to be paid off once economically viable fields were discovered. During the 1980s, the Russian production association

Table 10.13
Russian Far East Oil and Gas Reserves

Region	Proved Reserves: $A+B+C1^1$	Reserves Presumed to Exist:[2] C2	Percentage of Reserves Used Up A, B, C1 + C2	Probable Reserves: C3+D1+D2	Proved + Probable Reserves
			Oil		
	million tons		percent	million tons	
RFE Total	324.3	277.5	60.2	3,053.1	3,759.5
Sakha	131.3	131.5	0.2	2,635.0	2,908.0
Sakhalin	193.0	146.0	60.0	418.1	851.5
Land	63.0	12.7	60.0	116.4	286.5
Shelf	130.0	133.3	0	301.7	565.0
			Natural Gas		
	billion cubic meters		percent	billion cubic meters	
RFE Total	1,574.2	598.2		9,756.3	11,973.6
Sakha	959.0	375.0	1.9	9,075.0	10,427.5
Sakhalin	615.2	223.2	26.5	581.3	15,46.1
Land	73.1	19.0	26.5	180.6	299.1
Shelf	542.1	204.2	0	500.7	1,247.0

[1]A, B, C1, C2, C3, D1, and D2 are *categories of reserve*. These commonly used engineering categories reflect how fully stocks have been explored.

[2]Reserves are categorized as ``presumed to exist'' if for the particular area there are favorable geologic and geophysical data analogous to that for areas containing verified reserves.

Source: A. P. Marenkov and V. M. Malich, *Programma Razvitiia Energetiki Dalnekvostochnogo Ekonomicheskogo Raiona* (Irkuts-Khabarovsk, March 1993).

Sakhalinmorneftegas undertook further exploration resulting in the discovery of five additional, larger fields.[31]

In 1989±1990, the Soviet Ministry of Oil and Gas examined the feasibility of setting up a joint venture to develop the Piltun-Astokskoy and Lunskoy fields, containing 100 million tons of hydrocarbon liquids and 494 billion cubic meters of gas. Six consortia bid for the tender to explore these fields, and, in 1992, a Feasibility Study Agreement was signed with the MMMMS consortium (Marathon-McDermott-Mitsubishi-Mitsui-Shell). In 1993, the consortium created the Sakhalin Energy Investment Company to manage development of the fields, but the first phase of development was postponed until after Russia's Duma passed production-sharing legislation in December 1995.

The four fields currently proposed for development are located off the east coast of Sakhalin. Oil reserves lie within 15 miles of the coast in shallow water, but the Sakhalin shelf has difficult conditions for extraction. From October through June, it is icebound with frequent storms, powerful currents, and low temperatures.

The operating organization for Sakhalin-1 is Exxon Neftegas, an affiliate of the Exxon Corporation operating on behalf of an international consortium that includes two Russian affiliates of Rosneft, Rosneft-Sakhalin (17 percent) and Sakhalinmorneftegas-Shelf (23 percent); the Japanese company Sodeco (30 percent); and Exxon (30 percent).[32] The project is now referred to as Sodeco-2. Development of Sakhalin-2 will be carried out by the MMMMS Group. Initially, the Western consortium included Marathon, McDermott, Mitsubishi, Mitsui, and Shell, but, in 1997, McDermott offered its share of the project for sale, announcing that it would continue its involvement in Sakhalin as a contractor.

Although Russian production-sharing legislation still conflicts with some aspects of Russia's tax code, both Sakhalin-1 and Sakhalin-2 have moved ahead cautiously. Sakhalin-2 has contracted for a $45-million mobile drilling and production unit that is under construction by a military plant in Komsomolsk-na-Amur. Sakhalin-1 is drilling exploratory wells and undertaking 3-D seismic surveys. Additional exploratory drilling in a new area, called Sakhalin-3, has begun. By the end of 1997, total investment on the Sakhalin shelf was expected to reach $500 million.

In response to the demand that foreign oil companies provide funds for Sakhalin's infrastructure, Sakhalin-1 and Sakhalin-2 have created the Sakhalin Development Fund, dedicated to providing the social and economic infrastructure of the island. Each project will pay $20 million a year for the first five years after commencement of production, totaling $200 million.[33] Funding for Sakhalin-2 has been provided by the European Bank for Reconstruction and Development, and the Dutch Bank ABN-Amro is funding Rosneft-SMNG participation in Sakhalin-1.

If they were fully developed, the Sakhalin fields might provide 10 million tons per year of oil and 16 billion cubic meters per year of gas.[34] Natural gas could be delivered to Russia, South Korea, China, and Japan (Hokkaido) with liquefied natural gas being sold to countries in Northeast Asia. (See charts 10.10 and 10.11.)

CHART 10.10
Russian Far East Natural Gas Production, 1985±95

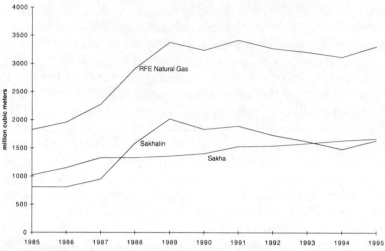

Source: *Promyshlennost'*, various years.

CHART 10.11
Russian Far East Oil Production, 1985±95

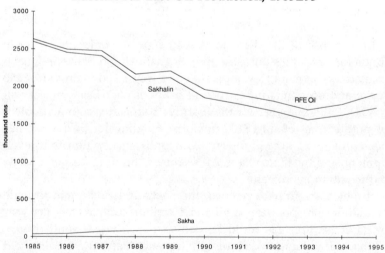

Source: *Promyshlennost'*, various years.

If China's growth remains high, then Chinese policy makers will have a growing interest in gaining access to Russian energy imports, as well. Oil output in China's Daquing field in Northeast China is falling gradually and China needs to shift energy consumption toward gas to compensate for declining quality and availability of coal. Gaining access to Siberia's energy appears to be considerably more feasible than China's recent proposals to transport Kazakh natural gas across mountainous terrain to southern China.

PLANS FOR REGIONAL COOPERATION

A second large proposal that could involve a major inflow of investment resources is the Tumen River Basin Development project moving forward (slowly) under the auspices of the UNDP. Initial plans envisaged creation of a seaport, construction of railways and airport, and establishment of a free trade zone on the Sea of Japan, in a region centered around the Tumen River where the borders of Russia, China, and North Korea converge. Opposition to early proposals by Primorskii Krai led to several variants encompassing a larger region.

The Tumen River is a shallow waterway winding through marsh and wetlands to empty into the Sea of Japan. At its mouth, the river demarcates the border between Russia and isolated North Korea, but a few kilometers upriver, China's Jilin Province occupies the river's western shores. Southern Primorsk is a long finger of land extending south along the coast of the Sea of Japan, separating China from direct access to the sea.[35] The Soviet Union's strategic concern with control of its Pacific region led it to restrict settlement in this border region, so, today, an international delegation taking a Russian ferry to Primorsk's small southern port of Zarubino sees open woodlands extending to rocky beaches, broken occasionally by subsistence farms or a state school for border guards. In the distance, the forested slopes of the low Bei Shan Mountains separate Russian territory from a densely populated Chinese hinterland.

Proposals to create a free economic zone in the Tumen region were first enunciated in academic papers at Hawaii's East-West Center.[36] The UNDP became interested in the proposal, preparing feasibility studies and a regional development plan and sponsoring regional conferences of the affected countries: China, North Korea, South Korea, Russia, Mongolia, and Japan.[37]

The level of interest of the participating countries varies widely. China, eager to gain access to the Sea of Japan, has given the proposals strong support, building roads, railroads, and infrastructure in the Hunchun region. Establishment of this key infrastructure link supports ambitious goals to create what China calls the ``Second Eurasian Continental Bridge,'' a rail link to Central Asia and Europe via the Chinese Eastern railway.[38] Mongolia, too, is interested in expanding rail and port links to Northeast Asia. North Korea would like to bring foreign investment to its ports of Sonbong and Rajin but on terms that do not diminish its sovereignty in the region. Japan and South Korea, which would be able to provide the capital for regional development, express strong interest. A Russian-Japanese joint venture with an authorized capital of $100,000 has been set up to upgrade the Khasan Commercial Port at Zarubino. Initial investments will be used to acquire new loading equipment and construct container and grain terminals.

Moscow and the territorial authorities in the Primorskiy region view developments in southern Primorsk differently. Their differences came to a head in spring 1997 when Moscow agreed to a demarcation of Russia's border with China that ceded to China a 300-square-hectare plot on the shores of the Tumen River that will give China easier access to the Sea of Japan.[39] Since then, the Primorsk leadership has lobbied for a program that would strengthen links between China and its port at Zarubino but that would limit the impact of population inflow on the fragile environment of the territory.

Regional leaders fear that an influx of population into Primorskii Krai would lead to eventual territorial claims. Given the difference in population size between the total RFE population of 7.5 million and the almost 100 million population of China's neighboring Heilongjiang, Jilin, and Liaoning, their hesitation is easy to understand.

ECONOMIC FORCES IN THE RUSSIAN-CHINESE ECONOMIC RELATIONSHIP

Thus, the future of Russian-Chinese economic cooperation seems to offer as much prospect of discord as of interdependence. In many respects, the problems raised by proposed development in the Tumen River region symbolize the broader underlying tensions between the economic interests of the two countries. China's leaders believe interaction with the world market is essential to continued economic growth, and continued economic growth is essential to continued political stability, while Russian decision makers perceive a tradeoff between increased openness to the world market and their political control over the sparsely populated Siberian and Far Eastern regions.

The primary engine of Chinese growth will be Western capital investment and technology, which will remain China's top priority. China will continue to attempt to build regional infrastructure in Northeast Asia and to gain access to Russia's energy and other natural resources, and it will continue to take advantage of the opportunity to acquire advanced Russian military technology on favorable terms, to the dismay of some of its smaller neighbors. But economic relations with the Asian region, Japan, the United States, and South Korea will remain more important to it than economic links to Russia.

Russian leaders, in contrast, are uncertain how to gain the benefits of integration into the Pacific market without losing political control over these regions. Yet, disintegration of Soviet-era production links and out-migration of unemployed workers leave Russia extremely vulnerable in its Eastern regions.

Hence, from the economic point of view, the forces fostering Sino-Russian cooperation are Russia's economic and military weakness, China's interest in profiting from a target of opportunity in Russia's military technology and raw materials, and the leverage that each hopes to get with the West from having access to an alternative partner. Still, neither these political considerations nor the genuine opportunities for economic cooperation that exist are likely to be sufficient to overcome the two countries' areas of competition.

There are many sources of potential contention—the immense population imbalance in Asia; persistent, if diminishing, border problems; and the prospect of competition for access to the energy resources of Central Asia. There is ample evidence that the sphere of common economic interest of the two countries remains limited, for example, in China's failure to purchase Russian energy equipment for its Three Gorges project and in Russia's eagerness to sell military hardware to other Asian states, including Taiwan.

To the economist, it appears likely that Moscow's and the RFE region's interest will be better served by a prosperous, dynamic

Pacific Russia than by a depressed and declining region. Furthermore, there seems to be no way to provide such prosperity except through trade, foreign investment, and technology transfer. Economic development based on the active involvement of investors from many countries could help to balance Russian fears of domination by strong neighbors like China and Japan.

Looking ahead, Russia's economy has not one but many possible futures in the coming years. Although there is a great deal of uncertainty about the probabilities of various outcomes, it is reasonably clear what policy choices and changes in expectations would be required to achieve each goal. So the key concept for thinking about Russia's future is ``contingency.'' The shape of Russia's economy in five years is contingent on choices that have not yet been made.

This is a time of opportunity but also a time of high risk. Russia's government appears to be committed to reform, and a large pool of domestic and foreign capital would respond rapidly if a stable and secure economic environment could be put in place. There is a large pool of well-educated people available to staff new ventures. The question that remains is whether Russia's Parliament and Russia's financial-industrial groups will be willing to support the policy choices that are needed to move beyond the institutions of political capitalism that currently impede success.

OPTIONS FOR U.S. POLICY

The United States and other Western governments, as well as the International Monetary Fund and World Bank, have been heavily engaged in supporting Russian reform. Since early 1992, the United States and other countries have provided humanitarian aid, extensive technical assistance, concessionary loans, and risk insurance for private lending. In March 1996, the IMF approved a three-year extended loan that will total more than $10 billion when it is fully exercised, bringing total IMF lending to Russia to more than $20 billion. The World Bank, including the International Finance Corporation, has provided more than $5 billion to date and has promised an annual Russian program of $3 billion, contingent on the process of Russian reform.[40] The European Bank for Reconstruction and Development has an active program in Russia, much of it coordinated with the European Union. The U.S. government support for financing commercial relations includes programs of the Export-Import Bank, the Overseas Private Investment Corporation, the Trade and Development Agency, USAID, and the Nunn-Lugar program for weapon dismantling. Yet, the amount of private capital flight from Russia continues to exceed the sum of multilateral assistance and private foreign investment. The IMF estimates that gross capital flows out of Russia equaled about $29 billion in 1996, resulting in an estimated net capital outflow of $22 billion.[41]

As Russia's tax base has shrunk, the government's ability to collect taxes has deteriorated. At the end of 1997, tax collections were running at 52 percent of planned levels, leaving the government unable to pay public employees or fund pension payments without rekindling inflation. In addition, Russia's financial sector remains extremely fragile. A decline in inflation and the end of many implicit government subsidies have eliminated many sources of profit for banks. Now, the undercapitalization of banks, their high operating costs, and the large share of nonperforming loans held by banks threaten a shakeout of many of them.

Moreover, the weakness in Asian capital markets spread to Russia. The Russian Central Bank announced drastic increases in interest rates, throttling a nascent expansion. Despite high interest rates, Russia is still unable to stem an outflow of capital, a development that has led to a breakdown of Russia's existing exchange rate system.

On top of short-run shocks, long-run institutional problems remain. The Russian Duma has not yet passed legislation supporting tax reform, production-sharing laws, or the full privatization of land. The existing regulatory regime is obtrusive, often contradicting underlying new legislation. Regulations may be enforced arbitrarily, corruptly, or not at all. Institutions for dispute resolution and enforcement of property rights are inadequate. The government itself is fragmented, with various agencies pursuing contradictory policies.

The implications of national disorder are unfortunate for both the center and the regions. When the centrally determined rules of the game are enforced unequally or are perceived to be confiscatory, then regional decision makers seek exceptions from the center or, in their absence, seek ways to evade the rules. Foreign corporations and affiliates of domestic firms choose to serve the Russian market from offshore.

The consequences of continued Russian decline and decapitalization of assets are likely to be particularly risky in Northeast Asia, where the level of militarization is high and a legacy of earlier conflicts still influences the popular mood. Institutional fragmentation in the Russian Far East would complicate a coordinated international response to a crisis in North Korea. But reversal of further decline depends mainly on domestic government policies.

There are many initiatives of the Russian central government that could enhance the region's role as a commercial link. An agrarian reform in the Russian Far East that provided the basis for private farming in the rich farm lands of Amur and Primorsk regions would slow the current exodus of population and improve regional supply of food. (Productivity per worker on the region's large collective farms is no higher today than the level that was achieved by peasant farmers in the region in 1910±1917.) Yet, implementation of nominal land privatization by means of land shares has resulted in little transfer of control rights over land from collective farm managers and local government authorities to households. A recent task force on agrarian reform found that regional governments impose high land taxes on newly privatized land and expropriate the land without compensation on grounds of non-use or ``irrational use.''[42] Thus, the government's uncertain commitment to reform creates the very uncertainty that could cause reforms to fail.

It is easy to say that the West has a large stake in Russia's reform and that it should remain engaged in supporting reform, but the emergence of political capitalism raises the probability that the Russian economy will be stuck in a partial and incomplete reform and that the Russian government may lose the support of its electorate and of private investors. In the face of this prospect, Western donors and multilateral institutions need to direct increased attention to the building of human capital and market-supporting institutions in Russia's regions, expanding the programs already under way. Most important, Russian government leaders need to understand that the success of economic reform hinges on their success in reforming government structures.

NOTES

[1] David Tarr, ``The Terms of Trade Effects of Moving to World Prices on Countries of the Former Soviet Union,'' *Journal of Comparative Economics*, no. 18 (1994), pp. 1±24.

[2]Vladimir Konovalov, ``Russian Trade Policy,'' in Constantine Michalopoulas and David Tarr, eds., *Trade in the New Independent States* (Washington, D.C.: The World Bank, 1994), pp. 29±51.

[3]Interview with Liu Chang Sheng, vice director of Jilin Province Planning Commission, Seattle, May 1997.

[4]Anthony Robinson, ``The Flywheel Gains Momentum,'' *Financial Times Survey*, April 11, 1997, p. 1.

[5]Lawrence H. Summers, ``The Global Stake in Russian Economic Reform,'' speech delivered to the U.S. Russia Business Council, April 1, 1997, reported in *Treasury News* (U.S. Department of the Treasury).

[6]Interview in Vladivostok, Russia, August 1996.

[7]Joseph Blasi, Maya Kroumova, and Douglas Kruse, *Kremlin Capitalism: Privatizing the Russian Economy* (Ithaca, N.Y.: Cornell University Press, 1997).

[8]U.S. Department of Commerce, BISNIS Briefs Electronic Broadcast, ``Russian Trade Statistics for January-December 1996,'' May 8, 1997.

[9]*Vneshneekonomicheskaia deiatel'nost' SNG* (Moscow: Gosudarstvennyi komitet Rossiiskoi Federatsii po statistike, 1996), p. 111.

[10]*China's Customs Statistics* (Hong Kong: EIA Publishing Ltd, 1996).

[11]``Economic Life in the Russian Far East'' (electronic subscription), International Technologies Laboratory, January 18, 1997.

[12]``Economic Life in the Russian Far East,'' May 17, 1997. In contrast, press reports in the region reported that an earlier sale of aircraft to China was concluded on the basis of barter, with the factory in Komsomolsk-na-Amur receiving partial payment in food products.

[13]In addition, there are several taxes, which are discussed later.

[14]Sub-units include 21 republics, 6 krais, 49 oblasts, 2 cities, 1 autonomous oblast, and 10 autonomous okrugs. The federal constitution gives republics the right to have their own constitutions and allows other units to write their own laws, which must not contradict the federal constitution.

[15]Alexander Lukin, ``Economic Life in the Russian Far East,'' International Technologies Laboratory, June 7, 1997, and June 14, 1997.

[16]*Russian Far East Update*, vol. 4, no. 3 (March 1994), p. 4.

[17]William Turner, ``Focus on the Russian Far East's Timber Industry,'' *Russian Far East Update*, vol. 4, no. 7 (July 1994), pp. 7±10.

[18]Alexander Sheingauz, Vladimir Karakin, and Vladimir Tyukalov, *Forest Sector of the Russian Far East: A Status Report* (Khabarovsk-Vladivostok: Economic Research Institute RAN, 1996), p. 14.

[19]The following details come from these sources: Sheingauz, Karakin, and Tyukalov, *Forest Sector of the Russian Far East*; Mark Wishnie, ``The Centrally Planned Timer Sector in the Russian Market Economy,'' paper (University of Washington Center for International Trade of Forest Products), Winter 1997; Nikita Rogachov, ``Forceful Methods Chosen to Reform Timber Industry,'' *The Current Digest of the Post-Soviet Press*, vol. 49, no. 3 (February 19,

1997), p. 19; K. Vishnepolski, ``Russia: Roslesprom to be Reorganized,'' *Commersant,* June 18, 1996, p. 9.

[20]*Business Moskovskie Novosti,* no. 33 (1995), p. 10 (cited in Sheingauz, Karakin, and Tyukalov, *Forest Sector of the Russian Far East,* p. 14).

[21]Sheingauz, Karakin, and Tyukalov, *Forest Sector of the Russian Far East,* p. 18.

[22]Ibid., p. 14.

[23]Visit to Dallesprom Caterpillar Sales Center, Khabarovsk, September 1996.

[24]Two Russian-Chinese joint ventures in Primorsk held harvesting leases for twenty-five to fifty years. These were Mudanjian-Kavalerogo, founded by a logging firm in Khrustalnyi Raion and the Heilongjian Foreign Trade Company, and See Da Flora in Dalnegorsk between the Russian firm Terneyles and the Bensin Company for Trade with CIS producing building materials.

[25]Sheingauz, Karakin, and Tyukalov, *Forest Sector of the Russian Far East,* p. 45.

[26]Kwang Il Tak, ``Foreign Investment in the Forest Sector in the Russian Far East and Potential Market Integration with Northeast Asia,'' working paper 94-92 (IIASA), November 1994, pp. 43±59.

[27]``Sino-Russia Summit: All Talk, No Action,'' *Wall Street Journal,* November 7, 1991, p. A16.

[28]Aleksey Balief, ``Great Friendship Growing through Kalashnikovs,'' *Rossiiskaya gazeta,* October 5, 1996, in *FBIS SOV-96-196;* and ``Pentagon Says Russians Sell Destroyers to China,'' *Washington Times,* January 10, 1997, p. 1.

[29]``Economic Life in the Russian Far East'' (electronic subscription), January 18, 1997.

[30]Michael Bradshaw, ``Sakhalin: The Right Place at the Right Time,'' *Russian and Euro-Asian Bulletin* (forthcoming).

[31]Piltun-Astokhskoye, Lunskoye, Arktun-Daginskoye, Yzllmetyevskoy, and Veninskoye fields.

[32]``Economic Life in the Russian Far East'' (electronic subscription), September 16, 1995.

[33]Bradshaw, ``Sakhalin: The Right Place at the Right Time,'' p. 5.

[34]David Cameron Wilson, *Eastern Bloc Energy* (June 1993), p. 3.

[35]*Russian Far East Update,* vol. 7, no. 2 (February 1997) provides maps and discussion of proposed infrastructure projects in the region.

[36]See conference proposals in an excellent volume edited by Mark Valencia, *The Russian Far East and the North Pacific Region: Emerging Issues in International Relations* (Honolulu: East-West Center, 1992).

[37]The reader can review current project proposals on the United Nations Development Project Web site on the Internet.

[38]Yang Faren, "Linkup of the Second Euroasian Continental Bridge and its Bearing on China's Opening Up as Well as on the Development of the Linkage between the Central Asian Nations and the Asia-Pacific Region" (working paper presented at a conference on Russia in Asia, organized by IREX and the Institute of East European, Russian, and Central Asian Studies, Chinese Academy of Social Sciences, Beijing, May 12–15, 1994).

[39]Lyudmila Sherova and Zakhar Vinogradov, "No More Than a Bit of Land . . . ," *Ogonek*, no. 9 (March 1997), p. 23, in *FBIS-SOV-97-0571*.

[40]John Hardt, "Russia's Opportunity to Enter a New Stage in Transition: Update," *CRS-33*, October 29, 1997.

[41]International Monetary Fund, "Russian Federation—Recent Economic Developments Staff Country Report No. 97/63," July 1997, p. 57.

[42]Bradley Rorem and Renee Giovarelli, "Agrarian Reform in the Russian Far East," *RDI Reports on Foreign Aid and Development*, no. 95 (October 1997).

11

The Far Eastern Challenge to Russian Federalism

Michael McFaul

Immediately after the collapse of the Soviet Union in August 1991, many analysts worried that the Russian Federation would share a similar fate.[1] Buoyed by their unique ethnic compositions, Russian republics, Chechnya and Tatarstan in particular, aggressively challenged the territorial integrity of the Russian Federation.[2] If Belarus could be an independent nation-state, then so could Tatarstan.

To date, however, only one republic—Chechnya—has attempted to leave the Russian Federation.[3] After reaching a nadir in center-republic relations in the summer of 1993, all other republics within the Russian Federation have sought to negotiate and compromise with Moscow rather than press for total independence. The federal compromise is not a static one, because rulers in Moscow and these republics constantly renegotiate the terms of their relationship. Yet, the threat of dissolution precipitated by republican defection has appeared to wane, not grow, with time.

Paradoxically, as the republican challenge to Russian federalism has subsided, the federal compromise between Moscow and Russian oblasts has grown increasingly strained. Initially, declarations of sovereignty by Russian oblasts looked like tactical moves designed to ensure that oblasts would receive the same bundle of benefits accorded to republics. The acquisition of symmetrical status with republics as specified at least on paper in the new Russian Constitution has not eliminated conflict between Moscow and Russia's regions. Most conflicts center on distributional issues regarding tax revenues, federal subsidies, and control over local properties. In some regions, however, conflict over political authority—the kind of conflict that helped to precipitate the Chechen War—has grown worse since 1993, not better.

The battles between Primorskii Krai and Moscow rank as some of the most contentious. Primorskii Krai is Russia's most defiant oblast today, as tensions between Moscow and Vladivostok over a whole range of political, economic, and foreign policy issues overshadow all other federal challenges in Russia, besides Chechnya and Dagestan.[4] Given the precarious international balance of power in the region, center-periphery conflict in this region of Russia might someday precipitate a larger international conflict. Together with the renewed military conflict in Chechnya and Dagestan, the Far East, because of its unique history, economy, distance from Moscow, and location on the outer reaches of the Russian state, poses the greatest challenge to Russian federalism. This center-periphery struggle significantly impacts on the larger Russo-Chinese relationship and generates important complications of the Sino-Russian regional interaction. Ethnic tensions and cross-border problems are often exploited in the internal struggle about the future of Russian federalism.

Ultimately, this essay dismisses the most dire predictions about the future of the Far East and Primorskii Krai, in particular, and argues instead that Russia's territorial integrity will be preserved, a fact that decreases sources of a potential Sino-Russian confrontation. The same factors that make the Far East such a challenge for federalism also create incentives, particularly political and security incentives, for Russians living in the area to maintain ties with Russians living farther west. At the same time, the conflicts between Primorskii Krai and Moscow have strengthened, however paradoxically, the institutionalization of federal norms in Russia and have constrained the power of the center. Moscow's attempts to discipline the region have failed, which in turn has undermined the center's authority throughout the Federation as a whole. Though a positive sign for federal power, the center's weakness has allowed local government officials to block democratization at the local level. The ongoing struggles between Moscow and Primorskii Krai illustrate a real paradox for those interested in state building and democratization; that is, progress in one arena—federalism—may impede progress in another arena—the consolidation of liberal democratic institutions at the local level.

To develop this argument, this chapter proceeds as follows. The first section provides an overview of the basic features and functions of federal states in general, providing an "ideal" framework from which to evaluate the evolution of Russian federalism. The second section outlines a brief history of the evolution of Russian federalism since the collapse of the Soviet Union. The third section addresses the specific relationship between Primorskii Krai and the Russian federal government, highlighting the political and economic developments that have exacerbated tensions between Moscow and Vladivostok. If the third section focuses on elite struggles, the fourth section sketches political attitudes of society writ large by tracing voting patterns in the region in 1989. Drawing together assessments from earlier sections, the fifth section offers a general evaluation of Russian federalism, highlighting those aspects that look robust and those factors that are either weak or missing.

FEDERAL DILEMMAS

Federal states are remarkable inventions. In essence, federal systems allow two governments to govern over the same territory. To be truly federal, the lower-level government cannot be merely the agent of the other but must have autonomous jurisdiction over certain issues. More precisely, a political system is considered federal when the following two conditions are satisfied: (1) There exists a *hierarchy* of governments with a *delineated scope of authority* (for example, between the national and the subnational governments) so that each government is autonomous in its own sphere of authority; (2) An *institutionalized degree of autonomy* imposes strong limits on the discretion of the national government so that it cannot unilaterally alter the distribution of authority between governments.[5]

Sustaining this precarious balance has been a fundamental challenge to all federal states that most have failed to meet at one point in history. Central authorities often seek to destroy federal structures by subordinating regional and local governments, while regional governments undermine federal structures both by exiting and by free-riding.[6] Moreover, the history of even the most robust federal states suggests that the balance of power between the center and the subnational governments cannot be assumed to be stable.[7] Although the Founding Fathers of the United States often are accorded genius status for penning a remarkable federal constitution, the first U.S. experience with federalism ended in civil war.[8] For decades, the Canadian federal system was thought to be an exemplary model for others to follow; yet, this brilliant design now appears to be on the verge of collapse. How do we know when (if ever) a federal system is stable? How can a stable federal system be preserved?

Even more difficult is the creation of a federal order from the ruins of a unitary state. In the case of the United States, sovereign states came together and agreed to surrender some portion of their individual sovereignty in order to generate public goods at a new federal level. First and foremost, leaders of the United States' first states sought to create benefits that could be acquired only collectively, including national defense, a common currency, and the creation of a common market (that is, the elimination of trade barriers between states).[9] In cases in which unitary states transform themselves into federal systems, the subnational governments *already* enjoy some of these benefits of cooperation; the trick is getting them to pay for these benefits in a voluntary way.

More generally, when unitary states move to decentralize political authority while also moving to decentralize economic authority, the result has often been increased conflict between constituent entities. In the postcommunist world, this problem of simultaneity in "federalizing" states usually has been resolved by state collapse and disintegration.[10] The Soviet Union, Yugoslavia, and Czechoslovakia all disappeared. Why should the Russian Federation be any different?

THE EVOLUTION OF RUSSIAN FEDERATION

Russia has moved close to the edge of dissolution. Ironically, Yeltsin-the-revolutionary fomented the central challenges to Yeltsin-the-Russian-president regarding Russian federalism even before Russia was an independent state. In organizing an opposition movement against the Soviet regime, Yeltsin and his political allies consciously and deliberately framed their struggle as one about sovereignty.[11] Soon after his election as chairman of the Russian Congress of People's Deputies in the spring of 1990, Boris Yeltsin declared that Russian sovereignty was a central aim of his political agenda and a necessary condition for achieving democratic and economic reform. As he stated in May 1990, "the problems of the [Russian] republic cannot be solved without full-blooded political sovereignty. This alone can enable relations between Russia and the Union and between the autonomous territories within Russia to be harmonized. The political sovereignty of Russia is also necessary in international affairs."[12] Two months after this speech, the Russian Congress of People's Deputies voted to declare the Russian Federation a sovereign state, defying Soviet "federalism." The declaration implicitly underscored that this act represented a reclamation of sovereignty lost: "The Sovereignty of the RSFSR is the natural and essential condition for the existence of Russian statehood, which has centuries of history, culture, and accumulated traditions."[13]

Of course, these declarations of sovereignty did not translate immediately into either de facto sovereign control over political and economic activities within the Russian Federation or de jure recognition by the international community. The battle for sovereignty raged for another year during the "war of laws" in the fall of 1990, the battle over the referendum on sovereignty in March 1991, the "9 + 1" federal accord in April 1991, the Russian presidential election in June 1991, and, finally and most dramatically, the standoff between Soviet troops and Russian citizens in August 1991.[14] Moreover, Yeltsin's own position on sovereignty remained ambiguous throughout this period as his definition of "full-blooded" sovereignty changed over time, depending on the political circumstances of the moment.[15] Nonetheless, early on in this contest for political power, the issue of Russian sovereignty assumed center stage.

Yeltsin employed the language of sovereignty in part to forge alliances with leaders of autonomous republics and oblasts within the Russian Federation, urging them in the summer of 1990 to "take as much sovereignty as you can handle."[16] Several of his allies in Democratic Russia advocated full independence for some of the republics within Russia.[17] After Soviet dissolution, however, these declarations came back to haunt Yeltsin. In invoking the language of sovereignty to broaden his domestic coalition opposing the Soviet regime, Yeltsin threatened to undermine the territorial integrity of *his* new state.[18] Immediately after the August 1991 coup attempt, Chechnya declared its independence. By the end of the year, almost every other autonomous republic within the Federation had followed Chechnya's lead and declared their own independence from

Moscow. In March 1992, Tatarstan made the threat of secession credible by holding a referendum on sovereignty that local voters approved.[19] Soon thereafter, Russian oblast governments also passed resolutions on sovereignty, complete with their own flags, customs agents, and threats of minting new currencies.[20] Like Gorbachev before him, Yeltsin attempted to craft a new federal treaty with republic leaders.[21] But Chechnya and Tatarstan refused to sign while attempts to incorporate this new federal compromise into a general constitutional document failed.[22] As negotiations dragged on without resolution, the Russian Federation looked increasingly prone to collapse.[23]

A New Constitutional Order

This constitutional crisis between center and periphery might have erupted into armed conflict had not the stalemate between executive and legislative branches of the central government proved to be even more dire—a standoff that precipitated military conflict in October 1993.[24] The tragic October standoff, however, created a new opportunity for designing more sustainable federal institutions.[25]

Closure regarding the federal debate did not come automatically after the ratification of the new constitution. In the weeks leading up to the October showdown, Yeltsin had pursued a series of co-optive, conciliatory strategies regarding regional leaders. Most saliently, he had signed the Federal Treaty, which accorded special rights and privileges to these republics. He also created a Federation Council, a new state organ comprising two representatives from each subject of the Federation. Upon creating this new state organ at a meeting with republican leaders in August 1993 in Petrozavodsk, Yeltsin hoped that this new body could approve an interim constitution and act as the legislative branch of government until new elections.[26]

After October 1993, however, the Federal Treaty was not included in the new constitutional draft, an omission that infuriated republican leaders and liberal advocates of asymmetric federalism.[27] Yeltsin's new constitution retained the Federation Council but members had to run for election.[28] Mintimer Shaimiev, the president of Tatarstan, complained that the new constitution intended to create a unitary state in Russia.[29] Chechen leaders rejected the new basic law full-stop.

Despite these objections, the "October events" and the subsequent ratification of a new constitution did reverse the devolution of the political power within the Russian Federation. On paper, the new constitution eliminated special privileges to republics, making them equal with other territorial units—krais, oblasts, and okrugs.[30] Ideas circulated earlier about the need to construct an asymmetric federal system were conspicuously absent from this new document.[31] Many "states' rights" (rights of the oblasts, krais, and republics) were still not assigned in the new basic law, but general principles regarding equality among subjects were spelled out clearly for the first time since Russia's independence.[32]

The new constitution also made no provision for secession, a constraint that all regional rulers except one—Chechnya—accepted. By the end of 1994, Chechnya's persistent claim to sovereignty became the exception, rather than the rule, providing hawks within Yeltsin's government with an allegedly compelling reason for military invasion in December 1994.[33] The war proved to be a disastrous mistake. Almost two years after the initial attack on Grozny, during which 100,000 Russians lost their lives, Russian soldiers went home in defeat.[34]

Again, however, the end of this first tragic conflict also fostered renewed optimism about the future of Russia's territorial integrity and federal development. Although Chechnya's status remains deliberately ambiguous, no other republic within the Russian Federation has moved to follow the Chechen example. Republics have continued to engage Moscow in a series of bilateral treaties as a way to exact more concessions.[35] During the 1996 election year, Yeltsin acquiesced to these "treaties" without hesitation, signing dozens of these accords with both republics and oblasts in the run-up to the June 1996 vote.[36] Several republic constitutions contradict federal law;[37] nonetheless, the threat of outright secession by any republic appeared to have passed.

While the threat of secession had waned since 1993, the balance of rights and responsibilities between the federal government and subnational units has remained volatile. The most recent influence on this delicate equilibrium has been the direct elections of regional executives. By the end of 1996, almost all regional heads of administrations had obtained a popular mandate from their local electorate.[38] For some regional leaders, especially the handful that govern in regions that, on balance, contribute to rather than draw from the federal budget, this electoral mandate has bolstered their negotiating leverage vis-à-vis Moscow.[39] For others, this electoral mandate has weakened their local position, because Moscow authorities no longer feel compelled to prop up local presidential appointees.[40] The continued state of ambiguity between center and region suggests that the consolidation of a stable Russian federalism is still in the distant future.

PRIMORSKII KRAI'S COLLISION COURSE WITH MOSCOW

Within the context of Russia's evolving federal structure, Primorskii Krai has played a particularly critical and difficult role. Only Chechnya has provided a greater challenge to the new contours of Russian federalism than Primorskii Krai. In contrast to Chechnya, however, Primorskii Krai's challenges to the center have provided a mix of positive and negative stimulants for the development of democracy and federalism in Russia.

Historically, Primorskii Krai always has carved a unique political profile compared with other Russian regions. Just as U.S. folklore developed a particular if not mythical image of the "Wild West," Primorskii Krai always has been Russia's "Wild East."[41] Thousands of miles away from Moscow and squeezed between China, Korea, and Japan, Russians living in the Far East developed a survivalist frontier mentality. Even throughout the Soviet period, the region maintained more independence from Moscow than most other regions within the Soviet Union.

Not surprisingly, therefore, the implosion of Soviet power in 1991 seemed to create permissive conditions for Primorskii Krai to finally develop and thrive *independently*. Under the leadership of the region's first head of administration,[42] Vladimir Kuznetsov, the first postcommunist Primorskii Krai government embarked on an ambitious, albeit vague, plan to integrate the local Russian economy with the thriving economies of its Asian neighbors. Kuznetsov was familiar with the economic successes of Asia's tigers, because he had studied them in his previous position as a research associate at the Moscow Institute of International Relations (IMEMO). In mimicking the Chinese coastal regions, Kuznetsov aimed to create a free economic zone called Greater Vladivostok.[43]

As an outsider, however, Kuznetsov quickly provoked resentment from local political and economic elites. For local industrialists in particular, Kuznetsov was nothing more than a Moscow intellectual (much like Prime Minister Yegor Gaidar at the national level) with no experience in either economic affairs or governance. During the constitutional crisis in Moscow in March and April 1993, when it became unclear whether the president or the Congress held ultimate national power, the Primorskii Krai Soviet moved to impeach Kuznetsov. After passing a resolution proclaiming that Kuznetsov's appointment was unlawful, the Soviet recommended Yevgeniy Nazdratenko for the position. Because Nazdratenko had developed important ties to presidential aide Viktor Iliushin and presidential bodyguard Aleksandr Korzhakov by this time, working as a RSFSR people's deputy in Moscow, the Kremlin put up little resistance to the local initiative. According to Nazdratenko, Yeltsin removed Kuznetsov and named him so that the new executive could fight crime and restore order.[44]

Rise of a Local Strong Man: Yevgeniy Nazdratenko

If these were the true motivations behind Nazdratenko's appointment, then Yeltsin made a very poor assessment of local conditions in the Far East, for no politician was more affiliated with "black business" than Nazdratenko. As the director of Vostok, a mining company in Dal'negorsk, Nazdratenko had developed a reputation as a hard-headed, no-nonsense *khozyain* (boss) well before entering politics. In the chaos of the initial market reforms in 1992, Nazdratenko organized more than 200 enterprise directors in the region to form PAKT in August 1992.[45] Though registered as a joint-stock company (Primorie Stock Company of Producers), PAKT quickly emerged as the region's industrial lobby with close ties to both military units and mafia organizations in the area. Soon after its creation, PAKT publicly endorsed Nazdratenko as the only politician in the region who could restore order and also maintain good relations with the Kremlin.[46] Yet, under Nazdratenko, crime statistics soared and conflicts with Moscow increased.[47]

With Nazdratenko at the helm, the Krai Soviet became more emboldened to challenge Moscow's authority. Angry that republics had accrued more power over their local affairs than oblasts or krais in the Federal Treaty of March 1992, Primorskii Krai deputies passed a resolution on July 8, 1993, that stated their intention to transform Primorskii Krai into a republic, thereby giving the region the same constitutional status as other republics in the Federation.[48] The move was motivated first and foremost by economic concerns, because deputies intended to retain locally all taxes collected in the krai.[49] Nazdratenko also supported this act of independence by arguing that his government morally could not transfer tax revenues back to Moscow when the federal government had not delivered subsidies owed to the region.

As noted above, this power struggle between Russian regions and Moscow might have escalated quickly into a major constitutional crisis had not the standoff between the president and Congress erupted in violence first. Initially, Nazdratenko and his allies in the Krai Soviet denounced Yeltsin's Decree No. 1400, which disbanded the Congress of People's Deputies in September 1993.[50] After Yeltsin used military force to enforce his decree, however, Nazdratenko suddenly changed his strategy. Rather than resisting Yeltsin, the Primorskii Krai governor instead mimicked his actions at the local level.

In following instructions from the Kremlin, Nazdratenko disbanded the Krai Soviet, the same Soviet that had pushed for his appointment just months earlier.[51] Just as Yeltsin used this interregnum to name a new government, Nazdratenko also cleaned house in the executive branch, naming many of his colleagues from PAKT to senior positions. In a matter of weeks, PAKT had asserted its political control over the only functioning part of the government, a new arrangement that created tremendous opportunities for rent-seeking and corruption.

As in most regions, new elections to the Krai Duma were scheduled for March 1994. Nazdratenko, however, unilaterally postponed these elections until October, allowing him to rule without any legislative check for more than a year. When these elections were eventually held on October 23, 1994, the governor and his allies did all that they could to discourage active participation.[52] Of the thirty-seven seats available, only twenty were filled, because the other seventeen either did not have two candidates or did not reach the minimum turnout level of 25 percent.

Eventually, the Krai Duma was filled after a second electoral round held in January 1995. By the end of this second round, Nazdratenko's allies dominated this new legislative body, as executive officials and industrialists constituted a solid majority. None of the candidates supported by local democratic parties won a seat in the new krai legislature.[53] Nazdratenko loyalist and PAKT founder Igor Lebedinits was elected chairman without challenge. But when Lebedinits began to use his new political base to challenge Nazdratenko in the summer of 1995, he was easily removed by the governor and replaced by another loyalist.[54]

Nazdratenko also neutralized the City Soviet in Vladivostok. It, too, was liquidated during the fall of 1993. When new elections finally occurred a year later, voters showed little enthusiasm for electoral politics in the krai's new authoritarian context. Turnout for the City Duma election, held at the same time, was even worse. Of the twenty-two electoral districts, the required 25 percent of registered voters showed up in only two districts.[55] Subsequently, the newly appointed mayor decided not to hold new elections but instead to rule by decree himself. Clearly, people understood that the election mattered not in the least. Nazdratenko was the new local czar.

During this same period, Nazdratenko's government also initiated a series of intimidation tactics against his critics in the local press, civic organizations, and political parties. Media outlets such as the newspapers *Utro Rossii*, *Tikhii Okean*, and *Bolshoi Vladivostok* and the private television network PKTV endured intimidation both to their operations and their staff for reporting on local corruption involving Nazdratenko's office.[56] The Dal Press group, an entity loyal to Nazdratenko that controls the only major printing press in the region, refused to publish articles critical of the governor.[57] Succumbing to the pressure, *Utro Rossii*'s liberal editor resigned in 1994 (soon after Cherepkov's removal, described below), while businesses loyal to Nazdratenko bought controlling positions in *Tikhii Okean* and *Bolshoi Vladivostok*.[58] Communist papers such as *Krasnoe Znamya* have been recurrently shut down. Leaders of local political parties also have been monitored and intimidated, making party development since Nazdratenko's appointment extremely difficult. Compared with cities of its size in other parts of Russia, party and civic group organization in Primorskii Krai is significantly underdeveloped.[59]

More generally, Nazdratenko has capitalized on ethnic tensions between Russians and Chinese to legitimize his regime's gross violation of individual human rights. Non-Russian residents and immigrants in the territory, especially Chinese and Korean, have been routinely arrested, jailed, or deported without any due process of law.[60] The region's border dispute with China has provided Nazdratenko with a convenient "nationalist" issue to rally local support behind his authoritarian regime. As stated in a pamphlet produced by the governor's office, "the transfer of even a small piece of land to China sends a signal that Russia is terminally enfeebled."[61] In the shadow of a superpower like China and thousands of miles away from Moscow, Nazdratenko's "tough guy" antics may seem like an asset to local Russians who may be worried more about the Chinese than about democracy.

Nazdratenko's most blatant abuse of democratic processes and the rule of law, however, was his physical removal of Vladivostok's elected mayor, Viktor Cherepkov. Elected in July 1993 as the leader of the city's democratic forces, Cherepkov came into the mayor's office with an ambitious agenda to fight corruption, streamline government, and foster market reform. Because Cherepkov had defeated eighteen other candidates in this election, including the PAKT-sponsored candidate, Boris Fadeev, his popular mandate posed a serious threat to Nazdratenko's rule in the region.

Only days after assuming power, Cherepkov had alienated the krai government with his brash rhetoric. A battle quickly ensued between the two levels of government. To undermine Cherepkov's local popularity, Nazdratenko's government switched off the city's electricity and water and then blamed the mayor's ineptitude for the interruption. According to Cherepkov, Nazdratenko resorted to more sinister tactics, including threats to his own life and an alleged kidnapping of the mayor's son.[62] While Cherepkov's paranoid and eccentric style helped to undermine his local support, it was Nazdratenko's intimidation that really left the mayor isolated and powerless. On March 17, 1994, Cherepkov, after being charged first with bribe-taking by the Ministry of Internal Affairs and then of being psychologically unfit to govern, was physically removed from his office after a three-week standoff in which the mayor literally lived in his office. In his place, Nazdratenko named Konstantin Tolstoshein, a PAKT member known locally for his intimate ties with regional mafia structures. Other Cherepkov loyalists were also removed from their government positions.[63] Throughout the rest of the year, Cherepkov fought the charges and tried to reassume his elected office. On December 23, 1994, Cherepkov's campaign for reinstatement received a major blow when President Yeltsin signed a decree removing him from office for his "long absence in fulfilling his executive responsibilities."[64]

In the fall of 1994, Nazdratenko then moved to consolidate his power through a direct but rigged election. Before 1994, several presidents of autonomous republics had been elected, but only a few heads of administrations in oblasts, cities, or krais had been given permission to hold elections. Rather than wait for Moscow's permission, Nazdratenko initiated the local election independently. In the run-up to the vote, however, it became clear that the governor had no intention of losing. He raised the signature requirements so that other viable candidates, Cherepkov and Igor Ustinov, were disqualified, while two dummy candidates picked by Nazdratenko were allowed on the ballot to give the election a fictitious sense of legitimacy.

The Center Strikes Back

Nazdratenko's authoritarian moves did not go unnoticed in Moscow. In the fall of 1994, liberal parties Russia's Choice and Yabloko sent delegations to the region to investigate these democratic irregularities. Because Cherepkov was a member of Russia's Choice, his dismissal mobilized fellow party member Deputy Prime Minister Anatoliy Chubais to his defense. The report issued by this independent special commission was scathing: it labeled the government in Primorskii Krai a "fascist regime."[65] Gaidar added personally that Primorie was "the most criminalized regime in Russia."[66] In a rare instance of cooperation, all major democratic leaders in Moscow, including Yegor Gaidar, Grigorii Yavlinsky, and Sergei Shakhrai, endorsed the report and urged Yeltsin to respond.

The publication of the report precipitated a major battle within the Kremlin between Nazdratenko's supporters (First Deputy Prime Minister Oleg Soskovets and Yeltsin bodyguard Aleksandr Korzhakov) and Nazdratenko's enemies (Yeltsin Chief of Staff Sergei Filatov and Deputy Prime Minister Anatoliy Chubais). Because Nazdratenko was a member of Yeltsin's Presidential Club and was considered a Yeltsin loyalist and an electoral asset for the coming presidential vote in 1996, his allies easily thwarted calls for his dismissal.

More generally, this group within the Kremlin, the so-called party of war that later initiated the military invasion in Chechnya, appreciated Nazdratenko's iron-hand style of ruling in this strategic part of the country.[67] For this group, impeding the Chinese onslaught was a much higher priority than fostering democracy. Allegedly, this group also had financial ties to PAKT and was particularly interested in ensuring that the region's ports and fishing industry remained in the hands of local authorities.

Those who advocated against Nazdratenko stood on principled ground, since no one could defend the governor's "democratic" record. In particular, Nazdratenko's removal of an elected official established an extremely dangerous precedent that no other elected official would want to see. In 1994, however, there were still very few elected officials in the executive branch of government at any level. Moreover, it must be remembered that Yeltsin had just removed legislative officials from office through the use of force the previous October, giving his government little moral authority in this local battle. Cherepkov's brief tenure as mayor had not been a very productive one, making it harder to argue his case on pragmatic grounds.

Moscow reformers and Chubais in particular had other motivations for acting against Nazdratenko. Most important, Chubais viewed Nazdratenko not simply as a threat to Primorskii democracy but also as an impediment to local market reform.[68] Early on in his tenure as governor, Nazdratenko prompted an open conflict over privatization when he attempted to renationalize some enterprises that had been privatized at only a fraction of their market value.[69] As Nazdratenko stated in an interview in 1995,

> I favor the expansion of the non-governmental sector. But why do they implement it in a way that our most efficient enterprises are sold dirt-cheap? A small shop in the center of Vladivostok was privatized for 700 million rubles, which is normal. But a huge berth in Nakhodka, 3.5 km long with all the port facilities was sold for 350 million rubles. . . . The Primorsk Shipping Line was privatized for 1 billion rubles. Lloyd's insurance company recently held an international audit which appraised the line at $1 billion.[70]

Like Moscow Mayor Yurii Luzhkov, Nazdratenko believed that local government authorities, not the federal government, should determine the form and pace of local privatization. More generally, his authoritarian and corrupt government encouraged rent-seeking, stymied local business development, and drained precious federal government financial resources.[71] While billions of dollars in trade flow through the region's ports, virtually none of it is taxed.[72] PAKT's monopolistic control over all local enterprises and markets also prevented Moscow financial groups and foreign investors from expanding into the region.[73] In their assessment of the region's potential, the Economist Intelligence Reports stated, "Infighting between authoritarian krai governor Yevgeniy Nazdratenko and city mayor Viktor Cherepkov has unsettled investors and hampered attempts to turn Vladivostok into a free economic zone."[74] Chubais sought to remove this political impediment to economic growth in a region that should be one of Russia's richest.

The first round of battle in Moscow over Nazdratenko ended in a compromise. Chubais and his allies succeeded in convincing Yeltsin to postpone the gubernatorial elections that Nazdratenko had scheduled for October 1994. At the same time, the "party of war" coalition in the Kremlin prevented the reinstatement of Cherepkov and actually enforced his removal with a presidential decree in December of 1994.[75] In a desperate move, Cherepkov left the region and sued the governor and the president in a Moscow court, where he remained embroiled in legal disputes for two years.[76]

Nazdratenko won the second round. The following year, Nazdratenko succeeded in holding "his" election, putting Primorie on a select list of regions that were granted permission to conduct gubernatorial elections on the same day as the national parliamentary election on December 17, 1995. Securing Moscow acquiescence in 1995 was much easier after the invasion of Chechnya because the "party of war" coalition in Moscow had assumed a much stronger position within the government.[77] Not surprisingly, Nazdratenko won this election in a landslide. With eleven candidates on the ballot, Nazdratenko garnered 69.9 percent of the vote, more than 50 percent more than runner-up candidate Cherepkov received. Local authoritarianism had been ratified by the people.

Moscow liberals (and their banker allies) did not write off the distant region completely. In the fall of 1996, Chubais launched yet another attack against the governor. In Moscow, the balance of power had shifted dramatically by this time. Because Chubais had orchestrated Yeltsin's reelection victory in July while Chubais's banker friends had financed the campaign, this constellation of interests dominated Yeltsin's new government after the election.[78] In assuming control, Chubais also managed to purge all Nazdratenko's Moscow allies including Soskovets, Korzhakov, and former Yeltsin chief of staff Nikolai Yegerov. Consequently, Chubais was in a much stronger position to settle old scores with his Primorskii nemesis. When strikes by miners and then power plant workers created a new crisis in Primorskii Krai, Chubais seized the moment to dethrone Nazdratenko.[79]

Miners and workers at Dal'nergo initially walked off the job to demand payment of back wages.[80] Quickly, however, these strikes took on an overtly political character of national importance.[81] Claiming that Nazdratenko had used federal money earmarked to pay their wages for his own personal use, strike committees (which had sprouted by this time beyond the power plant) issued a declaration on September 16, 1996, calling for direct presidential rule in the region.[82] Chubais and other reformist government officials and political organizations in Moscow sympathized with this demand by Primorie workers and urged Yeltsin to remove Nazdratenko based on his "criminal" behavior.

The governor countered by lambasting Moscow's interference in their local affairs, claiming that these attacks were not aimed toward him but the people of Primorskii Krai as a whole. Nazdratenko also intimated that Chubais and his associates had orchestrated the strikes at the power plant, thereby using power disruptions for the people of Primorie as a political weapon against the local government.[83] He denounced the claims of corruption and threatened to hold a referendum to let the people decide if they still trusted their governor.[84] Less publicly, Nazdratenko also flew to Moscow to meet personally with Yeltsin, pledge his loyalty, and urge the president to give him the chance to stabilize the situation. Yeltsin obliged. Nazdratenko returned home, found scapegoats at the power plant and in his government whom he fired, and then paid the back wages, ending this latest round of battle with the center.[85]

Observers, however, believed that Nazdratenko had been weakened by the fall crisis. Moscow's threat of dismissal had looked credible. The governor had been humiliated. Perhaps most important, people in Primorie learned that Nazdratenko was not invincible.

As part of the compromise to defuse this crisis, Cherepkov was reinstated as mayor.

Nonetheless, Nazdratenko was still in power, which incensed Chubais, frustrated Moscow financial groups, and troubled human rights groups and liberal political organizations. Consequently, after Yeltsin reshuffled his government yet again in March 1997 to the advantage of Chubais and his associates, Chubais sought to use his newly acquired position as first deputy prime minister to undermine his Far Eastern enemy for good. In drafting a 100-day plan to guide the new government in its first three months, the removal of Nazdratenko was on the list of political priorities.[86]

In May 1997, the federal government tried to reassert power in Primorie through the region's presidential representative, the local head of the Federal Security Service (FSB), Viktor Kondratov.[87] On paper issued from Moscow, Kondratov was given extraordinary new powers over the administration of the krai's energy system—the epicenter of strikes in the fall of 1996—as well as supervision and oversight of federal monies transferred to the region.[88] Local politicians claimed that Yeltsin's decree effectively created "dual power" in the region, a condition in Russia that historically has ended in bloodshed and revolution.[89]

To further intimidate Nazdratenko, Yeltsin's deputy chief of staff and former deputy chairman of the FSB, Yevgeniy Savostanyov, personally traveled to the krai to deliver Yeltsin's decree, warning Nazdratenko that the FSB had accumulated substantial evidence confirming the governor's corrupt use of federal money transferred to the region to pay back wages.[90] Just days after Savostanyov's visit, Kondratov ordered the search of Nazdratenko's office. Moscow authorities were certain that they had accumulated enough "compromat" (compromising materials) to force the governor to resign.[91]

On June 11, 1997, First Deputy Prime Minister Boris Nemtsov also visited the region. While Nazdratenko and Nemtsov both claimed to have productive discussions, Nemtsov returned to Moscow to recommend that Yeltsin call for new elections for both the governor's office and the mayor's office, a plan that Yeltsin apparently endorsed.[92] While Nemtsov was in the region, Chubais publicly asserted that Nazdratenko must be held accountable for the economic crisis in the region.[93]

In the latest battle between Moscow and center, however, Nazdratenko did not stand down his opponents alone. In a precedent-setting show of solidarity, governors and regional Duma chairmen in the Federation Council rallied to Nazdratenko's cause, voting 113-0 in support of a resolution to denounce as unconstitutional the government's attempt to remove the elected governor.[94] Although many of the governors who supported this resolution remained solid backers of the Yeltsin government, they also understood the long-term implications of this unconstitutional act for their own political futures.[95] Several powerful governors, including Sverdlovsk Governor Eduard Rossel, also denounced vehemently the appointment and powers granted to the Primorskii presidential representative and local FSB head, Viktor Kondratov, asserting that such appointments violated the electoral rights of local citizens.[96] Moscow Mayor Yurii Luzhkov concurred and urged the Federation Council to send a letter to Yeltsin calling for the renunciation of these new powers given to Kondratov.[97]

Yeltsin aides countered that the president had the constitutional right to do anything in the name of "defending the security of the nation." After the Federation Council vote, however, few analysts believed that even Russia's non-interventionist, pro-Yeltsin Constitutional Court would approve of this action.

Moreover, Nazdratenko welcomed the challenge of new elections, because he was certain he would win again.[98] In a surprise move, Cherepkov sided with Nazdratenko in this latest round of conflict with Moscow, perhaps realizing that this anticenter, pro-Nazdratenko position might bolster his reelection prospects should new elections actually be organized.[99] More generally, journalists in the region affirmed that Nazdratenko also had succeeded in rallying his constituents against Moscow. As one observer reported from the region,

> [T]he population is rather calm with respect to Nazdratenko. He is not liked, but "Moscow" is hated to such an extent that they will support Nazdratenko if only to spite the devil/reformers. He is also ranked among the mafia, but at the same time 'he is not the main mafioso; the main ones are in Moscow.' Almost everybody you ask says that if the governor is dismissed, things will get even worse.[100]

Reluctantly, Chubais's advisers concurred that even millions of dollars spent on a campaign against Nazdratenko would probably fail to oust the incumbent. In this latest battle, the center lost again. As Nazdratenko claimed triumphantly, "Beyond any doubt, it is me who has the power, just as I had before. They thought they would make me surrender and drive me mad. But I think that those who started this will be driven mad."[101]

POLITICAL ATTITUDES IN PRIMORSKII KRAI

The political struggle between Primorskii Krai and the Russian Federal government has had everything to do with elite politics and very little to do with popular attitudes. In reviewing electoral outcomes in the region over the past several years, the krai's population looks very similar to Russia as a whole. Even in contrast with its neighbors, residents of Primorskii Krai have not demonstrated a strong proclivity for supporting radical opposition leaders or movements. At the same time, the region's traditional distrust and disdain for faraway Moscow as well as the region's economic dependence on federal financial support have provided opportunities for local politicians—first and foremost, Yevgeniy Nazdratenko—to mobilize local support in a united front against federal interference. Over time, the krai's political and economic crises have been increasingly blamed on Moscow and not on local government officials, a situation that has served to bolster the electoral prospects of opposition parties in national elections and of Nazdratenko locally.

Elections in Primorskii Krai for deputies to the USSR Congress in 1989 and the Russian Congress in 1990 produced no striking results, but rather reflected national trends of the time. In 1989, 84 percent of eligible voters turned out to elect progressive deputies to the Soviet Congress. With an average of three candidates per seat, only Moscow boasted more competitive elections in 1989.[102]

In 1990, candidates who finished second or third in the previous election tended to perform well. As Russia's ideological spectrum was still poorly developed, most successful candidates simply ran on anti-*nomenklatura* platforms. Nazdratenko recorded his first electoral victory in this election. As a deputy in Moscow, he established cordial but distant relations with Democratic Russia and aides close to Boris Yeltsin. Other prominent deputies elected from the region included Svetlana Goryacheva, an outspoken critic of the Soviet system, who later became a deputy chairwoman in the Russian Congress and then sided against Boris Yeltsin during the polarized standoff between the president and Parliament in 1993. By 1995, she had gravitated to the Russian Communist Party and ran as one of the national leaders of the Communist Party's party list, along with Gennadii Zyuganov and Aman Tuleev. In 1990, however, Gorya-cheva closely identified with the "democrats." Strikingly, no one elected in 1990 represented the communist old guard.

In all the polarized elections between 1990 and December 1993, Primorskii Krai voters demonstrated solid support for Boris Yeltsin and his causes. In the March 1991 referendum on the preservation of the USSR, only 64 percent of Primorskii voters supported the preservation of the USSR, a percentage almost ten points below the national average. Three months later, a solid 61.5 percent voted for Boris Yeltsin, a level of support similar to that garnered by Yeltsin in Moscow. Despite the acute hardship brought to the region by the initiation of Gaidar's economic reforms in January 1992, the majority of Primorskii voters (56.6 percent) supported the new economic course in the April 1993 referendum, while an amazing 64.3 percent endorsed Yeltsin's leadership as president. In all these votes, Primor-skii voters demonstrated above-average support for Russia's reform course.[103]

In the December 1993 parliamentary elections, Primorskii Krai voters began to show signs of increasing dissatisfaction with the course of national events. Primorskii Krai electoral patterns on the 1993 party list vote generally reflected the balance of power between political forces in the country nationally. Vladimir Zhirinovsky, head of the Liberal Democratic Party of Russia (LDPR), scored a surprising and impressive victory in the krai, but the neonationalist's support in Primorskii was lower than his average in the Far East region as a whole. Centrists such as Women of Russia exceeded their national average in Primorskii Krai, while the Russian Communist Party and the rural comrades, the Agrarian Party, performed below their national average in the region. Not surprisingly, the progovernmen-tal electoral bloc, Russia's Choice, did particularly well in the capital, winning almost 40 percent of the popular vote in Vladivostok. Naz-dratenko's electoral machine was beginning to show signs of its effectiveness.

On the single-mandate side of the 1993 Duma vote, Primorskii Krai sent to Moscow representatives with solid reformist and centrist credentials. Deputy Mikhail Glubovskii from Vladivostok emerged in the Russian Parliament as one of Yabloko's most liberal spokespeople, while Igor Ustinov—after defecting from Russia's Choice—became a leader of the liberal faction "12 of December," headed by Boris Fyodorov and Irina Khakamada. Both established very liberal voting records. In the rating system established by Duma analyst Aleksandr Sobyanin, which ranged from 100 as the most reformist pole, -100 as the most conservative pole, and 0 as the center, Glubovskii's record was rated at 87 from 1993 to 1995, while Ustinov was rated at 78.[104] The third single-mandate seat was filled by Valerii Nesterenko, a factory director affiliated with the centrist Democratic Party of Russia. Nesterenko eventually allied with the proindustrial New Regional Policy faction, staking out a solid centrist profile.

In the election of representatives to the Federation Council or upper house, Nazdratenko won a seat solidly, winning 65 percent of the vote, while former USSR people's deputy and member of the reformist party Russian Movement for Democratic Reforms Evdokiya Gaer won the other seat, though with significantly less support (38.1 percent).[105] Again, no candidate firmly identified with an opposition party won.

The region's sustained economic depression coupled with protracted polarized elite politics described above appeared to influence Primorskii Krai voting patterns in the 1995 parliamentary elections. Voters sharply rejected both reformist parties and parties identified with Moscow. Gaidar's Democratic Choice of Russia won an abysmal 1.3 percent, while the new party of power, Prime Minister Viktor Chernomyrdin's Our Home Is Russia, garnered only 3.5 percent, well below its 10 percent national average. In contrast, Zhirinovsky maintained almost the same level of support in the krai as his 1993 showing, despite losing more than half of his support nationally. The Russian Communist Party more than doubled its 1993 share and almost reached its national average. Smaller communist and nationalist parties also fared better than average in the krai, while centrist parties did worse. Though a gross oversimplification to reduce forty-three parties into three categories, such a grouping nonetheless demonstrates a significant turn toward opposition parties in the 1995 elections. If "democrats" accounted for 19.7 percent of the total vote, and centrists won 24 percent, nationalists and communists captured a staggering 59.2 percent.[106]

THE FUTURE OF RUSSIAN FEDERALISM: AN INTERIM REPORT CARD IN LIGHT OF THE FAR EAST

The standoff between the Moscow federal government and the regional government in Primorskii Krai has devolved into the greatest affront to Russian federalism other than the Chechen Wars. Because the krai lacks the ethnic, historical, and cultural factors that divided Russia and Chechnya, this challenge in some ways looks even more dire than the Chechen case. If Primorskii Krai did take arms up against the Moscow government or declare its independence from Russia, the consequence would be civil war.[107]

The probabilities of such a scenario, however, remain low. As demonstrated above, this center-region conflict has resulted primarily from elite struggles for political power and economic resources. Personal rivalries, too, have figured prominently. Fears of secession, however, have been overplayed. As Nazdratenko himself declared, "As long as I am governor of the region, there won't be any republic. I support Russia's integrity."[108] Moreover, one can find little evidence of radical public attitudes among the region's people. As demonstrated in their voting behavior, people in Primorskii Krai have political views very similar to people in medium-sized cities in Russia. Above all else, the krai's geostrategic location ensures that Russians in this region will want to remain part of Russia. More than any other factor, the presence of 75 million Chinese living in the two provinces opposite the krai creates a strong incentive for Primorskii Krai to remain part of the Russian Federation.[109]

At the same time, the absence of a credible threat to secede has not limited the region's government—first and foremost the region's governor, Yevgeniy Nazdratenko—from assuming significant autonomy from Moscow. Although the Russian federal government repeatedly has attempted to undermine Nazdratenko personally and to limit the powers of his government generally, Moscow's efforts have failed. Primorskii Krai represents an extreme case, but the drama of conflict and resolution between center and region in this situation follows a more general pattern; every time Moscow government leaders have tried to assert greater control over their subnational constituents, they have exposed the weakness of the Russian federal state.

Moscow's inability to influence local political and economic affairs in Primorskii Krai bodes poorly for both democracy and market reform in the region. In striking contrast to the usual pattern of federal struggles in other countries, the center in this case represents the cause of liberal policies and institutions, while the regional government has erected an authoritarian regime damaging both to political pluralism and market competition.[110] Decentralization has allowed the Primorskii governor to consolidate a local authoritarian regime.

In the name of liberal reforms, however, the center in this case has deployed illiberal means. Paradoxically, the center's attempt to remove an elected governor may have fostered a more stable federal system in the long run. In rallying to Nazdratenko's cause, other elected regional leaders demonstrated for the first time in Russia's volatile postcommunist history that they are prepared to self-enforce the principle of federalism and limited central authority.[111] Only several years earlier, regional heads did not demonstrate such solidarity when elected governors in Bryansk (Lodkin) and Chelyabinsk (Sumin) were removed from office.

Since 1993, the political context has changed dramatically: Russia has a constitution. All local heads of administration are elected officials. Governors and their legislative counterparts now have their own coordinating institution, the Federation Council. The disastrous war in Chechnya has decreased the likelihood of military intervention by federal troops in the near future. Communist restoration is no longer a threat. Finally, federal budget transfers to local governments account for a smaller percentage of local economic activity. These factors have combined to give regional leaders more local autonomy, even in the absence of more conventional federal-preserving institutions such as national political parties or an independent judiciary.[112]

That regional heads would stand behind such an unpopular figure as Nazdratenko has demonstrated the increasing importance of principle, law, and precedent (reinforced, of course, by self-interest) and the decreasing salience of ideological or personal battles.[113] The Primorskii Krai battles with Moscow suggest that a hierarchy of governments does exist within the Russian Federation. At the same time, the scope of authority among these governments has not been institutionalized formally but is determined by the balance of power between center and region—a balance that is still in flux.

In the short run, gains in local autonomy in Primorskii Krai have not advanced the cause of liberal institutional development in the region in either politics or economics.[114] Nor have mutual gains from federal hierarchy been realized, which suggests that what we are witnessing in Russia is decentralization and not necessarily federalism. At the same time, the key principles of a federal order—autonomy and dual authority—have been reaffirmed in the standoff between Moscow and Primorskii Krai.[115] In the long run, this demonstration of central authority constraint may prove very beneficial to the development of federalism and the rule of law in Russia as a whole.

NOTES

[1]See Jessica Eve Stern, "Moscow Meltdown," *International Security*, vol. 18, no. 4 (Spring 1994), pp. 40–65; "Russia: Coming to Pieces?" *The Economist*, March 14, 1992, pp. 59–60; and Serge Schmemann, "Russia's Peril: Breakup," *New York Times*, March 15, 1993, p. 1.

[2]On the advantages that ethnically based republics enjoyed in this federal challenge, see Daniel Triesman, "Russia's 'Ethnic Revival': The Separatist Activism of Regional Leaders in a Post-Communist Order," *World Politics*, vol. 49, no. 2 (January 1997), pp. 212–49.

[3]In August 1996, Aleksandr Lebed, secretary of the Security Council, negotiated a peace settlement with Chechen leaders in which both sides agreed to postpone final settlement of Chechnya's independence for five years. Chechnya subsequently held presidential elections and acted as if it were an independent country. It has not obtained international law sovereignty but effectively acquired "Westphalian sovereignty"—the control over domestic affairs within its territory for a few years. Though peculiar, the world today (and the world of the past) has many similar cases of ambiguous sovereign status. See Steven Krasner, "Sovereignty and Intervention," in Gene Lyons and Michael Mastanduno, eds., *Beyond Westphalia?* (Baltimore: Johns Hopkins University Press, 1995). This "Westphalian sovereignty" is now, however, fundamentally challenged by the renewed military conflict between Russia and Chechnya and by Russia's plans to partition Chechnya's territory.

[4]Aleksandr Lebed's election to the office of governor in Krasnoyarsk in the spring of 1998 may push this region to the top of the list of troublemakers for Moscow.

[5]Yingyi Qian and Barry Weingast, *China's Transition to Markets: Market-Preserving Federalism, Chinese Style*, Essays in Public Policy (Stanford, Calif.: Hoover Institution Press, 1995), pp. 4–5.

[6]Rui de Figueiredo and Barry Weingast, "Self-Enforcing Federalism: Solving Two Fundamental Dilemmas," unpublished manuscript (Stanford University, Stanford, Calif.), April 1997.

[7]See William Riker, *Federalism: Origin, Operation, and Significance* (Boston: Little Brown, 1964).

[8]Jack Rakove, *Original Meanings: Politics and Ideas in the Making of the Constitution* (New York: Alfred Knopf, 1997).

[9]In other words, the drafters of the U.S. Constitution were "motivated by opportunities to capture gains from hierarchy" and believed that both national and state governments would be better off from the federal arrangement. See de Figueiredo and Weingast, "Self-Enforcing Federalism," p. 3.

[10]See Leonid Polishchuk, "Russian Federalism: Economic Reform and Political Behavior," unpublished manuscript (Moscow), February 1996; and Daniel Treisman, "Fiscal Politics and the Fate of Post-Communist Federations: Yugoslavia, the Soviet Union, Czechoslovakia—and Russia," unpublished manuscript (UCLA, Los Angeles, Calif.), 1996.

[11]John Dunlop, *The Rise of Russia and the Fall of the Soviet Empire* (Princeton, N.J.: Princeton University Press, 1993).

[12]Boris Yeltsin, speech to the Russian Federation Congress of People's Deputies, Moscow, May 22, 1990, reprinted in Alexander Dallin and Gail Lapidus, eds., *The Soviet System: From Crisis to Collapse* (Boulder, Colo.: Westview Press, 1995), p. 410.

[13]"Declaration on the State Sovereignty of the Russian Soviet Federation Socialist Republic," reprinted in Dallin and Lapidus, *The Soviet System,"* p. 404.

[14]*Gorbachev, Yeltsin: 1500 Dnei Politicheskogo Protivovostoyaniya* (Moscow: Terra, 1992).

[15]For instance, in the spring of 1991, when Yeltsin began negotiating with Gorbachev on the "9 + 1" accord, many of Yeltsin's allies in Democratic Russia felt that Yeltsin was selling out. See Michael Urban with Vyacheslav Igrunov and Sergei Mitrokhin, *The Rebirth of Politics in Russia* (Cambridge: Cambridge University Press, 1997). Similarly, on the referendum about whether to maintain the USSR, Democratic Russia urged its supporters to vote against the initiative, but Yeltsin refrained from taking a stand. Years later, Yeltsin claimed that he voted for preservation.

[16]See Dunlop, *"The Rise of Russia,"* pp. 54–58, 62–64.

[17]See *Materiali: II S'ezda Dvizheniya Demokraticheskoi Rossii* (Moscow: DR-Press, November 1991).

[18]For accounts of this period regarding federal issues, see Steven Solnick, "The Political Economy of Russian Federalism," *Problems of Post-Communism,* vol. 43, no. 6 (November-December 1996); and Gail Lapidus and

Edward Walker, "Nationalism, Regionalism, and Federalism: Center-Periphery Relations in Post-Communist Russia," in Gail Lapidus, ed., *The New Russia: Troubled Transformation* (Boulder, Colo.: Westview Press, 1995).

[19]On Tatarstan's unique interpretation of sovereignty and strategy for achieving it, see Raphael Khakimov, "Prospects of Federalism in Russia: A View from Tatarstan," *Security Dialogue*, vol. 27, no. 1 (1996); Edward Walker, "The Dog That Didn't Bite: Tatarstan and Asymmetrical Federalism in Russia," *Harriman Review* (1996); and John Slocum, "Russia's Regions and Republics as International Actors: The Case of Tatarstan," unpublished manuscript (University of Oklahoma, Norman, Okla.), February 1997.

[20]Lyudmila Pertsevaya, "Rodina Prezidenta Khochet Stat' Respublikoi," *Moskovskie Novosti*, July 4, 1993, p. 9A; and David Filipov, "Rebellion in Regions Threaten Charter," *The Moscow Times*, July 3, 1993, p. 1.

[21]For the provisions of the first treaty, see *Federatsiya*, no. 12 (March 18–24, 1992), in *FBIS-SOV-92-056*, March 23, 1992, pp. 40–42.

[22]See Elizabeth Teague, "Center-Periphery Relations in the Russian Federation," in Roman Szporluk, ed., *National Identity and Ethnicity in the New States of Eurasia* (Armonk, N.Y.: M.E. Sharpe, 1994).

[23]Gillian Tett, "Cold comfort in rebellious Saransk," *Financial Times*, April 23, 1993, p. 4; Gulchachak Khannanova, "Bashkortostan Decides to Be More Independent," *Kommersant' Daily*, April 28, 1993, p. 9, in *FBIS-SOV-93-080*, April 28, 1993, p. 44; Zhanna Trfimova, "Independence Is Recalled More and More Often," *Segodnya*, May 17, 1993, p. 3, in *FBIS-SOV-93-096*, May 20, 1993, p. 48.

[24]On the initial splits between Yeltsin and the Congress, see *Yeltsin-Khazbulatov: Edinstvo, Kompromiss, Bor'ba* (Moscow: Terra, 1994).

[25]Even Yeltsin's critics acknowledged as much. See the Expert Institute, *Russia's Regions in Transition* (Moscow: The Russian Union of Industrialists and Entrepreneurs, February 1994), p. 16.

[26]See Yeltsin's August 13, 1993, speech as quoted in *Yeltsin-Khazbulatov*, pp. 494–95.

[27]See Vladimir Lysenko, "Demokraty stanovyatsya gosudarstvennikami," *Nezavisimaya gazeta*, November 28, 1993, reprinted in Vladimir Lysenko, *Ot Tatarstana do Chechni (stanovlenie novogo rossiiskogo federalizma)* (Moscow: Institut Sovremennoi Politiki, 1995), pp. 87–89. The elimination of the Federal Treaty from the new constitution was one of the reasons that Yabloko did not endorse the new basic law.

[28]This procedure changed after the 1993 elections so that heads of administration and chairs of regional Dumas automatically became members of the Federation Council. See Michael McFaul, "Uncertainty, Institutional Design and Path Dependency during Transitions: Cases from Russia," working paper, no. 7 (Harvard University, Davis Center for Russian Studies, 1998), pp. 1–29.

[29]Shaimiev, November 3, 1993, as quoted in Robert Sharlet, "Russian Constitutional Crisis: Law and Politics Under Yeltsin," *Post-Soviet Affairs*, vol. 9, no. 4 (1993), p. 331.

[30]For a preliminary assessment, see Robert Sharlet, "Transitional Constitutionalism: Politics and the Law in the Second Russian Republic," *Wisconsin International Law Journal*, vol. 14, no. 3 (1996), pp. 495–521.

[31]Room for the development of asymmetric federalism, however, was contained in the constitution. See Ned Walker, "Federalism—Russian Style," *Problems of Post-Communism*, vol. 42, no. 4 (July-August 1995), pp. 3–12.

[32]Oblast governors still complain of their secondary status. See the remarks by Saratov Governor Dmitrii Ayatskov in "Governor Blasts 'Discrimination' Against Some Regions," *RFE/RL Newsline*, January 21, 1998.

[33]On the decision to intervene, see Michael McFaul, "Russian Politics After Chechnya," *Foreign Policy*, no. 99 (Summer 1995), pp. 149–65; L. A. Belyaeva, ed., *Chechenskii Krisis* (Moscow: TsSIiM, 1995); and George Breslauer, "Yeltsin's Political Leadership: Why Invade Chechnya?" in *Russian Political and Economic Development* (Claremont, Calif.: The Keck Center for International and Strategic Studies, McKenna College, 1995), no. 9, pp. 1–24.

[34]The number 100,000 comes from Grigory Yavlinsky, "Where Is Russia Headed? An Uncertain Prognosis," *Journal of Democracy*, vol. 8, no. 1 (January 1997), p. 4.

[35]Mikhail Yulin, "The Autonomous Republics Took Away as Much as They Could Grab," *Utro Rossii*, July 20–26, 1995, p. 4, in *What the Papers Say*, July 25, 1995, p. 12. Some believe that these treaties undermine federal stability and could even lead to federal dissolution. See Vladimir Lysenko, "Tatarstan, Bashkortostan, dalee bez ostanovok . . . ," *Rossiiskaya gazeta*, June 26, 1994, reprinted in Lysenko, *Ot Tatarstana do Chechni*, pp. 119–21.

[36]Steven Solnick, "Asymmetries and Federal Stability in Russia," unpublished manuscript (Columbia University, New York), May 1997.

[37]At a seminar at Stanford University in March 1998, Raphael Khakimov, adviser to the president of Tatarstan, reported that the Tatarstan Constitution is not subordinate to but equal to the Russian Constitution. For his views on federalism, see Khakimov, "Prospects of Federalism in Russia," pp. 69–80. On the contradictions between the Tuva and Russian Constitutions, see Steven Solnick, "Federal Bargaining in Russia," *East European Constitutional Review*, vol. 4, no. 4 (Fall 1995), pp. 52–53.

[38]See Michael McFaul and Nikolai Petrov, "Russian Electoral Politics after Transition: Regional and National Assessments," *Post-Soviet Geography and Economics*, vol. 38, no. 9 (November 1997), pp. 507–49.

[39]The divide between rich and poor regions has continued to grow since the Soviet collapse. One study reported that the average income in Moscow

is 1,630 percent higher than the average income in Ingushetiya. See Kamil Ivanov, "Gaps Between Regions Threaten Russia's Unity," *Ekonomika i Zhizn*, no. 8, (1997); cited here from Johnson's Russia List.

[40]During the 1996 presidential election, Yeltsin and his government felt compelled to foster close ties with all governors. After the election, however, this imperative no longer exists.

[41]John Stephan, *The Russian Far East: A History* (Stanford, Calif.: Stanford University Press, 1994).

[42]Fearful that the Russian Federation might follow a fate similar to that of the Soviet Union, Yeltsin decided to postpone local elections scheduled for December 1991 and instead created the new position of *Glava Administratsii* (Head of Administration) at the regional, city, and district level. Yeltsin assumed the right to appoint these local governors but often did so with consent of locally elected legislative bodies.

[43]Peter Kirkow, "The Siberian and Far Eastern Challenge to Centre-Periphery Relations in Russia: A Comparison between Altaiskii and Primorskiy Kray," in John Gibson and Philip Hanson, eds., *Transformation from Below: Local Power and the Political Economy of Post-Communist Transitions* (Cheltenham, UK: Edgar Elgar, 1995), p. 233.

[44]Interview with Nazdratenko in *Profil'*, no. 24 (June 30, 1997), p. 11.

[45]Michael McFaul and Nikolai Petrov, eds., *Politicheskii Almanakh Rossii 1995* (Moscow: Carnegie Endowment for International Peace, 1995), p. 294.

[46]Ibid., p. 294.

[47]On crime increases, see John Lloyd, "Challenge to Russian democracy on the waterfront," *Financial Times*, October 27, 1994, p. 3.; and Pyotr Yudin, "Vladivostok Shadowed by Crime," *The Moscow Times*, November 19, 1994, p. 4.

[48]John Lloyd, "Russia begins to fray at the edges, *Financial Times*, July 9, 1993, p. 2.

[49]David Filipov, "Far Eastern Region Calls Itself a Republic," *Moscow Times*, July 9, 1993, p. 5.

[50]Kirkow, "The Siberian and Far Eastern Challenge to Centre-Periphery Relations in Russia," p. 236.

[51]On the history of this council from 1990 to 1993, see Michael McFaul and Nikolai Petrov, eds., *Politicheskii Almanakh Rossii 1997* (Moscow: Carnegie Endowment for International Peace, 1997), pp. 390–92.

[52]For details of their activities, see McFaul and Petrov, *Politicheskii Almanakh Rossii 1995*, p. 298.

[53]Sokolovski, "Vladivostok Trip Report," p. 3. Former Vladivostok mayor Viktor Cherepkov ran for a seat in the first round and won the most votes in his district, but the turnout for the vote—17 percent—did not reach the required 25 percent to be valid.

[54]Oleg Kryuchek, "Predsedatelya Primorskoi dumy nizlozhili v ego otsytstvie," *Segodnya*, June 22, 1995, p. 3.

[55]McFaul and Petrov, *Politicheskii Almanakh Rossii 1995*, p. 298.

[56]Kirkow, "The Siberian and Far Eastern Challenge to Centre-Periphery Relations in Russia," pp. 238–39. In 1994, a local BBC journalist, Alexei Sadikov, was kidnapped and beaten, allegedly by thugs working on behalf of Nazdratenko.

[57]Alex Sokolovski, "Vladivostok Trip Report," National Democratic Institute, Moscow, mimeo, September 21, 1994, p. 4.

[58]Ibid.

[59]According to the assessment conducted by a Russia-based representative of the National Democratic Institute, a Western organization that has worked in dozens of regions throughout Russia, the only significant party presence in the region is Yabloko.

[60]For a typically anti-Asian account of ethnic tensions in the region, see Denis Demkin, "Primorskiy Kray: Investment Site or Battleground?" *Business in Russia*, no. 73 (January 1997), pp. 50–51.

[61]Quoted in Garth Jones, "Russia Far East Eyes Neighbors with Caution, Hope," *Reuters*, May 27, 1997.

[62]Lloyd, "Challenge to Russian democracy on the waterfront."

[63]For the list of those removed, see McFaul and Petrov, *Politicheskii Almanakh Rossii 1997*, pp. 393–94.

[64]Ibid., p. 392.

[65]The government also issued its own special report on the region's failure to pay its taxes. Called the Chubais-Karpov Commission, the federal investigation found dozens of illegal operations undertaken by the local government. The report, however, did not blame Nazdratenko specifically for any wrongdoing. See Valentina Voronova, "Otstupnik revizory," *Obshchaya gazeta*, June 29-July 5, 1995, p. 8.

[66]Quoted in Geoffrey York, "In Russia's Primorsky region, corruption runs rampant and the governors calls the shots," *The Globe and Mail*, July 11, 1997. Nazdratenko denounced the probe by "Gaidar and his stooges" as a provocation that "found nothing on me." See the interview with Nazdratenko, *Argumenty i Fakty*, no. 27 (July 1995), p. 9; quoted here from *What the Papers Say*, July 7, 1995, p. 7.

[67]This group, labeled the "party of war" by the Russian liberal press after the invasion, comprised several key Kremlin officials within or closely affiliated with the security ministries; they included Defense Minister Pavel Grachev, First Deputy Prime Minister Oleg Soskovets, Deputy Prime Minister Nikolai Yegorov, Security Council Chief Oleg Lobov, and Aleksandr Korzhakov, Yeltsin's personal bodyguard at the time. Although several of these officials had been in Yeltsin's government from the beginning, the

influence of this hawkish coalition grew while the influence of liberals and liberal interest groups declined throughout 1994. On the formation of this coalition, see Maksim Sokolov, "Razberis', kto prav, kto vinovat, da oboikh i nakazhi," *Kommersant' Daily*, December 8, 1994; Aleksandr Minkin, "Advokat shefa KGB Kriuchkova Zashchishchaet Prezidenta Yeltsina," *Moskovskii Komsmolets*, January 14, 1995, pp. 1–2; and John Dunlop, "The 'Party of War' and Russian Imperial Nationalism," *Problems of Post-Communism*, vol. 43, no. 2 (March-April 1996), pp. 29–34.

[68]Western reports have echoed Chubais's concern. See "Russia's Far East: Rotten to the Core," *The Economist*, October 18, 1997, p. 54. On the negative economic consequences of political decentralization in Russia more generally, see Darrell Slider, "Russia's Market-Distorting Federalism," *Post-Soviet Geography and Economics*, vol. 38, no. 9 (1997), pp. 489–504.

[69]Interview with Nazdratenko in *Profil'*, p. 11. Nazdratenko claims that his conflict with Chubais regarding privatization was very similar to Chubais's conflict with Luzhkov, the mayor of Moscow. The only the difference was that Chubais understood that he was not powerful enough to "teach" Luzhkov, whereas he thought he had more leverage over the smaller Primorie.

[70]Interview with Nazdratenko, *Argumenty i Fakty*, quoted here from *What the Papers Say*, p. 7.

[71]See Lloyd, "Challenge to Russian democracy on the waterfront," p. 3.

[72]York, "In Russia's Primorsky region, corruption runs rampant."

[73]For an in-depth analysis of Nazdratenko's ties to local financial groups and the conflicts between these regional economic groups and Moscow groups, see Stepan Kiselev, "S Primor'ya na Rossiyu nadvigayutsya sumerki," *Izvestiya*, October 8, 1997, pp. 1, 3.

[74]"Russia's Regions: The Far East," *Business Russia*, April 1997, p. 9.

[75]Nonetheless, conflicts between Cherepkov and the local administration continued throughout 1995. See Elena Tregubova, "Primorskie demokraty gotovyat 'isk za klevetu' protiv gubernatora Nazdratrenko," *Segodnya*, October 8, 1995, p. 3.

[76]Igor Korol'kov, "Viktor Cherepkov protiv Borisa Yelt'sina," *Izvestiya*, August 3, 1997, p. 1.

[77]McFaul, "Russian Politics After Chechnya," pp. 149–65.

[78]For details, see Michael McFaul, *Russia's 1996 Presidential Elections: The End of Polarized Politics* (Stanford, Calif.: Hoover Institution Press, 1997).

[79]"Shakhteram vydeleno 45 milliardov rubley is byudgeta," *Rossiiskie Vesti*, July 31, 1996, p. 3.

[80]"Shakhteri Primor'ya prodolzhayut massovuyu aktsiyu protesta," *Rossiiskie Vesti*, August 1, 1997, p. 2. Before the fall strikes, Nazdratenko's government had held energy prices well below prices found in other regions. The federal government eventually refused to subsidize the region's price-control policy, a move that led to a massive buildup of debt at the Dal'nergo

energy plant. The plant eventually was compelled to cut off electricity in the region for numerous hours a day as well as delay wage payments to workers. For details, see Galina Kovalskaya, "Polozhenie khuzhe Gubernatorskago," *Itogi*, June 10, 1997, pp. 12–16.

[81]For the center's view of the crisis, see Valerii Golovin, "Krisis v Primorie: kto avtor?" *Rossiiskie Vesti*, September 18, 1996, p. 1.

[82]On the claim that Nazdratenko had diverted federal funds, see Dmitrii Dokuchaev and Mikhail Berger, "AKT proverki v Primorie vse-taki podpisan, pretenzii k administratsii kraya ostayutstya," *Izvestiya*, August 15, 1996, p. 2; and Valerii Golovin, ". . . a popytki svoi grekhi spisat' na tsentr— zastavit otvechat'," *Rossiiskie Vesti*, August 15, 1997, p. 1.

[83]Interview with Nazdratenko in *Profil'*, p. 12.

[84]"Gubernator Primor'ya ne soglasen s Glavnym kontrol'nym upravelniam prezidenta," *Izvestiya*, August 16, 1997, p. 1; and "Primorskaya Duma otmenyaet referendum," *Rossiiskie Vesti*, September 19, 1997, p. 1.

[85]"V primorie edet komissiya," *Rossiiskie Vesti*, September 26, 1997, p. 1. The director of Dal'nergo as well as Nazdratenko's vice governor, Mikhail Savchenko, lost their jobs over this crisis. See Dmitrii Dokuchaev, "Grozovoe preduprezhndenie gubernatoru Primor'ya," *Izvestiya*, August 16, 1996, p. 3.

[86]Author's interview with an adviser to Chubais, Moscow, July 1997.

[87]Yeltsin invented this institution—the presidential representative—to parallel the activities of the heads of administration and thereby further fortify executive authority at the subnational level. Local officials referred to these people as Yeltsin's commissars. On the origins of this office, see Kathryn Stoner-Weiss, *Local Heros: The Political Economy of Russian Regional Governance* (Princeton, N.J.: Princeton University Press, 1997), pp. 74–75.

[88]Robert Orttung, "Moscow Intensifies Attack on Nazdratenko," *IEWS Russian Regional Report*, vol. 2, no. 21 (June 12, 1997). At the time, Chubais had a more general plan to strengthen central authority through these presidential representatives. He intended to create a dozen new territorial units run by presidential representatives to which republics, krais, and oblasts would report. The plan failed.

[89]Author's interview with Vladivostok political organizers, Moscow, July 1997. See also Orttung, "Moscow Intensifies Attack on Nazdratenko," and the interview with Nazdratenko in *Profil'*, p. 12.

[90]Orttung, "Moscow Intensifies Attack on Nazdratenko."

[91]Mikhail Streblev, "I bez boya sdat' Primorie," *Itogi*, June 24, 1997, p. 27.

[92]Ibid. Citing Kremlin sources, Streblev said the president endorsed the plan on June 16, 1997, and then waited for a request from the region's authorities to hold the election. Nazdratenko put the question before the Primorskii Krai Duma the following day. Duma Chairman Sergei Knyazev, however, refused to discuss the resolution, because the law allowed a new

election only if the governor resigned or was removed. In essence, Nazdratenko had forced Moscow to follow through with the unconstitutional act of removing him from office before the election would occur. Moscow backed down.

[93]Interfax, "Chubais Sees Primorie Governor As Chief Culprit in Crisis," June 11, 1997.

[94]Geoffrey York, "Russian Government Cannot Dictate to Primorsky's Powerful Governor," *The Globe and Mail,* July 10, 1997.

[95]For instance, governors considered loyal to the Kremlin, like Titov in Samara and Ayatskov in Saratov, sided with Nazdratenko in this latest dispute. Federation Council Chairman Yegor Stroev also denounced the Kremlin campaign against Nazdratenko and organized the coalition in the Federation Council that passed the resolution denouncing the act. See Lina Markus, "Yeshche raz o konstitutsionnom poryadke," *Itogi,* June 17, 1997, p. 18.

[96]Rossel, as quoted in Markus, "Yeshche raz o konstitutsionnom poryadke," p. 18.

[97]Robert Orttung, "Governors Defend Their Interests in Nazdratenko's Battle with Moscow," *IEWS Russian Regional Report,* vol. 2, no. 25 (July 10, 1997).

[98]Interview with Nazdratenko in *Profil',* p. 12.

[99]Streblev, "I bez boya sdat' Primorie," p. 28.

[100]Galina Kovalskaya, "Polozhenie khuzhe Gubernatorskago," *Itogi,* June 10, 1997, p. 15.

[101]Nazdratenko, as quoted in York, "Russian Government Cannot Dictate to Primorsky's Powerful Governor."

[102]McFaul and Petrov, *Politicheskii Almanakh Rossii 1995,* p. 296.

[103]Ibid., p. 296.

[104]Michael McFaul and Nikolai Petrov, *Previewing Russia's 1995 Parliamentary Elections* (Washington, D.C.: Carnegie Endowment for International Peace, 1995), p. 229.

[105]McFaul and Petrov, *Politicheskii Almanakh Rossii 1995,* p. 297. The electoral rules for this ballot allowed voters to cast two votes. The top two finishers were then elected to the Federation Council, which explains why Gaer could win a seat with only 38 percent of the popular vote.

[106]Figures all taken from Michael McFaul, *Russia Between Elections: What the December 1995 Elections Results Really Mean* (Washington, D.C.: Carnegie Endowment for International Peace, 1996), p. 60.

[107]In contrast, the war with Chechnya could be labeled a war of national liberation.

[108]Interview with Nazdratenko, *Argumenty i Fakty,* quoted here from *What the Papers Say,* p. 7. Of course, the fact that the governor must answer

questions about secession illustrates that some believed that the possibility was real.

[109]On migration issues in the region, see the edited volume *Migratsionnaya situatsiya na Dal'nem Vostoke i politika Rossii* (Moscow: Carnegie Endowment for International Peace, 1996).

[110]Similar assertions of local dictatorship have been levied against leaders in Tatarstan and Kalmykia.

[111]In other words, they overcame collective action problems to act in unity to check the discretionary power of the sovereign.

[112]For elaboration, see Solnick, "The Political Economy of Russian Federalism."

[113]For institutional arrangements such as federalism to persist, all actors must have incentives to abide by the rules. This situation provided a similar kind of incentive to constrain the center for every regional leader, no matter what his or her political orientation.

[114]In this regard, Primorskii Krai may be more the rule than the exception. See Mary McAuley, *Russia's Politics of Uncertainty* (Cambridge: Cambridge University Press, 1997), especially pp. 312–13.

[115]Theorists on democratization usually assume that all "democratic good things"—the rule of law, party development, checks and balances, federalism, civil society, free press, and so on—go together. This case suggests that this virtuous complementarity of democratic institutions may not always hold.

12
Chinese Migration into Russia

Galina Vitkovskaya,
Zhanna Zayonchkovskaya,
and Kathleen Newland

The thaw in relations between Russia and China after the collapse of the Soviet Union and the demilitarization of the 4,300-kilometer border between the two giants radically altered the migration dynamics of the border region. What had been a virtually closed and heavily militarized border became an open and essentially unregulated one in the early 1990s. To give just one example, the administration of the Amur Oblast counted 6,233 border crossings by foreigners, mostly Chinese, in 1988; in 1992, this number was 287,215.[1] The rapid change from virtually no Chinese presence in the Russian Far East to considerable numbers of Chinese traders, students, and contract laborers was highly visible, although very little accurate information is available on the actual numbers of Chinese migrants in the region or on their characteristics and activities. The information vacuum has been filled by highly speculative and often grotesquely alarmist estimations. To help fill this information vacuum, the Moscow Center of the Carnegie Endowment for International Peace carried out a large-scale scientific survey in the Far East and Eastern Siberia in 1996–1997. Local researchers participated in the survey, some of the early results of which are reflected in this chapter.[2] Another survey was conducted in 1998–1999 in Moscow, Khabarovsk, Vladivostok, and Ussuriysk.

Despite stark disagreements about the nature of the migration, no one doubts that there has been a substantial increase in the number of Chinese living, working, and traveling in the region. Several factors have contributed to the increase:

- Russian demand for consumer goods, arising from the collapse of subsidies for goods and transportation from European Russia, which encouraged cross-border trade
- demand for labor, mostly in agriculture and construction, spurred by increased economic activity and out-migration of the Russian population
- lack of border-control institutions, resources, and legal frameworks in Russia
- growing economic integration of the border regions
- high unemployment in the neighboring regions of China
- large discrepancies in population density on either side of the border.

Journalists, bureaucrats, intellectuals, and politicians have been among those claiming that Russia runs the risk of losing control of the region, characterizing Chinese migration to the region as an "invasion" and evoking sinister Beijing-sponsored plots to breach Russia's territorial integrity. In 1995, Pavel Grachev, who was then defense minister, warned that "people of Chinese nationality are trying to peacefully conquer the Russian Far East."[3] In 1997, Interior Ministry officials told a press briefing that Korean and Chinese illegal immigration into the Far East was a threat to Russia's national security, insisting that Chinese trading networks were trafficking arms, drugs, illegal migrants, and other contraband, as well as poaching, laundering money, and attacking Russian border guards.[4] Former dissident Alexander Solzhenitsyn and celebrated film director Nikita Mikhalkov have railed against Moscow's neglect of the provinces and the gradual silent "occupation" of the Far East by Chinese.[5]

The comments of Professor Alexander Yakovlev, leading researcher at the Institute of the Far East of the Russian Academy of Sciences, are perhaps characteristic:

> There are non-military threats to this country's integrity building up. In particular, the Chinese are intensifying their already massive infiltration of Siberia and the Russian Far

East, in which they are probably encouraged by Beijing. In the future, this could become a source of constant friction between Russia and China, to say nothing of the "infiltrants" acting as an added destabilizing factor in various parts of Russia's Asiatic part, especially in border areas, once their numbers have reached the critical mass. And this future is none too distant either.

The danger of masses of Chinese arriving and settling in the area is particularly great because the "infiltrants" are convinced that the lands where they are putting down new roots are no foreign country but China's historical territory lost a mere 150 years ago. . . . More is the pity that in today's China, which is supposed to be our friend, they continue to work with persistent zeal to prop up the claim with fresh "scientific" proof.[6]

In contrast to these voices, both within and outside of the Russian government, the Ministry of Foreign Affairs and the presidency have tried to calm the alarmist and exaggerated characterizations of migration in the Far East, emphasizing that the issue must be regulated through bilateral cooperation in the context of a many-faceted relationship with China. The deputy director of the first Asia Department of the Ministry of Foreign Affairs wrote, in February 1997, "official confirmation has been received from Beijing that China is not pursuing a policy of 'support for the penetration of citizens of the PRC into the Far East and Siberia,' and also that China is prepared to cooperate closely with Russia (including by initiating cooperation between the two countries' law enforcement agencies). . . ."[7]

Similarly, Russian Presidential Adviser Emil Pain has harshly criticized regional authorities in the Far East for fanning Sinophobia in the region in order to "shift some of the responsibility for the dismal situation in the region onto foreigners."[8] While acknowledging that illegal immigration is a problem that needs to be regulated, he argues that it is a limited aspect of Russian-Chinese relations. The Russian market as a whole is more important to China than is the Far East as a spillway for excess population. Pain states that "authorities in the Russian Far East have no right to play the 'Chinese card' and scare everyone with the threat of Chinese expansion in their own egotistical interests, for the purpose of creating a political image, in the process making the realization of Russian geopolitical interests involving China extremely difficult."[9] Pain also points out the importance of the Chinese migrants in supplying labor to agriculture and the construction industry, as well as the role of China as the Far East's second largest export market (after Japan). He quotes an estimate by Pavel Minaker of the Russian Academy of Sciences that the current Chinese population of the Far East makes up only about 3 percent of the total population, whereas at the turn of the past century a half-million Chinese in the Far East composed about one-third of the population.[10]

The scale of Chinese migration to the Far East and Eastern Siberia has been routinely exaggerated in the Russian press and in political debate. Estimates of as many as 2 million have commonly been cited. More sober local estimates were in the 100,000–200,000 range, not all of them (perhaps not even the majority) permanent. The Chinese government estimates that 300,000 Chinese reside in all the CIS (Commonwealth of Independent States) countries put together, and it has repeatedly felt compelled to deny any territorial ambitions in the Russian Far East. In February 1998, for example, Chinese Prime Minister Li Peng denied that Chinese workers were settling in Russia's Far East and establishing Chinatowns. He said Chinese citizens traveling or working in Russia must adhere to Russian regulations on obtaining visas, stressing that their presence in Russia does not constitute a "secret colonization."[11] A field study into the issue of Chinese migration was undertaken in 1998–1999 in Moscow, Khabarovsk, Vladivostok, and Ussuriysk.[12]

THE DEMOGRAPHIC IMBALANCE

While assessments of the size and significance of Chinese immigration vary wildly, what is not in doubt is the contrasting demographic facts on the two sides of the border. The Russian Far East has a population of about 8 million spread over 6.2 million square kilometers. The neighboring Chinese provinces have a population of 110 million crammed into 1.9 million square kilometers. To many people, these figures speak for themselves, and their message is an inevitable and irresistible spread of the Chinese into the demographic vacuum across the border. Few knowledgeable observers would dispute that the differences in "demographic potential" on the two sides of the

border are an important geopolitical factor, whose growing significance has not been much analyzed.

According to various estimates, the population density on the
Chinese side of the border is fifteen to twenty times higher than
that on the Russian side. This fact alone guarantees continuing pressure for Chinese expansion, particularly since Chinese immigration
to the South has exhausted itself. Can—and should—Russia resist
this pressure? This question is dominant in the discussion of migration in the Far East.

China's interests in providing the means of existence to its millions
of unemployed and poor citizens is presumed to lead it to favor
expansion of its population into the empty lands over the border. In
Russia, expert opinion is virtually unanimous that massive Chinese
expansion is not in the country's interests and that a restrictive
immigration policy is thus needed.

What are not taken into account in most portrayals of the issue—
which emphasize the large numerical superiority of the Chinese,
the underpopulation of the Russian border regions, and the crisis
of power in Russia—are Russia's future labor needs. After 2005,
Russia will experience a natural massive decline in the working-age
population, which according to various estimates will sink 15 percent
over the following decade—an extremely rapid drop in historical
terms. Many European countries have faced this situation and solved
the crisis by attracting immigrants. Russia, too, will not be able to
avoid this. As soon as the country's economy begins to recover, the
shortage of labor will make itself felt. It could act as a major constraint
on Russia's development in the next several decades. As a result,
Russia's capacity to absorb immigrants will be high, and its migration policy, increasingly, will focus on immigration.

In the Far East and Eastern Siberia, the effect of the natural
decrease of the population is exacerbated and accelerated by the
out-migration of existing residents. After the collapse of the Soviet
Union, migration flows in Russia started to move to the West. There
was an outflow of population from the Far East, probably for the
first time during the history of Russian expansion. In 1992–1996, the
region lost 559,000 people, or 7 percent of its population. Although
northern territories were hit the hardest, people are also leaving the
southern areas. Khabarovskii Krai and Amur Oblast lost 3.3 percent
of their population each, and Primorskii Krai lost 1.5 percent. Eastern

Siberia's Chita Oblast, which neighbors China, lost 3.1 percent of its population. Losses in internal migration are only partially (by approximately 30 percent) recovered through immigration from the other CIS countries. Most of these immigrants are Russian expatriates, reuniting with their relatives, or Koreans, returning from Central Asia and Kazakhstan where they were deported during World War II. Thus, Chinese immigration is developing against an unfavorable local demographic background.

Do the Chinese face competition from other potential emigrants to the Far East of Russia? Viewed in the CIS framework, traditional immigration from the overpopulated states of the Caucasus must be taken into account. These countries, however, are in a different "weight category" from China and cannot create serious competition. Immigration from Central Asia is also possible, but the region's indigenous population is not yet highly mobile and will take a considerable amount of time to develop the habit of migration. The Chinese, however, are ready to migrate at the first available opportunity. Over the past several years, refugees from Africa and South Asia have started to come to Russia, but their numbers are small. Russia would probably prefer to develop a labor migration system based on Chinese, with whom it is more familiar and who adapt more easily to its severe climate.

Chinese immigration is thus in both Russia's and China's interests over the medium and long terms. Not surprisingly, however, Russia is interested in maintaining an ethnic Russian majority in the border regions. In order to accomplish this, massive resettlements of Russians to Eastern Siberia and the Far East have been proposed. Vladimir Myasnikov, director of the Institute of the Far East in the Russian Academy of Science, for example, talks about resettling 2.5–3.0 million people. He appeals, as many authors of such proposals do, to the successful historic experience of such an approach, and he uses examples of both the recent Soviet experience and Stolypin's reforms in nineteenth-century imperial Russia, when Pyotr Stolypin (minister and later the head of government) moved large groups of people from the European part of Russia to the Far East. Contemporary conditions significantly differ from those of the past, however. If, at the turn of the past century, resettlement in Siberia solved a problem of overpopulation in the agrarian regions of western Russia, now the question is not where to move people but where to find people to move.

Demographers are unequivocal that in the foreseeable future Russian birthrates are not going to increase even to replacement level. Immigration is the only source of population growth. Currently, problems of overpopulation are nonexistent. Moreover, under the conditions of a surplus demand for labor, people have more opportunities to choose where they will live, and they are attracted to the regions that provide the most comfortable living conditions. The development of market relations has reoriented migration flows in Russia from the North and the East to the South and the Southwest of the country. In the near future, the labor market will be favorable for Russians not only in Russia but also in Ukraine. It is unrealistic to count on substantial population movement to Siberia and the Far East. Hopes for such developments are nothing more than an escape from reality, not the constructive solutions that their authors believe them to be.

The possibility of attracting Russian-speakers from the former Soviet republics does not provide much hope either, because the number of potential migrants from these countries is believed to be only about 2.5–4.0 million. At the higher end, this number would cover about half of the natural decline of the labor force. Over the past five years, the repatriation of Russians has accelerated, with Russia receiving more people from the other former republics than it had in the previous fifteen years, but not enough to compensate for the natural population decline. Moreover, people who move from the CIS countries and the Baltic States prefer to settle in the central, western, and southern regions of Russia, despite the higher unemployment rates in those areas. Very few people have moved to the East.[13]

Current Russian policy toward Chinese migration is aimed at control rather than management. Attempts at strict border control and occasional mass deportations hinder the economic integration of the Russian Far East with the economies of neighboring countries; indeed one might say that fear of the Russian Far East being overwhelmed by Chinese is itself a major constraint on the economic dynamism of the region, preventing both countries from taking advantage of the complementarities between them.

HISTORY

In 1858–1860, as a result of an agreement with China, territories on the left bank of the Amur River and on the right bank of the Ussuri

River were turned over to Russia. On their arrival, Russian settlers encountered a few indigenous people and several thousand Chinese (Manchu and Han Chinese).[14] Russia had little difficulty annexing the sparsely populated territories.[15]

Russian policy toward the Chinese in the region ranged from welcoming to intolerant depending on the need for cheap labor and the general political environment. The number of Chinese in the region varied accordingly. At the initial stage of the region's exploration in the second half of the nineteenth century, Russia was clearly interested in attracting the Chinese. They were allowed to live in Primorie and along the Amur River and to own land, and they were exempt from paying taxes for the first twenty years of residence. The first Chinese immigrants—construction workers, dockworkers, and servants—came to the region in the middle of the 1870s. According to the 1897 census, 57,000 Chinese lived in Russia, with 41,000 of them in the Far East. In 1910, 115,000 Chinese were registered, although their real number was estimated at 150,000.[16] At that time, the region was mostly populated by the "Stolypin migrants"[17] and Chinese accounted for just 10–12 percent of the population.[18]

Chinese greatly contributed to the initial exploration of the region. They occupied the hardest jobs of unskilled labor, accounting for 70–90 percent of workers in gold mines, coal mines, and on the docks.[19] Many also worked in construction. Trade and entrepreneurial occupations also played an extremely important role, with Chinese near parity with Russians in this sphere. In 1910, for example, 8,300 Chinese and 12,300 Russian enterprises existed in the region.[20]

The low wage rates of Chinese labor benefited Russian entrepreneurs enormously, but the Russian authorities were concerned with the rapid increase in the number of Chinese and Koreans in the Far East, with their entrepreneurial skills and eagerness to perform any task. The specter of the "yellow peril" was first raised after Moscow's defeat in the 1905 Russo-Japanese War, although Chinese migration was restricted for some years before that. In 1886, Chinese were banned from settling in the border regions and, in 1892, from acquiring land in that region. In 1910, employers were forbidden to hire Chinese as daily laborers. The policy was not successful, because restrictions on the use of Chinese labor resulted in great economic damage. The result was that legal Chinese migration was simply replaced by illegal Chinese migration.

Russia's policy changed again during World War I, when Chinese workers compensated for the general deficit of labor in the country. The vast majority of these Chinese workers remained in Russia even after the Bolshevik Revolution, because they did not have enough money to return to their homes. According to the 1926 census, 100,000 Chinese were living in Russia, 70 percent of them in the Far East. In 1928, 8,000 Chinese resided in Moscow.[21]

At first, the Bolsheviks were protective of all ethnic minorities, including the Chinese. Much was done to raise their literacy rates, develop their national culture, and assimilate them into Russian culture. These practices changed in the 1930s, however, because of the complicated political environment in the Soviet Far East. In keeping with the practices of the Stalinist regime, anti-Chinese measures were severe. In 1937, many Chinese were deported to China. Other ethnic minorities had similar fates. Some of the Koreans were sent to Korea and others to Central Asia and Kazakhstan.

During and right after World War II, Chinese immigration was virtually impossible. During the "Khrushchev thaw," the Soviet Union reopened its doors to Chinese college and graduate students, but as Russian-Chinese relations worsened again, even this interchange was lost. As early as 1959–1960, the students were recalled by China. At the same time, the Soviet mass media started an anti-Chinese campaign, which was particularly rigorous in the Far East. It created lasting anti-Chinese sentiment among the region's population.

THE PRESENT SITUATION

The regulation of border traffic declined dramatically after the thaw in relations between Russia and China in the Gorbachev era. The lack of control, especially after the introduction of a liberalized visa regime in 1988, spurred great anxiety in Russia as the volume of traffic of both people and goods picked up steam. Many Chinese immediately moved across the border to start a vibrant trade in consumer goods all over the Federation. Naturally, their presence was concentrated in the Far East. The rapid growth in the number of poor and hardworking Chinese highlighted Russia's lack of experience and legal means to control international migration or border disputes. This growth combined with a persistent public image of the "yellow peril" to raise the level of concern and apprehension on the part of the local population. Their anxiety was fanned and exploited by local politicians, who saw the Chinese migrants as pawns in their power struggles with Moscow and as scapegoats for various local problems such as housing shortages, corruption, crime, and so forth.

Central and local mass media persistently created an image of millions of Chinese living in Russia. Primorskii Krai newspaper *Vladivostok*[22] as well as the central *Izvestiya*[23] repeatedly estimated their number at 2 million. The press routinely claimed that "the Chinese population in the [Far East] border region is 1.5–2 times higher than the local [Russian]."[24] Television news anchors reported about some eastern Russian towns where the Chinese supposedly outnumbered the Russians.

Early results from the Carnegie Endowment research project indicate that the scale of Chinese immigration has been greatly exaggerated.[25] Survey data collected by local researchers in the framework of the Carnegie project are consistent with more moderate estimations. According to Pavel Minakir, head of the Institute of Economic Research of the Far Eastern branch of the Russian Academy of Sciences, Chinese immigrants in the Far East numbered no more than 50,000–80,000 in 1992–1993. Minakir's range includes 10,000–15,000 legal contract workers and 10,000–12,000 students who have received permission to study in the region for up to one year. It is hard to support claims that the actual number of illegal aliens was much higher. During operations carried out by the police and border patrol in the Primorskii and Khabarovskii Krais and Amur Oblast, no more than 5,000–6,000 illegal immigrants were deported from each of these territories.[26] Another assessment, produced jointly by L. L. Rybakovsky, director of the Center for Demography of the Moscow Institute of Socio-Political Research of the Russian Academy of Sciences, and V. V. Mindogulov, an official of the Khabarovskii Krai administration, places the number of immigrants in the Far East at approximately 100,000 people.[27]

In October 1996, the total number of Chinese in the Primorie and Khabarovsk regions was no more than tens of thousands of people. Many specialists believed 30,000–70,000 Chinese, including shuttle traders, lived in each of these territories.[28] The experts have unanimously rejected any estimates that placed their number at 2 million or even at hundreds of thousands. Chinese sources estimate the number of their countrymen in all the CIS states to be no more than 300,000, which is about 1 percent of the global Chinese diaspora.[29]

A NEW EMPHASIS ON RULE OF LAW AT THE BORDER

The de facto open-border regime of the early 1990s gave way, starting in 1993–1994, to attempts to restore control. In 1993, customs duties were imposed on imported goods and migration control was introduced at border checkpoints. These changes decreased the number of Chinese crossing the border, hindered economic integration of the border regions, and favored informal "suitcase" trading over formal cooperative trading relations.

A mechanism for licensing foreign workers was also created. Until 1994, there was no official data on the number of Chinese workers in the country. Published numbers ranged from 10,000 people in 1990 to 17,000–18,000 in 1992–1993. According to the Khabarovskii Krai administration, the region employed 707 Chinese workers in 1991; 1,175 in 1992; and 1,560 in 1993. In 1992, Chita Oblast led the region with 10,000 Chinese workers.[30] On December 16, 1993, President Yeltsin signed the decree On the Use of Foreign Labor in Russia, which established stricter control over the number of employed aliens. By mid-April 1994, the Federal Migration Service granted permission to 251 applicants to employ, in total, 15,000 Chinese workers, including 8,500 in the Far East region. Under such arrangements, 20,301 Chinese workers were employed in Russia in 1994;[31] 25,528 in 1995;[32] and 24,043 in 1996.[33] The quotas, however, were set higher than the actual number of workers. In Primorie, for example, the quota was set at 15,000 people, while in 1996 the actual number of foreign workers, including the Chinese, was 13,500.[34]

Rising tensions, accompanied by roundups and deportations of Chinese immigrants and by considerable xenophobic rhetoric, encouraged the Russian and Chinese governments to cooperate in devising a new visa regime in 1994 that abolished the kind of passport that enabled Chinese to travel to Russia without a visa. They declared a campaign against illegal migration, in which 9,500 Chinese were sent home from Vladivostok between 1994 and 1996. In 1995, Chinese authorities made Chinese tour-group operators responsible for bringing back all the travelers they took to Russia.

Chinese officials have been sensitive to Russian anxieties and have tried to soothe them with cooperative bilateral action to regulate the flow of migrants. They clearly are determined not to allow this issue to become a serious irritant in bilateral relations.

CHARACTERISTICS OF CHINESE WORKERS IN THE FAR EAST

A Carnegie Endowment research project in the Far East interviewed a sample of 244 Chinese aliens (49 percent were men and 51 percent were women) at markets; colleges and universities; dormitories; and agricultural, industrial, and transport enterprises. The results showed that 17 percent were under the age of twenty, 51 percent were between twenty and thirty years old, 25 percent were between thirty and forty, and only 7 percent were older than fifty. These results largely determined their marital status—58 percent were single, 64 percent had no children, and 73 percent of those with children had only one child.

It was an educated group—35 percent had a college degree, 48 percent had general high school, and 17 percent a specialized high school diploma. (The actual educational level of Chinese aliens is probably lower because educated people were more likely to agree to be interviewed. This characteristic was particularly noticeable at construction sites.) Their skills corresponded to their level of education: 57 percent had professions that require higher or specialized education, such as economists (18 percent), instructors (7 percent), engineers (7 percent), and interpreters (3 percent); 19 percent were doctors, lawyers, journalists, librarians, managers, marketing specialists, and such; 10 percent worked in construction and highly skilled manual occupations; and only 3 percent were peasants. Of the total, 17 percent did not provide any information. (Some overlap among categories accounts for totals over 100 percent.)

A total of 84 percent of the Chinese migrants were of urban origin, while 16 percent came from rural areas. The majority came from Heilongjiang Province, with 44 percent of the city dwellers coming from Harbin. The Girin Province, which neighbors Heilongjiang, was responsible for the second largest number of migrants. Together the Heilongjiang, Girin, Lyaonin, and Inner Mongolia Provinces accounted for 96 percent of Chinese migrants to the Russian Far East. According to a Chinese author, Heilongjiang, Sintzyan, Shensi, and Gansu are the four provinces responsible for most of Chinese immigration to all the CIS states.[35]

The survey showed that most Chinese travel to other parts of the region. The most common destinations were other cities in the Far East and Eastern Siberia, but many had also visited Western Siberia. Fully 13 percent had visited Moscow and 6 percent had been to St. Petersburg.

THE OCCUPATIONS AND ASPIRATIONS OF CHINESE MIGRANTS IN THE RUSSIAN FAR EAST

The data collected in the sample survey indicated that the qualifications of Chinese immigrants do not necessarily match their current occupations. Of those interviewed, 46 percent were working as traders and 40 percent were students or trainees. Some 14 percent were hired labor, including interpreters or instructors, enterprise workers (5 percent), and construction workers (4 percent). Only 2 percent were agricultural workers. Although none of the respondents described themselves as tourists, 45 percent had entered Russia on a tourist visa.

Two-thirds (68 percent) said they would like to have their own business in Russia. Of these, 72 percent wanted to open a store or trading firm, 15 percent would like to have a small production business, 11 percent would like to open a restaurant or a hotel, and 2 percent had not decided yet what kind of business they would like to own. In general, there was a clear tendency toward owning a trade-related business.

Despite the popular alarmist perception of a Chinese landgrab in the Far East, only 25 percent of the respondents said they would like to receive land for long-term lease. Only 11 percent would like to remain as workers in Russia.

Interest in trade and hotel businesses is characteristic of Chinese immigrants all over the world, but there are objective conditions in the Russian Far East that channel economic activity into these sectors. Russia still does not have a climate favorable to investment in and creation of joint enterprises. Despite the fact that numerous new Russian-Chinese joint ventures are registered, few are functional. Some experts interviewed thought that enterprises that register but do not do business, or continue to operate with a loss, are "spies" or fronts for Chinese businesses.

Existing labor relations can hardly be called a partnership. The use of Chinese labor falls far short of civilized standards. Despite an economic crisis and high unemployment, few local Russian residents are willing to perform the tasks of unskilled labor in construction and agriculture.[36] Employers are happy to hire Chinese workers to perform these tasks. The employers usually deal with Chinese labor-unit leaders. They are responsible for setting up a work schedule for their employees, who usually end up working very long hours without any days off or any possibility to see their families for the duration of their contracts, which usually are ten months long. Their relatives can visit only as tourists and have to pay their own expenses. Even if one works in Blagoveshchensk, it is not possible to go over the Amur River for a day off during a contract period.

Contracts must be renewed annually, which involves considerable expense. Chinese workers are paid half to three-quarters of what their Russian counterparts with similar skills earn.[37] Of those who work at these contract jobs, 86 percent say that they do not make much. But 40 percent of traders and 36 percent of "students" find their income satisfactory. Chinese contract workers get their salaries only after the completion of the contract period, often when they have returned to China. Some leaders of labor units do not give them any money while they are working in Russia and thus they are forced to take odd jobs illegally, mostly at night. In other cases, they are paid with a token sum. At one of the construction enterprises in Vladivostok, for example, the monthly allowance was 75,000 rubles (U.S.$18.00 at the time).

This state of affairs satisfies many local leaders and politicians because it provides cheap labor and demands no responsibility. And Russian employers are pleased with the industriousness and discipline of their Chinese work force.

The living conditions of Chinese laborers are far below local standards. Many Chinese workers live in hotels (38 percent of those polled), rented housing (9 percent), or dormitories (12 percent). Only 4 percent of the respondents bought their own house or apartment, and about 2 percent lived with relatives. According to local experts, providing housing for Chinese migrants has turned into a lucrative market, with wealthy Chinese serving as middlemen. Prices are usually set for a housing unit as a whole, and it is common for Chinese workers to live in crowded conditions with twenty to thirty people in an apartment. It is not surprising that the level of sanitation is low, but Chinese workers do not complain.

The pattern of Chinese immigrant experience has changed little since the early 1900s.[38] The typical Chinese migrant to Russia is poor, persevering, modest, hungry for earnings of any size, and brutally exploited by his own countrymen with the silent approval of the Russians. The model has reestablished itself at the first available opportunity, regardless of the Iron Curtain, revolutions in both countries, and the two world wars. Despite these unpromising conditions, 23 percent of Chinese migrants would like to become permanent residents of Russia, although their chances of doing so are very slim; 23 percent also want their children to live in Russia (a little more than a third of whom are among those who themselves want to live in Russia). Therefore, Russia can count on a continuing source of additional Chinese labor as needed.

CHINESE IN RUSSIAN PUBLIC OPINION

Open borders have radically changed the Russian Far East. The population has had a chance to see the world, its mobility has increased, and new sources of income have emerged. China probably receives the same number of Russian shuttle traders as Russia does Chinese. Active intercourse with China brought life to the border regions of Eastern Siberia and the Russian Far East, which during the Russian economic crisis have found themselves even more peripheral than before. Russian sentiments toward the Chinese, however, remain guarded at best. The Carnegie survey, like other research, shows that most inhabitants of the border regions as well as representatives of regional administrations support an increase in cooperation with China. But Russian attitudes toward the Chinese immigrants themselves cannot be called favorable, although they are not as hateful as some politicians claim.

The Carnegie project polled nearly 1,100 Russian residents of the Far East on their attitudes toward Chinese migrants. The picture that emerges is one of considerable ambivalence. A total of 59 percent felt that the presence of Chinese in their towns represented a net loss, 26 percent thought it was a benefit, and 15 percent saw both benefits and losses. Surprisingly, the main arguments against the Chinese workers did not involve threats of economic competition. Of those with negative views, one-quarter cited public health concerns (they believed Chinese were dirty and could spread diseases), which may reflect their reaction to the very poor living conditions of most migrants; one-fifth feared an uncontrollable influx of Chinese; and one sixth resented the low quality of Chinese goods. About 20 percent avoided buying Chinese goods. Only one-tenth of those with negative views (6 percent of the total sample) expressed a fear of competition from Chinese workers. Every seventh person in this group (9 percent of the total) used a typical Soviet argument that "they are getting richer at our expense." Almost none (four in the total sample) expressed concern about criminal or antisocial behavior on the part of Chinese migrants, although some felt that their presence stimulated Russian crime, rackets, and corruption in which Chinese are the victims.

The prevailing attitude toward immigrants is a result of current policy as well as of the state of Russian markets for housing, labor, and consumer goods. The conditions in which these workers are forced to exist do not comply with even elementary sanitary norms. And the lack of competition from local producers paves the way for the introduction of low-quality goods.

The younger generation shares public opinion only on the question of the spread of epidemics. Some 16 percent of the 1,182 students polled thought that Chinese migrants bring filth and epidemics to the region. The young, however, are far less threatened by their numbers and uncontrollability. Only 4 percent of students saw migrants as a threat to the region, which is one-third the proportion of the general population who felt that way. The students were also only half as likely to be afraid of the Chinese as competitors. During the poll of the general population, only two people believed that the Chinese presence increased possibilities for intercultural communication. Among the students, this number increased to twenty-four. Despite such small numbers, this fact can be regarded as hopeful.

Significantly, even people who were against any Chinese presence in the region rarely cited criminal activities as a reason. As a rule, none of those questioned in the Carnegie surveys had experienced Chinese criminal behavior. Only two respondents cited Chinese trade in illegal goods and two the "obnoxious behavior" of Chinese immigrants.

Forty-six students (4 percent of the sample) noted that Chinese immigration causes an increase in the crime rate—but not among the immigrants. This view is supported by expert opinion that the Chinese presence noticeably stimulates *Russian* crime, racketeering, and corruption. According to the Ministry of Internal Affairs, a new crime that has developed recently is stealing passports from Chinese citizens who are still in legal status and selling them to those who stay in the country illegally after expiration of their visas and hence cannot return to China. In 1996, the number of arrests for passport fraud was 1.5 times higher than in 1995.[39]

In general, most complaints about the Chinese are caused by appearances, worries about the future, or some stereotype created by the mass media. These complaints spotlight the influence of public opinion leaders—first of all, politicians and members of the press. Although many are unhappy with the low quality of Chinese merchandise, 25 percent of the polled population (80 percent of those who believe that their town has benefited from the Chinese presence and 60 percent of those who see both positive and negative influences) were convinced that Chinese get the credit for supplying the region with cheap and varied goods. Of those polled, 4 percent believed that Chinese competition is a positive factor in economic development.

Even the group that was most tolerant and friendly toward the Chinese and noted their industriousness, honesty, and sobriety would nonetheless like to see restrictions on their trade and their employment as cheap labor. A total of 79 percent believed that Chinese should be allowed to trade in Russia and 19 percent were against it. Although respondents were evenly split over the issue of allowing Chinese to work in Russia, only 31 percent supported the idea of allowing them to open their own enterprises; 65 percent opposed such a measure. Moreover, the Russian people in the sample were almost unanimous in their opinion that Chinese migrants should not be allowed to buy or build housing in Russia (83 percent against and 12 percent pro) or lease land for long terms (82 percent against and only 13 percent pro). The results of other polls, however, are somewhat more optimistic. According to them, the idea of creating temporary housing units for the Chinese aliens in the countryside was vigorously opposed by only 30 percent of the respondents.[40]

The Carnegie survey data depict a public ready for cooperation and with a good grasp of the need for it. But this attitude is combined with a desire to conduct such cooperation in a strict framework of temporary migration, under no circumstances allowing the Chinese to stay for long periods of time, much less to become permanent residents. A typical point of view of a local leader was voiced by A.B. Levinthal, deputy head of administration of the Khabarovskii Krai, in an interview with the journal *Vash Vybor*: "Without a doubt, some industries should use Chinese labor. Mostly it applies to agriculture and construction. Chinese produce some quality work and they labor very intensely and without any days off. However, I think that their numerous attempts to settle in Russia permanently should be restrained."[41]

The majority of the local population is against mixed marriages between their close relatives and Chinese (81 percent of the Carnegie sample were absolutely against, 12 percent thought such marriages to be normal, and 7 percent were indifferent). The younger generation again demonstrates a new outlook on the world. Only 49 percent of them were against such marriages, 33 percent believed them to be normal, and 18 percent were indifferent.

Clearly, the population does not approve of any steps that may lead toward Chinese settlement on Russian territory. They live in the shadow of the "Chinese threat," which 74 percent considered real, while only 20 percent believed that it is without substance.

Public opinion on this issue is stimulated by intermittent resurrection of the problem of the "yellow peril," which originated at the end of the nineteenth century. In 1908, Pyotr Stolypin, then head of the Russian government, noted during his speech to the Duma that the Far East would not remain sparsely populated next to an over-populated neighbor. Foreigners would slip through the borders, and if Russians did not settle there first, this Russian periphery would stay Russian only in name.[42] Since Chinese communities remained largely closed to outsiders, rumors spread about a system of underground societies. The view that Chinese were "spies" and even the "rear army" of the neighboring country were quite widespread.[43] Ninety years later, the same arguments are repeated by those who would resurrect the specter of the "yellow peril."

CONCLUSION

Chinese immigration to the Russian Far East is both a reality and a necessity—but it is not necessarily a threat. This realization calls for a radical change of perspective focused on immigration as a key element in resolving the serious labor deficit that will otherwise block Russia's economic development. The relevant strategic issue becomes not how to avoid immigration and cohabitation but how to organize it.

Dmitri Trenin of the Carnegie Moscow Center points out that "the Russian Far East is very vulnerable."[44] This vulnerability will persist and increase the longer Russian policy consists of separation without normalization at the border. Relations with China should be built from the perspective of the complementary interests of both countries in the next century rather than from the current hostile and defensive stance. It is much better to take a sober look at the situation and at Russia's potential. In order to avoid even the perception of a threat to Russia's territorial integrity, it might be wise to allow Chinese labor to migrate farther west in the country. This migration would more evenly distribute Chinese on Russian territory, instead of concentrating them in the Far East and especially in sparsely populated Eastern Siberia.

In the border regions, there is confusion over the supposed Chinese threat and heavy reliance on the old methods of coping with it—deportation and strict border control. Lacking the analytical tools to predict future developments, federal authorities also lack the ability to devise and implement what is most needed: a forward-looking migration policy that takes account of the needs of the region today and tomorrow.

NOTES

[1] This number represents the number of crossings rather than the number of individuals who crossed the border, as some people may have made multiple journeys into Russia and been counted each time.

[2] With the participation of local researchers, the Carnegie research project polled 244 Chinese migrants; 1,086 local residents; 1,182 students; and 466 migrants from the CIS countries. In addition, more than 100 interviews were conducted with representatives of local administrations, migration and employment agencies, migration control offices, managers of joint construction companies, professors, and journalists. References to expert opinion in the text are drawn from these interviews. The survey was carried out in three regions of the Far East: Khabarovskii Krai, Primorskii Krai, and Amur Oblast as well as in three regions of Eastern Siberia: Chita Oblast,

Irkutsk Oblast, and the Buryat Republic. The research was supported by grants from the Ford Foundation and the MacArthur Foundation.

[3]Paul J. Smith, "China's 'Immigration Card' is a Potent Psychological Weapon," *International Herald Tribune*, May 20, 1997.

[4]Mikhail Doronin, "Russia: Political Designs behind Korean, Chinese Immigration," *ITAR-TASS*, April 25, 1997.

[5]Vladimir Shlapentokh, "Russia, China and the Far East: Old Geopolitics or a New Peaceful Cooperation?" *Communist and Post-Communist Studies*, vol. 28, no. 3 (September 1995), pp. 307–18.

[6]Alexander Yakovlev, "Mezhdunarodnaya Politicheskaya Obstanovka v SVA i Polozheniye Rossii v Regione" (The International Political Situation in Northeast Asia and the Position of Russia in the Region), *Problemy Dalnevo Vostoka* (Far East Affairs), no. 2 (1995), pp. 3–16.

[7]Vladimir Olegovich Rakhmanin, "Russia, China: MFA Official Views RF-Chinese Cooperation," *Moscow Prolemy Dalnego Vostoka*, no. 1 (January–February 1997), pp. 10–14, FBIS translation *FBIS-SOV-97-91*.

[8]Emil Pain, "Problem: 'Illegals' on the Amur Shores: On Chinese Immigration to the Russian Far East," *Moscow Rossiyskiye Vesti*, May 6, 1997, p. 3, FBIS translation *FBIS-SOV-97-093*.

[9]Ibid.

[10]Ibid.

[11]*RFE/RL NEWSLINE*, vol. 2, no. 34, part I (February 19, 1998).

[12]Vilya Gelbras, "Predvaritelnye itogi uzucheniya problem kitaysk migratsii v Moskve, Khabarovske, Vladivostok, and Ussuriysk" (presentation at a Round Table in Vladivostok, June 28, 1999).

[13]See, also, Galina Vitkovskaya and Zhanna Zayonchkovskaya, "Novaya stolypinskaya politika na Delnem Vostoke Rossii: nadezhdy i realii," in Galina Vitkovskaya and Dmitri Trenin, eds., *Perspektivy Dalnevostochnogo Regiona Mezhstranovye vzaimodeistvia*, Carnegie Moscow Center (Moscow: Gandalf, 1999), pp. 80–120.

[14]A. Larin, "Retrospectiva: Kitaytsy v Russii" (Retrospective: Chinese in Russia), *Migratsiya* (Migration), no. 1 (1997), p. 21.

[15]I. Okul, "Politica Zaseleniya Dalnevo Vostoka i Migratsionnoye Dvizheniye evo Naseleniya (Istoriya Voprosa)" (Politics of the Populating of the Far East and Migration of its Population), *Demographicheskoye Razvitiye Dalnevo Vostoka i Formirivaniye Evo Trudovovo Potentsiala* (Demographic Development of the Far East and Formation of its Labor Force), Vladivostok (1991), pp. 113–19.

[16]Larin, "Retrospectiva: Kitaytsy v Russii," p. 22.

[17]In the nineteenth century, P. A. Stolypin, minister and later the head of government, moved large groups of people from the European part of Russia to the Far East.

[18]Larin, "Retrospectiva: Kitaytsy v Russii," p. 22.

[19]Ibid., p. 22.

[20]Ibid., p. 22.

[21]Ibid., p. 23.

[22]*Vladivostok*, February 19, 1994.

[23]*Izvestiya*, November 2, 1993, and November 30, 1994.

[24]"Kitaytsy na Rossiyskom Dalnem Vostoke" (Chinese in the Russian Far East), *Geographiya v Shkole* (Geography in School), no. 1 (1995), p. 31.

[25]See note 2.

[26]Pavel A. Minakir, "Chinese Immigration in the Russian Far East: Regional, National, and International Dimensions," in Jeremy R. Azrael and Emil A. Pain, eds., *Cooperation and Conflict in the Former Soviet Union: Implications for Migration* (Santa Monica, Calif.: RAND, 1996), p. 94.

[27]L. L. Rybakovsky, O. D. Zakharova, and V. V. Mindogulov, *Nelegalnaya Migratsiya v Prigranichnikh Rayonakh Dalnevo Vostoka: Istoriya, Sovremennost i Posledstviya* (Illegal Migration in the Far East Border Regions: Its History, Present Day, and Consequences) (Moscow: Institut Sotsialno-Politicheskikh Issledovaniy [Institute for Socio-Political Research of the Russian Academy of Sciences], 1994) p. 19.

[28]The authors interviewed twenty-six members of local administrations, migration and employment services, managers of joint construction ventures, university professors, and journalists.

[29]Tyan Czan, "Kitaytsy v Immigratsii" (Chinese Immigrants), *Rossiya i ATR* (Russia and the APR), no. 2 (1994), pp. 82–92.

[30]*Delpvaya Sibi* (Business Siberia), May 28–June 3, 1993.

[31]*Rossiiskaya gazeta*, September 16, 1995.

[32]*Informationny Bulletin Rossiyskoy Federalnoy Migratsionnoy Sluzhby* (Information Bulletin of the Russian Federal Migration Service), no. 1 (1996), p. 50.

[33]*Informationny Bulletin Rossiyskoy Federalnoy Migratsionnoy Sluzhby* (Information Bulletin of the Russian Federal Migration Service), no. 1 (1997), p. 53.

[34]Ibid., p. 52.

[35]Czan, "Kytaytsy v Immigratsii."

[36]"Kto i Zachem Budet Zhit na Dalnem Vostoke Rossii?" (Who Will Live in the Russian Far East and Why?) *Vash Vybor*, no. 1 (1995), p. 19.

[37]Ibid.

[38]Larin, "Retrospectiva: Kitaytsy v Russii."

[39]*Zabaikalsky Rabochiyr* (Trans-Baikal Worker), January 31, 1997.

[40]V. Mindogulov, "Chto Dumayut Zhiteli Dalnevo Vostoka o Rossiysko-Kytayskikh Pogranichnikh Otnosheniyakh?" (What Do Citizens of the Far East Think about the Russian-Chinese Border Relations?), *Sociologicheskiye Issledovaniya* (Sociological Research), no. 10 (1995), p. 117.

[41]"Kto i Zachem Budet Zhit na Dalnem Vostoke Rossii?" p. 19.

[42]P. A. Stolypin, "Nam Nuzhna Velikaya Rossiya" (We Need Great Russia), *Collection of Speeches* (Moscow: Molodaya Gvardiya, 1993).

[43]Larin, "Retrospectiva: Kitaytsy v Russii," p. 22.

[44]Dmitri Trenin, "Russia-Kitay: Voenny Aspect Otnosheniy" (Russia-China: The Military Aspect of Relations) (speech at the Carnegie Moscow Center, March 19, 1997).

PART FOUR

Central and East Asia

13
Russian-Chinese Relations and Central Asia

Martha Brill Olcott

A quick look at a map of the Central Asian states gives a vivid introduction to the geopolitics of the region. Central Asia is at the center of Eurasia—a bridge between Europe and Asia as President Nazarbayev of Kazakhstan likes to call it—which makes it an object of influence for all the more powerful states in the region. A vast area, with a small population and enormous natural resources, the states of Central Asia offer the prospect of rich reward to those who are able to dominate here. Moreover, the perceived weakness of the newly independent states makes the area seem ripe for domination both by the more powerful states bordering the region and by interested parties that are farther away.

These circumstances are nothing new. This area has been a magnet to many great powers in the past, who saw control of these lands either as an end in itself or as the key to control of the lands to Central Asia's east or west. Alexander the Great conquered part of this territory on his move north and eastward, as did the Arab commanders of the seventh century. Genghis Khan's troops were more successful yet and gained control of the entire region as part of a drive west and south, and their descendants managed to hold large parts of it for several hundred years.

The last great-power effort to gain control of these lands was made in the mid-nineteenth century, when England and Russia faced off in their efforts to establish secure boundaries for their imperial possessions. Russia and the USSR struggled to hold on to this region for 150 years, ultimately deciding that the prospect of retaining control of the region was not worth the price of the effort. The current competition for influence in Central Asia features both new and familiar actors: Russia, China, Iran, and Turkey. For today at least, Russia remains the most formidable foreign influence over the newly independent states of Central Asia. It is likely to remain so for the next several years, and maybe even for another generation. Privately, most of the region's leaders admit that they see an inevitable Russian retreat from the region. How complete the retreat will be is a question of great speculation, and the question of who might seek to fill Russia's gap is a quandary of even greater significance. This uncertainty creates a sort of guessing game for the region's leaders, all of whom seek to achieve balanced foreign policies in which good relations are maintained with various regional and more distant states, while all fear the prospect of being subjected to the will of a hegemon.

Given the potential wealth of the region, parties living outside Central Asia have discussed the "new great game" almost as much as parties within it have expressed fear of domination. The fascination of the Western press with the "new great game" has emphasized Turkey's and Iran's ambitions in the region. Few in the region, however, would credit either state with a serious chance of being an effective hegemon in Central Asia.

Revolutionary Iran is not an attractive model, and its international isolation has limited its potential to intervene economically. Turkey is a more alluring alternative, but although cultural affinity helps facilitate technology transfer, it is no substitute for large-scale economic investment. Turkish business has the know-how and capital sufficient for small and medium-sized projects, but Turkey is not robust enough economically to do much more than assist at the margins in the major reconstruction projects that these five states need to make a successful transition from Soviet satrapies to functioning economies.

These limitations do not mean that Central Asia will be free of outside intervention. Most discussions of the "great game" have largely ignored the likely role of another near neighbor, one whose prospective role in the region is potentially much greater: the People's Republic of China. China has strong interests in Central Asia, much greater potential for effecting development in the area, and a historic involvement in the region at least as significant as that of

either Turkey or Iran. China borders on three of the newly independent states in the region, and the border area on the Chinese side
includes millions of people who are the ethnic kin of the Central
Asians. For this reason, Central Asian independence has created a
potential security dilemma for the Chinese that is quite unlike the
new security opportunities created for either Turkey or Iran.

The mere existence of the Central Asian states does not create an
internal security dilemma for either Turkey or Iran. Turkey shares
no border with Central Asia, and the Turkmen diaspora population
in Iran is one that Teheran has little trouble accommodating. The
same is not true for China, where the Muslim peoples who live
along the Central Asian border have nationalist aspirations that have
been forcibly suppressed by the Chinese communists on several
occasions over the past fifty years. The Chinese government certainly
has a strong incentive to maintain friendly ties with the new Central
Asian states and make it worth their while to orient themselves
toward Beijing rather than toward the behavior of ethnic kin just
beyond their border.

Central Asian independence has its potential benefits for the Chinese as well, mostly in the form of major new economic opportunities. The Central Asian states are a new market for cheap Chinese
goods; a potential partner for complex technological transfer projects, especially in the area of light industry, where the Chinese have
much to offer; and a source of surplus energy and other raw materials
for the burgeoning Chinese economy.

The Central Asians also view the Chinese as a potential political
model, but few leaders are tempted to say so publicly. If they want
to maximize continued assistance from the United States and other
Western democracies, they must maintain at least a lip-service
endorsement of their desire to democratize their societies. Yet privately, many in Central Asia have admitted strong personal admira-
tion for a Chinese leadership that has shown skill in achieving rapid
and targeted economic development while maintaining firm control
over the reins of power.

Although all Central Asia's leaders have accepted the need to
transform their societies into market economies—albeit they advocate doing so at sharply different rates—even the most politically
tolerant of them are uncomfortable with the kind of political unpredictability that is associated with democratic societies. Even if only

secretly, most are envious of the Chinese for having avoided this problem. Given the uproar following Uzbek President Islam Karimov's September 1991 statement that he admired the Chinese model and hoped to implement it in his country, few would offer a similar public declaration. The fallout from this statement was such that even the hard-skinned Karimov backed away from advocacy of the Chinese model. A few days after making the original statement, Karimov somewhat disingenuously modified his remarks to say that Taiwan, and not Beijing, was the focus. He has, however, brazenly continued to defend the idea of Central Asia's "Asianness" as culturally more supportive of authoritarian, rather than democratic, political culture.

At the same time, however, the Central Asian states betray a certain nervousness about China, in part because of its size and potential strength and also because strong rulers from China have historically shown territorial ambitions toward Central Asia. A quick look at the map makes it obvious how easy it would be for China to lop off and then absorb any "offending" parts of these neighboring states, if the Central Asian societies lacked strong patrons. While the international community might express horror at such behavior and even seriously contemplate economic sanctions, it is unlikely to threaten military measures to combat a future act of Chinese aggression. The stronger defense would more likely come from closer to home: Russia has treaty obligations to respond militarily to an act of aggression launched against these CIS (Commonwealth of Independent States) member states. As long as Russia shares responsibility for guarding the former Soviet borders with the Central Asian states and has the capacity to do so, the prospects for direct Chinese intervention in Central Asia are remote.

The continued Russian military presence on the old Sino-Soviet border is a thorny issue for the Kyrgyz and Kazakh, who bristle at such a public display of their continued dependency. The leaders of these countries, however, simultaneously recognize that Russian withdrawal would of necessity lead to new accommodations with the Chinese, for even the appearance of a newly demilitarized border zone does not address the basic military inequality of go-it-alone Central Asian regimes facing China.

For now, given the choice between Russia and China, most in Central Asia would choose "the devil" they know over the one they do not know. But Central Asians also realize that Chinese interest in the region can work to the advantage of the Central Asian states as they seek ways to change their relations with Moscow from those of subjects to those of sovereign states.

The emergence of new strategic partners is likely to transform and even jeopardize relations with former close friends. The Central Asian states are conscious of Russia's potential response as they work out bilateral relations with China. The same is even truer of China's approach to the Central Asian states. The collapse of the USSR has created the opportunity for Beijing to reexamine relations with Moscow, and China's rulers must consider the impact of their evolving ties with the Central Asian states on Sino-Russian relations. Given the opportunities for technology transfer and arms procurements that improved ties with the Russians offer the Chinese, Beijing's rulers are unlikely to risk the current rapprochement with Moscow for uncertain advantage in Central Asia, especially since the possibility of long-term Chinese advantage in the Central Asian states is not compromised by allowing Russia near-term advantage in the region.

This paper explores the interplay of Russia and China in Central Asia from a variety of perspectives and looks at whether the pursuit of their respective interests in the region is likely to be a source of conflict or a basis of cooperation between the two. The paper pays more attention to Chinese relations with the Central Asian states than it does to Russia's efforts in Central Asia. By contrast, the question of what role China will play in Central Asia and whether it can supplant Russian influence in the region has been a far more neglected one. Finally, the paper tries to speculate on how these relationships are likely to be transformed with time and what key factors will either encourage or hamper the development of increasingly close ties between China and the various Central Asian states.

BORDERS AND POPULATION FLOWS

The demise of the USSR changed the shape of Moscow's relations with Beijing in a variety of ways. Not the least of these was the formal redefinition of the border, substituting five border states for the original two. Russia inherited most of the old Sino-Soviet border, but Kazakhstan, Kyrgyzstan, and Tajikistan all have borders with

China, as well. With these borders, the states also inherited the controversies surrounding them.

The communist government in Beijing raised the question of the legitimacy of China's borders in 1963 and called for border negotiations with all its neighboring states. By 1964, China had reached new agreements with all its neighbors except the Soviet Union and India. Negotiations with the Soviet Union resumed with the thawing of relations between the two states in the mid-1980s, but the formal boundaries between the two states were still not fully delimited when the Central Asian states inherited them in 1991. The Kazakh and Chinese governments have signed several agreements designed to regularize border arrangements both in April 1994 and in April 1996, when the five states signed an agreement on delimiting their common borders. In July 1998, Kazakhstan and China also signed an agreement dividing 944 square kilometers of disputed border territories.[1]

The provisions of the April 1996 agreement included plans for a 200-kilometer demilitarized zone with strict limitations placed on the stationing of troops and the numbers of men and equipment that can be brought in for military exercises. In the agreement on the implementation of this demilitarized zone, which was signed in April 1997, the five states agreed to reduce military forces in a 100-kilometer zone and set the number of tanks on the border at 3,900. Of all the CIS tanks, 3,810 would be along the border of the Russian Federation.[2] In the aftermath of the treaty, some small-scale military exchanges and promises of cooperation in limited numbers of officers have also occurred.

The 1996 border agreement is an important confidence-building measure for the Central Asian states, especially for Kyrgyzstan, whose border has historically been the most tendentious. Although China and Kyrgyzstan signed a border agreement in July 1996, work on border delimitation did not begin until April 1998, when President Akaev and President Zemin signed a joint statement in Beijing. The agreement is important because it means that China has now formally abandoned its earlier border claims against the Russian Empire, claims that were revived in the Soviet period when relations between the two communist giants became strained.

The current borders accept the old Sino-Soviet borders with some minor adjustments. The borders reflect the territorial divisions that were agreed to between the Russian imperial government and the Manchu rulers in China in the late nineteenth century, largely conforming to the provisions of the Treaty of St. Petersburg in 1881 and the subsequent elaboration of them in 1891 and 1895 at the time of the Russian and British demarcation of Afghanistan. Partly, the border issue is one of maintaining goodwill, because most of the border is drawn across the Pamir Mountains, where there are only a few easily passable points. In other words, close friends would not fight over this land, but unfriendly states would be willing to squabble to gain even the smallest advantage.

Significantly, there is no "natural" border between the Central Asian states and China, be it geographic or cultural, nor was there one between the Russian and Chinese possessions. The principal concern for the Soviets and the Chinese (as it had been for the Russians and Manchus before them) was one of security, of not having their possessions put at risk by events on the other side of the border.

The Manchus and Russians came into Central and Inner Asia at roughly the same time, in the middle of the eighteenth century. The Russians started their conquest with the Kazakh lands, which were acquired in part through treaties in 1731 and 1740; they then moved southward and introduced a full colonial administration over most of Russian Turkestan and the Kazakh Steppe in 1867 and 1868.[3]

The Manchus moved westward at roughly the same time, defeating the Oirat Mongols in 1755 (in Jungaria) and putting down the last great Uighur rebellion in Eastern Turkestan in 1878. But the Russians had a stronger military presence in the area than the Manchus did. In 1871, the Russians moved eastward beyond the territory that they now formally termed the Steppe Region of their empire to occupy the lands up to Kuldja (Yining) on the Ili River. They argued that the security of their own newly acquired possessions in Turkestan was at risk from the disorder in Eastern Turkestan, where Manchu officials had found it difficult to maintain order over local Muslim Uighurs and Kazakhs.

The Russian fears were not necessarily exaggerated ones. The main figure in the Kashgar revolt in these years, Yakub Beg, a native of Kokand, had fought against the Russians during their campaign to take Turkestan and then had fled east into China. If left unchecked, there would be nothing to stop a successful Yakub Beg from trying to expand "Kashgaria" westward onto Russian-held lands.[4] To prevent this expansion, the Russians pursued a complex strategy of initially supporting Yakub Beg and then helping achieve his defeat. For the Russians, however, Yakub Beg was simply a symptom of the larger problem: the rulers of Xinjiang (which was formally incorporated as a province of China in 1884) could not be relied on to effectively police their territory.

Thus, the 1881 treaty with China continued to recognize some rights of extraterritoriality for the Russians, as well as to oblige the Chinese rulers to pay reparations to the Russian government for the expenses it incurred in restoring order to the Chinese territory. The Treaty of St. Petersburg modified the territorial provisions of the 1879 Treaty of Livadia, which transformed the lands from Lake Zaisan (in Eastern Kazakhstan) to Kuldja into a virtual Russian protectorate. The 1881 treaty restored most of the land to China but did shift the traditional border eastward in Russia's favor, and parts of modern-day Kazakhstan and Kyrgyzstan were awarded to Russia. The Russian settlers, however, including the Cossacks, who had moved into the lands between the new border and Kuldja, remained on the Manchu territory to help protect Russian interests.

Thus, while the St. Petersburg Treaty led to a formal Russian withdrawal from China, it did not lead to an informal one. Russian security needs remained both acute and unresolved. Russia's leaders still felt empowered to act in China but did so through the use of indirect tools, such as the implicit threat of a large border presence (which was initially on both sides of the border) or the power acquired by the ownership of key economic assets.

THE SOVIETS CONTINUE THE IMPERIAL PATTERN

Russia's behavior was shaped by its perceived sense of strategic advantage, which continued throughout most of the Soviet era. For more than forty years, the Soviet leaders felt themselves able to exercise that advantage at will. Until the Communist Party came to power in China, the rulers in Moscow crossed the border into Xinjiang on numerous occasions, either because of political disturbances in Russian or Soviet Central Asia or because they believed that unstable conditions in Xinjiang were either threatening or could be manipulated to their own purposes.

In the years between the Bolshevik Revolution and World War II, the fate of the two Turkestans was particularly closely intertwined. Defeated Semireche Cossacks retreated across the Ili River into China in 1918. Although most of these troops were soon disarmed by Red forces chasing after them, the last White forces in Xinjiang were not "turned" until late 1933, just before Moscow sent two divisions of OGPU (Soviet Secret Police) troops across the border to help Sheng Shih Ts'ai, provincial warlord and eventual ruler of Xinjiang, break up the Turkish Islamic Republic of Eastern Turkestan.[5]

In fact, most historians treat Xinjiang from 1927 to 1942 as a virtual protectorate of Soviet Russia. The republican government of China never succeeded in acquiring effective control of this distant frontier province and was able to provide only minimal support for Xinjiang's various embattled rulers. Transportation and other forms of communication links were weakly established, and after the opening of the Turkestan-Siberian railroad link in 1927 it was economically more rational for those living in Xinjiang to reach the outside world through the Soviet Union than to move their goods eastward through China. For their part, the Soviets were not simply content to dictate the terms of trade; they also managed to dictate terms for the development of Xinjiang's raw materials, so that tin mines and oil fields were effectively turned into Soviet-dominated joint ventures. Although these Soviet efforts made merely a dent in Xinjiang's resource base, they provided Russia with critical raw materials and helped justify the presence of large security-dominated Soviet trading companies in the area.

The Soviets were also encouraged to intervene for another reason. The rule of the local warlords (loyal to the Chinese republican rulers) was being challenged from within, and they did not want instability in Xinjiang to further destabilize their own Central Asian republics, where they had found first the consolidation of their rule (1918–1924) and then the introduction of revolutionary social and economic reforms (1928–1932) quite difficult enough.

The religious revival and struggle with modernism that the Muslims of the late nineteenth century engaged in affected those living in Eastern as well as Western Turkestan. They struggled with these issues in different ways, in part in response to their own unique histories as well as because of the differing institutional and ideological makeup of their respective colonial regimes. By the early 1930s,

Islamic insurgents controlled Kuldja as well as much of the territory between Kuldja and Kashgar, lands near the Soviet border. The rebels' success was in part proof of the fluidity of the borders and the ease by which ideas as well as people moved from country to country and empire to empire.

The flow of political refugees also helped make these experiences common ones. Small numbers of Kyrgyz and Kazakhs crossed into China in the late nineteenth century at the time of the Russian conquest, and hundreds of thousands of them fled at the time of the 1916 uprising.[6] Some of them made their way to the ancestral Kazakh pasturelands along the Ili River, which the Oirats had forced them from in the seventeenth century. The next and smaller group came during the civil war, and another during the collectivization drives of the early 1930s, when tens of thousands of Kazakhs moved again into Jungaria, only to clash with the Chinese authorities who were trying to extend the rule of Urumchi to this territory.

Anti-Soviet resistance fighters were numbered among the refugees, including the "Basmachi" leader Kyrgyz Janibeg, who helped organize the disgruntled Kyrgyz of Xinjiang. Janibeg, along with the Uighurs, helped set up the short-lived Turkish-Islamic Republic of Eastern Turkestan. The Soviets opposed this first effort, intervening on the side of the local warlord. A decade later, however, they tried to use the history of this ill-fated effort to their own advantage.

After joining the Allied effort, the Soviets cooperated with the Nanking government in Xinjiang until the developing civil war helped convince them that they could once again advance their direct strategic advantage. The Soviet focus was the Ili Kazakh territory, which had never been fully pacified by the Chinese authorities and in which there had been fairly steady and escalating fighting since 1940. The Ili Kazakh territory (the districts of Ili, Chuguchak [Tarbagatai], and Altai) lay between Soviet Kazakhstan and the Mongolian People's Republic, giving the Soviets two possible points of intervention and pressure.

The Ili Kazakh territory—also known as the Jungar Plain or Jungaria—included traditional lands of the Great Horde (Ili and Chuguchak) as well as the Middle Horde (Altai). The Kazakhs had begun moving back into these territories in the late eighteenth and nineteenth centuries when the Manchus defeated the Kalmyk (Oirats). The Middle Horde Kazakhs of Jungaria were in increasingly more attenuated contact with the rest of the Horde from the mid-nine-teenth century on (although they initially maintained some ties to the Kazakhs of Mongolia while the new transit links across the two empires kept those of the Great Horde in closer contact with one another). On the Soviet side, the Great Horde Kazakhs were also the dominant group in the postpurge Communist Party, and so it was their representatives who played the key role in liaising with the Eastern Turkestan Republic, which the Soviets helped sponsor in the mid-1940s.

Much of the planning for this effort was done by the Xinjiang People's National Liberation Committee, which was organized in Mongolia in 1943 and was then responsible for the November 7, 1944, "coup" in Kuldja (Yining).[7] The Eastern Turkestan Republic (ETR) brought to power a coalition of pro-Soviet Kazakhs, Uighurs, and Uzbeks, who were all nominally local citizens but whose leader-ship was far closer to the Soviet authorities across the border than to the local political elite. The rule of this government lasted only until August 1945, when, under risk of a formal Soviet-Chinese rift, the ETR negotiated a power-sharing agreement with the Nanking government. The dual authority that was provided, however, was never fully implemented. Instead, Xinjiang was a place with divided authority between the Kuomintang (KMT, commonly known as Nationalist) government and the pro-Soviet ETR, which continued to dominate much of the Ili Kazakh territory. In the territory under their influence, the Soviets were once again quite free to extract resources, including the now highly valuable uranium.[8] This state of affairs remained intact until the People's Liberation Army of the Chinese Communist Party reached the area in 1949.

THE ADVANTAGE BEGINS TO SHIFT

After the Communist Party came to power in China, the Soviet influence in Xinjiang started to erode rapidly, and the flow of refu-gees reversed from what it had been over the past half century. The Soviets withdrew their support from the Eastern Turkestan Republic, which formally collapsed in 1949 when a plane crash claimed the lives of many of its principal leaders who were en route to the first All-Chinese People's Meeting in Beijing. Stalin then accepted the success of Mao's effort to absorb Eastern Turkestan into the Xinjiang

Autonomous Region. Tens of thousands of Ili Kazakhs fled from China to Mongolia after the communist takeover, while others remained and offered small-scale armed resistance to the Chinese communist authorities until 1954, when they were forced to flee. By then the only escape route available was across the Himalayas, and the fleeing Kazakhs began a two-year trek that took them from China over the mountains to Srinigar and then (after an airlift) on to Turkey.[9] Some of their descendants were resettled in Kazakhstan in the early 1990s, as the Great Leap Forward and Cultural Revolution—when nationalists and non-Han in general were viewed with suspicion—and the collectivization campaign, combined with resettlement projects, had left Uighurs and Kazakhs alike feeling pushed out.

Tight border controls on the Chinese side meant that probably fewer than 100,000 Uighurs and Kazakhs were able to flee to the Soviet Central Asian republics.[10] Uighur nationalist groups offer a much higher figure and argue that most of the nearly 300,000 Uighurs who are citizens of the various Central Asian states crossed the border to their new homes after riots in Xinjiang in 1962.[11] The policy changes in the early 1960s had driven many prominent Uighurs (and Kazakhs) from the Chinese Communist Party. Given the deteriorating state of Sino-Soviet relations, those former communists who managed to make it across the borders to the Soviet Union were given a warm welcome by the local authorities. One of the forms this welcome took was Soviet support of a revived Free Turkestan Movement, which was reputed to include an underground Turkestan Liberation Army that was headed by Zunam Taipov, the Uighur leader of the 1944 revolt and later an army general in the PRC.

The Chinese then shut the local Soviet consulates, all but closed the border with the Soviet republics, and added a much increased military presence to the border region. The border was formally closed in 1972 and remained so until November 1983, and even then the USSR and China made little effort to develop plans for large-scale movement of people or freight for five more years.

The opening of the borders and the steady increase in the movement of people and freight observed since 1988 have not led to a normal unfettered contact of peoples across borders nor changed the fact that the fates of the ethnic communities of the two Turkestans remain quite dissimilar ones.

This continued divided quality of many Central Asian nationalities makes the border questions contentious and creates the current asymmetry of relations between Central Asians and Chinese. The Central Asian states have received their independence, but the Central Asian peoples of China have not. The systematic immigration of Han Chinese into Xinjiang has meant that the Uighurs no longer constitute the majority of the population of that province. In the early 1990s, the Uighurs (7.2 million people) accounted for 37.6 percent of Xinjiang's population, Kazakhs (1.2 million) 7.3 percent, Kyrgyz and Mongols less than 1 percent each, and Han Chinese 37.6 percent.[12]

The creation of independent states just across the border certainly helped increase the level of dissatisfaction among Xinjiang's Uighur population, but more than enough was going on in China to stimulate their growing political activism. In the 1980s, China, too, was experiencing a political reform process, which brought with it a liberalized attitude toward Islam. When Uighur and other Muslim activists tried to test the limits of this attitude in public protests, however, including at Tiananmen Square, authorities were quick to crack down. Uighur activists responded to the arrests by going underground and organizing a series of violent antigovernment acts.

This pattern of periodic acts of terror followed by government crackdowns has continued into the present, with demonstrations by the Islamic Party of Eastern Turkestan being organized in 1985, in 1989, and again in April 1990. Substantial force was used to put down the latter demonstrations (in Baren township), resulting in twenty-three deaths. Some claimed that the separatists received their arms from Afghanistan, while others claimed that recent demonstrations in Dushanbe had served as a catalyst.[13] The latter claim, however, seems tenuous. The Chinese authorities did close the border to local travel in retaliation for several months and once again made it considerably more difficult for Uighurs to receive local relatives in Urumchi (which had been allowed to become a meeting point for family reunions since 1985).[14]

There was more unrest in Xinjiang just after the signing of the five-partite treaty in April 1996, and then a more serious wave of violent actions by separatist groups in early 1997, when the Uighurs struck within and then outside of Xinjiang. During the month of February, exiled Uighur groups in Kazakhstan carried out three bus bombings in Urumchi, in which nine people died and seventy-four were injured. Then in March, a Uighur separatist group, called Eastern Turkestan Liberation Organization–Feddayin of Beijing, claimed responsibility for two bombings in Beijing.[15] The violence in Xinjiang was the most serious in several years, with twenty-five Uighurs reported shot by police, fifty-five Chinese civilians killed by the demonstrators, and thirty activists publicly executed.[16]

It is difficult to know how much active support the Uighur separatists get from their conationals in Central Asia, because the Kazakh and Kyrgyz border with China is now closely regulated. The Chinese-Afghan border seems to be more porous. Those knowledgeable about the Afghan scene privately maintain that some Uighur activists received training in camps run by Gulbudine Hekmatyar, the former Afghan prime minister who is now a leader of the opposition to the dominant Taliban movement. Since those loyal to Taliban have taken over, the amount of assistance, if any, that Uighur separatists have been given is uncertain. After the successful Taliban campaign of winter-spring 1997, however, the Chinese authorities instituted a "special regime" on the border with Afghanistan. The effectiveness of such a measure is unknown, because shortly after the new border regime was announced rumors circulated that Taliban supporter Osama Bin-Ladin was planning to shift his center of operations to Xinjiang. These rumors began circulating after a series of Islamist groups gathered at a London meeting sponsored by the Syrian-based Harakat al-Mujaharin (the Emigrants Movement) to talk about supporting a jihad in China.[17]

In the long run, the situation in Afghanistan may present an even greater threat to stability in Xinjiang than developments in the newly independent states of Central Asia. The former has served as an important meeting point where Islamic activists from both Eastern and Western Central Asia can expand their contacts with international Islamic radical and terrorist groups. This being said, notably, absolutely no evidence suggests that the central and local authorities in China feel themselves unable to isolate and contain the threat that Uighur and other Muslim separatist communities pose in Xinjiang. Forty years of settling Han Chinese in this region have created new demographic realities in the region, and the regime has grown ever more competent during this period as well.

The Chinese authorities are very capable of making targeted and effective use of force. They are also wise enough to make advantageous use of "the carrot" along with "the stick" in their efforts to retain control of, and better use, the valuable resources of Xinjiang. The resources include 1.5 billion tons of petroleum, 370 billion cubic meters of natural gas, 4 billion tons of coal, 120 tons of gold, as well as nearly a half-million tons of cotton per year. As a result, in recent years official concern over the need to speed up the economic growth process in Xinjiang has grown. Since the unrest of the spring of 1997, local party leaders have been calling for further speeding up of government investment in resource extraction projects, industry, and agriculture in the region, as well as further investment in improving transport from Xinjiang to the rest of China and through Xinjiang to the outside world.[18]

TRANSPORT AND TRADE FLOW

The issue of improved transport links from Europe to Asia through Central Asia and China is one of great interest to all those in the area. While significant hope of improving transport through the region exists, there is also the realization that the development of transportation links between Central Asians and Chinese is likely to be a slow and costly process. Concerted efforts are being made to better the transport of freight by both road and rail, as well as to expand the available airline connections.

Improvements to both the road and rail links come under the Transport Corridor Europe Caucasus Asia (TRACECA) program. This program is a cooperative effort by the European Union and the states of Central Asia and Mongolia to rebuild historic transport routes between their two regions. It has strong support from the United Nations, the European Bank for Reconstruction and Development (EBRD), the Asian Development Bank, and various donor nations interested in Central Asia. Yet although steady progress is being made, the full "opening" of this region to foreign trade remains decades away.

The major rail link across the region (from Druzhba in Kazakhstan to Urumchi in China) was opened in 1992, although until 1996 freight going from China through Central Asia to Europe had to go through Russia (at least as far as the Caucasian republics). The principal routing remains the same even now, because the rail link across Turkestan (Tedjen) to Iran (Meshed), which opened in May 1996, can handle only about a quarter-million tons of freight per year. The facilities at Druzhba can easily handle a million tons, but through 1994 there was still insufficient demand to test this capacity.[19] Plans call for this capacity to be increased to 3 million tons annually. In September 1998, President Rakhmonov of Tajikistan opened a 54-kilometer stretch of Qurghanteppa-Kulob broad-gauge railway that will link up with the Karakaroum Highway. The Central Asian states negotiated port rights at the rail head in Lianyungang, but the cost of moving freight across China was 30 percent higher than through Russia to its Pacific ports. Unfortunately, no figures on how much "through freight" was shipped across China from Central Asia exist, but anecdotal evidence suggests that given their greater familiarity and lingering contacts with the old Soviet port officials, the Central Asia states still preferred to ship goods across Russia.

Over time, the new rail link through China across Central Asia into Iran and on to Turkey and Europe is sure to become more popular, because it will cut several days off the shipping schedule. Even with all the difficulties of using the old Soviet rail, however, the new routing is unlikely to eclipse the old. Not only is it likely that the quantity of freight will support two separate routings, but the new route will need adjustments, first on the Chinese border and then again on the Iranian border, in order for freight to move along the wider CIS rails. Unfortunately, those responsible for building the new freight facilities at both Druzhba and Serakhs (Turkmenistan-Iran border) have chosen to deal with this problem in the traditional way—by switching wheels—while the Brest crossing is experimenting with a container transfer system.

Highway connections through Central Asia into China are also extremely difficult. They, too, are improving and slated for even further progress, but the harsh climate combined with the difficult terrain of the Kyrgyz and Chinese mountains are certain to continue constraining the ability to move freight during the winter. Key to the transport link is the upgrading of the Karakaroum Highway, which extends from Urumchi to Pakistan. In March 1995, a quadripartite trade agreement on the transport of freight was signed between Kazakhstan, Kyrgyzstan, Pakistan, and China in which the signatories agreed to a uniform customs policy along the highway.

A three-year highway improvement project was launched with a ceremonial four-nation truck convoy in October 1996. Once the upgrade project is completed, the highway is supposed to be fit for year-round travel (as opposed to the May through October regime of the past). In November 1998, the four countries signed another agreement on "traffic in transit." It aims to increase cooperation through the upgrade of roads connecting Almaty, Kazakhstan, with Karachi, Pakistan.[20] But with mountain passes that top out at nearly 10,000 feet, road closings due to snow and glacial erosion are likely to remain commonplace.

A linkup from Bishkek to Karakaroum Highway through Turugart already exists, and the TRACECA program helps pay for upgrades to the road from Osh through Sary-Tash to meet a road that the Chinese are cutting through to the border at Erkecham. In July 1997, the prime ministers of Uzbekistan and Kyrgyzstan as well as senior Chinese officials attended a ceremonial opening of the new customs point, which is a centuries-old trade route that is being widened and resurfaced for truck traffic and will primarily serve Southern Kyrgyzstan, Southern Kazakhstan, and Uzbekistan. Moreover, a highway link connects (as weather permits) Bishkek to Karshi (via Naryn to Turugart) and then on to the Karakaroum Highway, which is the shortest way to get from Almaty to China. This route lacks freight storage facilities, however, and so is used primarily by local traders. In February 1998, China, Uzbekistan, and Kyrgyzstan signed an automobile transportation agreement, pledging to complete upgrades on the highway by October 1998. There are two other crossing points for Kazakhstan, at Pakhtu (from Semipalatinsk) and Khorgos (from Almaty). The Chinese are trying to turn their side of the latter border into a major freight storage and forwarding facility, as well as a free enterprise zone designed especially for joint ventures with Kazakhstan. Although the latter effort has been well publicized for what it will mean for the future of Kazakh-Chinese economic relations, for the present, at least, it still falls far short of being a major international freight terminus.

This effort has serious consequences for the development of international trade through the region, because for the moment the Karakaroum Highway is still the only feasible way to move freight from Central Asia to the ports of the Indian Ocean. The alternative routing goes through from Termez (Uzbekistan) or Kushka (Turkmenistan) through Afghanistan and into Pakistan. These highways have been virtually destroyed by nearly twenty years of fighting and will not be rebuilt until peace prevails.

The countries also aim at increasing their air transport communication. In May 1998, China and Kyrgyzstan inaugurated nonstop flights between their territories, while China and Kazakhstan agreed to open an international air route linking Urumchi, capital city of China's Xinjiang Uighur Autonomous Region, with Ayaguz of Kazakhstan (Urumchi-Almaty route is already operational).

Partnership with China in transport is important, but the costs of surmounting the difficulties (and the continuing state subsidies needed to surmount them) mean that multiple routes—including those through Russia—will continue to make economic and political sense well into the future. China is potentially a trading partner of enormous importance for the Central Asian states. China is no less capable than Russia of distorting the development of the Central Asian economies, since it serves as a vast market for Central Asian goods, especially energy, and has committed billions of dollars of investment in Central Asia's energy resources. Since April 1998, Kyrgyzstan and China have been examining a possibility for Kyrgyzstan to supply electricity to China or to a third country via the Chinese territory.

The real level of trade between the various Central Asian states and China is hard to know because so much of the trade evades duty and border regulation. This difficulty is particularly true of trade between China and Kyrgyzstan and Kazakhstan, both of which have direct borders with China and seemingly well-deserved reputations for corruption on them. China has become Kyrgyzstan's fourth largest trading partner after Russia, Kazakhstan, and Uzbekistan, and in 1997 the value of Kyrgyz-Chinese trade rose 47 percent over that in 1996.[21] Kazakhstan and Uzbekistan are China's two largest trade partners in the region. Trade with Uzbekistan has grown, and while in 1995 the total trade turnover between Uzbekistan and China was still half that of China-Kyrgyzstan and a third that of China-Kazakhstan, in 1997 its total trade turnover was almost twice as high as that of China-Kyrgyzstan, though still remained about a third of that of China-Kazakhstan. However, trade with China represents only 4.4 percent of Uzbekistan's exports and 2 percent of its imports; included in this trade is Chinese purchase of Uzbek-produced military cargo aircraft. Trade between China and both Turkmenistan and Tajikistan is still insignificant.

The future shape of trade relations between China and its Central Asian neighbors is still unknown. Chinese trade statistics show a continuing decline in exports to Kazakhstan, $228 million in 1992 to $75.5 million in 1995,[22] which represents a 2 percent share of Kazakhstan's imports, as they are reported in official statistics. By contrast, exports to Kyrgyzstan have increased steadily from $18.8 million in 1992 to $107.5 million in 1995.[23] International Monetary Fund (IMF) statistics for Kazakhstan and Kyrgyzstan show a similar pattern, albeit there are discrepancies between the figures they provide in the Chinese trade chart and the Central Asian trade charts. According to the Kazakhstan trade chart, imports from China have declined from $245 million in 1992 to $36 million in 1996, while the figures for exports to Kazakhstan in the Chinese chart are $222 million and $95 million, respectively.[24] This discrepancy only serves to highlight the problem of unreliable trade statistics from this region.

The pattern of decreasing Chinese imports to Kazakhstan is an interesting one. In part, it reflects more stringent visa requirements put in effect for travel between the two states in 1994. It also is a sign of the growing vitality of Kazakhstan's economy, for most observers report that demand for higher quality European and other Asian imports are making the Chinese consumer goods less competitive, which is certainly the impression one gets from press accounts. Coverage of the Chinese "beer scandal" of 1995 featured reports of mass poisonings in Almaty caused by bad beer imported from China. The tainted beer was portrayed as indicative of the poor quality of Chinese goods more generally. The media also offers good coverage of joint ventures that fail, such as the planned Taldy-Kurgan paper factory, which collapsed when the investors from the PRC defaulted.[25] Discussions in the local press make clear that these goods are viewed as low-quality ones.

By contrast, exports from Kazakhstan to China have been growing steadily, from $141.1 million in 1992 to $453 million in 1997. The latter figure represents 7 percent of Kazakhstan's exports. Exports from Kyrgyzstan to China have also increased, from $28 million in 1992 to $34 million in 1997, or 6 percent of Kyrgyzstan's exports.[26]

Whether these exports to China represent the development of sustainable economic ties is still difficult to know. To some degree, these statistics reflect the activity of new joint ventures between Chinese and local partners. The economic significance of these enterprises is unknown because little information is published about their operation, except the fanfare when they open. Again, although the press offers little discussion about these joint ventures, the figures for 1993 and 1994, at least, reflect the sell-off of Soviet-era stockpiles of raw materials, like aluminum, copper, and even cement, a practice that continued through part of 1995. At first, this trade was almost exclusively a barter one, and these figures include the value of goods traded rather than cash transfers between the parties. Certainly, Chinese enterprises may remain a customer for Central Asia's raw materials, but as these resources are transferred to private hands and production is restored, the Central Asian partners are pressing for trade to be transformed into currency-based transactions. It is still too soon to know what impact this change will have on current levels of exports to China.

One other critically important area of future cooperation between Central Asia and China is the development of Central Asian oil and gas deposits. China is a critical transit point for shipment of oil and gas reserves to Japan, a very expensive prospect but one that is not technically infeasible. In August 1995, Exxon, Mitsubishi, and the Chinese National Oil Company signed an agreement with Turkmenistan to export gas to Japan via Uzbekistan, Kazakhstan, and China. This projected 6,000-kilometer pipeline would cost an estimated $10 billion. While the construction of this pipeline is not an immediate priority for either Exxon or Mitsubishi, both continue to maintain that it is a serious project for future development, and Exxon is developing new technologies that would make the transport of gas over such distances more feasible.[27]

Plans for cooperation with China in the development of Central Asian oil reserves are further along and are of more immediate interest to the Chinese. In 1997, the Chinese State Oil Company was allowed to buy a 60 percent share of Aktubminneft, the formerly state-owned oil company in Aktubinsk. The deal included a Chinese commitment to invest in the development of two oil fields and to help raise capital for the building of a pipeline east into China. As of May 1998 the company was extracting 2.6 million tons of oil per year.[28]

In September 1997, the Chinese State Oil Company was also given the right to develop the Kazakh oil field at Uzen, which had earlier been transferred to a Western consortium. Development of the field will cost about $4.4 billion. At the same time, plans for a 3,000-kilometer pipeline stretching from Uzen to Western Xinjiang were firmed up between the two governments. If these projects move forward as planned, the Chinese investment in Kazakhstan's economy will be $9.5 billion, which will put Beijing in a commanding position vis-à-vis the Kazakhs.[29] During President Niyazov's August 1998 official visit to China, the two sides signed an agreement according to which China's Import and Export Bank pledged to provide Turkmenistan's oil enterprises with a 100 million yuan ($12 million) credit.

Military cooperation between the Central Asian states and China is moving at a much slower pace and is unlikely to go much further in the near future. A meeting in April 1997 between Kazakhstan's President Nursultan Nazarbayev, Kyrgyzstan's President Askar Akaev, Tajikistan's President Imomali Rakhmonov, Russia's President Boris Yeltsin, and China's President Jiang Zemin, after a similar meeting the year before, produced an agreement that reduced military forces along the CIS-China border. During the July 1998 five-nations summit in Almaty, the leaders praised the 1996 and 1997 agreements and vowed to refrain from using their territory to engage in activities damaging to state sovereignty, security, and social order of any of the five nations. But with Russian border troops still stationed in three of the Central Asian countries (Kazakhstan, Kyrgyzstan, and Tajikistan) and the lingering fears of Uighur nationalism, bilateral China–Central Asia military projects are unlikely to be significant any time soon.

BEIJING AND THE CENTRAL ASIAN STATES

While the Central Asian states may be stuck between two great powers, the problem of working out bilateral relations with China has been a very different challenge for the leaders of the newly independent states than development of bilateral and multilateral relations with Russia has been. While Central Asia's leaders are engaged in subtle games of jockeying for position and influence with the Russian leaders, whom they usually personally know well and can communicate with freely, dealing with the Chinese leadership has been quite a different experience.

Before independence, the Central Asian leaders had very little direct contact with Chinese officials, although the level of contact was changing at the end of Soviet rule as states sought to increase their spheres of autonomy. With the dramatic out-migration of Russians in the first years of independence, the Central Asian states had room to explore foreign policy strategies that were not exclusively focused on Russia.[30] The Kazakhs and the Kyrgyz were particularly interested in developing relations with China. They defined their relation as national sub-unit to national sub-unit (Soviet republic to Chinese autonomous region), and so both Soviet republics began initiatives with the Xinjiang Autonomous Region. In 1990, a delegation from Xinjiang went to Kazakhstan to discuss the establishment of trade ties and cooperative economic ventures between the two regions. In July 1991, Kazakhstan President Nazarbayev accepted the invitation of the Xinjiang authorities to visit their region and country but created a mild diplomatic stir by his decision to visit Urumchi before paying his respects to the government in Beijing.

The granting of independence to the Central Asian states made it much harder for them to engage in bilateral relations with Xinjiang, for now they were to deal on a state-to-state basis with the government in Beijing. This change in status created far more opportunities than it terminated. Given their uncertainty about China, and probably also because most viewed it as an interesting and exotic destination, Central Asia's leaders made state visits to Beijing soon after independence.

The first major reciprocal visit by the Chinese was Prime Minister Li Peng's visit to Turkmenistan and Kyrgyzstan in April 1994. During his well-publicized trip to the region in April 1995, Li delivered a major address in Tashkent, elaborating the four principles of Chinese relations with the Central Asian states: (1) peaceful coexistence and the maintenance of good-neighbor relations; (2) the promotion of mutually beneficial cooperation; (3) no interference in the political affairs of these states, so as to assure the independent choice of political systems; and (4) respect for the independence and sovereignty of states as the formula for attaining regional stability. These principles closely follow China's stated strategy for dealing with most other states, and the risk of internal interference refers to the

United States and not to Russia, although of course it would technically apply to Russia as well.

During his visit to Central Asia in July 1996, President Jiang Zemin reaffirmed an elaborated version of these principles in a series of bilateral agreements with Kyrgyzstan, Kazakhstan, and Uzbekistan. In addition, these agreements called for strengthened cooperation in a vast variety of sectors, including economic, cultural, and social service spheres. They also talked of creating joint ventures in heavy and light industry, transport, and agriculture. The need to cooperate in the sphere of drug trafficking and organized crime was also discussed, but implementation plans for these goals were minimal.

Currently, few tense issues exist in the relationships of the Central Asian states with China, partly because the expectations of depth in the "friendship" are still low, driven by the pragmatic awareness of its necessity. All the Central Asian leaders realize that in China they have a powerful and potentially dangerous neighbor, particularly if they deal with China without a close security relationship with Russia. All are cognizant that the side with the perceived strategic advantage has always felt that it was reasonable to help shape events in the "other Turkestan"—with the use of troops if necessary—as long as no perceived risk of retaliation from a stronger power existed. For now, of course, the risk of Russian retaliation remains, but as the Central Asian states look forward to weaning themselves from Russia, there is real incentive to build in the habits of caution.

Consequently, the Central Asian states in general, and Kazakhstan and Kyrgyzstan in particular, have worked hard to downplay potentially controversial issues in their relationship with China. Potential problem areas, however, have not been fully avoided. One that has arisen from time to time is Chinese nuclear testing at Lob Nor, an issue of great sensitivity in both states but especially so in Kazakhstan, which was itself a long-time nuclear weapons test site.[31] Critical statements about China's testing program have appeared periodically in the Kazakh and Kyrgyz press, and demonstrations were organized by Nevada Semipalatinsk Anti-Nuclear Movement (a quasi-official group) at the time of Li Peng's 1994 visit to Kazakhstan. When China engaged in or prepared for renewed nuclear testing in 1994, 1995, and 1996, the foreign ministers of Kazakhstan and

Kyrgyzstan issued formal and tersely worded expressions of official displeasure. During the July 1998 summit, the leaders of Kazakhstan, Kyrgyzstan, Tajikistan, Russia, and China passed a resolution on preventing nuclear proliferation and a nuclear arms race. This issue defines for Central Asians all the difficulties inherent in having a strong neighbor next door. Not only are environmental conditions in their countries put at risk by the testing program, but also the testing puts at more direct risk their ethnic kin who live on the Chinese side of the border.

In their dealings with the Chinese government over the past seven years, the leaders of all five republics have been primarily concerned with maximizing state-to-state relations with Beijing and have been less concerned about the fate of their ethnic kin across the border. Ample evidence of this attitude was apparent during the signing of the military provisions of the border treaties (and at similar official visits) when the leaders of Kazakhstan, Kyrgyzstan, and Tajikistan all made statements condemning Muslim extremism and activities of separatist groups. All five Central Asian states have also signed bilateral agreements with China supporting the territorial integrity of the signatory states (as well as statements in support of a single China). Because all the states face potential separatist movements within their own borders, gaining Chinese support for *their* territorial integrity is at least as important as effectively disavowing Uighur territorial ambitions. There is certainly an inequality to these statements. Central Asia is a potential launching point for Uighur separatism, whereas, for now at least, China is likely to provide potentially powerful diplomatic, rather than military, assistance. In the future, however, these circumstances could change.

Currently, maintaining good diplomatic relations with China is sufficiently important to the leaders of the Central Asian states for them to limit the sphere of political action of radical Uighur groups. Such activity is a particular problem in Kazakhstan and Kyrgyzstan, because both have diaspora Uighur populations that often live in ethnic enclaves and are highly politicized. These countries also have relatively liberal rules of assembly and organization, even though informal political groups generally lack a decisive role in the political process.

For now at least, the Kazakhs and Kyrgyz are successfully managing their Uighur problem. The total number of Uighurs remains insignificant compared to the population as a whole. According to the 1989 Soviet census figures, there were 185,301 Uighurs in Kazakhstan, 36,779 Uighurs in Kyrgyzstan, and 35,762 Uighurs in Uzbekistan.[32]

The Kazakhs, Kyrgyz, and Uzbeks encourage the development of Uighur cultural organizations, such as state-sponsored (or closely monitored) radio stations and newspapers, but these media must not have a political agenda. Nonetheless, the Uighur separatists groups (which in 1997 merged into the single United Revolutionary National Front) are well represented among the local diaspora Uighur population, and they even regularly held press conferences in Almaty during the disturbances in Xinjiang in winter-spring 1997.

A reasonable assumption is that the separatist organizations that are physically (though not legally) represented in Central Asia have been successfully infiltrated by local security forces and that their activities are closely monitored. To date, no anti-Chinese terrorist acts have occurred on the territory of any of the Central Asian states. There were, however, small (and unsanctioned) protests by Uighur nationalists at the time of Li Peng's first visit to Central Asia and during the execution of the Uighur nationalists in April 1997 who had been charged with responsibility for the February 1997 riots.[33]

While the leadership of the Central Asian states tries to minimize coverage of their ethnic kin across the border, critical articles about their harsh treatment at Chinese hands do periodically emerge, and the plight of these people never slips too far from public consciousness.[34] The theme of the persecution of the separatist Uighurs must be approached with real caution in the Central Asian press. Even in Kyrgyzstan, the Uighur opposition has been denied licensing for their publication, while the Uighur Freedom Organization in Kyrgyzstan (Ittipak) had a great deal of difficulty getting registration, only to get itself suspended in 1996 for separatist activities.[35]

At the same time, representatives of the separatist organizations do live in Central Asia and maintain a public presence in both Kazakhstan and Kyrgyzstan. While these political organizations are not registered, the Almaty office in particular has been used for issuing press statements and was often quoted during the 1997 bombings and subsequent arrests and trials in Xinjiang. Yet the position of the Kazakh government remains clear: they are unwilling to support the cause of Uighur separatism or see it openly advanced from their territory.[36]

Quite obviously, the Kazakh government has even greater sympathy for the plight of the Kazakh population in China, although the press deliberately neglects this theme. While the newspapers have been full of articles about the need for the ingathering of the Kazakh people, most of the new settlers from outside the CIS have come from Mongolia. In fact, the official statistics on settlement of Kazakhs do not even include a category of new residents from China,[37] although presumably there are some Kazakhs returning to Kazakhstan. It seems likely that the official silence on this issue is to divert attention from the trickle of ethnic Kazakh immigration that does exist.[38] Of course, some of the "Mongol" Kazakhs may in fact come from China, a phenomenon that a Kazakh government sensitive to Chinese government feelings is, in fact, concealing. Regardless, there has not been a mass migration of Kazakhs returning from China.

The Kazakh government would have mixed feelings about such an immigration, for it would mean that China's Kazakhs had simply abandoned traditional Kazakh lands to the full control of the Han Chinese who have been settling there in increasing numbers. China's part of the Ili Valley (the Ili Kazakh Autonomous Region) is considered by the Kazakhs as part of their historic territory, because it was the easternmost land in which the Kazakhs of the Middle Horde and Great Horde pastured their land.

At no time in modern history have the Kazakhs had easy access to this territory or the opportunity to interact freely with those kin (generic and specific) that lived in the region. The opening of the border with China in 1983 was not synonymous with the easing of difficulties associated with Kazakh visits to their kin in Xinjiang. At first, Kazakhs had to travel to Beijing to meet with family members, and it was only in 1990 that they were allowed to hold these meetings in Xinjiang. Even now, the Chinese government remains reluctant to suspend visa requirements fully, for fear of what could happen if exchanges between Central Asians and the minority nationalities of Xinjiang occurred in an unhampered fashion. The visa requirements, however, have impeded the travel of ethnic Kazakhs to Kazakhstan, because the requirements have forced most unofficial travelers to get a visa from the Kazakhstan embassy in Beijing.[39]

The Kazakh government, too, has very complicated attitudes concerning the ideal visa regime with China, and the need for reuniting families is still of small importance. The government is nervous about even the current loose visa requirements, because numerous officials claim that many Han Chinese are entering the country with the intent to stay and form a "fifth column" in Kazakhstan. In 1993, the Kazakh press was nearly hysterical about the issue when tales of hundreds of thousands of illegal Chinese émigrés began to circulate in Kazakh nationalist circles.[40] While these tales contained serious exaggerations, thousands of Chinese have indeed remained in Kazakhstan illegally; some remain in Kazakhstan legally by "buying" local brides. Most seem to do so for the trading advantages that citizenship offers them, and a smaller number of the others do so to help facilitate organized criminal activities across the Kazakh territory.

Although there is probably some truth in these allegations, the scale of immigration from China is dramatically overstated by the Kazakh nationalists. Nonetheless, fear of illegal migration from China is undoubtedly one of the reasons why the Kazakh government accepted the tighter visa provisions that were put in place in 1994. These regulations also had the advantage of decreasing the amount of unregulated "suitcase" trade between the two countries, which is something that Kazakh authorities sought. The better regulation of Chinese-Kazakh trade was also something that Russian officials were pressing Kazakhstan for, because Chinese goods were seeping into Russia through Kazakhstan.

Kyrgyzstan has voiced similar complaints about unregulated Chinese migration. In November 1993, a less strict but nonetheless formal regime (complete with entrance and exit visas) was introduced as part of an effort to curb illegal migration to Kyrgyzstan, which was said to include some 2,000 ethnic Kyrgyz who had emigrated from China to Kyrgyzstan and unspecified but allegedly larger numbers of Han Chinese.[41] The free economic zone in the border oblast of Naryn was said to be a particular target, and the quasi-opposition group Asaba even held demonstrations to protest this migration in 1995.[42]

Given the continued pattern of Han Chinese settlement in Xinjiang, the cause for the fantasies of the Kazakh or Kyrgyz nationalists is not hard to imagine. But while Beijing would unquestionably be capable of "seeding" all of Central Asia with surplus population, and while a subsequent regime might even do so in the future, no evidence currently shows that China is doing this today. Criticism of the settlement of Han Chinese in Kazakh territory across the border, however, has caused occasional comment in Kazakhstan's press.[43]

While both Kazakhstan and Kyrgyzstan have diaspora populations just across the border in China, the problem is more particular for the Kazakhs because of the greater size of that population and because they believe that a part of ancestral Kazakh lands lie across the border. Yet, Kazakhstan's current leadership does not let these issues become the subject of any sort of public debate because such debate would be certain to threaten the current cordial state of relations with China.

LOOKING AHEAD

The position of the communists-turned-nationalists who currently head the Central Asian regimes is not hard to maintain. Even if one credits these leaders with undergoing sincere political conversions, each nonetheless is a consummate politician, and backing Beijing over the separatists makes good political sense for the survival of new states with limited defensive capacities. Moreover, these leaders are all intuitively distrustful of spontaneous or unregulated political groupings, which the Uighur groups have clearly represented since their reorganization after perestroika into something other than the Soviet front organizations that they initially were.

How subsequent governments will react when confronted with similar challenges is harder to know, especially if the current leaders are succeeded by a group of committed nationalist figures, and especially if these new leaders lack the political acumen or diplomatic savvy of their predecessors. A strongly pro-Islamic government in Central Asia might also feel pressed to support the cause of their co-religionists in China against the "infidels" that rule them. A pro-Islamic government in Tajikistan that was in alliance with an Islamic Afghanistan could serve as a conduit for arms and assistance to the Uighurs, as well.

The Chinese would not tolerate a security risk developing just across their borders, which is precisely what would happen if the Central Asian leaders formally supported the cause of the Uighur nationalists. The Chinese government would view itself as similarly aggrieved should a Kazakh nationalist regime call for the reannexation of the Jungar Plain and Ili Valley or even provide clandestine assistance to any underground Kazakh nationalist opposition that might develop in Xinjiang.

Russia, however, could decide to sit quietly by and let China deal with such security risks. Even more likely is a scenario in which the Chinese encourage Russia to deal with what both perceive as a shared security threat arising from one of the Central Asian states. Russia would not likely view a strong nationalist government in either Kyrgyzstan or Kazakhstan with any sympathy. This sentiment is especially true of a Kazakh nationalist government, for such a regime would likely try to push out the country's Russian population well before it began a proactive policy in China. Russia would also feel directly threatened by the existence of an Islamic government in any of the Central Asian states, because it would pose a risk to regional stability and to the loyalty of Russia's own Muslim population.

For the foreseeable future at least, the Chinese have little incentive to pursue a strategy in Central Asia that would put them at odds with Moscow's rulers. Moscow still sees these five states as falling within its part of the world, and for the foreseeable future China has no incentive to put its relationship with Russia at risk for the sake of changing the status quo. Moscow can provide valuable military technology to China, while it is unclear what the Central Asian states have to offer that Beijing would be willing to risk offending Moscow by accepting. China does not provide the same risk to trade between Russia and the Central Asian states that the United States, Europe, and the Asian democracies do. Pipelines east are unlikely to take appreciable revenue away from those that ship oil and gas through Russia to Europe, and they are certain to be far slower in developing than alternate routes to Europe.

For now at least, China has more than enough challenges to face within Xinjiang without looking for more trouble just beyond its borders. Some future ruler in Beijing, who has insured the loyalty of Xinjiang's population through placating them or simply "drowning" them in a "sea" of Han Chinese may feel differently. By then, Xinjiang's resources are sure to have been more fully exploited, while those in Central Asia may not, or, if they are, Central Asia might once again be an attractive path westward to the underutilized treasures and lands of Russia itself.

China is a state still in its ascendancy, while Russia—even after shedding its Soviet republics—is a state in decline. What Russia's continuing decline could mean in Central Asia is still difficult to predict.

The fate of the two "Turkestans" can never be fully separated. Beijing is unwilling to see its empire suffer the Soviets' fate, and planned investment in Xinjiang will only harden this position. The Chinese may not have welcomed the collapse of the Soviet Union, but their relations with Moscow and the successor states are predicated on the continuation of the status quo. If these regimes begin to totter from within and Russia is no longer able to police Central Asia, then the Chinese authorities may be tempted to step in. With every passing year, this temptation is likely to increase, especially after the new pipelines begin pumping oil and gas eastward.

History provides some indications of what Chinese actions may be if disorder is allowed to reign in this part of the world. When its security was threatened, and China was weak, Russia treated Western China as a backyard to trample at will. If the reverse situation were to develop in the next decade or two, the Chinese could well act with the same abandon.

NOTES

[1] According to the agreement, Kazakhstan retained 442 square kilometers in the Zurek Mountains and in the Chogan-Obo River Valley and 442 square kilometers in Keregentas. The Chinese border will be moved 187 square kilometers further out. As a result, Kazakhstan retained 56.9 percent of the disputed territory and China 43.1 percent. "Kazakhstan Parliament Ratifies Border Agreement with China," Moscow *Interfax* (in English) 1403 GMT, February 3, 1999.

[2] "CIS-Chinese Border Agreement Signed," *RFE/RL Newsline*, vol. 1, no. 18, part I, April 24, 1997.

[3] Although Tashkent fell to the Russians on June 9, 1865, the two pieces of legislation that divided and ruled the Kazakh Steppe were enacted in 1867 and 1868. The Provisional Statute on the Administration of the Semire-che'e and Syr Darya Oblasts was adopted July 11, 1867, and the Provisional Statute on the Administration of the Turgai, Akmolinsk, Uralsk, and Semipalatinsk Oblasts was adopted October 21, 1868. A note on historical geography: What used to be Russian Turkestan is today made up of Southern Kazakhstan and parts of Uzbekistan and Kyrgyzstan. The former Eastern Turkestan is the modern-day Xinjiang Province in Western China.

[4] C. Y. Immanuel, *The Ili Crisis: A Study in Sino-Russian Diplomacy* (Oxford: The Clarendon Press, 1965).

[5] Andrew Forbes, *Warlords and Muslims in Chinese Central Asia* (Cambridge: Cambridge University Press, 1986), p. 116.

[6] In the last days of the czarist regime, Russian policies toward the Steppe Region were especially severe. From late June through November 1916, the

Kazakhs staged several episodes of resistance, reacting to policies of forced conscription and land seizures, and against the general economic deprivation caused by World War I. The Russians imposed a similarly harsh truce once the revolt had finally been put down. For more discussion on this topic, see Martha Olcott, *The Kazakhs,* 2nd ed. (Stanford, Calif.: Hoover Institution Press, 1995), pp. 118–26.

[7]Forbes, *Warlords and Muslims,* p. 151.

[8]Ibid., p. 194; D. Holloway, *Stalin and the Bomb* (New Haven, Conn.: Yale University Press, 1994), p. 177.

[9]G. Lias, *Kazakh Exodus* (London: Evans Bros, 1956).

[10]Mosely puts the figure at 50,000. See G. Mosely, *A Sino-Soviet Cultural Frontier: The Ili Kazakhh Autonomous Chou,* Harvard East Asian Monologues (Cambridge, Mass.: Harvard University Press, 1966).

[11]M. Sharipzhan, "Kazakhs of Eastern Turkestan in Threshold of 21 Century," *BITIG Journal of the Turkish World,* January 1997, p. 20.

[12]Peter Ferdinand, *The New States of Central Asia and their Neighbors* (New York: Council on Foreign Relations Press, 1994), p. 96.

[13]R. Israeli, "A New Wave of Muslim Revivalism in Mainland China," *Issues and Studies 33,* no. 3 (March 1997), p. 30.

[14]J. J. Rudelson, "The Uighurs in the Future of Central Asia," *Nationalities Papers,* vol. 22, no. 2 (1994), p. 304.

[15]*Agence France-Presse,* Hong Kong, "Beijing Bus Bomb Reportedly Work of Uighur Separatists," *FBIS-TOT-97-069,* March 11, 1997.

[16]*Agence France-Presse,* Hong Kong, February 11, 1997, *FBIS-CHI-97-029.*

[17]*Al-Watan Al-Arabi,* Paris, May 23, 1997, *FBIS-NES-97-102.*

[18]*Kuang Chiao Ching,* Hong Kong, May 10, 1997, *FBIS-CHI-97-110.*

[19]*Delovoi Mir,* May 15, 1996.

[20]"Traffic in transit" begins in Almaty, Kazakhstan, goes through Bishkek, Kyrgyzstan, to Kashgar, China, and then on to Khunjera Pass, Pakistan. The total length of the road system is approximately 3,000 kilometers.

[21]"The Kyrgyz Prime Minister Hails Sino-Kyrgyz Ties," *Xinhua* Hong Kong Service (in Chinese) 1237 GMT, May 17, 1998.

[22]Chinese customs statistics quoted by G. Walker, "China Builds Trade Ties Across its Western Border," *Transition,* vol. 2, no. 17 (August 23, 1996), p. 30.

[23]Ibid.

[24]International Monetary Fund, *Direction of Trade Statistics Yearbook 1989–1996* (Washington, D.C.: IMF, 1997), pp. 158–59, 272. It should be noted, however, that the Chinese chart shows an increase of exports to Kazakhstan from 1995 to 1996, from $75 million to $95 million.

[25]*Delovoy Mir,* October 9–15, 1995.

[26]International Monetary Fund, *Direction of Trade Statistics Yearbook* (Washington, D.C.: IMF, 1998), p. 285.

[27]S. Agafonov, "Central Asia Is Closer to Japan than Russia Is," *Izvestia*, August 30, 1995, p. 3.

[28]"Kazakh-China Oil Deal Questioned," *Delovaia Nedelia*, May 8, 1998, pp. 8–9.

[29]Moscow *ITAR-TASS*, "Nazarbayev, China's Li Peng Sign 'Deal of the Century,'" *FBIS-SOV-97-267*, September 24, 1997.

[30]More than half a million ethnic Russians have left Kazakhstan alone, and the wave seems far from over. See Martha Olcott, "Unlocking the Assets: Energy and the Future of Central Asia and the Caucasus," *Baker Report* (April 1998), p. 10.

[31]A total of 470 nuclear tests, 118 of which were above ground, were made between 1949 and 1989 in the northeast region of Kazakhstan. See "Forlorn the Victims of Soviet Nuclear Tests," *The Guardian*, March 19, 1998.

[32]Sean Roberts and Sahimi Dautura, "A Nation Across Borders," *Living Together*, vol. 13, no. 3 (August 1995), pp. 50, 51.

[33]*Agence France-Presse*, Hong Kong, "50 Uighur Demonstrators Arrested in Almaty," *FBIS-SOV-97-118*, April 28, 1997.

[34]"Nationalities: Leaders of the Uygur Community Believe that the Shanghai Treaty on the Borders Between the PRC and the Post-Soviet States Has Allowed the Repression of Uygurs in the Xinjiang-Uygur Autonomous Region," *Panorama*, June 7, 1996, p. 5.

[35]B. Dave, "Temporary Ban on Uighur Society in Kyrgyzstan," *OMRI Daily Digest*, April 9, 1996, p. 3.

[36]"Tokaev Warned Against Uighur Separation," *Krasnaya Zvezda*, July 18, 1996, p. 3.

[37]According to *Interfax*, by 1992 some 40,000 ethnic Kazakhhs had immigrated to Kazakhhstan from Mongolia (*FBIS-SOV-92-206*, October 23, 1992).

[38]According to Ross Munro, some 30,000 ethnic Kazakhhs have immigrated to Kazakhhstan from Xinjiang. See R. Munro, "Central Asia and China," in M. Mandelbaum, ed., *Central Asia and the World* (New York: Council on Foreign Relations Press, 1994), p. 232. It should be emphasized, however, that Munro's figure not only is hard to verify, since no other available source exists, but also is unofficial and approximate, since it is based on the author's private conversations with Kazakhh officials.

[39]*Aziya*, no. 44 (October 1993), pp. 1, 3.

[40]Victor Kiyanitsa and Vladimir Gubarev, "Chinese Immigrants Find a Foothold in Kazakhstan," *Moscow News*, no. 38 (September 17, 1993).

[41]*Radio Mayak*, November 19, 1993, *FBIS-SOV-93-222*.

[42]"Paper Notes Anti-Chinese Activity by Asaba Party," *Delo No*, April 26, 1995, p. 3, *FBIS-SOV-95-087*.

[43]Quoted by K. Martin, "China and Central Asia Between Seduction and Suspicion," *Transition*, vol. 3, no. 25 (June 24, 1994), p. 33.

14

The Changing Asian Arena

Harry Gelman

The current phase in the relationship between Russia and China reflects the third swing of the pendulum in the past half-century, from formal alliance to vituperative enmity to the present "partnership." At each stage in the past, the relationship has conditioned the strategic environment in East Asia. And each time, too, changes in the Asian landscape in their turn had an impact on the behavior of Moscow and Beijing toward each other and helped (along with other factors) to change the relationship.[1] These observations still appear to apply today in the era of the alleged Sino-Russian "strategic partnership."

While Russian dealings with China have been evolving toward this new stage over the past few years, other changes have been taking place in Asia that may prove equally important—in some cases more so. Overlapping all other considerations was the emergence of financial crisis throughout East Asia after the spring of 1997, seriously affecting many economies hitherto considered invulnerable—not to mention the Russian economy, which was only too vulnerable. Meanwhile, this recent spread of economic malaise was superimposed on several major political changes already in train. Fundamental, long-delayed geopolitical shifts have now begun at several points around the periphery of the Sino-Russian landmass, from Korea to the Caspian Sea. Some of these broad changes have begun to interact with each other and with the new Sino-Russian relationship in ways that will complicate that relationship.

Among the ingredients in this mix are the Russian transfer of advanced military technology to China; Taiwan's drift toward permanent separation from China, along with Beijing's reaction to that drift; Japan's refocusing of its strategic concerns southward and broadening of its alliance with the United States; and, finally, the historical discontinuities that have begun to emerge in the Korean peninsula.

THE KOREAN PENINSULA

To trace the thread linking these disparate elements, we may begin with the last, Korea, where the accumulating changes have already been spectacular, and where further drastic movement might pose new challenges for the Sino-Russian relationship. Here the underlying question for the long term is the effect that eventual reunification of the Korean peninsula could have on the U.S. military presence in the region, and the consequences this effect could bring for China and Russia. In this connection, some symptoms of radical future change are visible today in the South Korean reaction to Russia's efforts to escape from its present marginal position in the peninsula.

Russia's Weakness in the Korean Peninsula

Russia, like Korea's other immediate neighbor China, and like the United States and Japan, is now faced with the problem of helping to manage the dangerous period of transition created by the protracted internal economic crisis of the heavily armed, traditionally pugnacious North Korean regime and the possibility of North Korea's eventual collapse and absorption by South Korea. But while the dangers for Russia are real if the management process fails and an explosion occurs, the humiliating fact is that the Russian government has thus far had only a marginal say in that process.

For a number of years, Russia has been the least influential of the four major powers interacting on the peninsula. In contrast, Russia's new partner China is important in both halves of the peninsula. These facts were dramatized, for example, by Russia's insignificant role, and China's meaningful role, during the United States's tortuous diplomatic struggle in 1993–1994 to head off North Korean completion of its nuclear weapons program.[2] Similarly, Russia was ignored as the United States sought to persuade Pyongyang to enter four-power talks on the status of the peninsula that have since begun, conspicuously including China but not Russia. Many in the Russian foreign policy elite have long been resentful of the contrast between the Chinese and Russian roles.

The reasons for this anomaly, this disparity between the inherent risks to this large bordering state and Russia's share of the diplomatic action, are generally taken for granted but are worth spelling out. ' The disparity stems, in the first place, from the simple fact of Russia's economic and military weakness in the post-Soviet era. The "sick man of Asia" inherently has fewer relevant assets to bring to the table than the other large powers. In addition to its weakness, Russia has poor bilateral relations with the North Korean regime and a correct but not strong relationship with South Korea.

In North Korea (DPRK), Russia's present lack of influence has a long train of well-known historical causes. On Moscow's side, there was, in the first place, resentment at what was perceived as North Korea's ingratitude and betrayal. Despite the fact that Moscow created the Pyongyang regime a half-century ago and later provided very significant economic and military inputs (notably in the early Brezhnev years), the DPRK leaned toward China during the years of the Sino-Soviet dispute and, in general, has been less distant from China than from anyone else throughout most of the regime's history.[3] Added to this circumstance was the Soviet perception, which grew in importance as dealings with the United States multiplied in the 1970s and 1980s, that North Korean behavior was dangerous, irrational, and, worst of all, unpredictable and could drag Moscow into undesired conflict with the United States. Finally, in the Gorbachev era came the belated realization that relations with the rapidly modernizing and expanding South Korean economy offered far more potential benefit than the tie to the contracting economy of the self-isolated Stalinist regime in Pyongyang.

North Korean attitudes at every stage represented the other side of the coin. The fact that Stalin had placed Kim Il-sung in power was not reason for gratitude, but rather reason to break free from Soviet control and tutelage after Stalin died and it became feasible to do so. In the 1960s, Chinese rejection of Soviet authority was convenient for this purpose. Mao's attacks on Khrushchev's domestic "revisionism" and on the notion of détente with the United States also coincided with the needs of the DPRK, since Kim's rigid regime anathematized internal change and saw its central external goal as the removal of the U.S. obstacle to the absorption of South Korea by the North. Later, the North Korean government was understandably aggrieved when the evolution of Soviet policy gradually made the mutual defense clause of the 1961 Soviet-DPRK treaty a dead letter. Still later, Kim Il-sung was infuriated by Gorbachev's 1990 recognition of Seoul in pursuit of economic benefits, an act that was a fundamental blow to Kim's denial of the legitimacy of the Republic of Korea (ROK) and, therefore, to his ambitions in the peninsula. And after the fall of the Soviet Union, North Korea was further injured by a precipitous drop in imports from Russia, as the result of Russian inability—and unwillingness—to continue traditional exports that had little prospect of repayment.

Finally, in addition to all these practical considerations, in the background there has always been the cultural factor, which, while intangible, is far from trivial. Other things being equal, the pulling power of centuries of links to Chinese civilization has always tended to draw both North and South Koreans toward China, and not toward Russia.

In the past few years, the Russian government has taken steps attempting to redefine and revive relations with the North. In 1993, Moscow unilaterally renounced the defense assistance clauses of the 1961 Soviet–North Korean Treaty, and in 1995 Moscow informed North Korea that it did not intend to renew the treaty. At that time, however, Moscow presented Pyongyang with a draft for a new bilateral friendship treaty with no military aspect, supposedly shaped along the lines of Russia's present treaty with Vietnam, emphasizing economic and cultural matters. In early 1997, the two sides for the first time examined opposing drafts together in detail, but important differences remained, apparently owing in large part to North Korea's reluctance to abandon either the mutual military commitment or the "ideological assessments . . . inconsistent with modern realities" found in the old treaty.[4] It seems possible, however, that agreement will be reached within the next few years, since the beleaguered North Korean government now has some stake in reviving a relationship, however limited, with Moscow.

From the Russian perspective, the best opportunity to implant a significant new presence in North Korea was lost in 1994 when South Korea and the United States rejected out of hand Moscow's proposal—supported by North Korea—that Russia supply the nuclear power plants that under the U.S.–North Korean agreement are to be furnished to the DPRK as compensation for abandoning Pyongyang's nuclear weapons program. Despite Moscow's bitter complaints, the Russian government had been well aware that this proposal was a forlorn hope, because South Korea—providing the main funds for the project—would certainly refuse to do so unless the Republic of Korea also provided the nuclear facilities.

In the absence of this bonanza, the Russian economic relationship with North Korea is likely to remain limited.[5] North Korea has already sought new lines of credit to revive Russian deliveries. But given Pyongyang's inability to pay for significant imports from Russia, and given the existence of a very large accumulated North Korean debt to Russia with no prospect of repayment, the essential issue is how far any Russian government will be prepared to go in sending commodities like petroleum products to North Korea as perpetually unpaid "political loss leaders," in the old Soviet style. Most Russian leaders are likely to be skeptical about going far down this road.[6]

The Main Arena: South Korea

All these circumstances, however, are now of secondary importance to Moscow, a hedge rather than a main bet, because the question of the relationship with Pyongyang could in any case suddenly become moot. The more important issue for all foreigners in the peninsula today is clearly the relationship with South Korea, where the future lies, and here the results for Russia so far have been disappointing. Despite considerable effort and some marginal progress since Gorbachev's recognition of Seoul, Russian economic dealings with the ROK have remained much less significant than those of China, let alone the United States and Japan.

Beijing's relative advantage over Moscow in the Republic of Korea derives, in the first place, from the fact that Russia came late to the party. China began both significant movement toward a market economy and significant trade with South Korea well before the Soviet Union. From the beginning, the Chinese economic reform process, for all its defects, proved successful enough to make China's "opening up" to foreign investment credible and attractive. In contrast, Russia has up to now remained handicapped in dealing with the South Koreans, as with the Japanese and the West generally, by the Russian systemic political and economic problems that hamper exports and seriously constrain direct foreign investment.

Greatly compounding these problems has been a specific bilateral burden Russia has inherited from the Soviet Union: the very large debt to Seoul, most of it still unpaid, that Gorbachev had incurred by extracting massive South Korean loans to Moscow in 1991 in return for diplomatic recognition. Seoul agreed at the time to lend the Soviet Union $3 billion in cash and goods. But after the first tranche of $1.47 billion had been released, the Soviet Union collapsed, Russia proved unable to meet interest payments, and Seoul halted further disbursement. Since then, accumulated interest has raised the amount owed by another third. Although Russian–South Korean trade (notably with the Russian Far East) has grown, largely on a barter basis, on the whole, Korean credits and investments are still greatly inhibited by the debt issue.[7]

Russia's effort to deal with that debt has recently had suggestive consequences. As with some Russian debts to other countries, a partial solution has been discovered in the large unneeded arms stocks inherited from the Soviet Union and in the surplus production of Russian weapons plants, very little of whose output can now be absorbed by the impoverished Russian armed forces. In 1993, Russia announced that it was prepared to supply the Republic of Korea with so-called defensive weapons to help pay principal and interest on the debt. In return, Moscow expected Seoul to revive investment in Russia. After extensive negotiation, South Korea announced in April 1995 that it had consented to accept a mixture of weapons and commodities to offset a portion of the debt, and in July 1995 it signed an agreement to that effect. Some of the allegedly defensive weapons, such as T-80 tanks and infantry fighting vehicles, began arriving in 1996, much to the indignation of North Korea, and were deployed in separate South Korean units.

The Russian government, hoping to make more significant inroads on the debt, has naturally sought to expand on this beginning, with encouragement from South Korea. An agreement on bilateral military cooperation was signed in the fall of 1996, and extensive public discussion ensued in both countries about the possibility that the ROK would next procure defensive missiles or even fighter aircraft from Moscow—the sponsor of its opponent in the Korean War— rather than from its traditional supplier and ally and rescuer in that war, the United States. The South Korean government, understandably attracted by the enormous prospective cost savings, let it be known that it was seriously considering, in particular, whether it should turn to the Russian SA-12 missile rather than to the U.S. Patriot to counter the North Korean SCUD threat.[8] The United States government reacted sharply, particularly in public statements in Seoul by the U.S. secretary of defense, to which the Korean press responded in kind.

Regardless of the choices made on specific issues, such squabbles marked a watershed, though not primarily because of their military significance, and still less because of the consequences for Russia's relations with South Korea—which at least over the next few years are not likely to reach the breakthrough Moscow craves, despite Russian hopeful rhetoric. Rather, the emerging, assertively independent South Korean posture on such particular arms procurement issues was symbolically significant because of what it suggested about the future of the larger ROK relationship with the United States, particularly if North Korea does eventually collapse and reunification occurs.

Long-Term Consequences of Changes in the ROK-U.S. Relationship

In recent years, a variety of other such signs has shown that the Republic of Korea is maturing as an ally, chafing at its traditional dependence on the United States, and increasingly resistant of restrictions and deference hitherto tolerated as part of the alliance relationship. Among other things, differences of opinion have surfaced more sharply and more frequently in the past few years over how to deal with North Korea.

This problem for the alliance became particularly serious in 1993–1994, when Pyongyang attempted to use negotiations with Washington over its nuclear program to lever the United States into establishing and gradually broadening an economic and diplomatic relationship with North Korea from which South Korea would be excluded. As the bilateral negotiations went on, Seoul deeply resented what it saw as the Clinton administration's tacit acquiescence in this North Korean effort because of its failure to give a higher priority to insisting on North Korean talks with the South.[9]

These bilateral tensions did not disappear after the signing of the Washington-Pyongyang nuclear agreement. In the fall of 1996, officials and analysts in both the United States and the ROK were cited as saying that relations between the two countries had reached their lowest point in years, particularly because of differences over how to deal with North Korea in the wake of an incursion of a North Korean submarine on a terrorist mission at the very time that Pyongyang was loudly demanding food from the world.[10] This point of tension in the relationship between Washington and Seoul was passed, for the time being, when the United States induced a desperate North Korea to apologize.

Even after economic desperation in 1997 compelled North Korea to agree to four-power talks including South Korea, Pyongyang's behavior at the initial preparatory session of these talks made it clear that it had not abandoned its hope of "bilateralizing" its relations with the United States to the exclusion of bilateral talks with South Korea. Differences between Washington and Seoul over behavior toward Pyongyang are therefore unlikely to go away, and enduring resentments will probably continue to surface sporadically in different forms of assertive South Korean behavior affecting the bilateral relationship.[11] Ironically, even after the 1998 election of the liberal reformist Kim Dae-jung as president of the Republic of Korea, tensions over policy toward North Korea reemerged in a new form, with Kim urging the United States to conciliate Pyongyang by unilaterally halting economic sanctions against North Korea, and Washington at least initially declining to do so.

The growing problems in the U.S. relationship with South Korea are in a sense inevitable, an inescapable consequence of South Korea's emergence as an industrializing, globally respected modern state with a sizable middle class. There has for some time been a natural tension between these changes and the continued dependence of the Republic of Korea on the U.S. alliance in the face of North Korean hostility. Meanwhile, over the past decade, first the demise of the Soviet Union and then the visible incremental weakening of the economic base of the North Korean regime have cumulatively weakened South Korean perception of danger. And more recently, the relationship with the United States has been further strained by considerable South Korean resentment over the hardships imposed by the United States and the International Monetary Fund in dealing with South Korea's own economic crisis.

These factors do not mean that the alliance is likely to be threatened in the immediate future. So long as the menacing North Korean regime endures—and there is neither a total collapse in Pyongyang nor a magical transformation of that regime sufficient to produce a final peace treaty and total elimination of the military threat to South Korea—in short, so long as there is neither a "hard landing" nor a "soft landing" leading toward reunification, the South Korean elite consensus will continue to see a vital need for the military tie to the United States, and the U.S. consensus will also probably remain supportive of that tie and the U.S. military presence in South Korea. Moreover, as a practical matter, the new economic difficulties experienced by the Republic of Korea since 1997 reversed the earlier trend and rendered South Korea more dependent on the U.S. relationship.

Over the next decade, therefore, friction in the U.S.–South Korean alliance and dissent over the need for the U.S. military presence will probably grow but will most likely remain contained.[12] If and when, however, the North Korean regime does suddenly collapse and reunification occurs on that basis, there almost certainly will be radical and quite rapid changes in the political equation that now maintains the alliance.[13]

Whether or not this contingency is probable, it is not extremely unlikely. Because of the economic catastrophe in the DPRK, in recent years many in the United States, both inside and outside the U.S. government, have come to the conclusion that a total North Korean collapse could happen much sooner than previously expected. Certainly the South Korean elite is by no means eager to see this happen, particularly in view of its own great economic difficulties. Yet the past decade has already seen even greater historical discontinuities, notably in the demise of the Warsaw Pact and the end of the Soviet Union.

But if the Korean peninsula were indeed to be abruptly reunified by the South as a result of a breakdown in the North, it seems unlikely that either the Korean or the U.S. publics would long support the continued presence of U.S. forces in Korea. Even if the Korean–U.S. alliance itself remained in existence—like NATO, a vestige of a former day, its old raison d'être gone, searching for a new rationale—no bland diplomatic formula is likely to override the pressure of Korean nationalism and the almost inevitable demand in the U.S. Congress to remove the troops. Close relations of other kinds between the United States and the Republic of Korea would surely remain, in view of the existing close economic relationship and the many ties of friendship, not to mention the likely South Korean need—magnified by Seoul's own economic problems—for major international assistance in coping with the grave task of assimilating the North. Nevertheless, something very important would have been subtracted from the relationship. Although this much seems quite likely (given the uncertain assumption of a North Korean collapse), the possible further consequences for Russia and China are more conjectural.

So far as Russia is concerned, some in Moscow may very possibly look forward to this eventuality and count on such altered circumstances—the diminished U.S. influence and presence—to facilitate an expansion of the Russian relationship with Korea. Those who harbor such hopes no doubt see Russian arms transfers as the entering wedge in this process and have promoted Yeltsin visits to Seoul to help push the process along, in advance of any events that might bring about reunification.

If reunification did bring in its train elimination of the U.S. military presence in Korea, there could conceivably be an increase in Korea's readiness to accept essentially cost-free weapons transfers from Russia to be charged against the otherwise uncollectable Russian debt (assuming that the weapons in question remained relevant to Korea's procurement needs in the new situation). But even if this exchange happened, it is by no means clear that it would, in turn, result in the quantum leap in Korean investment in Russia that is the key Russian desire. The most important question here is Moscow's ability—particularly after the Russian financial collapse of August 1998—to put an end to the profound unpredictability of the domestic economic and political environment that constrains direct foreign investment in Russia by Korean firms, and by the firms of other states. Russian foreign policy planners have no control at all over this factor, and the prospects for an early solution are dubious at best.

Consequently, it seems likely that China will retain its existing advantage in the Korean peninsula over its supposed strategic colleague Russia whether or not the North Korean regime collapses in the next decade. If that regime hangs on despite economic calamities and declining elite morale, as is quite possible, Russia's relationship with both Koreas will probably remain marginal, and its competitive position will continue to be handicapped by China's "insider" role in joint negotiations, by China's somewhat closer relationship with the North, and by its much broader economic relationship with the South.

If, however, the sudden North Korean collapse that many in the West have anticipated does occur in the next decade, and the ensuing reunification brings in its train a reduction in U.S. military presence and influence in the Korean peninsula, competition between Moscow and Beijing is likely to intensify, each seeking to take advantage of this change.[14] Again, however, China, and not Russia, is likely to be the major gainer. Over the years, the expansion and gradual modernization of the Chinese economy and the steady growth of Chinese geopolitical weight in Asia will probably continue to exert a magnetic pull on Korean exports and investments. This pull will continue to dwarf the relationship with Russia unless a radical change occurs in the investment environment in Russia.

Noteworthy in this connection is Seoul's apparent disinclination to view Chinese military modernization aided by Russia with the same degree of concern as do Japan or the United States. Indeed, once all danger from the North has finally vanished, the instinctive Korean tendency may be to look with greater suspicion on Japanese, rather than Chinese, defense policy.[15] Visceral Korean hostility to Japan lies close to the surface and is likely to emerge more openly if the North Korean threat has disappeared—particularly if Japan, influenced by its perception of long-term trends in Chinese behavior, adopts a less constrained defense posture. Needless to say, this change will greatly complicate the problems of U.S. policy makers.[16]

The Effect on Japan's Strategic Posture

These circumstances bring us to the consequences of a Korean reunification for the U.S., Russian, and Chinese relationships with Japan. Other things being equal—which they are not—the withdrawal of U.S. forces from the Korean peninsula as a result of Korean reunification might be expected to have a major negative impact on the Japanese-U.S. alliance. Once the United States had totally withdrawn its Korean military presence, the main rationale for the continued U.S. presence in Japan accepted by much of U.S. public opinion (if not necessarily by the U.S. government)—its function as the essential support base for Korean operations—would be undermined.[17]

The Japanese public would also no doubt be impressed by the vanishing of the putative North Korean missile threat to Japan, which, since the decline of the danger from Russia, is the primary concrete military danger to Japan that the Japanese government—unable for political reasons to articulate the full extent of its worries about China—can publicly acknowledge as justification for an enhanced security relationship with the United States. In a sense, North Korea has recently become the "cover" for Tokyo's long-term concerns about the PRC. With reunification, that cover would vanish.

At the very least, therefore, reunification of Korea and the subsequent withdrawal of U.S. forces from the peninsula would surely rekindle vehement public discussion in both Japan and the United States on the purpose and appropriate nature of the alliance. This discussion is all the more likely in view of the bilateral friction that has arisen in recent years over the U.S. troop presence, notably in Okinawa.

If Japanese-U.S. military cooperation nevertheless does continue and expands its scope in the next decade even if North Korea collapses, it will be because the geopolitical environment outside the Korean peninsula has also begun to change in ways that seriously concern the majority in both elites. In a nutshell, military cooperation between Japan and the United States is likely to endure and grow even after Korean reunification because new long-term worries and uncertainties are emerging elsewhere in East Asia—particularly about China—to replace the vanished traditional worry about Soviet and Russian military power.

JAPAN AND THE BELATED DEMISE OF THE RUSSIAN THREAT

How did the Japanese shift in focus from North to South come about? In the first place, it has been a gradual process. Eventually, Japanese strategic perceptions were, of course, greatly affected by what happened in the past decade to the Soviet Union and Russia, but this reevaluation was slow in coming. During the Gorbachev years, Japan's relationship with the USSR had remained very cold long after Moscow's relations with the United States, Western Europe, and China began to grow warmer. This lag existed largely because, despite various cosmetic overtures to Japan, Gorbachev never was in a position to offer Tokyo concrete concessions to Japanese national interests remotely comparable in scope to those major geopolitical concessions that he presented in the late 1980s to the United States, Western Europe, and China.

Thus, while Gorbachev eventually found it possible to yield to U.S. demands for the "zero option" to obtain an Intermediate-Range Nuclear Force (INF) settlement, and to NATO demands for drastically assymetrical force reductions to obtain a Conventional Forces in Europe (CFE) settlement, because of internal pressures and his own priorities Gorbachev could not yield to Japanese demands for return of the "Northern Territories," the four islands north of Hokkaido that have been the focus of Japanese irredentist claims since World War II.

In addition, the change the Gorbachev years brought about in the scope of the concrete military threat confronting Japan in the Soviet Far East, while significant (largely because of the deterioration of the local Soviet naval forces), was much less overwhelming than the geopolitical earthquake accomplished in Europe, first by the asymmetrical CFE reductions, then by Soviet acceptance of the loss of its East European empire, and finally, of course, by the breakup of the Soviet Union. What happened to Soviet forces in Primorskii Krai (the locus of the strongest concentration of forces facing Japan) was hardly comparable to what happened to the Soviet forces in East Germany, or to Russia's military position in Ukraine, Poland, and the Baltic States. Consequently, while by the start of the Yeltsin era the European evaluation of the military threat from the East had retreated to zero, the Japanese Defense Agency in 1992 was still calling Russian forces in the Far East a "factor promoting instability in the region" and even as recently as 1996 was still describing their activities as "unpredictable."[18]

The resulting gap between Tokyo's attitude toward Moscow and that held by the United States, Western Europe, and China persisted in the first years of the Yeltsin regime. Although Yeltsin, like Gorbachev (and Khrushchev) before him, toyed with the notion of offering Japan the two least important of the four disputed islands in return for a territorial settlement and a peace treaty, it remained clear that this offer was unacceptable to Japan, while on the Russian side the domestic political costs to Yeltsin of offering even this much also remained unacceptable.[19] The nadir of Moscow's post-Soviet relationship with Japan came in the fall of 1992, when Yeltsin abruptly cancelled a scheduled visit at the last minute rather than face the consequences of the continued impasse.[20]

Meanwhile, the divergence between Washington's and Tokyo's attitudes toward Yeltsin came into dramatic prominence during the run-up to the G-7 meeting of July 1992, when the Bush administration reversed its position to support international help to the Yeltsin regime despite vehement Japanese resistance. The Japanese felt that this U.S. shift was a betrayal that would weaken their negotiating position with the Russians over the Northern Territories and believed that the United States—for the first time since World War II—had chosen to sacrifice a Japanese national interest to a Russian interest.[21]

Hashimoto's Shift

By the summer of 1997, however, there had been a perceptible change in the Japanese attitude. Despite the fact that the Northern Territories issue was still unresolved (and in the opinion of this writer is likely to remain so indefinitely), the Japanese government finally began to significantly soften its rigid posture toward Russia. This change had been developing incrementally by fits and starts over the previous two years, under the aegis of Japanese Prime Minister Ryutaro Hashimoto, and it now apparently accelerated.

In the spring of 1996, the director general of the Japanese Defense Agency (JDA) for the first time visited Moscow for conversations with Russian military leaders, and he signed a mutual cooperation protocol providing for confidence-building measures such as advance notice of military exercises and exchanges of information, as well as mutual training missions and naval port visits.[22] Later that year, the annual JDA white paper ratcheted downward its threat evaluation of the Russian force posture in the Far East from "promoting instability" to merely "unpredictable." Severe irritants in the bilateral relationship persisted, however, notably over fishing near the disputed territories; and in summer 1996, as in years before, Japan vainly sought to prevent Russian participation in the 1996 G-7 meeting. But in November, Tokyo announced that it would resume disbursing some $500 million in export-import bank loans to Russia frozen since the fall of the Soviet Union. Originally intended as "humanitarian aid," they would now be available for commercial and industrial projects.[23]

In May 1997, Russian Minister of Defense Igor Rodionov paid a return visit to the Japanese Defense Agency in Tokyo, and during this visit he made a remarkable statement, to which we shall return later, to the effect that he had no objection to the strengthening of the Japanese-U.S. military alliance.

Next, Japan, in the summer of 1997, finally gave up its usual futile resistance to Yeltsin's participation in G-7 meetings and subsequently made it clear that this change was not merely accommodation to a fait accompli, but reflected a new Japanese strategy toward the Russians. The shift was articulated and symbolized in a new formula on Japanese policy adopted soon thereafter by Prime Minister Hashimoto, who declared on July 24, 1997, that Tokyo's guiding principles in dealing with Russia would henceforth be "trust, mutual interest, and long-term perspective."[24]

This revised formula seems to have been intended to imply that the Japanese government would now take a somewhat more forthcoming attitude toward Japanese investment in Russia in advance of any territorial settlement, as part of a series of confidence-building initiatives—which the Russians were expected to reciprocate—leading toward a solution of the territorial issue, which Hashimoto said he wanted to see by the time his term ended in 1999. A series of semiannual Hashimoto meetings with Yeltsin, beginning with a November 1997 meeting in Krasnoyarsk, was inaugurated to try to move the process forward.

At the time of Hashimoto's July 1997 statement, Japanese diplomats briefing the press played up the statement as a watershed event, and the Japanese press interpreted the change as rendering the economic relationship no longer hostage to a Northern Territories settlement.[25] But a territorial solution did not, in fact, emerge by 1999, and it remains uncertain how far Japan will, in practice, move to expand investment in Russia in the absence of such a political payoff.

While he remained in office, Hashimoto put down some markers in this regard. He gave the Russians a memorandum specifying Japanese general requirements for increased investment in Russia, and he agreed to establish a joint commission to consider energy development in the Russian Far East. He also alluded in his July 1997 speech to an interest not only in further joint development of oil and gas resources in the Sakhalin shelf area—where two Russian-Japanese-U.S. consortia are already involved—but also in exploiting the gas resources of the Irkutsk region and of Yakutia.[26] By implication, the Japanese government might be less reluctant to offer trade insurance and export-import bank credits for selective, large, new Japanese deals with Russia.

The biggest question mark, however, remains how far the Japanese business community is likely to respond and whether the Hashimoto initiative can be sustained in the next administration. For in practice, up to now the greatest hindrance to Japanese investment in Russia has not been the political obstacle (the Northern Territories issue) but rather the perception by Japanese business leaders that Russia is a frustrating and inhospitable and generally unpromising target for investment, however enticing Russian energy supplies may be.[27] In Japan, as in Korea, this perception is likely to be difficult to change, especially since the Russian financial disaster in 1998. One major factor working to change that Japanese perception had been Hashimoto himself. Since his departure, Japan's own economic problems have made it all the more uncertain whether his successor, Keizo Obuchi, will be inclined to invest similar personal political capital in Japanese-Russian relations.

Japanese Worries about China

Regardless of how much movement in the Russian-Japanese relationship emerges, the question remains why Hashimoto thought it desirable to take an initiative in this direction. Russians have suggested that the rise of the PRC has had much to do with Japan's decision to begin mending fences with Russia,[28] which indeed seems to be the case, and the Chinese press has drawn the same conclusion.[29] Meanwhile, the same concerns about Beijing have also prompted more important adjustments to Japan's alliance with the United States, and dealing with China's reaction to these changes has become a difficult problem for Japanese politicans.

There seems to be little doubt that as Japan's security worries about Russia have gradually eased since the collapse of the Soviet Union, Tokyo's long-term concerns about China have grown. A long list of factors contributes to these concerns:

- the extremely rapid growth of the Chinese economy over the past decade, impelled by inputs from Japan and the West

- the increased proportion of the published budget acknowledged as going to the Chinese military over the past few years, while the budgetary pie meanwhile continues to grow

- Russian weapons transfers to the PRC, and the important ongoing contributions of many Russian specialists to long-term Chinese military modernization

- the signs of increased military influence in decision making by a divided and weakened Chinese political leadership as the Deng Xiaoping era came to an end

- the growth of China's geopolitical weight in Asia and visible self-confidence as a direct result of the advance of China's economic and military strength

- evidence suggesting to some onlookers that this self-confidence was producing a Chinese tendency toward regional assertiveness born of an unvoiced conviction that China's size confers natural and legitimate geopolitical rights.

The Taiwan Issue and Japan

All these concerns were, of course, sharpened by China's behavior regarding Taiwan in 1995 and 1996. This conduct was apparently affected by the views of the Chinese military leadership, who had pressed for the issue of Taiwan reunification to be given a higher priority.

From the perspective of Beijing's leaders, the measures the PRC adopted in the year after the visit of Taiwan President Lee Teng-wei to the United States in 1995 were reasonably successful in their primary aims. That is, China's naval maneuvers, missile firings, and associated beating of the propaganda drum vividly reminded Taiwan of the military dangers attached to any attempt to convert Taiwan's status from de facto to de jure independence; and, more important, they made the United States much more hestitant to take any future actions—such as its decision in 1995 to permit Lee to visit the United States—that would help an effort by Taiwan to formalize its independent status.

The PRC paid (and is still paying) a grievous political price for these achievements, however, in the long-term reactions of the United States as well as Japan and much of the rest of East Asia to what was seen as military bullying of Taiwan.[30] The demonstrative Chinese military maneuvers near Taiwan in the spring of 1996, and particularly the ostentatious missile firings in Taiwan's vicinity, raised hackles all around China's eastern periphery. These actions seemed at the time to confirm forebodings about China's possible behavior in future years when its economic strength may have grown much further (thanks in large part to help from Japan and the West) and its military modernization program building on that economic base may have taken on more serious proportions (thanks in part to help from Russia).

Even before the 1996 events in the Taiwan Straits, Japanese strategic analysts were inclined to take a grave view of the implications of present trends. In 1995, an analysis prepared for the Japanese Defense Agency predicted that within the next twenty years, Korea would be reunified, U.S. influence in Northeast Asia would be (apparently in consequence) "greatly compromised," the Taiwan problem would still not be resolved, but the PRC would become a political, economic, and military superpower. The conclusion drawn was the need for Japan to strengthen cooperation with the United States to balance the expected growth of Chinese power.[31]

In July 1997, the annual white paper issued by the Japan Defense Agency stressed a need for Japan to pay close attention to the evolution of China's maritime activity, particularly in the Taiwan Straits, as well as to the Chinese military modernization process. While acknowledging that the advance of that process would remain gradual, the JDA complained about a lack of transparency in Chinese defense policy and pointed out that the defense spending made public by the PRC was only a fraction of the total amount. The conclusion the JDA drew from this and from other Japanese defense concerns (notably regarding the North Korea missile threat) was that Japan should prepare new guidelines for the self-defense forces to allow for a wider range of regional contingencies and a heightened Japanese role in security cooperation with the United States.[32]

Such revised guidelines had, in fact, been under active discussion between Japan and the United States since President Clinton's visit to Japan in 1996, and the process of fleshing them out has made evident the deep divisions in Japanese society—and within the governing Liberal Democratic Party itself—between those who wanted Japan to cooperate with the United States to help constrain China from undesired actions and those who did not. One key point at issue was whether the guidelines should specify the region around Taiwan as an area of potential U.S.-Japanese cooperation. Although the United States and important forces in the Liberal Democratic

Party originally wished to do so, in the end agreement was reached to avoid mentioning Taiwan—or any specific geographic area—in order to placate Beijing and avoid a political showdown in Japan. Thus, while the present Japanese leadership apparently has a tacit understanding that the United States could expect Japanese cooperation if a crisis in the Taiwan Straits, in fact, materialized, the policy on handling this contingency has not been made explicit or given formal legal status. Because of this ambiguity, it is still possible, depending on the future alignment of internal Japanese political forces, that Japan might not cooperate if this contingency someday arose.

Nevertheless, the likelihood that under the new guidelines Japan would, in fact, cooperate by facilitating U.S. military operations in the Taiwan Straits has now become strong enough to generate considerable Chinese alarm. Chinese disquiet has been increased by Japanese conversations with others in East Asia, notably Australia, who have also shown a disposition to improve security cooperation with the United States.[33] Since 1996, the PRC leadership and press have therefore voiced a long series of protests about the implications of revision of the Japanese security guidelines. The essence of the matter, in China's view, was summed up by one Chinese analyst as follows:

> The strengthened U.S.-Japan and U.S.-Australia alliances are intended to pin down the PRC. The short-term goal of the alliances is to deal with "instability" in the Taiwan Straits, the South China Sea and on the Korean Peninsula. The long-term goal is to deal with the imaginary "troubles" made by an economically and militarily stronger China.[34]

While this statement has an element of the truth, it is not the whole truth, for the practical evolution of these alliances will be greatly influenced by China's future behavior in the Taiwan Straits and its demeanor toward its smaller neighbors. Moreover, Japanese and U.S. authorities are well aware that, despite Russian assistance and despite Chinese intelligence collection efforts, the difficulties of Chinese military modernization are so great as to impose severe limitations on China's capabilities for at least a number of years to come.[35]

Meanwhile, Sino-U.S. bilateral tensions have multiplied in recent years—over transfer of satellite technology to China, over alleged

Chinese espionage, over allegations that the PRC had sought to interfere in the U.S. political process, and over the NATO bombing of the Chinese embassy in Belgrade. Yet despite all these tensions, both Washington and Tokyo retain a vested national interest in attempting to preserve a civil atmosphere and a useful working relationship with the PRC. Japan and the United States are China's two largest trade partners and are major investors in China. Each now has a significant and influential business constituency with a strong interest in calm and "normal" relations with the PRC. Moreover, obtaining the cooperation of the PRC is important to the United States on many diplomatic issues, notably regarding Korea. And, finally, many in the Japanese elite are perpetually on the psychological defensive in dealing with China because of Japan's behavior toward China earlier in the century.

For these reasons, both the United States and Japan in recent years have made repeated efforts to reassure Beijing about their alliance while retaining a security arrangement that has China very much in mind. Hashimoto, in particular, sought while he was in office to offer both material and spiritual compensation for the offense he intended to commit. Thus, by late 1996 his government had decided to resume billions of dollars worth of loans to the PRC that had been suspended or delayed because of various items of past bilateral friction, including Hashimoto's irritation over China's 1995 resumption of nuclear testing.[36] Moreover, Hashimoto and his representatives several times during visits to China in 1997 took the occasion to repeat apologies to China for past Japanese aggression. Finally, in high-level contacts in 1997 and 1998, both Japan and the United States repeatedly sought to assure China that the revised U.S.-Japanese security arrangements did not have China and the Taiwan issue specifically in mind. These bland assurances, of course, were not believed, nor were they expected to be believed. But like the big Japanese loans, they served as additional salve for what is likely to be ongoing Chinese resentment over being "contained."

Russia and the U.S.-Japanese Alliance

Meanwhile, these trends have already begun to have an impact on the Sino-Russian relationship, because Russia now has an embarrassing problem regarding what line to take toward the emerging revisions in the Japanese-U.S. alliance. Over the long term, Russia and

China may possibly be in the process of trading traditional positions on this question.

On the Chinese side, for a quarter-century the dominant view had been that this alliance was, on balance, a good thing, initially because it helped counterbalance the Soviet danger to China, and later, after that danger had abated, because the Washington-Tokyo security relationship was seen as helping to deflect Japan from entering on a path of independent rearmament and unrestrained assertive nationalism. Though never stated publicly in so many words, this mild blessing for the Japanese-U.S. connection was repeated many times over the years in private conversations by the Chinese.

In the past few years, however, this view has changed in response to the shift southward in the focus of this alliance. For the first time since the beginning of the 1970s, Chinese officials and the Chinese press have now begun to attack the alliance outright, and to call—like North Korea—for U.S. forces to withdraw from the region. This reaction is not surprising under the circumstances.

The response of Beijing's new "strategic partner" has been somewhat confused. Throughout the years of the Cold War, Moscow had naturally regarded as anathema the Japanese-U.S. alliance directed against Soviet power in East Asia. During the Gorbachev years, this view became greatly attenuated as "new thinking" advanced, and in the Yeltsin era, until recently, little had been said about the alliance officially, although individual political forces had on occasion expressed a variety of contrasting opinions. With the growth of the Sino-Russian relationship professing a broad solidarity of views, however, and with China's simultaneous turn toward denunciation of the Japanese-U.S. military alliance, the Russian government apparently came under some pressure to make clear where it stood.

In November 1996, therefore, Russian Ambassador to China Igor Rogachev took the occasion at a press conference in Beijing to state that Russia shared China's worries that the new U.S.-Japanese defense agreement might be used to bring pressure on neighboring Asia-Pacific countries.[37] A week later, however, the commander of the Russian Pacific Fleet, in Tokyo for a joint naval symposium, evaded the issue when asked his opinion of China's attitude toward the Japanese-U.S. alliance.[38] And by May 1997, as already noted, Minister of Defense Igor Rodionov, in Tokyo with a large delegation for official conversations with Japan, went so far as to assure the

Japanese that he had no problems at all with closer U.S.-Japanese security relations and, in fact, supported the revision of the guidelines that the United States was seeking.[39] The PRC was certainly not happy about this.

It is difficult to believe, even given the perpetual confusion in the Russian leadership, that this important statement, which drew a great deal of attention in the three countries, was not coordinated in Moscow with Foreign Minister Primakov. To be sure, Rodionov was known to be personally concerned about the possibility of a future Chinese threat, and he has since been replaced (for other reasons) as minister of defense. The future may very well see further wavering back and forth by Russia on the question of the U.S. alliance with Japan. Certainly the Russian sale to China of modern missile-firing destroyers that can be used against any U.S. warships operating in the Taiwan Straits with Japanese logistical support is an ironic commentary on Rodionov's statement. Nevertheless, this episode vividly demonstrated the strain that Russian policy in East Asia is likely to experience under the opposing pressures generated by the relationships with China and Japan above all, if Japanese investment in Russia does, in fact, improve.

Finally, there are other ways in which Japanese defense arrangements could come to evoke what used to be called "contradictions" between Russia and China. In the summer of 1996, for example, the Russian press reported that Moscow, ever eager to peddle at all costs the SA-12 antimissile weapon it was already offering to South Korea, had proposed to Japan that it adopt this Russian weapon as part of a regional Theater Missile Defense (TMD) system in which, the Russians allegedly said, the United States might conceivably also play a part. This remarkable suggestion was evidently ignored.[40] Japan had long been considering a proposal strongly urged by the United States for development of a joint TMD system, and the PRC had viewed the notion as extremely contrary to its strategic interests.[41]

CONCLUSIONS

What conclusions can be drawn for the Russian-Chinese relationship from these trends in East Asia? First, discontinuities in the regional geopolitical environment have already begun to create a new divergence of underlying Russian and Chinese interests. The trend has just begun, and much will depend on the pace of further change. Among the many variables at play, three should be stressed.

The first variable is whether the North Korean regime will collapse, and if so, when. For the reasons discussed, this event, if it comes, is likely to trigger a series of events beginning with Korean reunification and soon leading to the removal of U.S. forces from the peninsula, a fresh public reexamination of the U.S. alliance with Japan, and heightened attention to (and controversy over) the fact that the main concerns of that alliance will now more than ever be directed southward. At the same time, reunification would probably bring more open competition between the PRC and Russia for influence in Korea, with China probably retaining a substantial advantage.

The second variable is whether new, large-scale Korean and Japanese investment in Russia materializes in the next decade. For the reasons given, this investment will mostly depend on whether the Russian government can eventually create a much more hospitable climate for foreign investment, which is problematical at best. Future trends in the Korean and Japanese economies, which were both beginning to emerge from deep recession in 1999, will obviously also be a factor. At the same time, the scope of Japanese investment in Russia will also be influenced by how far the Japanese government now wishes to push the issue, for new geopolitical as well as economic reasons. Japan's shift of focus in its security concerns from Russia to China certainly represents a discontinuity with the past. The various consequences for policy toward Russia, however, are still being explored.[42] To the degree that an important Russian stake in the economic relationship with Japan eventually does materialize, it is likely to generate commensurate difficulty for Russia's relationship with China over the question of the Japanese-U.S. alliance.[43]

The third variable is whether the Chinese government can reconcile itself to the de facto independence of Taiwan as a long-term reality. Here the fundamental issue is not really whether the United States will again cooperate with Taiwan's efforts to expand its international presence, which is not likely to happen. Rather, it is whether the Chinese leadership over time can accept defeat at the hands of demographic trends on Taiwan for its fading hopes to persuade Taiwan to accept a status similar to Hong Kong's. Despite Taiwan's economic ties with China, the political forces on Taiwan opposing any such solution and insisting on preservation of de facto Taiwanese independence are likely to get only stronger as leaders born in Taiwan increasingly come to the fore.[44] This problem will be compounded as the existing tendency to accept democratic norms simultaneously becomes stronger in Taiwan, in contrast to trends in China.

As the years go by, how patient the dominant forces in Beijing will be in the face of this phenomenon is unclear. It should be noted that the issue is not limited to the question of whether China will someday attempt to invade Taiwan. Far short of that, any Chinese renewed military demonstrations in the Taiwan Straits along the lines of those carried out in 1996 would evoke a reaction that would "tighten the screws" further everywhere in East Asia—reinforcing the tendency by some regional forces to coalesce to contain China and further increasing the conflicting pressures on Russia over its attitude toward the Japanese-U.S. alliance. Although the Jiang Zemin leadership appears to have recognized the adverse consequences of its 1996 behavior, the long-term persistence of Chinese restraint regarding Taiwan remains problematical.

A second broad conclusion flows from the emergence of East Asian discontinuities. These changes may now, for the first time, compel Russia to come to grips with the limitations of its reliance on China to open the way in East Asia. China is very much the "middle kingdom" in the region, the focal point of economic and political relationships, fears, attachments, and animosities, an inevitable major factor in all regional disputes. Russia is the perpetual outsider clamoring to participate in the economic and political life of the region, forever seeking broad international fora unwanted by others as a means of conjuring up a role that continues to be missing. Despite the hopes of some Russians, the "strategic partnership" with China has not altered these realities. Nor has the PRC lifted a finger to try to change them.

Meanwhile, the PRC is a valuable customer for Russian military hardware and a useful supplier of food and textiles, but it cannot be a major source of investment funds or advanced technology. Yet the Russian economy desperately needs more investment, and particularly much more direct foreign investment, which is especially true of the Russian Far East. In East Asia, not China but Korea and especially Japan are the prospective sources for such investment.[45]

Despite the recent recession in the Japanese economy, Japan, and not China, remains the key to Russian hopes for a revitalized relationship with East Asia. To be sure, for the time being the Russian impulse toward cooperation with China has been strengthened by the reaction of both to U.S. policy in the 1999 Kosovo crisis. Moreover, in any case there is no way that the Russian military, desperate for cash, and the Russian military industry, desperate for customers, can soon be expected to halt the sale of weapons to the PRC. But the domination of Russian policy by this fixation on weapons sales remains disastrous for the Russian economy and the Russian Far East. Despite all the talk about shifting the emphasis of Russian foreign policy toward greater cultivation of Asia, it seems unlikely that such a shift will ever be fruitful without a breakthrough in the relationship with the most important East Asian economy. The evidence examined in this chapter suggests that regional discontinuities acting together have now, for the first time, opened at least the possibility of such a breakthrough. This breakthrough will, however, require far-reaching adjustments in both Russian domestic policy—to facilitate investment—and Russian foreign policy to carry out a broad shift in emphasis from cultivation of China to conciliation of Japan. The Yeltsin regime has thus far failed on both counts. It remains to be seen whether any future Russian government can perceive what is at stake and seize the opportunity.

NOTES

[1]Thus, for example, the supposedly eternal Sino-Soviet alliance established after Mao took power was undermined within a decade by a number of factors, but none more important than the fortuitous emergence of a U.S. commitment to Taiwan as a by-product of the North Korean attack on South Korea, followed by the Chinese discovery, during the Taiwan Straits crisis of 1958, that the Soviet leadership was unwilling to accept serious risks of military conflict with the United States to help its ally fulfill its fundamental goal of regaining control of Taiwan.

[2]See H. Gelman, "The Future of Northeast Asia: An American Perspective," *NBR Analysis*, National Bureau of Asian Research, vol. 6, no. 2 (August 1995).

[3]H. Gelman and N. D. Levin, *The Future of Soviet-North Korean Relations*, R-3159-AF (Santa Monica, Calif.: RAND, 1984).

[4]*Izvestiya*, January 28, 1997, and *Kommersant*, June 19, 1997.

[5] In June 1997, the two sides reportedly agreed to cooperate on a few minor projects. *ITAR-TASS*, June 17, 1997. North Korean labor has also made an increased appearance in Eastern Siberia, presumably to help pay for imports from Russia.

[6] In 1996, Russia dropped from fifth to seventh place as a North Korean trading partner, accounting for 3.1 percent of all North Korean trade. China remained in first place, accounting for 28.5 percent of all trade. South Korea was a close second. *Korea Times* (Seoul), August 31, 1997, citing Japan External Trade Organization.

[7] *New York Times*, July 3, 1996.

[8] The ROK was also obviously pleased with the bargaining leverage over U.S. suppliers that the Russian proposals furnished to Seoul. In 1999, South Korea similarly raised the possibility of procuring Russian submarines.

[9] The United States, for its part, felt that South Korea underestimated the danger of North Korean acquisition of nuclear weapons and the priority that should be given to heading it off. Some U.S. observers believed this attitude was fortified by an assumption by some in Seoul that, at the end of the day, South Korea would inherit whatever capability the North had acquired.

[10] *Wall Street Journal Interactive Edition*, October 31, 1996.

[11] Among other things, for example, in 1997 Seoul allegedly delayed for a considerable time furnishing U.S. interrogators with access to a senior North Korean defector, prompting indignant public protests from U.S officials.

[12] Such pressure on the U.S. presence would be particularly likely if Pyongyang, in the course of the protracted negotiations that have now begun, should someday choose to reverse itself and offer dramatic political concessions to Seoul (for example, joint formal recognition) in return for a U.S. withdrawal. The present North Korean position is far removed from this, however, since Pyongyang has never desired U.S. withdrawal solely for its own sake, but above all as a prerequisite to the undermining of the South Korean state. From North Korea's perspective, such fundamental concessions to Seoul would obviate much of the point of obtaining a U.S. withdrawal.

[13] In the opinion of this observer, the alternative scenario, positing a long, drawn-out transformation of the North Korean regime sufficient eventually to permit a peaceful reunification of the peninsula, is quite unlikely.

[14] The PRC is also apparently keeping that contingency in mind and, while by no means abandoning its relationship with Pyongyang, has taken pains to protect its good relations with Seoul. Thus, in 1997, China eventually agreed to the staged release to South Korea of a senior North Korean defector with only limited concessions to save North Korea's face.

[15]This suspicion may already be the perception in some Japanese quarters. In late 1996, a Tokyo newspaper published a report that the ROK was increasing its military spending and long-term military capabilities "with a view that Japan will become the ROK's most threatening potential adversary after DPRK threats disappear in the twenty-first century." The report asserted that the Japanese government was well aware of this alleged ROK belief. *Hankyoreh Shinmun* (Seoul), November 28, 1996, citing a *Defense News* article quoted by *Sankei Shimbun*.

[16]In 1997, Seoul's reaction to the prospect of wider U.S.-Japanese military cooperation under revised guidelines furnished a mild foretaste of the more serious problems that may lie ahead if North Korea collapses. Seoul urged Japan to stick to its defense-only principles and focus on rear support activities, "in consideration of neighboring countries' concerns over Japan's expanded military role." The ROK also asked Japan and the United States to closely consult with it and obtain its prior agreement when implementing any joint defense activities affecting Korean interests. *Korea Herald*, August 20, 1997.

[17]Aware of this connection, North Korea at the first preliminary session of the four-power talks took the occasion not only to reiterate its traditional demand that the United States leave the Korean peninsula, but also to add that the United States must leave Japan as well. *Nikkei Shimbun* (Tokyo), August 20, 1997. Pyongyang is likely to step up its propaganda emphasis on this point in the future.

[18]The Russians, however, regarded the 1996 Japanese white paper appraisal as a big improvement. *ITAR-TASS*, June 13, 1966.

[19]See H. Gelman, *Russo-Japanese Relations and the Future of the U.S.-Japanese Alliance*, MR-168-AF (Santa Monica, Calif.: RAND, 1993), pp. 11–17, 63–79.

[20]Despite the fact that Yeltsin subsequently did make a fairly successful visit to Japan in 1993, the mutual hostility between Tokyo and Moscow persisted and at times surfaced in astonishing form. As recently as May 1995, Yeltsin rudely refused a Japanese offer of assistance to Russians suffering from a devastating earthquake on Sakhalin, alleging that Japan would only make use of such help to bolster its claim to the disputed islands.

[21]Japanese Foreign Ministry officials in the spring of 1992 gave unattributed interviews agonizing over the consequences the new international decisions would have for their territorial negotiations with Moscow. There had been "a U.S. policy change," they said, that would have "a very negative effect on the negotiations being conducted between Japan and Russia." See Gelman, *Russo-Japanese Relations and the Future of the U.S.-Japanese Alliance*, pp. 52–63.

[22]The adoption of such confidence-building measures had been proposed to Japan a year earlier during a visit to Tokyo by Colonel General Boris Gromov, the former Russian deputy defense minister who had become adviser to Foreign Minister Kozyrev. *ITAR-TASS*, March 3, 1995.

[23]*ITAR-TASS*, November 16, 1996.

[24]"Hashimoto Announces New Foreign Policy Toward Russia," *Yomiuri Shimbun*, July 25, 1997.

[25]Ibid. At the beginning of the year, Hashimoto had sent a letter to Yeltsin saying he would like to begin a new political dialogue, but after this information was leaked to the press, the Japanese Foreign Ministry hastened to deny that there had been a change in Japanese policy. *Yomiuri Shimbun*, January 4, 1997; *Kyodo*, January 4, 1997. By July, the Foreign Ministry's public posture was quite different.

[26]*Izvestiya*, July 26, 1997. A year earlier, Japanese officials had announced that they had some interest in participating in development of a large natural gas field near Irkutsk. *UPI*, June 5, 1996.

[27]For a summary of trends that have discouraged Western oil and gas investment in Russia (as distinguished from investment in the Caspian Sea and Central Asia), see Michael Gordon, "From Gusher to Trickle: Oil Boom in Russia Fails to Materialize," *New York Times*, September 5, 1997.

[28]*Izvestiya*, August 16, 1997.

[29]*Wen Hui Daily*, May 21, 1998.

[30]Moreover, Beijing was certainly discomfited by the U.S. response in deploying large naval units near the Taiwan Straits. This reaction was not because those deployments inhibited China from doing anything it had intended to do on this occasion—they did not—but rather because the U.S. response somewhat weakened the intimidating lesson about Chinese strength that the PRC was seeking to convey to Taiwan (and less directly to others elsewhere in East Asia).

[31]*Sankei Shinbun* (Tokyo), January 7, 1996. One press report alleged that the same analysis also urged Japan, for similar reasons, to strengthen its relationship with Russia. *Hankyoreh Shinmun*, January 7, 1996.

[32]*Reuters*, July 15, 1997.

[33]In the spring of 1997, one Chinese commentary described Hashimoto's recent visits to the United States and Australia as creating a pincer aimed at China, joining together the "northern anchor" of the U.S. regional security position with the "southern anchor." *China Daily*, May 27, 1997.

[34]Zhao Jequi in *China Daily*, May 27, 1997.

[35]See David Shambaugh, "China's Military: Real or Paper Tiger?" *The Washington Quarterly*, vol. 19, no. 2 (Spring 1996), pp. 19–36.

[36]The new commitments included more than $5 billion in loans for projects in China over the 1996–1998 period, as well as a smaller amount in frozen "untied" funds. *China Daily*, December 4, 1996; *Yomiuri Shimbun*, February 7, 1997. While the resumption of this massive lending by Japan to China was probably inevitable in any case, Hashimoto certainly expected that it would be a useful reminder to Beijing of China's stake in the economic relationship with Japan.

[37] *Kommersant*, November 23, 1996.

[38] *Sankei Shinbum*, November 30, 1996.

[39] *Sevodnya*, May 19, 1997; *Asahi Shimbun*, May 17, 1997. These statements were duly noted by the strategic partner. *China Daily* on May 19, 1997, quoted Rodionov's remarks and concluded that Rodionov had "given Moscow's blessing to closer U.S.-Japanese military ties."

[40] *Nezavisimoye Voyennoye Obozreniye* supplement to *Nezavisimaya gazeta,* October 10, 1996. In May 1995, Yeltsin and President Clinton had, in fact, issued a joint statement raising the possibility of cooperative efforts in theater missile defense research and development, technology, and exercises. This statement has so far also come to nothing. See the discussion in L. Gronlund, D. Wright, and Y. Liu, "China and a Fissile Material Production Cut-Off," *Survival* (Winter 1995–1996), p. 154.

[41] In addition, Japanese defense officials in August 1996 disclosed that they had sought Russian permission to send several pilots to Russia to familiarize themselves with the SU-27 fighter, the aircraft that Russia is supplying to China and that is the centerpiece of PRC plans to modernize its air force. *Reuters* and *UPI*, August 23, 1996. A year later, the JDA was at least considering purchasing a few SU-27s for "research purposes," presumably again with China in mind.

[42] One straw in the wind was Japan's consent to join the United States in supporting Russia's admission to the Asia-Pacific Economic Cooperation Forum, in return for which Yeltsin indicated, at the Krasnoyarsk Summit in November 1997, that Russia would support Japan's effort to win a permanent seat on the UN Security Council, which the Chinese appear to oppose.

[43] Some sections of the Russian press have welcomed the possibility of significantly increased Japanese investment in Siberia not only for its own sake, but also as a means of neutralizing what they depict as an almost inevitable future expansion of Chinese influence there. *Sevodnya*, November 4, 1998.

[44] "The old KMT mandarins from the mainland are gone, replaced by a new generation raised and rooted on the island. Most of this generation takes de facto independence as a given in discussing Taiwan's future, although the question of de jure independence remains contentious. . . ." See Evan A. Feigenbaum, *Change in Taiwan and Potential Adversity in the Strait*, MR-558-1-OSD (Santa Monica, Calif.: RAND, 1995), p. xi.

[45] In March 1996, a delegation headed by the industrial leader Arkady Volskiy presented to Japanese business leaders a long-range program for development of the Russian Far East. Major goals were to develop export-oriented industries and to integrate Russia's Far East into the world economy. The total cost was estimated at $70 billion, of which the Russian government would, of course, contribute only a small portion. *ITAR-TASS*, March 28, 1996. Unfortunately, Russian authorities have not yet shown awareness of the implications for them of what they were asking of Japan.

THE CONTRIBUTORS

SHERMAN W. GARNETT is the Dean of James Madison College of Michigan State University and a former senior associate at the Carnegie Endowment for International Peace. Between 1984–1994, he held various positions in the Office of the Secretary of Defense and served as acting deputy assistant secretary of defense between 1993 and 1994.

HARRY GELMAN is a consultant and former senior staff member of the Rand Corporation, and previously worked for many years in assessment of Soviet foreign and domestic policy for the Central Intelligence Agency. His last position in Washington was in the National Intelligence Council as assistant national intelligence officer for the Soviet Union.

LI JINGJIE is director of and professor at the Institute of East European, Russian, and Central Asian Studies of the Chinese Academy of Sciences. He specializes in international relations.

LU NANQUAN is chairman of the Center for Russian Studies at the Chinese Academy of Social Sciences. He has also taught and worked at the Institute of East European, Russian, and Central Asian Studies.

MICHAEL MCFAUL is an assistant professor of political science at Stanford University and a research fellow at the Hoover Institution. He is also a research associate at the Center for International Security and Arms Control and a senior associate at the Carnegie Endowment for International Peace.

KATHLEEN NEWLAND is a senior associate at the Carnegie Endowment for International Peace. Before coming to Carnegie, she was an independent consultant to the UN High Commissioner for Refugees, the

Secretary General of the United Nations, and the World Bank. She was also a member of the international relations faculty of the London School of Economics.

MARTHA BRILL OLCOTT is a professor of political science at Colgate University, the director of the Central Asian American Enterprise Fund, and a senior associate at the Carnegie Endowment for International Peace. She has served as a special consultant to Acting Secretary of State Lawrence Eagleburger.

GILBERT ROZMAN is Musgrave Professor of Sociology at Princeton University. In the 1980s he published books on Soviet debates about China and Chinese debates about Soviet socialism. In the 1990s, with support from the United States Institute of Peace, he studied regionalism in Northeast Asia, including Sino-Russian cross-border relations. Lately he has focused his work on great-power relations.

JUDITH THORNTON is a professor of economics at the University of Washington. Since 1996 she has been head of the International Advisory Board of the Eurasia Foundation. She has also served on the Committee on Behavioral and Social Sciences of the National Academy of Sciences.

DMITRI TRENIN is the deputy director of the Carnegie Moscow Center. He is also a senior research fellow at the Institute of Europe of the Russian Academy of Sciences and a member of the International Institute for Strategic Studies. Between 1972 and 1993, he held various positions in the Soviet and Russian armed forces.

TAMARA TROYAKOVA is a senior researcher at the Institute of History, Archaeology and Ethnology of the Far Eastern Branch of the Russian Academy of Sciences in Vladivostok. She was a visiting fellow at the Monterey Institute of International Studies in Monterey, Calif.

GALINA VITKOVSKAYA is a scholar-in-residence and a program associate of the Carnegie Moscow Center. She is also a senior researcher at the Laboratory for Migration Studies of the Institute for Economic Forecasting of the Russian Academy of Sciences.

ALEXEI VOSKRESSENSKI is deputy head and senior research fellow of the Russia-China Center of the Institute of Far Eastern Studies in Moscow and honorary research fellow of the Center for Post-Soviet Studies of the University of Reading.

ELIZABETH WISHNICK is a research associate in the Department of Political Science at Barnard College, Columbia University. She has written articles about Russia's Asia policy and the Russian Far East, and a book about Sino-Russian relations.

ZHANNA ZAYONCHKOVSKAYA is the head of the Laboratory of Migration of the Institute of Economic Forecasting of the Russian Academy of Sciences. She also serves as the chair of the Independent Research Council of CIS and Baltic Countries on Migration and as the chief of the CIS Research Center on Forced Migration, a regional public organization based in Moscow.